Consideration
Educational Technology Integration

THE BEST OF JRTE

EDITED BY LYNNE SCHRUM

International Society for Technology in Education
EUGENE, OREGON • WASHINGTON, DC

Considerations on Educational Technology Integration

The Best of JRTE

EDITED BY LYNNE SCHRUM

Director of Book Publishing: *Courtney Burkholder*
Acquisitions Editor: *Jeff V. Bolkan*
Production Editors: *Lynda Gansel, Tina Wells*
Production Coordinator: *Rachel Williams*
Graphic Designer: *Signe Landin*
Copy Editor: *Barbara Hewick*
Proofreader: *Diane Durrett*
Indexer: *Potomac Indexing LLC*
Cover Design: *Signe Landin*
Book Design and Production: *Kathy Sturtevant*

Library of Congress Cataloging-in-Publication Data

Considerations on educational technology integration : the best of JRTE / edited by Lynne Schrum. — 1st ed.
p. cm.
Includes bibliographical references and index.
ISBN 978-1-56484-300-5 (pbk.)
1. Educational technology—United States. 2. Education—Effect of technological innovations on—United States. I. Schrum, Lynne. II.Journal of research on technology in education.
LB1028.3.C6635 2011
371.33—dc23

2011023158

First Edition
ISBN: 978-1-56484-300-5
Printed in the United States of America

About ISTE

The International Society for Technology in Education (ISTE) is the trusted source for professional development, knowledge generation, advocacy, and leadership for innovation. ISTE is the premier membership association for educators and education leaders engaged in improving teaching and learning by advancing the effective use of technology in PK–12 and teacher education.

Home of the National Educational Technology Standards (NETS) and ISTE's annual conference and exposition (formerly known as NECC), ISTE represents more than 100,000 professionals worldwide. We support our members with information, networking opportunities, and guidance as they face the challenge of transforming education. To find out more about these and other ISTE initiatives, visit our website at www.iste.org.

As part of our mission, ISTE Book Publishing works with experienced educators to develop and produce practical resources for classroom teachers, teacher educators, and technology leaders. Every manuscript we select for publication is carefully peer-reviewed and professionally edited. We value your feedback on this book and other ISTE products. E-mail us at books@iste.org.

International Society for Technology in Education

Washington, DC, Office:
1710 Rhode Island Ave. NW, Suite 900, Washington, DC 20036-3132

Eugene, Oregon, Office:
180 West 8th Ave., Suite 300, Eugene, OR 97401-2916

Order Desk: 1.800.336.5191
Order Fax: 1.541.302.3778
Customer Service: orders@iste.org
Book Publishing: books@iste.org
Book Sales and Marketing: booksmarketing@iste.org
Web: www.iste.org

About the Editor and Contributors

EDITOR

Lynne Schrum is a professor and coordinator of elementary education in the College of Education and Human Development at George Mason University. Her research and teaching focus on appropriate uses of information technology, online and distance learning, and preparing teachers for the 21st century. She has written five books and numerous articles on these subjects; the most recent are *Web 2.0 How-To for Educators* and *Leading a 21st-Century School: Harnessing Technology for Engagement and Achievement*. Lynne is currently chair of AERA's Annual Meeting Policies and Procedures Committee, is editor of the *Journal of Research on Technology in Education (JRTE)* (2002–2011), and is a past president of the International Society for Technology in Education (ISTE).

CONTRIBUTORS

Charoula Angeli is associate professor of instructional technology at the University of Cyprus. She has undergraduate and graduate studies at Indiana University-Bloomington (BS in computer science, 1991, MS in computer science, 1993, and PhD in instructional systems technology, 1999). Her research interests include technological pedagogical content knowledge, distributed cognition, adaptive learning, educational software design, online learning, and the design of learning environments for the development of critical and scientific thinking skills.

Ann E. Barron is a professor in the instructional technology program at the University of South Florida. Her research focuses on the integration of technology in education and the design and development of web-based instruction.

Randall Boone is a professor of instructional and assistive technologies at the University of Nevada, Las Vegas. His research focuses on technology supports for persons with mild disabilities.

Amy C. Bradshaw is an associate professor of instructional technology in the Educational Psychology Department at the University of Oklahoma. Her interests include instructional visuals and visualization, problem solving, and social and cultural implications of technology. She received her PhD from Arizona State University.

Ching-Huei Chen received her PhD from the program of instructional psychology and technology at the University of Oklahoma, where she also worked as a teaching and research assistant. She currently is working as an assistant professor in the Graduate Institute of e-Learning, National Changhua University of Education, Taiwan. Her education and scholarly interests include instructional design and technology across disciplines, evaluation of professional development, and problem solving.

Karee E. Cox (Dunn), previously at the University of Memphis, is an assistant professor in the Department of Educational Statistics and Research Methods at the University of Arkansas where she teaches courses in educational psychology and statistics. Her research reflects a three-fold interconnected research agenda. The three components of her research include teacher beliefs, student motivation, and data-driven decision making.

Loretta Donovan is an associate professor in the Department of Elementary and Bilingual Education at California State University, Fullerton. Her current research interests address the effective implementation of one-to-one programs in K–12 and teacher education. She is involved in program evaluation of one-to-one laptop initiatives in California and Nevada.

Valerie S. Fields, previously at Louisiana Campus Compact, teaches technology-related courses in the doctoral program in the School of Graduate Studies and teaches in the Department of Education at South Carolina State University.

Lauren B. Goldenberg is a senior research associate at the EDC's Center for Children and Technology. Her research interests include the role of technology in teacher learning and using computers for language learning.

Christine Harmes is a consultant on research and evaluation with the Florida Center for Instructional Technology at the University of South Florida. Her research interests focus on computer-based testing and teacher use of technology.

Kendall Hartley is an associate professor of educational computing and technology in the College of Education at the University of Nevada, Las Vegas. His research involves the use of computer-based technologies in teaching and learning.

Dj Himes, instructional technology specialist at University of Wisconsin-Milwaukee, received his master's degree from North Carolina State University. He teaches courses in instructional technology.

Kimberly S. Kalaydjian is an instructional designer and senior program manager for online undergraduate and graduate degree programs. Her interests are in online education and adult learning.

Kate Kemker, previously at the University of South Florida, is the director of technology and learning innovation for the Florida Department of Education. Her research interests focus on the integration of technology in the curriculum and student technology literacy.

Karla V. Kingsley is an assistant professor of educational computing and instructional technology in the Department of Teacher Education at the University of New Mexico. She teaches courses in multimedia literacy, digital game-based learning, educational research, and K–12 teacher education. Her research interests include interactive digital learning environments, technology-supported social studies education, critical pedagogy, and technology for equity and social justice.

Annette Kratcoski is a researcher at Kent State University's Research Center for Educational Technology (RCET). In this capacity, she studies teachers' and students' use of technology in the AT&T Classroom. Annette is also part of RCET's project team on the Thinking with Data project, a grant funded by the National Science Foundation. Prior to joining RCET in fall 2000, she worked as a speech-language pathologist in clinical and school settings and also in special education and curriculum coordination in the public schools. She holds bachelors and masters degrees in special education and earned her PhD from Kent State University in speech-language pathology and curriculum.

Yiping Lou is an associate professor in the educational technology graduate programs, Department of Educational Theory, Policy, and Practice, Louisiana State University. Her interests include instructional design and development, technology integration in K–12 and higher education, science inquiry learning and assessment, distance education, and computer-supported collaborative learning.

S. Kim MacGregor is an associate professor of educational research and coordinates the graduate program in applied research, measurement and evaluation in the Department of Educational Theory, Policy, and Practice at Louisiana State University. Her research interests focus on the development and evaluation of programs designed to facilitate student engagement, university-community partnerships, and the implementation of technology in educational contexts.

Barbara Means directs SRI's Center for Technology in Learning. Her research focuses on ways in which technology can support students' learning of advanced skills and the revitalization of classrooms and schools. She specializes in defining issues and approaches for evaluating the implementation and efficacy of technology-supported educational innovations.

James W. Pellegrino is a liberal arts and sciences distinguished professor and distinguished professor of education at the University of Illinois at Chicago, where he also codirects the Learning Sciences Research Institute.

William R. Penuel is director of evaluation research at the Center for Technology in Learning at SRI International. His research focuses on how technology can support classroom assessment and on the implementation and scaling of technology-supported innovations in science and mathematics education.

Marleen C. Pugach is a professor of teacher education in the School of Education and Leadership at the University of Wisconsin-Milwaukee. Her research interests include collaboration between the preparation of general and special education teachers, teacher preparation for urban schools, teacher education policy, and qualitative research methods.

Edys S. Quellmalz is the director of technology-enhanced assessments and learning systems in the Science, Technology, Engineering, and Mathematics Program at WestEd.

Glenda Rakes is a professor of instructional technology at the University of Tennessee at Martin where she teaches courses in instructional technology and educational research. Her current research focuses on motivation and self-regulated learning as it applies to instructional strategies that can be integrated into online graduate teacher education programs.

Amy Staples is an associate professor in the College of Education at the University of Northern Iowa. Her research interests include literacy learning in individuals with significant disabilities, and the role technology (including assistive technology) can play in supporting learning in inclusive settings.

Neal Strudler is a professor of educational technology at the University of Nevada, Las Vegas. His research focuses on the implementation of electronic portfolios and technology integration in teacher education and K–12 schools.

Karen Swan, previously at Kent State University, is the Stukel Professor of Educational Leadership at the University of Illinois, Springfield. Karen's research has been focused mainly in the general area of electronic media and learning. She has authored over 90 journal articles and book chapters, produced several hypermedia programs, and co-edited two books on educational technology topics. Her current research interests include online learning, ubiquitous computing, and data literacy.

Bill Tally is senior research scientist at EDC's Center for Children & Technology in New York City. His work focuses on understanding the roles that digital media can play in improving K–16 student and teacher learning in the humanities.

Darlene Unger, previously at Virginia Commonwealth University, is an associate professor of special education at DePaul University. Her clinical experiences and research have focused on the education and transition of secondary age youth with disabilities to postsecondary education and employment. She has also assisted K–12 teachers with technology integration and implementing the practices of universal design for learning to address the needs of diverse learners.

Nicos Valanides is associate professor of science education at the University of Cyprus. He has undergraduate studies at the Aristotelian University of Thessaloniki (BA in physics, 1969, and BA in law, 1985). He has graduate studies at the American University of Beirut (teaching diploma, 1980, and MA in education: teaching sciences, 1981) and at the University of Albany, State University of New York, SUNY—Albany (MSc in instructional supervision 1986, and PhD in curriculum and instruction and educational research, 1990). His research interests include teacher training, methodology of teaching and curricula for science education, development of logical and scientific thinking, science-and-technology literacy, the utilization of ICT in science education, technological pedagogical content knowledge, blended learning, and the design of educational interventions and learning environments.

Mark van 't Hooft, PhD, is a researcher and technology specialist for the Research Center for Educational Technology at Kent State University, and is the editor of the *Journal of the Research Center for Educational Technology* (RCETJ). He is a founding member and former chair of ISTE's Special Interest Group for Mobile Learning (SIGML). His research focuses on ubiquitous computing and the use of mobile technology in K–12 education, especially in the social studies. Prior to his work at RCET, Mark taught middle and high school social studies and language arts. He holds a BA in American studies from the Radboud Universiteit of Nijmegen, the Netherlands, and an MA in history from Texas State University. He received his doctoral degree with a dual major in curriculum and instruction, and evaluation and measurement from Kent State University in 2005.

ACKNOWLEDGMENT

This book would not have been possible without the efforts of many authors, teachers, learners, and school leaders who continue to participate in important research to help us understand the potential of technology in teaching and learning. In addition, I would like to thank the ISTE office and editors/reviewers who helped make this manuscript a valuable contribution to the field. Finally, to Mary English, graduate student extraordinaire, my deep gratitude.

DEDICATION

I dedicate this book to my family who do so much to make me laugh and bring joy.

Contents

INTRODUCTION

Revisioning a Proactive Approach to an Educational Technology Research Agenda 1

Lynne Schrum

CHAPTER 1

Rethinking the Technology Integration Challenge:
Cases from Three Urban Elementary Schools 9

Amy Staples, Marleen C. Pugach, Dj Himes
Spring 2005: Volume 37 Number 3

Author Update 36
Appendix 40

CHAPTER 2

Fostering Historical Thinking with Digitized Primary Sources 41

Bill Tally, Lauren B. Goldenberg
Fall 2005: Volume 38 Number 1

Author Update 61

Appendix 64

CHAPTER 3

Uses and Effects of Mobile Computing Devices in K–8 Classrooms 67

Karen Swan, Mark van 't Hooft, Annette Kratcoski, Darlene Unger
Fall 2005: Volume 38 Number 1

Author Update 81

CHAPTER 4

Large-Scale Research Study on Technology in K–12 Schools:
Technology Integration as It Relates to the National Technology Standards 83

Ann E. Barron, Kate Kemker, Christine Harmes, Kimberly Kalaydjian
Summer 2003: Volume 35 Number 4

Author Update 102

CHAPTER 5

Implementation and Effects of One-to-One Computing Initiatives: A Research Synthesis 105

William R. Penuel
Spring 2006: Volume 38 Number 3

Author Update 123

CHAPTER 6

The Influence of Teachers' Technology Use on Instructional Practices 129

Glenda C. Rakes, Valerie S. Fields, Karee E. Cox
Summer 2006: Volume 38 Number 4

Author Update 145

CHAPTER 7

Teacher Concerns During Initial Implementation of a One-to-One Laptop Initiative at the Middle School Level 149

Loretta Donovan, Kendall Hartley, Neal Strudler
Spring 2007: Volume 39 Number 3

Author Update 171
Appendix 174

CHAPTER 8

Web-Based Learning: How Task Scaffolding and Website Design Support Knowledge Acquisition 177

S. Kim MacGregor, Yiping Lou
Winter 2004–2005: Volume 37 Number 2

Author Update 193

CHAPTER 9

The Effect of Web-Based Question Prompts on Scaffolding Knowledge Integration and Ill-Structured Problem Solving 197

Ching-Huei Chen, Amy C. Bradshaw
Summer 2007: Volume 39 Number 4

Author Update 213

CHAPTER 10

Effects of Multimedia Software on Achievement of Middle School Students in an American History Class 217

Karla V. Kingsley, Randall Boone
Winter 2008–2009: Volume 41 Number 2

Author Update 233

CHAPTER 11

The Effect of Electronic Scaffolding for Technology Integration on Perceived Task Effort and Confidence of Primary Student Teachers 239

Charoula Angeli, Nicos Valanides
Fall 2004: Volume 37 Number 1

Author Update 254

CHAPTER 12

Technology and Education Change: Focus on Student Learning 257

Barbara Means
Spring 2010: Volume 42 Number 3

Author Update 280

CHAPTER 13

Perspectives on the Integration of Technology and Assessment 285

James W. Pellegrino, Edys S. Quellmalz
Winter 2010: Volume 43 Number 2

Author Update 300

INTRODUCTION

Revisioning a Proactive Approach to an Educational Technology Research Agenda

Lynne Schrum | George Mason University

In 2005, five educational technology editors and researchers (Bull, Knezek, Roblyer, Schrum, & Thompson, 2005) wrote an editorial that was designed both as a call for educational researchers to identify the pressures toward one model of research methodology and as a call for the joint creation of an agenda that respected the way schools work, the challenges of learning technology, and the impact of pressure to demonstrate academic achievement directly tied to the use of technology. This introduction is designed to revive the conversation, and also to expand the agenda in new ways.

During the past 30 years, technological advances have exceeded even the most optimistic expectations. The steady advance in speed and capacity has produced powerful computers available at modest prices, along with a wide variety of handheld technologies that can accomplish remarkable tasks. This wider accessibility has resulted in wider usage. A recent Pew study found that 93% of teens ages 12–17 now use the Internet, up from 73% in 2000 (Pew Internet & American Life Project, 2007). Additionally, this study found that 69% of online Americans have used "cloud computing" applications (basically Web 2.0 tools) (Jones & Fox, 2009).

Those of us who have committed our professional lives to investigating this educational arena have anticipated that the advances in technological capacity would be matched by parallel enhancements in learning. Recently, we have witnessed a remarkable expansion of Web 2.0 tools and their uses in educational settings. And research on teaching and learning is blending activities inside and beyond the classroom in innovative uses of technology, (2009), such as the "Innovative Digital Media and Learning Projects" (The MacArthur Foundation, www.macfound.org/atf/cf/%7Bb0386ce3-8b29-4162-8098-e466fb856794%7D/DMLCOMP2009-PR-090416.PDF).

Technology has had a positive impact on education, even if it has not yet resulted in wholesale educational transformation. However, there are larger issues that have not yet been addressed: for example, disparities in educational outcomes still exist, too many of our youth still drop out of school and do not reach their potential, and students are often disengaged from content and learning. Perhaps our research is unable to answer the questions, or perhaps we are asking the wrong questions. It appears that our conversations are not yet as broad, deep, or inclusive as they will need to be for us to see the type of transformation we desire. An effective return on future investments in educational technology is more likely to be realized to the extent that research captures past impact and provides directions for future use. Best approaches to educational research have been the focus of a major emphasis by the U.S. Department of Education. There is no area in which well-conceived and effectively implemented research could be of greater value than in the area of technological innovation. Our research is about technology; we now must let others see how it is about learners of all ages, teaching, and the future of our democracy.

Challenges for Educational Technology Research

A review of educational technology journals provides an opportunity to survey the landscape of the published research in this area. It raises a concern about our efforts to mentor the next generation of researchers. For example, in 2009 approximately 85% of submissions to the *Journal of Research on Technology in Education (JRTE)* were ultimately rejected for two main reasons. The primary reason was related to quality, methods, and focus. But many were rejected because they did not deepen, expand, or push the envelope on our literature base, nor did they help develop new knowledge that added to what we already know.

Every researcher undertakes a study with the hope of making a substantive contribution to the field. Each of the submissions represents months or years of effort and commitment on the part of one or more authors. A publication process that results in inefficiencies of 80% or more clearly cries out for improvement.

We stand at a crossroads as the U.S. Department of Education is beginning to recognize that not all randomized studies are valuable, and that other types of studies may offer insights and knowledge worth having. At the same time, the funding will still go only to educational researchers who offer strong and worthwhile research designs that are based on sound background literature, theoretical constructs, deep and important research questions, and accepted methods of data collection and analysis.

Some of the reasons for the ongoing challenge, presented when the editorial first was published, are still useful and unfortunately, operational, so they are repeated here:

> ***Unrealistic expectations for technology-based reform.*** Technologies brought about such high-profile reforms in other areas of society that many educators and researchers came to expect similarly widespread impact in education. Other areas of society faced similar challenges. For example, researchers were not able to capture any relationship between investments in technology and increases in productivity throughout the 1980s. Business continued to invest, and eventually the investment in technology was associated with gains in productivity in the 1990s. Education represents an unparalleled set of problems and complexities. In retrospect, it seems apparent that expectations should be based on a more realistic, theory-based appraisal of specific learning problems for which technology applications might be a good solution. Research should have focused on confirming that these applications were instructional strategies of choice and on providing guidelines for conditions under which this was true.
>
> ***Lack of consensus on research questions and methodologies.*** For the first 20 years, educational technology research focused on the question: "Is a technology-based method better than a non-technology-based one?" Eventually, this approach was deemed ill-conceived and unproductive. Yet no more useful paradigm has emerged to take its place. Future research must focus on yet-to-be-articulated research questions.
>
> ***Diminished role of research in school reform.*** Even published studies do not typically result in any change in educational practice. Some educators have argued that this is due in no small part to a "disconnect" between the interests of researchers and the needs of teachers and schools. A more practical, focused research agenda is an essential need, as are strategies for coordinating research efforts and findings across researchers and research centers. (Bull et al., 2005, pp. 218–219)

A New Challenge for Our Design-Based and Collaborative Research

Since this original editorial was written, new Web 2.0 tools, which offer greater potential to increase interactivity and perhaps better address the digital divide, have become commonplace, and almost all use of these tools is voluntary (Alexander, 2008; Solomon & Schrum, 2010). Now we are tasked with investigating their purposeful educational uses and identifying ways these new tools may affect student engagement and academic achievement; the hope is that we have learned about creating a unified research agenda to help guide us.

We are beginning to see research that examines a new type of activity, epistemic games; they are "explicitly based on theory of learning in the digital age and are designed to allow learners to develop domain-specific expertise under realistic constraints" (Rupp et al., 2009, p. 4). The goal is to have learners experience what it is like to really think and act like "journalists, artists, business managers, or engineers by using digital learning technologies to solve realistic complex performance tasks" (p. 4). We might consider this somewhat analogous to an authentic practicum or internship, and these models have been created in a variety of content areas, including history (Johnson & Levine, 2008; Squire, DeVane, & Durga, 2008) with research suggesting powerful and positive results in engaging learners. Research on these tools offers an opportunity to be both formative as well as design based, because reflection on the data leads to modification of the tools. If, as Barab, Thomas, Dodge, Carteaux, and Tuzun suggest, these types of activities sit at the "intersection of education, entertainment, and social commitment" (2005, p. 86), then what are the implications for our research? Annetta (2008) suggests, "These educational games commonly require the use of logic, memory, problem-solving, critical thinking skills, visualization, and discovery" (p. 261). What requirements are placed on researchers to examine the constructs in and out of school? Squire, Giovanetto, DeVane, and Durga (2005) posit, "To date, we actually know relatively little about the consequences of game play on the cognition of those who play them" (p. 35).

More importantly, some research has begun to show that students are really learning in this environment. Hickey, Ingram-Goble, and Jameson (2009), for example, have seen this in their research. In two studies of Quest Atlantis, they found sixth grade students making "larger gains in understanding and achievement" than in classes that used expository text to learn the same concepts and skills (p. 187). In a study of a similar type of project, Ketelhut (2007) found that her results "suggest that embedding science inquiry curricula in novel platforms like a MUVE might act as a catalyst for change in students' self-efficacy and learning processes" (p. 99). Kyza (2009) conducted a multiple-case study looking at middle school students' reasoning in an investigation of data-rich, scientific problems scaffolded by software, the task, and the teacher. Although she found statistically significant growth in learning and that the scaffolding contributed to the inquiry, she also found that they required "epistemologically targeted discourse along-side guided inquiry experiences" to be able to really understand alternative hypotheses and to support their scientific reasoning processes (p. 377).

We hear a great deal about the preparation of teachers these days, and how many still are not changing their teaching to take advantage of technology. Recently some researchers have begun to reexamine the preparation and role of school leaders and their need for specific types of preparation to lead our 21st-century schools (Schrum, Galizio, & Ledesma, 2011; Schrum & Levin, 2009). The reality is that without support, leadership, and commitment from all stakeholders in a school system, the type of learning we have often dreamed of may not be realized. The need then is for a comprehensive plan with complementary comprehensive research to document what we find.

Are these studies and efforts the beginning of a new research agenda? Are they perhaps the beginning of a new effort to demonstrate that in certain circumstances, under particular conditions, technology may assist in enhancing learning outcomes? Or will we again see that real systemic changes happen only with funding, and that well-designed projects are not scalable or applicable in other situations?

A Renewed Proposal for a Proactive Research Agenda

One editorial function is to serve as a nexus for quality control. However, being an editor also offers an opportunity to provide leadership, either implicitly by what is published, or explicitly by purposefully seeking important and thoughtful additions to our literature base. Discussions regarding the potential value of a proactive approach to research continue within this context. After many years as editor of *JRTE*, I consider it important to explicate the importance of what needs to be published, to explore ways to influence the conversation, and to encourage new scholars to join us; such discussion also allows us to courageously draw a deep line in the sand to only approve and accept rigorous and valuable research.

An effective conversation must include discourse among leading educational technology researchers. However, to be successful, it will be equally important to involve other stakeholders to ensure strong linkages between applied research and explicit connections and value to schools. It is also important to include input from corporate partners, the K–12 school community, developers, and policy makers in the questions we ask, in the research we conduct, and in the interpretations and policy that ensue.

Two further outcomes may emerge from this dialogue. The process of preparing doctoral students to design, conduct, and analyze good research is a nontrivial task, and yet we continue to see less funding, fewer full-time positions, and thus less time for faculty to devote to this important goal. If educational technology researchers and journal editors can proactively work toward a measure of consensus on productive directions for future research, it may be possible to increase the positive outcomes for our future colleagues.

Second, as previously addressed, the introduction of technology into our schools has not resulted in the expected educational reform. One reason for that may be the missing relationship between educators and their burning questions and the questions educational researchers choose to investigate. If we can assist in creating a dialogue, stronger collaboration, and recursive conversation between these two groups, that too would be an excellent outcome. After all, teaching and learning require support from the teacher in designing an educational environment, and technology must be embedded in thoughtfully planned ongoing instruction to be effective in supporting student outcomes. Educators and researchers have common goals, and synergy between them would benefit all.

Conclusions

The purpose of this compilation of research articles from *JRTE* is to provide a context and trail of where we have been and what our research base has established thus far. At present the technological capacity available to schools exceeds our ability to use it effectively to enhance learning. A proactive approach to establishing a research agenda can potentially provide guidance to future investigators. The substantial continuing cost of technology in schools makes it important to ensure that research produced is relevant. Providing researchers with context and guidelines will increase the likelihood that efforts are productively directed. Barab, Dodge, Thomas, Jackson, and Tuzun (2007) suggest that a larger purpose may result from the community of educational researchers, if they decide to work together to build true transformative materials and move theory into directions that take advantage of our collective knowledge. They state that a collective effort would be

> significantly heightened if we as a community embrace the critical agendas that are central to so many discussions in anthropology, philosophy, or even curriculum development more generally. Instead of simply building an artifact to help individuals accomplish a particular task, or to meet a specific standard, the focus of critical design work is to develop sociotechnical structures that facilitate individuals in critiquing and improving themselves and the societies in which they function, and

then we use our understanding of participation with these structures to advance theory. (p. 264)

A consensus on every point will not be reached, nor is that the intent. There will always be diverse perspectives within an academic community. However, the dialogue will encourage more sharply articulated research objectives and guidelines. The result should facilitate much needed research in this area.

References

Alexander, B. (2008). Web 2.0 and emergent multiliteracies. *Theory into Practice, 47*(2), 150–160.

Annetta, L. A. (2008). Video games in education: Why they should be used and how they are being used. *Theory into Practice, 47*(3), 229–239.

Barab, S., Dodge, T., Thomas, M. K., Jackson, C., & Tuzun, H. (2007). Our designs and the social agendas they carry. *Journal of the Learning Sciences, 16*(2), 263–305.

Barab, S., Thomas, M., Dodge, T., Carteaux, R., & Tuzun, H. (2005). Making learning fun: Quest Atlantis, a game without guns. *Educational Technology Research and Development, 53*(1), 86–107.

Bull, G., Knezek, G., Roblyer, M. D., Schrum, L., & Thompson, A. (2005). A proactive approach to a research agenda for educational technology. *Journal of Research on Technology in Education, 37*(3), 217–220.

Digital Learning Environments. (2009). *Technology's Impact on Learning.* Retrieved August 14, 2009, from www.guide2digitallearning.com

Dodge, T., Barab, S., & Stuckey, B. (2008). Children's sense of self: Learning and meaning in the digital age. *Journal of Interactive Learning Research, 19*(2), 225–249.

Hickey, D. T., Ingram-Goble, A. A., & Jameson, E. M. (2009). Designing assessments and assessing designs in virtual educational environments. *Journal of Science Education and Technology, 18,* 187–208.

Johnson, L. F., & Levine, A. H. (2008). Virtual worlds: Inherently immersive, highly social learning spaces. *Theory into Practice, 47*(2), 161–170.

Jones, S., & Fox, S. (2009). Generations online in 2009. *Pew Internet and American Life Project.* Retrieved October 25, 2009, from www.pewInternet.org/~/media//Files/Reports/2009/PIP_Generations_2009.pdf

Ketelhut, D. J. (2007). The impact of student self-efficacy on scientific inquiry skills: An exploratory investigation of River City, a multi-user virtual environment. *Journal of Science Education and Technology, 16*(1), 99–111.

Kyza, E. A. (2009). Middle-school students' reasoning about alternative hypotheses in a scaffolded, software-based inquiry investigation. *Cognition and Instruction, 27*(4), 277–311.

Pew Internet & American Life Project. (2007). *Teens and social media.* Retrieved March 15, 2009, from http://pewInternet.org/PPF/r/230/report_display.asp

Rupp, A., Choi, Y., Gushta, M., Mislevy, R., Thies, M. C., Bagley, E., et al. (2009). Modeling learning progressions in epistemic games with epistemic network analysis: Principles for data analysis and generation. Paper presented at the Learning Progressions in Science conference (LeaPS), Iowa City, IA, USA. Retrieved August 1, 2009, from http://epistemicgames.org/eg/wp-content/uploads/leaps-learning-progressions-paper-rupp-et-al-2009-leaps-format1.pdf

Schrum, L., Galizio, L. M., & Ledesma, P. (2011). Educational leadership and technology integration: An investigation into preparation, experiences, and roles. *Journal of School Leadership, 21*, 241–261.

Schrum, L., & Levin, B. (2009). *Leading 21st century schools: Harnessing technology for engagement and achievement.* Thousand Oaks, CA: Corwin Press.

Solomon, G. & Schrum, L. (2010). *Web 2.0 how-to for educators.* Eugene, OR: International Society for Technology in Education.

Squire, K. D., DeVane, B., & Durga, S. (2008). Designing centers of expertise for academic learning through video games. *Theory into Practice, 47*(3), 240–251.

Squire, K. D., Giovanetto, L., DeVane, B., & Durga, S. (2005). From users to designers: Building a self-organizing game-based learning environment. *TechTrends, 49*(5), 34–42, 74.

CHAPTER

1

Rethinking the Technology Integration Challenge: Cases from Three Urban Elementary Schools

Amy Staples | University of Northern Iowa

Marleen C. Pugach | University of Wisconsin-Milwaukee

Dj Himes | University of Wisconsin-Milwaukee

Case studies of three urban elementary schools were conducted to document the integration of technology given identical resources from a local university's PT[3] grant. Data sources for this qualitative study included participant observers' field notes and journal entries, school personnel interviews, timeline and chronicle of technology-related priorities and events, and children's and teachers' technology artifacts. Cases were summarized with respect to prior technology context, agents of growth and development, and changes and future directions. The analysis identified three scaffolds that appear to have a significant influence on—and redefine the challenge of—technology integration: alignment with the curriculum/mission, teacher leadership, and public/private roles for technology recognition.

During the 1990s, schools began spending more money on technology than capital goods (Trilling & Hood, 1999). The rapid growth in the types of available technological tools, paired with the decline in the price of these resources, captivated schools and parents alike, who wanted to prepare their children for a society where learning and employment were increasingly dependent on digital access and expertise. Prior to the 1990s, many schools had computers, perhaps one or two per classroom, but the flood of technology acquisition in the 1990s created a different context and opportunity for learning. Computers, the Internet, and software became increasingly available to more and more students.

The task for schools became that of determining how technology and curriculum would operate to strengthen student learning. Companies offering games, educational software, networking equipment, accessories and the like sprang up overnight, offering a multitude of options from which to choose for teachers and administrators. Acquisition, however, was not the end of the road. Teachers, administrators, and researchers alike were coupling their excitement concerning the possibilities and potential power of technology with the underlying question of whether technology was truly needed or beneficial. Studies began to be conducted that examined the effectiveness of technology use in various contexts. Teachers and schools adhering to constructivist orientations seemed to reap the benefits of technology quickly. For example, Wenglinsky (1998), in a large-scale study, found that students who used computers in constructivist ways to learn mathematics (e.g., using simulations and spreadsheets) scored significantly higher on math achievement assessments than students whose only exposure was to computer-based drill-and-practice programs. These simulations and spreadsheets enabled students to relate information to real life and solve problems logically.

Despite studies documenting the effectiveness of technology to support student learning, barriers to technology integration have been identified. For example, the issue of preparedness of teachers to respond to the influx of technology resources, and of schools to keep up with the mechanical functioning and maintenance of equipment, was one major barrier. Further, many teachers had not been prepared to utilize technology in their teacher preparation programs. The U.S. Office of Technology Assessment (1995) found that schools devoted no more than 15% of their technology budgets to professional development. More recently, Carvin (2000) suggested that professional development should be closer to 30%, but unfortunately was as low as 3% in some districts. Without time and monetary resources devoted to increasing staff expertise in technology use, effective integration was a struggle. Still, optimism regarding the power of technology remained.

Barriers to technology integration have been identified that span practical issues of time for professional development (Jones, 1998), lack of systemic planning (Cradler, n.d.), and lack of support for networks and hardware at individual school sites (Fulton & Sibley, 2003). However, although much of what is written regarding technology integration focuses on barriers to its use, others have theorized conditions under which integration might best occur (Chang et al., 1998; Gooler, Kautzer, & Knuth, 2000; WestEd, 2002; White, Ringstad, & Kelly, 2002), namely, providing ample professional development for teachers, making certain that technology supports the curriculum, and providing a solid infrastructure to support the technology itself. Still other researchers have examined particular technologies with students in specific content areas, measuring the effect of technology on achievement (Butzin, 2001; Zhang, 2000; Doty, Popplewell, & Byers, 2001).

So although instructional technology has been a routine part of the educational landscape for several decades, the integration of technology in classrooms still lags behind expectations for its use (Cuban, 2001; Jones, 1998; Rogers, 2000), and especially for traditionally underserved populations (Solomon, Allen, & Resta, 2003). For example, in 1999, in schools where the free lunch rate was 70% or higher, only 39% of classrooms had Internet access, while schools where free lunch was less than 11% reported that 74% of classrooms had Internet access (Solomon et al., 2003). Even though Hativa (1988), in a meta-analysis of the use of computer-based drill-and-practice in arithmetic, determined that it was widening the gap between high- and low-achieving students, teachers continue to use technology as a drill-and-practice remediation tool, particularly with students of color. Similarly, researchers have noted that teachers in poorer schools utilize technology to reinforce basic skills, rather than to support higher-order thinking (CEO Forum, 2001).

Fewer research studies, however, have paid close attention to contextual variables and factors that might affect the nature and degree of technology integration in schools, particularly urban schools. One longitudinal research effort examining systemic reform in Union City, New Jersey, determined that in the absence of school reform, technology would not have a sustained positive effect on learning (Honey, Culp, & Carrigg, 2000). In particular, they found that variables such as instructional leadership, extensive professional development, a whole-language approach to learning, establishment of libraries, de-emphasis on remediation, and emphasis on fostering student creativity were necessary to maximize the effect of technology on student learning.

The purpose of this study was to describe the ways in which three urban elementary schools, in partnership with a local, publicly funded multipurpose university, used a similar array of material and human resources to improve their integration of technology. This paper is framed from the perspective of how new technology resources are absorbed into an existing, normative ecosystem, namely, the school culture (Bronfenbrenner, 1994; Sarason, 1982) in each of these buildings. Our interest in framing the study from this perspective was to capture the different aspects of these three school cultures that might contribute to increases in the use of technology. We were interested in how these differences inform our understanding of what it means to prepare schools, administrators, and teachers to use instructional technology effectively. In particular, the following research questions guided the study:

> *How do schools use fiscal and human resources to support technology use?*
>
> *How does the existing culture or ecosystem of the school affect technology integration?*
>
> *What factors mediate decisions regarding technology integration in schools?*

The three sites in the study represent an interesting array of urban schools. One is a multi-site year-round neighborhood school with roughly 700 students, 85% of whom are African American and 83% of whom qualify for free or reduced lunch. Their students with disabilities are integrated into general education settings. The second is a school whose 650 students are largely African American (72%). Two-thirds of the student body qualifies for free or reduced lunch. The school has adopted a social justice orientation to its curriculum. And the third is a 350-student, multi-age classroom school committed to discovery project-based learning that began as a single early childhood site. Its students with disabilities, comprising 20% of the school population, are included in general education settings. As with the other schools, most of its students are African American (80%) and most qualify for free or reduced lunch (80%). All three sites were, or were in the process of becoming, K–8 schools.

Using qualitative methods of research, we conducted a case study of technology integration at each school to describe each local school context and document in detail how each school used the technology resources made available to it through its partnership with the local university. This technology-focused partnership was funded through the U.S. Department of Education's Preparing Tomorrow's Teachers to Use Technology (PT^3) initiative. We were principally interested in documenting changes that occurred during the three-year period of the effort, from 1999–2002. At the start of the project, each of the three participating schools had low levels of technology integration.

The significance of this study lies in its ability to provide detailed descriptions of local urban school contexts where technology integration is occurring in the context of an active partnership between the university and the schools as part of a larger community-wide PK–16 effort. Further, it provides not only individual cases, but a cross-case analysis that addresses how schools might more effectively plan for the introduction and integration of technology. It is especially important because of the continued digital divide and the need to ensure that children in urban schools are prepared to draw on technology as a regular, transparent part not only of their education, but of their future work. Although the literature has documented difficulties with technology integration, prior studies often focus on surveys of technology use by individual teachers or groups of teachers rather than a cultural view of technology integration in the school ecosystem. Finally, few studies focus on technology integration in the context of urban school partnerships.

Context

The context for this study was a mid-sized urban school district in the Midwest. The partnership between the three schools and the university involved in this study is part of a larger community-wide partnership to improve urban education under the auspices of an active local PK–16 council whose members are committed to sharing the work of achieving student success. The three schools that were selected had a history of partnerships with the university.

For each of three years of the federal PT^3 grant, these three partner schools were provided with $32,000 each to support hiring a half-time technology specialist at their school. One morning per week of consultative support from a university-employed instructional technology specialist who coordinated the federal grant further supported the schools as they implemented new instructional technology activities. In addition, the three technology support specialists hired at the schools with project funds networked on a monthly basis under the leadership and guidance of the university technology grant coordinator. At the same time that these technology initiatives were taking place in these three partner schools—also as part of the same PT^3 grant—the university's preservice programs were undergoing significant redesign to improve technology preparation for their teacher candidates. Several preservice students were regularly placed in the three project partner schools for early field experiences as well as for student teaching.

Although throughout this project each of the three partner schools was provided with the same technology resources, each utilized those resources in very different ways. Prior to the project, all three principals had prioritized the acquisition of computer equipment for their teachers and students, resulting in an average of five computers per classroom as well as a computer lab. None of the schools, however, was wired for Internet access beyond a single connection in the building. At the outset of the project, survey data indicated that although teachers reported a high belief in the value of technology integration, they acknowledged that their belief was inconsistent with their practice, and that they were not using technology often or well. Computer use ranged from free choice periods to transferring students' "sloppy copies" to word-processed essays and reports. The modal use, however, was for skill-and-drill or free-time activities, rather than computer use directly connected to or integrated with the curriculum and classroom instruction. Also, prior to receiving funds through the federal grant, none of the three schools had a full-time instructional technology support person.

In addition, shortly after the PT^3 grant had begun, one of the project directors wrote grants to support three additional technology projects, one in each of these buildings, funded through a state-level competition that focused on technology in PK–16 partnerships. Working directly with the technology specialists, the schools identified projects they valued that were specifically connected to the relationship between technology and learning to be funded by these supplemental grants.

The budgeting process in the district in which these schools were located was decentralized for the purchase of hardware, software, and local network support. The district housed a centralized technology division that brought an Internet connection into each building and that provided various centralized professional development opportunities. The plan for wiring the buildings began with high schools, then middle schools, and then the elementary schools. At the start of this project the wave of wiring was just beginning to reach the elementary schools. Schoolwide Internet use was dependent on building-based administrator decisions regarding local hardware and networking capacity. On a districtwide basis, although every employee was eligible for an e-mail account, the use of e-mail was not well established in most buildings, and it was difficult for teachers to meet district criteria for its use. Communication between the centralized district resources and schools was dependent on the initiative of the local school principal, and individual teacher priorities and decision making.

Method and Data Sources

Qualitative research methods were used to examine how a common set of technology support resources made available through the grant were used at three different urban elementary schools within one urban school district. Multiple sources of data were gathered across the three years of the project to support the three case studies, including (1) field notes and logs from participant observers, (2) interviews with school personnel, (3) timeline and chronicle of technology-related priorities and events, and (4) a compilation of technology artifacts produced by the children and teachers. Each of these data sources was used to validate and cross-check findings within and across the schools.

Field notes and logs reflecting observations in classrooms, staff development activities, discussions with principals and teachers, and meetings and school events were compiled by two individuals who were participant observers: the grant coordinator and one of the grant's principal investigators. These individuals were involved in providing staff development and also providing ongoing support to the grant-funded technology coordinators in each building. The grant coordinator was the key participant observer at one of the schools; the principal investigator was the key participant observer at another school, and they shared the participant observer role at the third school. Situations they observed included classrooms, technology laboratories, staff development/retreats, and monthly collaboration meetings with the technology coordinators from each school. Additionally, participant observers had ongoing, regular interactions during the three years with the building principals and at least weekly meetings with the technology coordinators.

Interviews with key school personnel, both during and at the conclusion of the project, were conducted and then transcribed for analysis. Interviews conducted during the course of the project were informal, unstructured interviews (Merriam, 1998); formal semi-structured interviews were conducted at the close of the project, in the beginning of the year that followed the project's conclusion. Interviewees included the building principals, technology coordinators (two per building as each school had a change in this position during the course of the project), one classroom teacher nominated by project staff as a technology-using teacher, and one classroom teacher nominated by project staff as a technology-novice teacher. In all, a total of 15 formal, semi-structured interviews were conducted. A common interview schedule was used for all those interviewed, with additional questions for building principals and classroom teachers. The interview schedule for the formal interviews appears in Appendix 1.A. These interviews were conducted either by one of the grant's principal investigators, the grant coordinator, or two graduate students who were trained for this role. Graduate students working with the grant transcribed all interviews to convert them to text for analysis.

For each school, a timeline summarizing schoolwide technology goals and their implementation was developed, as well as a chronology of other technology-related events to clarify within- and cross-school efforts. Initial drafts of these documents were developed by the grant coordinator and one of the principal investigators and then reviewed by both principal investigators. Finally, a list of technology artifacts such as iMovies, slide shows, computerized drawings, and written work were compiled by the grant coordinator to provide an understanding of student outcomes related to the project's technology efforts.

Data were then assembled by school. Each piece of data, which existed primarily as written text, was read and analyzed by one of the principal investigators. Interviews were read and coded first, then field notes, followed by the timeline and compilation of artifacts. Preliminary drafts of the three cases were prepared by the principal investigators as a departure point for discussing within-case themes. All discussions included the two principal investigators and the project coordinator. As tentative themes surfaced from the data, each theme was discussed, sources of evidence were located within the data to support the proposed theme, and alternate explanations were proposed and discussed to determine whether the theme held up across the various data sources available to support the thematic analyses. In particular, during the analysis stage the authors actively sought out negative cases and nonconfirming evidence to challenge the interpretations being posed and to suggest alternative explanations. Once consensus was reached for each case, the next draft of the case was prepared. Based on readings and rereadings of the second draft of each case, the cross-case analysis was conducted. To develop the cross-case analysis, prominent issues in each individual case were discussed and noted. Then, each issue was discussed in depth to determine whether or not the particular issue held up and/or was represented over the three cases. Through this analysis, a finite set of themes was developed that characterized all three cases. Again, the researchers actively challenged each theme to determine whether evidence existed to support it; themes were discarded until the final set of themes was determined.

Results: The Case Studies

Each of the three case studies begins with a brief description of the school, followed by the technology context that existed prior to the inception of the grant. We then describe agents of technology growth and development that occurred during the project period. Each case concludes with a discussion of changes and future directions for the school. Following the individual cases, we offer a cross-case analysis. In order to protect the identity of the schools, pseudonyms replace the actual school names.

CASE 1: ROSA PARKS ELEMENTARY

The first school was Rosa Parks Elementary School. Approximately 80% of its 350 students qualified for free or reduced lunch at the time of the study, and approximately 70% of the students were bused in from other neighborhoods in the city. The school is diverse, inclusive, project oriented, and family focused. Although most of its students are African American (80%), 5% are Hmong, and the remaining 15% are Caucasian, with a very small number of Native American students. Additionally, Rosa Parks provides an inclusive education for the 20% of its population who qualify for special education services. These children's disabilities include emotional disturbance, cognitive disability, learning disability, attention deficit hyperactivity disorder, and other health impairments such as cerebral palsy. The school is committed to strengthening its ties to key major figures within the urban community. The school's philosophy of constructivist education and project-based learning is emphasized with the goal of empowering its children through applied learning about themselves, their community, and the world.

Technology context prior to the project

When the project began, the single technology lab at Rosa Parks had older Macintosh computers. The library and the lab also housed a few newer models. There were older black-and-white laser printers and a server, primarily for the skill-and-drill program that the computer lab was designed to support. Although there was a wiring closet in the school, nothing had been connected or set up at the start of the project. A new server had been delivered, but with no assistance from the district as to how to set it up. Wiring had been started at the school during a changeover in contractors the district hired. As a result, the school had been left in the middle of the wiring job and had been placed at the bottom of the list for wiring for two reasons: first, it was an elementary school and not a top priority, and second, on paper it was already listed as having been wired. In addition to the computers, the school had purchased digital cameras for the teachers that required a connection to the computer to view, edit, or print images. The school also had a standing technology committee prior to the start of the project.

Teachers used the computer class/lab as a drop-off point; it was treated as a "special" parallel to music or physical education, and teachers were not expected to remain in the lab with their students. The lab teacher supervised the students' use of a required skill-and-drill program. Students worked at their own pace, and the results of their work were recorded in a central database from which teachers could print progress reports at a later time. The office at Rosa Parks housed a variety of Macintosh and Windows machines. The principal and one of the secretaries each used newer Macintosh computers. The rest of the administrative staff used Windows-based machines.

Agents of technology growth and development

This school chose to use its project funds to support teachers who were already employed by the school. A teacher with an interest in technology became the official technology specialist, shifting from her role as a part-time physical education teacher and part-time technology support person. She took on the primary responsibility of supporting the network and maintaining the working condition of the technology resources in the school. An instructional technology consultant to the school, funded through a prior early childhood technology grant, continued her services. The presence of these two individuals enabled a complementary sharing of technology support. One person focused on the mechanical and systemwide use of technology while the other person worked with teachers to assist with integrating technology into the curriculum.

The PT^3 grant coordinator provided support in a number of ways. Because of his previous experience as a network manager, he worked with the technology specialist to ensure that the network and computers were working, that software was installed properly and legally, and consulted with her regarding software purchases. He also worked with the instructional technology specialist to develop ideas for sound, high-quality technology projects at the school, as well as to provide staff development so the teachers felt capable of using technology effectively.

The grant coordinator met weekly with the technology staff to develop new projects, plan and provide staff development with input from the technology specialist, and support the growing use of technology in the school. Staff development was offered prior to the start of the school day and on weekends. Before-school staff development opportunities were often attended not only by teachers but also by students. Staff development and technology projects were always considered within the context of current themes and projects at the school. Topics included, for example: HyperStudio, KidPix, iMovie, digital imaging, and how to integrate iMovie and HyperStudio. In effect, the coordinator served as a facilitator while the school technology staff served as support and change agents. The coordinator was welcomed as a part of the school community, was visible to teachers and staff, and was invited to school events, including an annual two-day retreat.

The principal at Rosa Parks welcomed the opportunity to continue to support the integration of technology into the school through this grant. She empowered the two technology specialists whose work was supported by the grant to take a joint leadership role in the school for technology. To extend the grant's reach, she utilized the permanent school budget to purchase new hardware and software for the school, including new Macintosh computers for the computer lab. With the additional state-sponsored grant funds mentioned earlier, four digital cameras, two digital video cameras, and a scanner were purchased to support technology use at the school. She also understood that staff development time was required in order for teachers to learn how to use technology and worked with the technology specialists to make this time available. She noted, "We have been able ourselves to purchase a number of new machines, the hardware, so we've really taken on the responsibility of the hardware for the program. The grant afforded us the opportunity to understand how to use it better." As agendas for staff development got squeezed, the time originally set for technology was sometimes reduced in these formal staff development workshops/activities.

The principal described technology as a tool to help teachers integrate the curriculum, which is foundational to the school's philosophy. She believed that it was important that teachers have newer and better equipped computers; digital cameras and iMovie were also now available for teachers to use as they chose interdisciplinary projects for their students that incorporated some aspect of technology use.

The principal also supported opportunities for students' uses of technology to be shared on a schoolwide basis. She used public opportunities that already existed within the school's culture for technology to be featured—for example, at regularly scheduled schoolwide gatherings whose purpose was to celebrate various strides the school and its students were making. This gave technology a visible platform in the school across all grade levels, and alongside the technology specialists, the principal became a "cheer-leader" for technology. These public occasions also provided an opportunity for students who had become heavily involved with technology and who had joined the school's new Technology Club to display their accomplishments.

The role of teachers was defined generally by the expectation the principal set that each teacher would use technology to have students support their required interdisciplinary projects. The specific relationship of technology to particular aspects of the curriculum, however, was not identified from the top down. It was up to the teachers themselves to figure out the most appropriate ways to integrate technology. To the extent that a high value was placed on project-based learning, technology was aligned with the curriculum for this requirement. There was no discussion about the specific ways technology could actually be used to advance student learning in particular content areas of the curriculum.

In other words, it was up to the individual teacher to determine how far he or she wished to go with technology use within the general parameter of the schoolwide commitment to project-based learning. Teachers could get involved to a greater or lesser extent depending on their personal interest and motivation, as long as technology use showed up in their projects. This might range from a simple use of technology for typing a written assignment to a complex use, such as the development of a PowerPoint presentation on a famous leader in the Civil Rights movement with an iMovie embedded in the presentation. The technology specialists and grant coordinator provided ongoing opportunities for teachers to develop their skills in a variety of works, painting, and graphic organizer software packages. For example, one high–technology-use teacher created a movie of a field trip.

On a schoolwide basis, students played a major role in technology use. An active Technology Club was formed that was empowered to document various events of importance to the school and the community. These activities included, for example, filming an urban technology exposition featuring work from all three partner schools and filming a bird count at a local urban nature center. Also, as noted above, consistent with the culture of the school, technology was given the same berth on the school's regular public celebration as other issues and developments considered to be of schoolwide importance. Students were empowered to share the fruits of their technology labor at these events; this public sharing also served to make sure that teachers and other students became familiar with the students who were knowledgeable about technology. They could then draw on these students as resources to further support technology use.

Changes and future directions

Describing the effect of this project, the principal noted, "In the beginning our computers collected dust. Our partnership allowed us an opportunity, afforded us an opportunity to begin some real staff development ... and because now teachers are able to access it more readily, and have a better understanding of how to use it, it is being used more often." One of the technology specialists stated a similar sentiment: "Getting to use the computer was more or less the goal [rather] than learning something on the computer. So the whole focus of the use of the computer has changed. It's now become a tool for learning rather than a Game Boy. And we've pulled a lot of programs off of our computers after analyzing whether they were really meeting the curriculum goals of the school."

In other words, the school leadership—both from the perspective of the administration and of technology teacher leaders—noted and were encouraged by the increased use of technology. With the end of the project in sight, however, the motivation for the staff to go on growing with regard to technology use seems to have waned. Although hard money from the school budget was used to bolster and update hardware, insufficient funding was available in the face of serious budget cuts to provide support teachers needed to move ahead with technology integration.

One of the former technology specialists did note that the school was moving to online performance assessments in certain content areas. However, in the absence of targeted funds for staff development and for funding an individual for network support, she doubted whether any other new technology projects could be launched. The principal believes that budgetary constraints hamper setting long-term technology goals. Her hope in terms of extending staff development is that enough "staff who really want to be pioneers" will be hired into the school to keep pushing technology use forward. Internal leadership among teachers, based on a "star teacher" technology model, then, is her best hope for an ongoing commitment to integrating technology.

CASE 2: CENTRAL ELEMENTARY

The second site was Central Elementary School, whose 650 students also reside in the largely poor urban center of a Midwestern city. Approximately 80% of the students are bused from other neighborhoods to this school, with 68% of the student population qualifying for free or reduced lunch. At Central, literacy is a schoolwide priority. Seventy-two percent of the students are African American, 16% are Caucasian, and the remainder are Native American, Asian, or Hispanic. The curriculum focus of the school is social justice.

Prior technology context

At the start of the project, Central Elementary had older Macintosh equipment and inkjet printers. Computers were grouped into small local networks to maximize the few printers. The lab, located just off the library, had the most up-to-date computers, which were Macintoshes. Every class had scheduled time in the lab for about 45 minutes per week, but this period functioned as a "special" and teachers were not expected to stay in the lab with their students. A technology committee was in existence prior to the start of the project.

The equipment and programs were very old; teachers reported this made using them difficult for other than an "extra" activity. Software that was available was mostly of the skill-and-drill variety and also included several games. The school had the beginnings of a wiring closet. The frame for the server and routers were there, but the final wiring to a fast connection to the district network had not been established.

Agents of technology growth and development

Several years prior to the funding of the PT^3 grant, the school had employed a technology specialist. That individual departed two years prior to the PT^3 grant and was not replaced. The principal used her PT^3 funds to hire a knowledgeable person to serve as a full-time technology specialist. He installed and maintained a network server, warehoused ancient or broken equipment, made sure software licenses were up to date, and removed programs that he believed had no educational benefit. He worked with teachers to increase their technology skills as well. The third year of the grant brought a new technology specialist to the school. This individual spent a significant amount of time maintaining the network and technology, as well as trying to provide instructional support for the teachers and students.

Each school determined how they utilized the grant coordinator's services. In the case of this school, the PT^3 coordinator worked with the technology specialist in a much more behind-the-scenes fashion. He communicated regularly with the technology specialist through face-to-face meetings or e-mail. He was not called upon to help teachers develop projects, provide staff development, or to have a visible presence in the building. During the third year, the new technology specialist chose not to make use of the grant coordinator, but he did attend monthly meetings led by the grant coordinator along with the specialists from the other partner schools.

Central's principal served as a facilitator and guide for her teachers and staff and relied on the expertise of the technology specialist and her classroom teachers to guide her in decision making. The technology specialist was encouraged to develop both short- and long-term plans for technology acquisition and use. The principal supported his decisions to shift the lab from a special class to a place in which students could work on an as-needed basis. As a result, the lab was used more often—and more effectively—by those who wanted to integrate technology into their curriculum. When the principal at Central talked about technology, she did so in the context of the curriculum goals of the school. In this way, she did not treat technology as a separate, fragmented activity in the school. She seemed to believe that technology had the potential to improve instruction.

The commitment to curriculum was evident in how new initiatives were supported. Central's principal encouraged her teaching and support staff to propose new projects and acquisitions. Her criterion for responding to these requests was the degree to which they made sense given the school's philosophy, curriculum focus on social justice, and academic needs of the students. For example, when the technology specialist proposed securing interactive white boards, wireless laptop carts, and wiring the upper grade classrooms, the initiative was funded. The principal understood that wireless Internet access and portable computers could strengthen students' research and composition skills and enable them to access content relevant to social justice themes.

In another example, as kindergarten, first, and second grade teachers worked with university professors to write a supplemental grant to bring wireless laptop computers into balanced literacy instruction, the principal not only supported the project philosophically, but also committed matching funds for a portion of the project and reserved staff development days so that the teachers could become familiar with the new technology and how it could best be integrated into their literacy instruction. If grant funds were not available, she paid for the technology specialist to attend these meetings so that he could absorb supporting the maintenance and use of the equipment into his duties.

Despite the leadership of the principal, teachers at Central varied in their technology interest, use, and expertise. Available technology resources were public knowledge in the school. Technology growth took place from the classroom level up, based on teachers' individual decisions to integrate technology. The teachers used technology in ways and at times that seemed sensible to them given their instructional goals and technology knowledge. If technology was perceived by them to increase the power of their instruction, they used it; if it did not, they chose not to use it. Teachers were not required to use technology for any predetermined length of time or manner, nor were they expected to document or publicly display their students' progress in this area. Each grade level seemed to have at least one strong technology-using teacher. Other teachers sought out these grade-level experts for ideas on how to use technology with their students.

Students used technology to support their learning in a variety of ways. Although for some students technology was more often a replacement for paper and pencil work or a reward, for others it was a tool for pursuing questions, learning content at a deeper level, and sharing what was learned. By the time the grant ended, more students at all grade levels in the school were using technology to support their learning of content and were demonstrating the ability to use all of the technologies available to them.

Changes and future directions

At the start of the project, teachers reported that technology was viewed as an add-on. It was used to reward students, to keep them busy, and to teach basic computing skills. As time passed and personnel and hardware resources were committed, more teachers began integrating technology into their curriculum. Evidence can be seen in video productions created by upper grade students, the study of African-American poets by second graders with disabilities, lost pet books developed by first graders, and research on Mother Jones conducted and disseminated by second graders. Technology-based activities supported content. Some teachers used technology to supplant usual instruction, others used it to augment or follow up instruction. Technology shifted from being used three to four students at a time to being used in whole group instruction as well as small group, paired, and independent use. At this school, technology became a tool for collaborative learning, a tool made increasingly available through lab and wireless resources.

At Central, the principal relied on the expertise of the technology coordinator to provide the knowledge and skills to make widespread technology use possible. Working with two different technology coordinators during the span of this project, the principal trusted their judgment. As a result, she supported the first technology coordinator in bringing network capacity to the school as a means of getting the Internet into the hands of the students well before the district had scheduled it. She took her direction from her technology-savvy staff as they made recommendations for purchases of hardware and software. Her criterion for responding to these requests was the degree to which they made sense given the school's philosophy, curriculum focus on social justice, and academic needs of the students.

CASE 3: MICHIGAN STREET ELEMENTARY

The third school was Michigan Street Elementary School, which enrolls approximately 700 students, of whom 88% are African American, 8% are Caucasian, and 4% are Southeast Asian. Approximately 83% of its children qualify for free or reduced lunch. Only about 9% of the students at this school are bused in from other neighborhoods; it is therefore essentially a neighborhood school. Michigan Street has a philosophy of integration of students with disabilities and houses a high population of students with autism.

Prior technology context

At the start of the project, Michigan Street had a computer lab with approximately 30 basic Windows machines. The lab was used as a drop-off point and teachers were not required to stay with their students during the time they were in the computer lab. During these periods, the lab teacher, previously an early childhood teacher, supervised the students' use of a skill and activities program. The students worked at their own pace and the results were recorded in a central database that teachers could print out at a later time. Much of the software consisted of single-use licenses. The principal connected to the Internet through her own service provider using a phone line and a Macintosh laptop. No standing technology committee existed at Michigan Street prior to the project.

In general, the classrooms themselves housed older Macintoshes. Each teacher in the building had a Windows machine at his or her desk that was wired to a television monitor suspended from the wall. The platform of this computer, as well as the software, was inconsistent with the student-used computers. Software spanned skill-and-drill, works programs, and paint programs. Students were allowed to use computers as a reward in learning centers, or for typing up their writing. In other words, computers were not integrated into classroom instruction, but rather functioned as an add-on activity. One classroom, however, was equipped with newer Macintosh computers. In that classroom, each student had his or her own station. There was no server connecting them, although a server had been purchased to do so. The teacher in the classroom was attempting to integrate technology into the curriculum using word processing and HyperStudio. Classroom printers were largely inkjet, but the computer lab had a color laser printer and a black and white laser printer, as well as a printer that would enable teachers to print posters and banners.

In addition to the computers, the school had a range of other technology equipment such as a cart with portable word processors, video equipment, and a digital camera. Teachers were not made aware of this equipment and as a result it was rarely used during the time of the PT^3 grant.

Agents of technology growth and development

During the course of the grant, the school purchased newer Windows machines for the computer lab, keeping the Macintoshes in the classroom. Technology staff worked to develop a database of technology hardware and software throughout the school. A server was purchased and connected so that the classroom computers were connected to one another. The lab computers were connected to a separate server. As a result, work that students began in the lab could not easily be finished in the classroom and vice versa.

As a result of PT^3 grant funds, a teacher was shifted from the classroom to the role of technology specialist. This teacher had an interest in technology and was viewed as a leader by her principal but was by no means an expert regarding hardware and software and had no knowledge of networks. In addition to her role as a technology specialist, which she assumed as half of her job, she also worked to write grants and secure funds for additional projects at the school. The degree of her communication/collaboration with the computer lab instructor was somewhat low.

The grant coordinator met with this individual on a nearly weekly basis, either at the university or at the school to discuss hardware and curricular issues. There was no clear focus or direction to these discussions. Ideas were discussed about workshop topics for teachers or how to make the server work. The grant coordinator provided five staff development workshops on video editing, databases, web design, and how to use the electronic report cards that were developed as part of the grant. These workshops, with the exception of the electronic report cards, were not directly connected to any curricular goal.

During the third year of the grant, a new technology specialist was named. A former classroom teacher at this school, also assigned to this role half-time, this individual sought the support of the grant coordinator on a regular basis to support the teachers' administrative needs. The technology specialist had a basic knowledge of how technology might support instruction but had a narrow range of expertise regarding software and hardware. She was very eager to learn, however, and spent a considerable amount of time broadening her knowledge base. Although the bulk of the work focused on developing online report cards for teachers, occasional workshops demonstrating software use were held as well.

The principal at Michigan Street viewed her role as developing teacher leaders. She supported teachers' staff development through their attendance at local and national conferences. Michigan Street's principal trusted that her teachers knew what they needed to develop as professionals and what their students needed to grow academically. She encouraged her teachers to conceptualize innovative projects and seek funds to support their implementation. In other words, she put great faith in her staff's ability to follow through on whatever she and/or they committed to and intervened only when problems were brought to her attention. With regard to technology, the principal was interested in acquiring media and materials she thought would benefit her teachers and students. The teachers were to make a choice whether to learn about and take advantage of the resources. No common mission or thread connected these initiatives, however, and once monies were obtained, there was inconsistent administrative support to ensure that projects were carried out as they were intended.

In response to receiving grant funds from the PT^3 grant, the principal placed one of her teachers in the role of school-based technology specialist. A computer lab instructor was already in place. The grant-funded position was to serve as a conduit between the university and school. The person was to learn about technology, collaborate with the other technology partner schools, conceptualize projects for the school that might support technology integration, and so on. In other words, this person was to become a technology leader.

The teachers at Michigan Street were committed to their students. They consciously worked toward inclusion of all their students and celebration of individual differences. Much of the staff was also involved in one of the many after-school programs offered for the students at the school. Regarding technology, each teacher had several computers in the classroom and access to the school's technology lab. Teachers differed in their use of technology. Technology was viewed by the principal as a valued tool teachers were to utilize as they deemed appropriate. Although most teachers utilized low-end technology such as tape recorders or VCRs and some of the teachers supported the high-end technology needed by the students with special needs such as augmentative communication devices, for most teachers computer technology was not integrated into their curriculum.

Many of the teachers reported feeling uncertain, however, about how to use technology effectively and felt their own skills were weak. For example, in the after-school program developed to focus on students learning to use computer-based graphic organizers to support their writing, some teachers checked out laptop computers loaded with the educational software so they could become more familiar with the technology. Other teachers abandoned the technology component of the after-school program and used paper-based organizers.

The students at Michigan Street were exposed to a wide array of learning and personal growth experiences. During the school day they learned about basic content but also engaged in thematic learning such as their annual World Fest projects. After school they could take advantage of several programs, from athletic teams to literacy/writing groups to camp. Essentially, they were provided with a fertile landscape upon which to grow. Students approached these opportunities in a cafeteria fashion, taking what they liked and leaving the rest. With regard to technology, they appeared to enjoy using technology such as computers and digital cameras. These resources were utilized sporadically as the teachers made them available.

Changes and future directions

At the outset of the grant, teachers' views of technology at Michigan Street were consistent with the view of the teachers at the other schools regarding its role and use. It appeared that the principal saw technology as a way to level the playing field for her largely poor urban students. Her goal was to provide them with exposure to technology tools to close the digital divide. Students used technology as a free choice item, to write final composition drafts, and to learn basic skills. Teachers reported that they believed in the notion of technology integration but admittedly were not practicing it. The inconsistencies in availability, connectivity, and compatibility of technology throughout the school made it challenging to use technology across multiple learning environments.

During the course of the grant, technology was addressed on a range of fronts, primarily at the administrative and system level. The first point of business was to get servers working properly so that teachers could communicate with one another and have a secure place to store files. The second activity of the grant involved creating online report cards. At the end of the grant, the school was connected to the Internet at the classroom level and teachers began thinking more about how to integrate technology into their instruction. In response to this interest, workshops on digital video production, graphic organizers, and other software programs were provided by the grant coordinator.

More efforts were made to try to link what was happening in the computer lab to what was happening in the classrooms, and vice versa. The lab at Michigan Street shifted from a place for special instruction to a place where teachers could take their students to work on classroom-related projects. In the classroom, upper grade students created book reports with multimedia software, e-mailed children in a foreign country, and used graphic organizers to support their writing. Younger students used phonemic awareness skill-and-drill programs to support their reading while teachers worked with small reading groups. Once the school became wired at the classroom level for Internet use, children began to use online reference sources as well. These were decontextualized projects however, not aligned with curriculum. The enduring focus of technology reform at this school was electronic report cards.

Scaffolding Technology Integration

One of the most commonly held beliefs about implementing technology across a school is that the commitment and leadership of the principal is essential to reaching this goal. These cases portray three principals who were all committed to implementing technology and who voiced their commitment in terms of support for the project itself and for their technology-savvy teachers. The three principals also made time for university-based project staff, were respectful of project staff and, although to different degrees, welcomed them into their buildings. Technology was viewed positively at all three sites. Professional development for technology was definitely "on the radar screen" in each building, with resources that were augmented through the auxiliary grants funded for each school through the state university grant program.

In addition, all three principals used funds from their regular school budgets to purchase hardware and software, as well as to make decisions regarding funding technology support personnel beyond the small contributions made through the PT^3 grant. By most measures, these actions by the schools' three leaders suggest that leadership was in place in every site. Follow-up interviews with each principal also attested to their valuing of technology and their contributions to enhancing the technology environment in their particular building.

However, despite the general valuing of technology, as well as the local investment in technology resources, each school had very different results. In this analysis, we suggest that beyond a generalized support for and investment in technology, both in terms of hardware and professional development, other considerations appear important to technology integration and use, and serve in a sense as scaffolds in this regard. The analysis of qualitative data from these three sites suggests three scaffolds that support technology integration. They are: (1) alignment with the school's curriculum/mission, (2) teacher leadership, and (3) public/private roles for technology recognition.

ALIGNMENT WITH THE CURRICULUM/MISSION OF THE SCHOOL

In each of the three schools, the principals viewed the relationship between technology and the curriculum/mission in three very different ways. The degree to which this *alignment* was recognized and embraced by the school leader resulted in different technology implementation trajectories.

At Rosa Parks, technology was connected to the broad mission of project-based learning. When teachers were able to begin using technology for student presentations, they were using it to meet the school's mission of project-based learning. Further, the public displays of technology skill and activity that were initiated through this project were consistent with the family/community orientation of the school. The specific relationship between technology and particular content areas was not well articulated, however. In fact, the goal for the students was to use technology to demonstrate learning rather than enhance learning. Although some teachers noticed that learning was deepened through the use of technology, these were individual rather than schoolwide insights. The principal at Rosa Parks talked about technology in relationship to curriculum as a general concept, but did not discuss the specific connection between technology and content areas. Although technology was aligned with the general school mission, it did not appear to be well aligned with the curriculum itself.

At Central, the principal talked about technology as a means of moving the students ahead in the curriculum. She discussed technology and literacy, technology and writing, and technology and student research. She seemed to view technology as a means of improving instruction and, in the long run, as a means of improving student achievement. The alignment with the school's social justice mission was not discussed, but the alignment with day-to-day instruction was articulated well. Although individual teachers could determine the degree to which they used technology, there was an expectation from the principal that its use should serve the curriculum goals of the school.

At Michigan Street, technology was not discussed in relationship to a specific direction of the curriculum or the school. Rather, it was viewed as another new project that was not necessarily connected to other initiatives at the school. Although very supportive of the project, the principal did not discuss technology specifically in relationship to its potential in any given curriculum area. Student achievement was conceptualized more in terms of test scores than in terms of curriculum goals. Although individual teachers used technology—and if they were particularly interested, they were recognized by the principal for doing so—the primary, lasting use was in the administrative work of creating electronic report cards. Staff development to provide technology expertise included specific software that featured graphic organizers; the potential for its use, however, was not discussed from an administrative level. The alignment between technology and the curriculum was loosely coupled.

These differences appear to indicate that the question of alignment is a critical one for the implementation of technology. Whether it is seen as central to the work of teaching relies on the degree to which the principal and the teachers recognize and affirm the alignment. From the outset the discussion of technology integration must first be a discussion of the curriculum—and the leadership role has to be curriculum-based. The initial discussion of technology makes sense only insofar as it is directly related to the curriculum and is not focused on the acquisition of technology resources—either hardware or software.

In other words, the real leadership act regarding technology may be to *resist* the temptation to acquire hardware and software decontextualized from a specific curricular goal and instead to commit to limited purchases and to doing a few things well with technology as a first step. For technology to have an enduring effect, principals themselves have to take an active role in defining and communicating a *sensible* role for technology integration. For example, it might be prudent to limit the scope of software acquisition to a few packages that enable high levels of student communication (e.g., painting, works, and graphic organizers) as a specific starting point. A school could, for example, purchase three good software programs to begin with, and ensure that teachers master those as they relate directly to the curriculum—and look toward increased student learning as a result. This is not meant to suggest that teachers who see themselves as "techies" are held back, but rather that teachers who might otherwise be reticent might be willing to learn to do a few things well technologically and be reinforced by results related to student learning. Principals themselves do not at first need to be technology experts, but they do need to understand the alignment issues and the importance of the curriculum connection. A commitment to the curriculum is one critical scaffold for integrating technology.

At the same time, because they are responsible for the fiscal well being of the school, principals also need to be concerned with the practical aspects of supporting hardware, networks, and so on, both from a human and fiscal resource basis—even if initial technology resources are limited purposefully. They also need to be prepared to expand technology resources on a regular basis as teachers practice how technology specifically enhances the curriculum and begin to see its uses and use it effectively.

These alignment issues had different implications at the three schools. The principal at Central used the grant as a catalyst to embed technology more permanently as a means of advancing the curriculum goals of the school. The principal at Rosa Parks realized the potential of technology in a more general way; in her school, technology leadership was not permanently planned for although new hardware and software had been purchased and there were high hopes for its use. At Michigan Street, a systematic understanding of the potential of technology vis-à-vis the curriculum was not in place; rather, the enduring effect was the administrative decision to create electronic report cards.

TEACHER LEADERSHIP

The leadership function of principals, however, can only go so far. A second scaffold we believe may hold importance across these case studies is *teacher leadership*. The principal at Rosa Parks talked eloquently about the role of teacher leadership in the future of the school. In the face of budget cuts, she chose to discontinue a dedicated technology specialist. Instead, she discussed the importance of hiring staff members who were technology savvy as a means to moving the school ahead.

During the course of the project, the leadership for technology resided in the staff that was made available during the project, including the project coordinator, who was a major player in technology at the school. The visibility of technology was brokered by the grant staff much more than it was by permanent staff at Rosa Parks. All teachers at the school were mandated to use technology in their students' project-based work; it was a top-down imperative but ample support was provided for teachers to acquire the skills to produce the ends the principal desired. Teachers at the school responded to and participated in technology workshops but did not determine independently how they wished to use it. The principal trusted the teachers to learn how to use the technology, but she prescribed the conditions under which it had to be used. She empowered the technology project staff and held a very high degree of respect for their expertise, but their charge was directly related to the goal of public presentations associated with project-based learning.

A different situation existed at Central, where the teachers could approach either the technology specialist or the principal with an idea about technology—and were encouraged to do so. If they could justify their idea in relation to the curriculum and student learning, the principal was prepared to give it serious consideration and respond positively and from a permanent funding and staffing perspective. In other words, once teachers understood the potential of technology and got more involved in using it, they had an avenue for pursuing it and could expect that such use would likely be supported. Further, the principal at Central deferred to the expertise of the technology specialist, but sought justification for suggestions that were made. This put the responsibility on the teachers for creating the pathways for technology and arguing for the resources to support it. At Rosa Parks, that avenue was effectively closed off once the project ended and there was no internal leadership for technology. Therefore, the future of technology seemed to lie in the chance hiring of staff who were technology savvy.

At Michigan Street, the decision to get involved with technology remained with individual teachers. They could choose whether to participate in workshops and whether to use technology heavily. A similar situation existed at Central, but at Central the principal talked about technology use in relationship to the curriculum and saw it as a potential source of instruction across the staff. She created a context in which technology became an integral part of the school's culture. At Michigan Street, teachers who used technology might be rewarded by having the principal arrange for them to attend a technology conference and feature the school publicly. Although there was a fair amount of technology activity during the grant, technology seemed to remain an add-on, except in the case of electronic report cards, which persisted after the grant ended. Teacher leadership was anticipated while the grant resources were available, but occurred on an individual basis. When the grant was able to provide the resources, technology was a high priority. With the end of the grant, the potential was recognized but supporting it was not viewed as a priority.

The teacher leadership scaffold is an important consideration for several reasons. First, it is unlikely that principals themselves will possess the technology expertise required to move a school ahead. Therefore, principals must often look to teacher leaders to inform and guide technology integration. Next, the relationship between classroom teachers who use technology well and the school itself is an important aspect of teacher leadership; in other words, how does the expertise of classroom teachers get shared? A formal structure for technology-using teachers to share their expertise and coach their peers should be implemented. Finally, what is the relationship between technology experts and technology-using classroom teachers in implementing technology in a focused manner? How often are technology specialists—teachers themselves—expected to be professional development leaders rather than custodians of equipment?

PUBLIC/PRIVATE ROLES FOR TECHNOLOGY

A third scaffold for technology integration in these cases is public/private roles for technology related to teacher and student empowerment. In terms of the students, the most public roles existed at Rosa Parks, where public recognition was integrated into the regular recognition avenues that were practiced in that school. Everyone knew that technology was being used in new and exciting ways and this accomplishment was celebrated publicly. The recognition was showered on the students rather than the teachers. In many ways, the students were carrying the technology ball, so to speak, along with the technology specialists. Certainly individual teachers were beginning to use technology, but in the context of the principal's mandate.

At Michigan Street, it was individual teachers who were recognized more than the students. There was not schoolwide public recognition, but rather those teachers who were ahead in technology integration were asked to present their work publicly outside of the school at conferences. Within the school, technology was not featured publicly on a regular basis. The absence of recognition within the school conveyed the message that technology was not a high priority.

At Central, it was also the case that there was not schoolwide public recognition of technology in the way it existed at Rosa Parks, for example. However, once technology was on the principal's radar screen, she began to talk about instances of technology use in her regular descriptions of the school's progress. She herself began to integrate the discussion about technology, not as an add-on, but more as an integral part of her understanding of the school. She knew which teachers were technology savvy and at some level could talk about how they were using technology, their students' accomplishments, and so on. Once the teachers began to demonstrate leadership in technology integration, she in effect praised their work as part of her regular praise of her staff and their accomplishments. She also discussed student use of technology across content areas.

It may be the case that different levels of recognition for students and teachers alike are needed to support technology integration. These various kinds of recognition may not necessarily need to be connected with flashy uses of technology, however. Rather, they may be day-to-day uses that demonstrate higher levels of student understanding and achievement.

Conclusion

A dichotomy is often invoked in discussing the implementation of technology in the schools. In this dichotomy, the purchase and upkeep of hardware and software is pitted against investing in professional development for teachers. The conventional wisdom is that the investment in professional development is almost always slighted in favor of the acquisition of equipment and software—which is then used inappropriately or inadequately. Although we agree with this analysis, we believe that these three case studies illustrate a more complex situation with regard to technology integration. This analysis suggests that the ability of a school staff, through professional development activities, to use technology well—defined here as using technology in the service of the curriculum—is not simply the flip side of investing in hardware and software.

Preparing a school well for technology integration appears to represent a special instance of professional development, one that has a unique identity requiring a unique kind of stewardship. To use technology effectively, principals and other technology leaders who contribute to decision making regarding how a school will invest in technology first need a solid understanding of the difference between technology use to enhance learning of the curriculum and technology use for productivity—as well as the ability to make distinctions in the various kinds of supports that will be required for each. We would argue that it is not a case of privileging professional development over acquisition, but rather that in planning for technology integration, professional development and acquisition considerations need to take place simultaneously. Curriculum needs to be the overriding framework for these deliberations. In other words, good planning for technology integration takes a special understanding of the acquisition of hardware and software specifically *as it relates to the curriculum*. This requires graduated staff development that anchors technology in the curriculum, but that also recognizes the need for teachers to have the opportunity to learn the technology well so that it can be used easily and transparently to support the curriculum. It goes without saying that teachers must be deeply informed about content and pedagogy in a particular content area to use technology to enhance learning effectively. Neither can be shortchanged. In short, preparing for technology integration requires a much more nuanced understanding of what it means to provide leadership and professional development at a school site, with the ability to move back and forth in a very sophisticated manner between learning technology itself and the curriculum. But why is this the case?

Traditionally, professional development encourages teachers to change their practice within a relatively familiar zone of operation. New approaches to literacy, mathematics, writing across the curriculum, block scheduling, or project-based learning all pose challenges—but they exist within a relatively safe, traditional classroom structure and school context that is known to the players. As technology is introduced, teachers and principals *must always juggle multiple levels of professional development and expertise*, moving back and forth between the technology itself and the curriculum. Simply put, the territory becomes much more complex for teachers and administrators alike. The reality is that although technology always needs to serve the curriculum first, it also requires administrators and teachers to invest real time and effort, real fiscal and human resources in acquiring and learning to use the technology itself and keeping up the technology precisely so that it can serve the curriculum.

Without a clear vision of the goal of technology as it relates directly to the curriculum, it is possible to get distracted along the way with the details of acquisition, with productivity goals, or with generalized uses of technology—but not uses that are specific to various aspects of the curriculum. Administrators who themselves may feel insecure about technology may take technology advice that will not serve the curriculum well (Wasser, 1996; Radlick, 1998; Thomas, 1999). Planning for technology should directly address the complexities of this endeavor, the juggling act between acquisition, network support, professional development directly related to the curriculum, and technology for professional productivity.

Technology integration may be likely to pose a special challenge in urban schools, which tend to be under-resourced to begin with. When the budgetary chips are down, so to speak, the failure to support technology may be tempting, and in the face of shrinking dollars technology may quickly be seen as a real stretch, an unaffordable luxury. This stance may be mitigated when administrators and teachers anchor their understanding of technology deep within the curriculum. But it is also made more complex with the reality that schools will need to update technology not only to serve the curriculum, but also to continue supporting professional productivity.

We have argued that the initial understanding on the part of the principal of the complexity of technology is crucial to a measured, reasonable introduction to the goals and progress of technology integration. Although the principal may set the tone, it is equally important to have a trusted technology leader in the school who knows technology itself. This technology knowledge then needs to be aligned strongly with the curriculum, based on a sound understanding of the curriculum itself. Where there is strong technology knowledge but a weak sense of alignment, technology may absorb scarce resources but not add substantially to students' progress. When principals and technology leaders themselves connect all discussions about technology acquisition to the curriculum, the alignment is much more likely to take place. It seems important that schools identify and understand their school context and mission, identify curricular goals for the future, and consider how technology growth and development goals would serve curricular goals. Both agendas, technology acquisition and use and curriculum, need to move forward simultaneously, with the understanding that quite often the two will be intertwined, reciprocally supporting one another.

However, technology integration is not simply a top-down affair. When either a principal or a technology leader in a school is more focused on technology acquisition and less focused on alignment, it will be critical to have a teacher leader who can step up to address the curriculum question. Leadership from teachers and children can support, and in some cases drive, schoolwide technology and curricular agendas. The enthusiasm of children and thoughtful risk-taking of teachers can combine to create atmospheres of a mutually defined learning space—a space where children have a broader array of tools to explore ideas and demonstrate skill. When schools make these innovations public, even to themselves, the opportunity for increased use and collaboration becomes more likely. For this to occur, technology must permeate all aspects of a school's ecological system, including students, teachers, classrooms, and administrative leaders.

The analysis of these cases provides a greater understanding of the complex interplay of curriculum, technology, and professional growth and development activities. The study illustrates some of the subtleties associated with planning for and implementing technology integration in the schools—subtleties that often go unvoiced at the school level, where principals and teachers make important decisions about the role of technology. These three cases illustrate a range of understanding of what it takes to integrate technology on the part of principals who all considered themselves to be—and were, to some extent—technology supporters.

What are the implications for future research? Case studies of how principals make decisions regarding technology purchases, guided by the role of the curriculum in these decisions, is one area that could be explored. Further research could also be structured to look at the existing matches between technology and the curriculum and the presence or lack of alignment. Finally, research could also be conducted on whether or how technology and curriculum are connected in the process of professional development.

To be integrated successfully, there must be a clear understanding that technology creates a new layer for professional development. It is not just another resource to be added and considered haphazardly, with its promise and commitment easily falling away in times of fiscal crisis. Instead, technology can be a powerful tool for moving schools toward their fundamental goals of supporting student learning. What seems critical for this to happen, however, is a deep understanding of how technology relates to curricular goals, how professional development must be layered to embrace both technology learning and curricular alignment in relationship to one another, and how carefully constructed professional development can support technology's most judicious use.

Acknowledgments

This paper was prepared as part of the Technology and Urban Teaching Project at the University of Wisconsin-Milwaukee funded by the U.S. Department of Education's PT[3] program. This paper does not necessarily represent the policy of the U.S. Department of Education or imply endorsement by the Federal Government.

Author Update

In the years since this research was conducted, conversations around technology integration in schools have continued, with the current trend being to match technology use outside of school (e.g., social networking, gaming consoles, smartphones) to its use in school as a means of engaging students in the curriculum. Because technology is already integrated in meaningful ways throughout students' lives, with children regularly using multiple types of technology as tools for communication, entertainment, learning, and the like, maintaining that use across settings to enhance learning should be a goal.

A competing reality in the schools, however, is the use of technology to develop rote and test-taking skills in an effort to improve school-wide test scores. This underscores the challenge we raised in our

Continued

study, namely, that school officials in leadership roles must prioritize technology as a tool to enhance learning of the curriculum rather than using it primarily for short-term achievement test gain. But this narrow use of technology also says something about the often narrow perception of the needs of children in urban schools, as well as the lack of funding for high-end technology in these same schools.

A second finding from our study was the importance of teachers as leaders. Personnel preparation programs must work harder to integrate technology effectively in ways that encourage university and college students to use it to enhance not only their learning of academic content, but also to support children's learning. Clearly, electronic portfolios, PowerPoint, and electronic courseware are insufficient to achieve the goals of integrating technology for enhancing the learning of prospective teachers and of PK–12 students. Rather, we need to encourage preservice teachers to use the technology they most often use anyway in interesting, engaging ways to serve the curriculum.

The increase in access to the Internet combined with free tools to provide access for individuals with print-based disabilities can do much to narrow the gap that often exists between urban schools and more affluent ones. Still, leaders must educate themselves, pursue a vision of learning based on the trust that testing results will follow rather than lead decisions, and support teacher leaders in technology use in their schools. Technology is becoming increasingly affordable, portable, and powerful. Still, many schools do not introduce technology at the elementary level and continue to use technology in very stilted ways, resulting in an ever expanding disconnect between school-based and community learning.

References

Bronfenbrenner, U. (1994). Ecological models of human development. In T. Husen & T. N. Postlethwaite (Eds.), *The international encyclopedia of education* (2nd ed., pp. 1643–1647). New York, NY: Elsevier Science.

Butzin, S. M. (2001). Using instructional technology in transformed learning environments: An evaluation of Project CHILD. *Journal of Research on Computing in Education, 33*(4), 367–373.

Carvin, A. (2000). More than just access: Fitting literacy and content into the digital divide equation. *Educause Review, 35*(6), 38–47.

CEO Forum on Education and Technology (2001). *Key building blocks for student achievement in the 21st century: Assessment, alignment, accountability, access and analysis. Year 4 report.* Retrieved December 13, 2003, from www.ceoforum.org

Chang, H., Henriquez, A., Honey, M., Light, D., Moeller, B., & Ross, N. (1998). *The Union City story.* New York, NY: Education Development Center, Center for Children and Technology.

Cradler, J. (n.d.). *Implementing technology in education: Recent findings from research and evaluation studies.* Far West Laboratory. Retrieved July 23, 2002, from www.wested.org/techpolicy/recapproach.html

Cuban, L. (2001). Why are most teachers infrequent and restrained users of computers in their classrooms? In J. Woodward & L. Cuban (Eds.), *Technology, curriculum, and professional development* (pp. 121–137). Thousand Oaks, CA: Corwin Press.

Doty, D. E., Popplewell, S. R., & Byers, G. O. (2001). Interactive CD-ROM storybooks and young readers' reading comprehension. *Journal of Research on Computing in Education, 33*(4), 374–385.

Fulton, K., & Sibley, R. (2003). Barriers to equity. In G. Solomon, N. J. Allen, & P. Resta (Eds.), *Toward digital equity* (pp. 14–24). New York, NY: Allyn and Bacon.

Gooler, D., Kautzer, K., & Knuth, R. (2000). *Teacher competence in using technologies: The next big question. PREL briefing paper.* Honolulu, HI: Pacific Resources for Education and Learning.

Hativa, N. (1988). Computer-based drill and practice in arithmetic—widening the gap between high and low achieving students. *American Educational Research Journal, 25*(3), 366–397.

Honey, M., Culp, K. M., & Carrigg, F. (2000). Perspectives on technology and education research: Lessons from the past and present. *Journal of Educational Computing Research, 23*(1), 5–14.

Jones, B. F. (1998). *Learning with technology: Integrating new technologies into classroom instruction.* Washington, DC: U.S. Department of Education and North Central Regional Education Laboratory.

Merriam. S. B. (1998). *Qualitative research and case study applications in education.* San Francisco, CA: Jossey-Bass.

Radlick, M. S. (1998). Hardware, software, vaporware, and wetware: A cautionary tale for superintendents. In R. R. Spillane & P. Regnier (Eds.), *The superintendent of the future: strategy and actions for achieving academic excellence* (pp. 237–266). Gaithersburg, MD: Aspen.

Rogers, P. L. (2000). Barriers to adopting emerging technologies in education. *Journal of Educational Computing Research, 22*, 455–472.

Sarason, S. B. (1982). *The culture of the school and the problem of change* (2nd ed.). Boston, MA: Allyn and Bacon.

Solomon, G., Allen, N. J., & Resta, P. (Eds.). (2003). *Toward digital equity.* New York, NY: Allyn and Bacon.

Thomas, W. R. (1999). *Educational technology: Are school administrators ready for it?* Atlanta, GA: Southern Regional Education Board. Available at www.sreb.org/page/1295/publications.html

Trilling, B., & Hood, P. (1999). Learning, technology, and education reform in the knowledge age or "We're wired, webbed, and windowed, now what?" *Educational Technology, 39*(3), 5–18.

U.S. Congress, Office of Technology Assessment. (1995). *Teachers & technology: Making the connection. OTA report summary.* Washington, DC: Government Printing Office.

Wasser, J. D. (1996). Reform, restructuring, and technology infusion. In *Technology infusion and school change: Perspectives and practices* (pp. xxiv–lvi). Cambridge, MA: TERC.

Wenglinskey, H. (1998). *Does it compute? The relationship between educational technology and student achievement in mathematics.* Princeton, NJ: Educational Testing Service Policy Information Center.

WestEd. (2002). *Investing in technology: The learning return. Technology policy brief.* San Francisco, CA: Author.

White, N., Ringstaff, C., & Kelley, L. (2002). *Getting the most from technology in schools. Knowledge brief.* San Francisco, CA: WestEd.

Zhang, Y. (2000). Technology and the writing skills of students with learning disabilities. *Journal of Research on Computing in Education, 32*(4), 467–478.

APPENDIX
1.A

Formal Interview Schedule

QUESTIONS ASKED OF ALL INTERVIEWEES:

- Describe how technology is used in your school.
- Describe how technology is used to support instruction in your school.
- Describe how the use of technology has changed over the past three years.
- Describe how the use of technology resources has changed over the past three years.
- What are your future plans with regard to technology? Short term? Long term?
- What might help or hinder reaching these goals?

ADDITIONAL QUESTIONS FOR BUILDING ADMINISTRATORS:

- What role did you play in the changes you described?
- What were your goals for the school?
- What did you accomplish?

ADDITIONAL QUESTION FOR TEACHERS:

- Give us an example of technology use in your classroom and/or in the technology lab (if applicable).

CHAPTER

2

Fostering Historical Thinking with Digitized Primary Sources

Bill Tally | Education Development Center, Center for Children & Technology

Lauren B. Goldenberg | Education Development Center, Center for Children & Technology

This pilot study examined middle school and high school student performance on an online historical thinking assessment task. After their teachers received training in the use of digital historical archives, students from all groups engaged in historical thinking behaviors (e.g., observation, sourcing, inferencing, evidence, question-posing, and corroboration) in response to an open-ended document analysis exercise. The types of thinking they did are described, and differences between AP-level and non-AP students are discussed. Challenges teachers face in developing students' historical thinking around visual documents are also discussed. Educators seeking to take advantage of digitized primary source documents need activities with clear curriculum linkages and small exercises that give students guidance in working with different kinds of documents (visual, textual, and audio). In addition, students and teachers need far more practice in learning to make meaning from primary source documents—in beginning to think like historians.

Introduction

You know my method, Watson. It is founded upon the observation of trifles.

—Sherlock Holmes, *The Boscombe Valley Mystery*

A growing body of research suggests that educators face a key challenge with students across the curriculum: fostering active habits of mind in working with primary source materials (Bass, 2003; Bransford, Brown, & Cocking, 2000; Perkins, 2003; Seixas, 1998; Stearns, Seixas, & Wineburg, 2000). This research suggests that if primary source documents are going to significantly enhance students' understanding of content, students need to be both cognitively active and emotionally engaged when working with them. In particular, some of the things that students need to do are:

- closely observe the documents' features
- bring prior knowledge to bear
- speculate about causes and consequences
- make personal connections, and
- use evidence to support their speculations.

There is evidence that learners who develop and practice these habits with primary source materials perform better whether the domain is language arts, social studies, or science, and whether the grade level is upper elementary or high school (Brown, 2000). The reason is that these intellectual (and emotional) habits with sources and data are at the heart of how critical thinking is defined in every area of the sciences and humanities, and now, in the information-rich workplace as well (Levy & Murnane, 2004). Indeed, the centrality of these skills is a key reason why digital archives of primary sources, such as those from the Library of Congress and elsewhere, have important roles to play in improving elementary, middle, and secondary teaching and learning across the curriculum.

The data we discuss here are derived from students' performance in an online document-analysis task. The task is part of our evaluation of a professional development program, An Adventure of the American Mind (AAM), aimed at helping teachers use online primary source materials in their teaching. AAM, a program of the Library of Congress, works in colleges of education and school districts in several states and regions to help K–12 teachers integrate primary sources from the online *American Memory* collections (memory.loc.gov) into their teaching. The task is also part of a larger inquiry into how students learn a particular discipline—history—using new technologies and primary sources, especially visual sources. Here we present the student performance data as suggestive of ways in which students can and do think historically with visual documents when given effective supports, including teacher guidance and software scaffolding.

It may be useful to briefly review some of the thinking and research that led us to hypothesize that well-designed software could support teachers and students in working closely with documentary sources, and thereby improve history teaching and learning. Our work has been shaped by three developments: recent cognitively-oriented scholarship in history learning, the growth of digitized history archives that put vast collections of searchable visual and textual documents at teachers' and students' fingertips, and our own professional development work with teachers that has underscored their relative lack of skill and confidence in interpreting visual sources.

First, the work of scholar Sam Wineburg and his colleagues has been extremely influential in helping educators and researchers understand how students learn well from documents and how teachers teach well with them. A cognitive psychologist who specializes in history teaching and learning, Wineburg has studied document-based learning among novices and experts, children and adults, students, teachers, and historians (Wilson & Wineburg, 2001; Wineburg, 1991, 2000, 2001). For example, Wilson and Wineburg (2001) found that successful history teachers construct activities in which students encounter documents for multiple purposes, such as noting point of view and bias and thinking about why different accounts vary, whereas less successful teachers construct activities in which students encounter documents for a much more narrow and restricted set of purposes, such as illustrating an idea or event, or finding the author's bias. For Wineburg, what is most important is giving children opportunities to explore primary and secondary sources in depth in order to figure out the "truth" of differing accounts. It is then that they are engaged both cognitively and emotionally, and it is then that their thinking—full of speculation and guessing based on what they can observe in the images and texts—most approaches that of expert historians (Wineburg, 2001). This kind of reasoned "messing around" with documents is also, he notes, precisely what we rarely allow students to do in history classrooms.

Second, the growth of online archives of primary sources (such as those maintained by the Library of Congress, the National Archives, and countless universities, museums, and libraries) has made rich documentary materials widely available, and provided an extensive laboratory for teacher and curriculum development. These archives have formed the basis of much curriculum development and professional development during the past decade, from the *American Memory Fellows Program* at the Library of Congress, to the *Digital Classroom* at the National Archives, to *Edsitement* at the National Endowment for the Humanities, to *History Matters* teaching resources at George Mason

University, and countless websites and institutes hosted for teachers by other cultural and academic organizations.

Several things are clear from these projects and the growing literature about them (Bass & Eynon, 1998; Tally, 1996). First, using primary documents gives students a sense of the reality and complexity of the past; the archives thus represent an opportunity to go beyond the sterile, seamless quality of most textbook presentations to engage with real people and authentic problems. Second, the fragmentary, idiosyncratic, and often contradictory nature of primary documents can help students understand the problematic nature of historical evidence and the need for critical thinking about sources and bias. Third, the multimedia nature of most digital archives—the way they combine textual, audio, and image formats—offers students with diverse learning styles multiple pathways into thinking about historical and cultural problems. Finally, the search engines that accompany most digital archives—for example, full-text searches on oral history archives or subject-based searching on photographic archives—enable students to query materials in novel ways that only experts have been able to do before now. Together, these capacities enable what Bass (2003) calls "the novice in the archive," the ability of students to work in ways similar to practitioners in the field, yet as novices rather than experts. "These kinds of activities—searching, examining patterns, discovering connections among artifacts—are all germane to the authentic thinking processes of historians and scholars of society and culture" (Bass & Rosenzweig, 1999, p. 6). The promise of digital image archives is that they can make it possible for students and teachers to engage directly and routinely in these more *authentic historical thinking* processes en route to acquiring a narrative grasp of history.

Historical images, in particular, are a useful point of entry for many students, for unlike historical texts—which often present archaic language that children must decode before they can begin to construct meaning—photos, lithographs, cartoons, and maps present instantly recognizable features and information, and easily evoke background knowledge that children can begin using to build an interpretation. In our own work with history teachers and students around these digital archives, we have seen their promise as well as the challenges teachers face in using them. To cite just two examples of digital historical image use as part of more active and rigorous history classrooms, seventh graders in several Virginia classrooms we worked with created period "newspaper" articles to accompany photos they selected and carefully researched from the Library of Congress collection of *Selected Civil War Photos* (Ridgway & Donelly, 1998–1999). And in an eleventh grade Michigan classroom, students compared and connected portraits of Depression-era life in John Steinbeck's novel *Grapes of Wrath* with those in interviews conducted by WPA writers and pictures taken by Farm Security Administration photographers (Federspiel, 1998–1999).

Yet teachers as well as students face challenges in using visual historical sources well. For many teachers, it is common to use historical images simply as *illustrations* of established fact, rather than as data from which to reason about the past. (This is understandable: it is exactly how most history textbooks use imagery.) What gets overlooked in such cases is the often contradictory information images contain, the purposes they might have served for their creator, and the understandings that viewers might have brought to them.

Based on the insights gained from working with historians and skilled history teachers, we created a set of inquiry tools and templates whose purpose is twofold: (1) to support and scaffold image-based history learning in the online environment; and (2) to make visible and comparable the thinking processes of students, teachers, and historians as they interpret documents—both for teaching purposes, and for research. The software inquiry tools can be found on a website titled *Picturing Modern America* (http://cct2.edc.org/PMA/), which helps students and teachers explore historical documents related to the building of modern America from 1880–1920. The word "picturing" refers both to the prevalence of mass-produced imagery (lithographs, photographs, films, panoramas, etc.) that were characteristic of the period (and that enable students to learn about it), and also to students' active historical imagination.

Although research into student thinking with documents and images is growing, thus far we know of no studies that have examined students' historical thinking behavior with software tools designed to support them. It is this issue that we explore in the current pilot study.

Research Questions

Our research questions in this pilot study were:

1. How do students describe their current history or social studies class (given that it was taught by a teacher trained to use primary documents)? Sub-questions include: Do they see it as different from prior history/social studies classes? Do students, according to their self-reports, learn more history, and like history more, as a result of their current class?

2. What historical thinking skills do these students exhibit?

Methods

Drawing from parts of the *Picturing Modern America* website, we constructed an online historical interpretation task for middle and high school students to complete. The task asked students to look closely at a historical image from the *American Memory* website, take notes on details they observed, and draw conclusions based on their observations and prior knowledge. Students could choose one of three images from the turn of the 20th century: a photograph, a panoramic map, or a political cartoon. The online assessment task led students step-by-step through the reading of a primary document they had not previously seen. The task served as a scaffold upon which students might—or might not—display historical thinking behaviors. Students were asked to assume the role of "history detectives." First, they were asked to select a question to answer about the image, or invited to write their own question. Then, by clicking on the image, they were able to "gather clues" about the details they noticed in the image. Finally, they were asked to draw conclusions based on their observations (responses to the "clues") of the image. Students also completed a brief questionnaire that asked them about their experiences in their history classes compared to previous classes. These data—the questions students posed, the descriptive details they noted in the clues, the conclusions they drew, and their responses to the questionnaire—were captured by our servers. (See Appendix 2.A for sample screens from the task and the questionnaire items.)

We contacted teachers who had participated in a professional development program whose aim was to encourage the use of the Library of Congress's *American Memory* collections in K–12 classrooms. Using data from a survey of 358 of these teachers, and information provided by professional development staff, we sought teachers who met several criteria: they needed to be teachers of the humanities (i.e., history, social studies, or language arts), they needed to be at the middle or high school level, they needed to have worked with students around primary sources to some extent during the past year, and if possible they needed to teach humanities courses for remedial as well as advanced students.

Based on these criteria, we invited seven middle and high school teachers from public and private schools to participate; five were able to schedule their students to complete the task in the time frame allotted. Teachers received instructions for administering the task to their students, including a standard introduction to be read before students began the task, telling the students the purpose of the task, what would happen to the data collected, that the activity was not going to be graded, and that there were no right or wrong answers. Students completed the task within one class period. Most teachers had their students complete the task in a computer lab setting, with each student working alone at a workstation.

Because the professional development program in which the teachers participated was focused on the use of primary sources and new technologies for learning, we reasoned that in history classrooms where the teachers used these strategies a great deal, students would likely perform better on such a task than students in classrooms where teachers did not use these strategies a great deal. Accordingly, we sought to recruit middle and high school history teachers who were ranked "high" and "low" in the use of primary sources and new technologies with students, by virtue of their responses to a teacher survey administered to participants in the professional development program. In the time allotted, however, we were only able to recruit teachers whose use of primary sources and new technologies was relatively high, making the high/low comparison moot. However, the five classrooms varied in other, interesting ways. Subject matter taught was one: three were history classes, one an English class, and one a geography class. Another was grade level: two were middle school classrooms and three were high school classrooms. Finally, classrooms represented contrasting academic ability levels: one was an AP/Honors class, three were regular history or English classes, and one was a history class attended by low-achieving students. Thus, the student task became a pilot assessment of students' historical thinking, as revealed through the software, across all these variations.

A total of 159 middle and high school students from four different schools completed the online activity. The respondents came from six classrooms in four schools. (See Table 2.1.) The students represent a mix of genders (53% were female, 47% male), grade levels (47% were in grades 6–8 and 53% in grades 9–12), and academic ability levels (80% were in regular history classes or non-AP social studies classes, and 20% were in honors or AP history classes).

Table 2.1 School and Participant Overview

	Grade Level	Type of Class*	No. of Students
School A			
Public high school, urban area	11 11/12	AP/Honors "Remedial"	23 36
School B			
Public middle school, urban area	6	Heterogeneous	26
School C			
Public middle school, rural area	7 8	Heterogeneous Heterogeneous	21 26
School D			
K–12 religious school, rural area	10, 11, 12	Heterogeneous	24
TOTAL			156**

** Some students in heterogeneous classes indicated that they were AP or Honors students.*

*** 159 students completed the exercise, but some students provided incomplete demographic data.*

The data consisted of students' responses to the activity and questionnaire, as described above. Data were compiled in a spreadsheet and analyzed for trends related to each group's context. Categories of analysis were derived from the work of Wineburg (2001), Seixas (1998), and others (e.g., Stearns et al., 2000) on how people develop as historical thinkers. This research has found that historians approach the reading of documentary sources differently from novices, regardless of whether the novices are children or adults. Novices tend not to engage in the following kinds of behavior that constitute reflexive "habits of mind" for experts in the humanities:

- ***Observation***: Scanning and parsing the document, observing details
- *Sourcing*: Considering who made the document and what their motives are
- *Inferencing*: Making inferences, speculating, guessing about meaning
- ***Evidence***: Citing evidence when making inferences or drawing conclusions
- *Question posing*: Cultivating puzzlement, keeping track of one's questions
- *Corroboration*: Comparing what is found to what one already knows, other documents, etc. (Stearns et al., 2000)

Thirty-two students chose the political cartoon, 33 chose the panoramic map, and 94 chose the photograph.

Results

QUESTION 1:

How do students describe their current history or social studies class? Do they see it as different from prior history/social studies classes? Do students learn more history, and like history more, as a result of their current class?

More than two-thirds of students (68%) said that their current class (taught by a teacher trained to use primary sources) was different than previous history classes they had taken. Students consistently cited three things that made their current class different: (a) using technologies to learn in new ways, (b) working with primary sources to gain deeper understanding of history, and (c) learning independently as well as in small groups. Students said that in one way or another all three of these practices are important to them because of how they differ from typical history class, which they characterize as over-reliant on a single textbook, lecture-driven, and providing few opportunities to discuss or debate ideas. There was one more distinguishing trait of these classrooms: lots of work. Students consistently reported that they have more work in their current history classroom than in prior classes—but as the next section indicates, they still like it more.

Following are characteristic student statements about what made their current history or social studies classroom different from previous classrooms.

Using new technologies to learn differently

The greatest percentage of students (nearly half) said that their current class is different because of the roles that technologies play. Significantly, however, they did not just say they liked using computers in their classes, but they also connected their use of computers to more active, interesting assignments, resources, and activities. The following student writing excerpts are produced verbatim, with idiosyncratic capitalization and punctuation as well as spelling errors intact. It is interesting to note that the middle school students relied heavily on the written vernacular common in online interactions such as instant messaging.

> We use the computers a lot more than we ever did in my other history classes. Our assignments are always more interesting when we use the computers, and I'm learning how to research things more efficiently.
>
> —11th grade female, School A

> This year, we were assigned to pick a particular American Memory collection to study and build a project from. I chose the Wright Brothers Collection, which I found very interesting. I built a 4ft replica of the first plane, which was a very different project, which I greatly enjoyed.
>
> —11th grade male, School D

> We are using computers and getting information that you just can't get from the books. We are learning valuable things through pictures, and understanding what has gone on in the past.
>
> —11th grade male, School A

> It is differnt b/c i have never done anything on a computer and it is more interesting.
>
> —7th grade male, School C

> I was used to always using the textbook and movies. Now we have computers and we can participate more. Better assignments.
>
> —12th grade female, School A

> It is cool to have a lap top computer so it makes learning more hands on exspeshly with the projecter.
>
> —8th grade male, School C

Using primary sources for a deeper understanding of history

About a quarter of students said that their current class feels different because it involved materials besides the textbook. Many cited primary sources as an important element, using terms such as "in-depth," "seeing things for myself firsthand," and learning "the whole picture" of history.

> We have more in depth topics and projects and discussions. We use more primary resources, which I haven't used much before in my other history classes.
>
> —11th grade female, School A

> We not only use our textbooks, but also use many resources to expound on what we are learning. For example, if we are learning about a specific President we integrate other information from AAM to enhance what we are learning not only about his Presidency, but also things about his every day lifestyle.
>
> —6th grade female, School D

> It helpz me learn more bc i see pictures and it is different bc textbooks r boring and i dont think u learn that good bc u dont pay attention but with the computer and showing pictures i know i have learn a lot.
>
> —8th grade female, School C

> Seeing the primary source documents has helped me be more interested in history. Also, when we just read textbooks, we did not learn the whole picture of history. History books do not always tell what happened the way we have been able to learn it.
>
> —6th grade female, School D

More independent and group work

About a fifth of students say they spend their time in their current classes differently than in prior history classes. They say they are doing more independent and group work, and less lecture and seatwork.

> In the other history classes I have taken, most of the time I am reading out of a book or listening to a teacher talk.
>
> —11th grade male, School A

> In the past years I have just read about this stuff and this year I got to make things and do projects and I actually got to have a war (with paper bullets and bombs of course.
>
> —8th grade male, School B

> We tend to do a lot more group work and projects. It isn't so much reading out of the book.
>
> —11th grade female, School A

> It's more interesting in this class. We do more by ourselves and I like that better than last year, when the teacher always just stood up in front of the class and talked.
>
> —12th grade female, School A

Learning—and liking?—history

Nearly nine out of 10 students in these five classrooms (87%) said they had learned more history in their current class compared to prior years. And almost three-quarters of the students (72%) said they now liked history more as a result.

These are remarkably robust numbers. Before looking at the details, it is worth asking:

How much can we trust these kinds of positive self-reports, coming from two-thirds of student respondents? How likely is it that some students felt inclined to write more positively than they felt, for example, imagining it might reflect well on them or their teacher? This is possible and even likely in some instances. However, if students were being generally honest, we would expect at least a few in each group to report no difference in their classroom, and no greater learning or liking of history as a result. The reason is individual differences: students who truly dislike history or have had negative experiences with it in the past should not report a positive change due to one classroom experience. And this is the case; in each classroom, between 10–25% of students said that their history classrooms were still uninteresting to them. Far from casting doubt on the largely positive findings reported, these kinds of responses confirm that students felt free to answer honestly—i.e., that the task did not skew findings too heavily in the positive direction. Here is a sample of these comments:

> Last year was the same as this year. We both were reading out of a book. And just talking about what we read.
>
> —6th grade female, School C

> I am not liking history any more than in the previous classes. I am not a big fan of studying history, because I believe that the past is the past, and we should leave it there.
>
> —12th grade male, School A

> I hate having to learn everything straight from the book.
>
> —11th grade male, School A

> History is pretty much the same way as before. It's just not interesting to me.
>
> —8th grade male, School C

> I don't like history class because its based on nothing but memorizing the material. I like a class more like math where you memorize the method or methods and then apply yourself and your own knowledge.
>
> —12th grade female, School A

> I am learning a little more about history but I don't like history any more than I used to.
>
> —11th grade female, School D

What do students learn, and like, in their history classes? Two interconnected themes emerge from the examples students provided. First, they described having a sense of competence because they had mastered a body of knowledge in greater detail than usual. It is possible that the newly-trained teachers are asking their students to do "more with less"—to slow down and spend time working closely with a few documents from one event or time period, rather than moving through a lot of material in an effort to "cover it." This "depth over breadth" approach goes against the typical grain of history teaching, and appears to have real benefits for students. In their comments, students explicitly cited greater understanding and list many specific areas of knowledge they have studied and mastered.

> I understand more [this year], and it feels good.
>
> —8th grade female, School C

> In the past I may have been too young or not listening all the time because now since in the 7th grade I understand history and like it much more. I used to think it was boring but now I am beginning to think it's not.
>
> —7th grade female, School C

> I have learned more about the settlement of Virginia in the 15 and 1600s. I have liked learning more about the founding of our country.
>
> —11th grade male, School D

> It was hard at first but now it is not. i have learned a lot about the children that was Jewish and was killed at camps bc of germans.
>
> —8th grade male, School C

Second, students, especially those in the older grades, said they enjoyed learning to work with different media and materials, including primary source materials and *American Memory*. They say that the online primary documents offer greater ease of doing research, a more vivid understanding of the past, and more opportunities to think for themselves.

> I think it is easier to learn and remember when you can see the original papers, pictures and documents. American Memory has divided things into collections, which makes it easier to find a specific thing when you are doing a research.
>
> —12th grade female, School A, Honors

> In history class this year, I learned more about Western expansion and the hardships of it through the American Memory Collection "Utah and Western Migration."
>
> —11th grade female, School D

> I like when we have done research on a specific topic, created a powerpoint presentation, and built an exhibition piece about what we are leaning.
>
> —11th grade male, School D

QUESTION 2:

What historical thinking skills do these students exhibit?

At the heart of our inquiry was finding out what historical thinking skills the students exhibited. Our question was: Did these students engage in historical thinking behaviors (e.g., observation, sources, inferencing, evidence, question posing, and corroboration) when confronted with a primary document they had not seen before? The short answer from this pilot study of five classrooms is yes, and to a surprising degree, they did so across all groups.

As might be expected, high school students in AP and honors classes exhibited these behaviors to the greatest degree. These advanced classes are usually the only places where students are exposed to primary source-based research and critical thinking about documents. What is significant is that students who were in regular and even history classrooms labeled "remedial" and students of middle-school age displayed aspects of good historical thinking as well. Their responses often contained less background knowledge of the period and less sophisticated language than the advanced students. Nevertheless, they approached documents actively, noting details, drawing inferences, and using evidence.

Below we describe the kinds of historical thinking students displayed in response to the digital images. Although students displayed multiple types of thinking in response to all three images, for reasons of space we present responses to two of the documents—the photograph, which elicited a wide variety of *observations* and *inferences,* and the panoramic map, which elicited examples of *sourcing* and *corroboration.*

Historical Skills: Observation and Drawing Inferences

Figure 2.1 reproduces the photograph. It is of a street scene from the Detroit Publishing Co. collection titled "The Close of a Career in New York" (Library of Congress, 2005). By clicking on the picture, students "gathered clues" about it (details were highlighted onscreen, and a "notebook" appeared for students to write down what they saw). Some details that students could select for comment are also pictured.

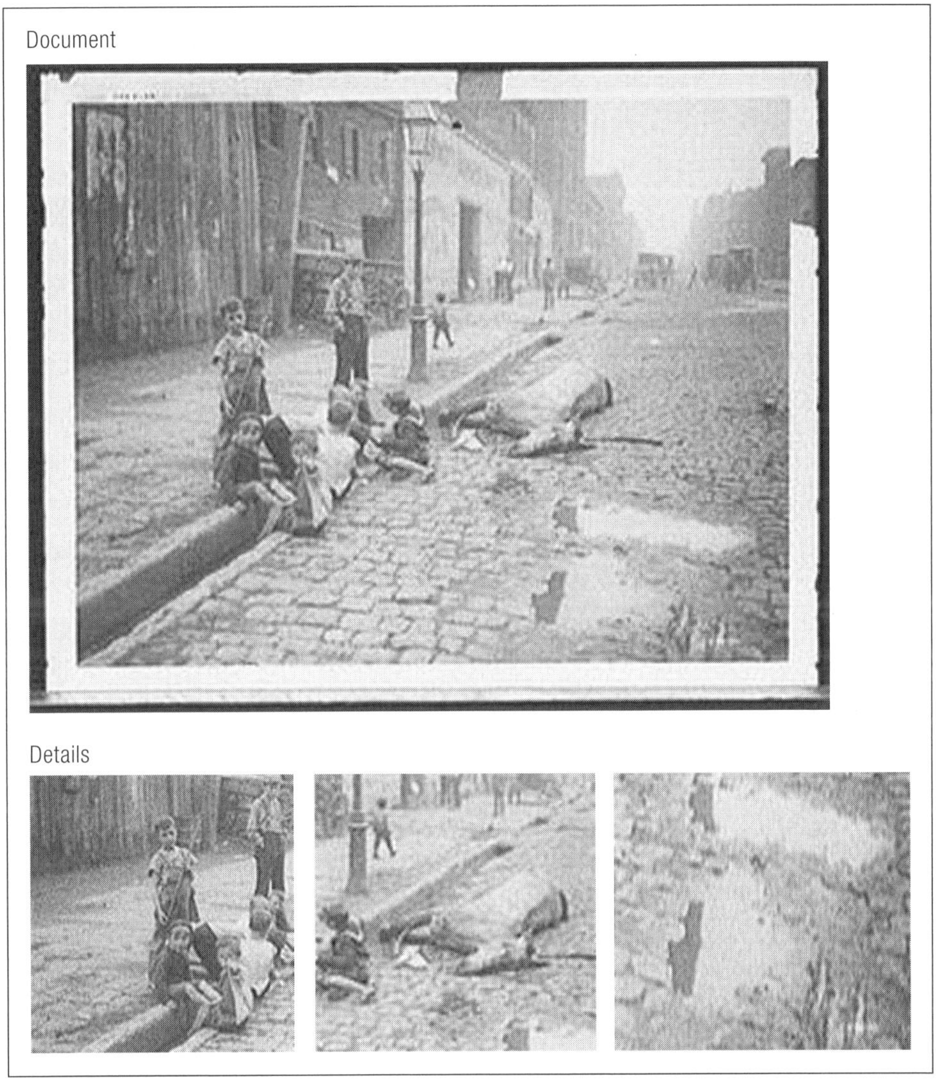

Figure 2.1 Document 1—Photograph from the American Memory collection

Here are some of the observations that high school AP/Honors students made about selected portions of the document. Even in simply recording what they saw, these students carefully noted details, posed questions, and made inferences from the visual information before them.

> There are little kids sitting on the side of the road near a dead horse, they have their feet in what looks like drain water. None of them seem to be well dressed. [noting detail]

> Water means it rained or the road has poor drainage. Great place for bacteria to grow. [inference]
>
> The road has water puddles in it so it has been raining. Also, the road having puddles means it's uneven or cracked. [inference; noting detail]
>
> There are cars up ahead, looks like the very first model T's. [corroboration]
>
> There are cars, so what is a horse doing on the road? [cultivating puzzlement]
>
> You see the big difference between the business-looking environment of the background and the dead horse laying in the road in the foreground. I think someone made this to show the gap between the rich and poor during the 1900's. [sourcing]
>
> The buildings up the street seem to be more well kept. Are the people richer in that direction? [inference; question-posing]

If we compare the observations above to those of regular and remedial history students at the high school level, we see less background knowledge overall and often less grammatical writing present. However, we also see evidence of parallel historical thinking processes:

> The horse is dead in the street. Maybe there was a riot, or maybe there is a lack of food. [inference]
>
> Is this a dead cow? Isn't that something a child should not play near? [inference]
>
> A Dead Horse. There isn't lot of money to feed the horse, or take care of it. It's very unsanitary conditions. [inference]
>
> Puddle. Maybe the horse stumbled in the pothole and broke its ankle and the owner left it there to die. [inference]
>
> A bunch of scary children. They don't seem to mind the horse being there. Maybe they dont know any better. [noting detail; inference]
>
> People and carriages. Don't seem worried that the horse is dead and the kids are playing near it. [inference]

Middle school students, too, actively read the document and exhibited good strategies of historical thinking as they encountered it, particularly in noting detail and drawing simple inferences. But at their age, they do not scan the document as completely nor do they bring as much background knowledge of the period to bear:

> Looks like they're sittin there hungry and they're pointing to the camera. [inference, noting detail]
>
> I see six Childern sitting and one standing up.I think that the kids are talking about the died horse. [noting details; speculation]
>
> the children are living on the street probably with no shelter and they probably don't get to eat a lot. [inference]
>
> i see a dead horse and a little boy, and he has a stick in his hand that has a sharpe porint on the end. did they kill the horse? [noting detail; speculation]

Historical Skills: Corroboration and Citing Evidence

Corroboration entails comparing what one finds in a new document to what one already knows, from other documents, from experience, or from prior study of the period. Using evidence means pointing out the reasons for one's inferences and conclusions, and grounding them in the document. Here again, comparing the performance of high school AP/Honors students to the less academically oriented as well as the younger students suggests that students at all levels displayed good historical thinking skills.

For example, students displayed their skills at corroboration and using evidence when they drew conclusions about the following Panoramic Map of Seymour, Connecticut, in 1879 (Figure 2.2) (Library of Congress, 2005).

When a high school AP/Honors student drew a conclusion about what most people in Seymour did for a living, she synthesized her observations of the map:

> I think most people in Seymour, Ct. make their living in 1879 by working in the mills and factories located close to the river.

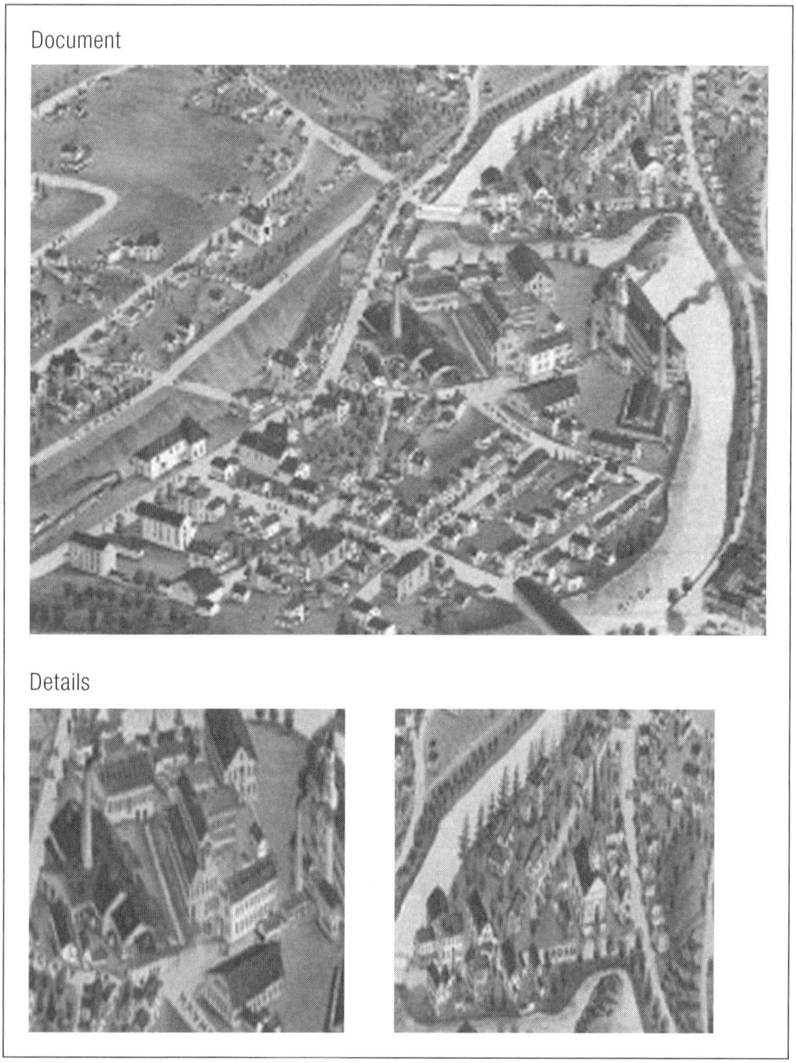

Figure 2.2 Document 2—Map of Seymour, CT, from the American Memory collection

And she then went on to cite corroborating knowledge from her prior studies about industrial America, and evidence she found in the picture:

> From the picture, it looks as if there were large factories close to the river, in which the mills could generate power from the river. It also looked as if there were houses close to the factory possibly of those who worked at the factory. [corroboration; evidence]

In comparison, when an 8th grade student reached for a conclusion about what people in Seymour did for a living, she said:

> They had to work in mills all their lives, and other factories.

She also drew on what she knew for corroboration, but it was far more immediate knowledge:

> My uncle worked in a factory, like the one they got in the picture. With smoke all coming out. And that is why I think that.

Conclusions and Implications

What does our investigation into how students "read" digital images reveal about historical thinking and how it may be fostered? Our findings underscore several things.

First, it appears that students can apply historical thinking behaviors to primary sources even without prior direct teaching about the historical era or context. In this case, students approached images about turn of the 20th century American life simply as "historical detectives," apart from any curricular unit they were studying. This may indicate that students have learned skills of document analysis (from teachers who themselves were trained in these skills) that are *transportable* across historical topics. Alternately, this may signify that the supports built into the software tool to scaffold historical thinking may have worked. A deeper, rigorous investigation into what helps students exhibit historical thinking behaviors is needed.

Second, students' comments about their resource-rich history classrooms echo what we have long known about "hands-on" learning in other parts of the curriculum, notably science and mathematics: When students have structured opportunities to construct meaning from primary materials, and critically examine those meanings, they feel more invested in the results. This suggests that as artifacts in multiple media enter into the history classroom we may see shifts in learning and motivation associated with the rise of "hands-on" learning in science and math (Anderman & Midgley, 1997; Bransford et al., 2000; Lumsden, 1994; National Research Council, 2000).

In sum, this pilot investigation of student performance on a digital image analysis task indicates that in classrooms where teachers are using primary sources to actively engage students, students are learning important skills of historical interpretation and document analysis. Scaffolded exercises of the sort described here, coupled with classroom instruction, help students integrate acquisition of historical content knowledge and development of historical thinking skills and immerse students and teachers in building knowledge from documents, in ways that reflect disciplinary perspectives.

This study contributes to a growing body of literature on the skills that teachers and students need to "read" and make meaning from a wide variety of source materials, whether photographs, maps, quilts, music, speeches, or cartoons (Bass, 2003; Seixas, 1998; Wineburg, 2001). These skills include things such as close observation and document parsing, sourcing (asking about the maker and his/her motivations), inferencing (making guesses, speculating, posing questions), and corroboration (comparing what you find to what you know from other sources) (Wineburg, 2001).

We offer several conclusions that might help educators and researchers foster historical thinking in middle and high school students using digitized visual images. Professional development programs in history and the humanities need to build teachers' skills in analyzing documents and images, as well as improving teachers' content knowledge of history. Also, software programs that scaffold image analysis can be useful tools for teachers. By "slowing down" the process of image analysis and sequencing it through stages of observation, information gathering, making inferences, and posing questions, they can help make student thinking visible—to students themselves, to teachers, and to researchers.

The next stage of software tool development includes enabling learners to go beyond their individual interpretations of documents. This next generation of scaffolds and supports should enable students and teachers to compare their own novice interpretations to those of other novices as well as expert historians, and learn from them; and enable students to "curate" and publish on websites their own historical exhibitions, and to engage in conversations with other students and teachers using web-based forums about the meaning of their work. Making student work public in new media formats will create opportunities for review by broader professional and public audiences.

A question remains about whether students, when analyzing documents, are practicing true historical thinking behaviors (i.e., habits of mind that help them sympathetically yet critically imagine the world of the past), or simply repeating a heuristic routine in a formulaic way. This is an issue we plan to explore in future work. Fostering the historical thinking behaviors we have documented here is just one small piece of the larger challenge that history teachers face—helping students develop the sympathetic yet critical imagination that characterizes historical inquiry as practiced by professional historians.

Author Update

Our article about digital archives and historical thinking focused on evaluation research we conducted in 2004 in collaboration with the Library of Congress, using historical thinking tools developed with funding from the National Endowment for the Humanities. We have continued to explore the roles that rich online sources, and tools for examining them, can play in improving humanities, social studies, and science education. Our work since then has developed in several directions. First: What alternatives to the ubiquitous online lesson plan can help teachers teach effectively with primary data? Working with WGBH's Teachers' Domain, National Geographic, and others, we have been investigating how teachers use more modular, just-in-time supports for using primary data and digital resources with students. Second: How can we help students and teachers get a better grasp on the kinds of thinking that historians do? In evaluating professional development for history teachers run by colleagues at the City University of New York, we are seeing the value of explicitly teaching students not only historians' distinctive reading habits (which cognitive psychologist Sam Wineburg (1999) and his colleagues have named sourcing, contextualizing, close reading, and corroborating), but also the distinctive kinds of questions that historians ask (Mandell & Malone, 2008). Third: How do digital tools help support literacy in the content areas for struggling readers as well as proficient readers? At the Educational Development Center (EDC), researchers have been studying how digital readers such as the Thinking Reader software can support struggling adolescent readers in literacy, science, and social studies. Finally: How does renewed interest in video games as learning media create opportunities for better history and social studies teaching and learning? As part of the Corporation for Public Broadcasting's American History and Civics Initiative, we are part of a collaborative team headed by Thirteen/WNET that is designing and studying a suite of web-based adventure and role-playing games, titled Mission US, specifically created to help middle school teachers deepen students' understanding of key moments in American history (see http://mission-us.org).

Acknowledgments

This paper is based on work supported by the Library of Congress, the National Endowment for the Humanities, and the Education and Research Consortium's Adventure of the American Mind Project. Any opinions, findings, and conclusions expressed in this material are those of the authors and do not necessarily reflect the positions or policies of these funders.

References

Anderman, L. H., & Midgley, C. (1997). Motivation and middle school students. In J. L. Irvin (Ed.), *What current research says to the middle level practitioner* (pp. 41–48). Columbus, OH: National Middle School Association.

Bass, R. (2003). *The garden in the machine: The impact of American studies on new technologies.* [Online document]. Retrieved May 25, 2003, from www9.georgetown.edu/faculty/bassr/garden.html#novice

Bass, R., & Eynon, B. (1998). Teaching culture, learning culture, and new media technologies: An introduction and framework. *Works and Days 16*(1/2), 11–96.

Bass, R., & Rosenzweig, R. (1999). *Rewriting the history and social studies classroom needs, frameworks, dangers, and proposals.* White Papers on the Future of Technology in Education: U.S. Department of Education. [Online]. Available at www.eric.ed.gov

Bransford, J. D., Brown, A. L., & Cocking, R. R. (Eds.). (2000). *How people learn: Brain, mind, experience and school* (Expanded ed.). Washington, DC: National Academy Press.

Brown, J. S. (2000). Growing up digital: The web and a new learning ecology. *Change*, March/April 2000, 10–20.

Federspiel, M. (1998–1999). The great depression in your classroom: Creating successful student lessons around American memory. Available at http://cct2.edc.org/NDL/1999/institute/activities/depression.html

Levy, F., & Murnane, R. (2004). *The new division of labor: How computers are creating the next job market.* Princeton, NJ: Princeton University Press.

Library of Congress. (2005). *American memory collections.* Available at http://memory.loc.gov/ammem

Lumsden, L. S. (1994). *Student motivation to learn.* (ERIC Digest Report No. 92). Eugene, OR: ERIC Clearinghouse on Educational Management.

Mandell, N., & Malone, B. (2008). *Thinking like a historian: Rethinking history instruction.* Madison, WI: Wisconsin Historical Society Press.

National Research Council. (2000). *Inquiry and the National Science Education Standards.* Washington, DC: National Academy Press.

Perkins, D. (2003, December). *Making thinking visible.* New Horizons for Learning. Retrieved from http://education.jhu.edu/newhorizons/strategies/topics/thinking-skills/visible

Ridgeway, E., & Donelly, A. (1998–1999). "Civil war newspaper project," Grade 7 student project in English and American History at Williamsburg Middle School in Arlington, VA. Retrieved from http://lcweb2.loc.gov:8081/learn/lessons/98/brady/home.html

Seixas, P. (1998). Student teachers thinking historically. *Theory and research in social education, 26*(3), 310–341.

Stearns, P., Seixas, P., & Wineburg, S. (Eds.). (2000). *Knowing, teaching, and learning history.* New York, NY: New York University Press.

Tally, W. (1996, September). History goes digital: Teaching when the web is in the Classroom. *D-Lib Magazine.* Retrieved March 31, 2004, from www.dlib.org/dlib/september96/09tally.html

Wilson, S. M., Shulman, L. S., & Richert, A. E. (1987). '150 different ways' of knowing: Representation of knowledge in teaching. In J. Calderhead (Ed.), *Exploring teachers' thinking* (pp. 104–124). London, UK: Cassell.

Wilson, S., & Wineburg, S. (2001). Wrinkles in time and place: Using performance assessments to understand the knowledge of history teachers. In S. Wineburg (Ed.), *Historical thinking and other unnatural acts: Charting the future of teaching the past* (pp. 173–214). Philadelphia, PA: Temple University Press.

Wineburg, S. (1991). Historical problem solving: A study of the cognitive processes used in the evaluation of documentary and pictorial evidence. *Journal of Educational Psychology, 83,* 73–87.

Wineburg, S. (1999). *Historical thinking and other unnatural acts.* Phi Delta Kappan, *80*(7), 488–499.

Wineburg, S. (2000). Making historical sense. In P. N. Stearns, P. Seixas, & S. Wineburg (Eds.), *Knowing teaching & learning history: National and international perspectives* (pp. 306–326). New York, NY: New York University Press.

Wineburg, S. (Ed.) (2001). *Historical thinking and other unnatural acts: Charting the future of teaching the past.* Philadelphia, PA: Temple University Press.

APPENDIX

2.A

Student Activity: Sample Screens and Student Questionnaire

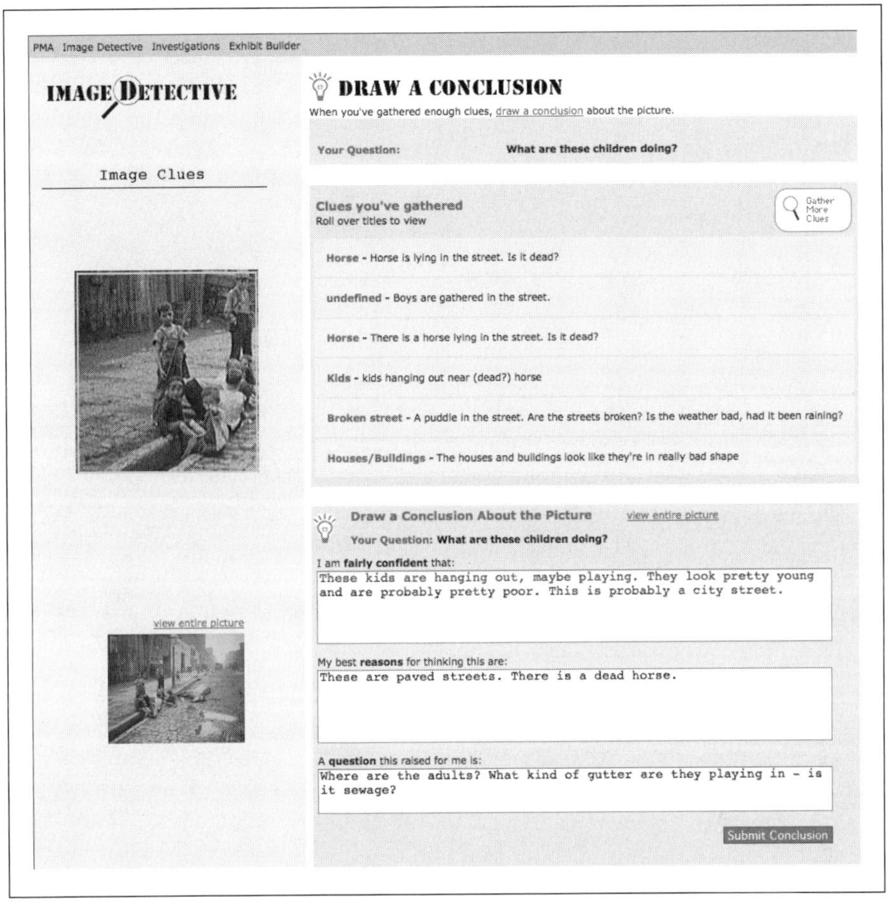

1. Is the way you are learning history THIS year different from how you have learned it before, in other classes? ○ yes ○ no

   If yes, how is it different? (Please be as specific as you can. For example, you might say how the *topics*, or the *assignments*, or the *materials*, or the *activities* you do are different.)

2. Does the way you are learning history this year work for YOU?

   Are you learning more history? ○ yes ○ no

   Do you like history more? ○ yes ○ no

   If yes, please tell us an *example* of something you have learned, or something you have liked in your history class.

CHAPTER

3

Uses and Effects of Mobile Computing Devices in K–8 Classrooms

Karen Swan | Kent State University
Mark van 't Hooft | Kent State University
Annette Kratcoski | Kent State University
Darlene Unger | Virginia Commonwealth University

This preliminary study employed mixed methodologies to explore students' use of mobile computing devices and its effects on their motivation to learn, engagement in learning activities, and support for learning processes. Data collected from students in four elementary and two seventh grade science classes in Northeast Ohio included usage logs, student work samples, student and teacher interviews, and classroom observations. Findings highlight the personalization of learning afforded by such devices both in terms of individuals and individual classroom cultures, as well as their usefulness in extending learning beyond the classroom. They also suggest that increased motivation due to mobile device use leads to increases in the quality and quantity of student work.

Background

More than a decade ago, Mark Weiser (1991) wrote that we live in a society in which technology is so pervasive that we do not notice it anymore when used for everyday tasks such as information retrieval, communication, and entertainment. Defining this environment as ubiquitous computing, he described it more as a state of mind, as "a new way of thinking about computers in the world ... [that] allows the computers themselves to vanish into the background ... [and] become indistinguishable from everyday life" (p. 94). As a result, the current generation of K–12 students is growing up more technologically literate than children their age were a decade ago, with access to an increasing number of devices and services such as video game consoles, mobile gaming devices, cell phones, the Internet, and instant messaging. Interestingly enough, even though many students know and use these technologies as integral parts of their lives, they learned to do so mostly outside of school (U.S. Department of Education, 2004), and teachers are struggling to integrate technology into their curriculum.

However, there are signs that the idea of ubiquitous computing is starting to get a foothold in K–12 settings, as a vision of classrooms filled with many computing devices designed for differing purposes and to be used as needed in the same ways as pencils and paper and books are used now. This vision is accompanied by a need for systematic research to investigate its effect, which is especially important given the argument that technology can play a more significant role in education and everyday life if it becomes more human-centered and less visible. For learning, the implication is that the smaller and less disruptive the device, the more of a chance it stands of becoming a lifelong-learning tool for anyone, anywhere, anytime (Inkpen, 2001; Sharples, 2000).

Given this theoretical framework and their relatively low cost, handheld computers are becoming an increasingly compelling choice of technology for K–12 classrooms because they enable a transition from the occasional, supplemental use of classroom computers and school computer labs to the frequent, integral use of portable computational devices (Soloway et al., 2001; Tinker & Krajcik, 2001). Early evaluations indicate that teachers and students respond favorably to handheld devices, and suggest handheld computers have the potential to affect student learning positively across curricular topics and instructional activities. Teachers, for example, have indicated that students are more motivated, spend more time using technology, collaborate and communicate more, and benefit from having a portable and readily accessible tool (Vahey & Crawford, 2002). Students, in turn, have found handhelds easy to use, fun, and a useful tool for learning (van 't Hooft, Diaz, & Swan, 2004).

Perhaps more important, some researchers argue that classrooms with handheld computers differ fundamentally from more traditional desktop computing environments in that users interacting with handheld computers can also interact with each other and other computing devices at the same time (Cole & Stanton, 2003; Danesh, Inkpen, Lau, Shu, & Booth, 2001; Mandryk, Inkpen, Bilezkjian, Klemmer, & Landay, 2001). Handheld computers thus have the potential to support both personalized and collaborative learning. Roschelle and Pea (2002), for example, highlight three ways handheld devices have been used to increase learning collaboratively—classroom response systems, participatory simulations, and collaborative data gathering—and suggest there are many more such uses (Danesh et al., 2001; Mandryk et al., 2001; Roschelle, 2003).

Finally, because of their small size, handheld computing devices no longer constrain users in the way desktop computers or even laptops do. As such, handheld computers support learning outside the classroom, twenty-four hours a day, seven days a week. They thus have the potential to support lifelong-learning anywhere, anytime (Bannasch, 1999; Inkpen, 2001; Sharples, 2000; Soloway et al., 2001; Staudt & Hsi, 1999; Tinker, 1997).

However, the limited size of most handhelds may be a disadvantage as well as an advantage (van 't Hooft et al., 2004). Screen size is an issue for some, but text input on handheld computers is a more pressing one, especially at the elementary level. Unless students attach an external keyboard, which costs more money, takes up space, and affects mobility, text input is limited to the onscreen keyboard or text recognition software (Vahey & Crawford, 2002). Primary teachers, in particular, believe that text recognition software can confuse students who are learning to write (van 't Hooft et al., 2004). In contrast, mobile computing devices such as the ones used in this study (AlphaSmart's Dana) may be the best of both worlds. On one hand, they feature a handheld-specific operating system, integrated wireless capabilities, and a full-size keyboard, and therefore function like handheld computers without the text input issues. On the other hand, they are relatively small and lightweight, and are cheaper and easier to use than full-blown laptop computers. The devices used in the study were donated by AlphaSmart as part of a research grant, and are referred to as "mobile computing devices" throughout the remainder of this article.

Research on the effects of mobile computers on teaching and learning is still relatively scarce (van 't Hooft et al., 2004). This preliminary study was designed to begin exploring the use of mobile computing devices and its effects on student learning. The following questions were addressed:

1. How do students use mobile computing devices?
2. Does the use of mobile computing devices affect students' motivation to learn and engagement in learning?
3. Does students' use of mobile computing devices support learning processes?

Methodology

SUBJECTS AND SETTINGS

Data were collected from subjects at two sites during the 2003–2004 school year. The first site was a technology-rich laboratory classroom at a state university in northeast Ohio where local teachers (who are nominated by their administrators and subjected to a selection process) bring their classes to complete regular units of study in a ubiquitous computing environment. Classes spend half a day every day for six weeks in the classroom, with access to desktops, wireless laptops, and handheld computers (1:1), a document camera, a presentation system, scanners, printers, digital cameras, teleconferencing equipment, video and audio recorders, VCRs, video editing equipment, CD and DVD burners, digital microscopes, scientific probes, wireless writing pads, and a wide variety of software to support teaching and learning.

Classes and subjects involved at the first site included one sixth grade class ($n = 28$), two fourth grade classes ($n = 41$), and one third grade class ($n = 16$). The sixth grade class's work centered on a biography project; one of the fourth grade classes studied plants and the environment; the other fourth grade and third grade classes, both from the same district, worked on identical projects organized around a study of flight. All students were given mobile computing devices to use and take home for the six-week period their classes spent in the laboratory classroom. In this part of the study, we were especially interested in the ways in which the use of mobile computing devices might support student development of conceptual understanding. Thus, representative students (high achieving, middle, low, special needs) in each class were closely followed. Representative students were identified by their teachers.

The second site was a suburban middle school in northeast Ohio whose student population of approximately 380 is drawn from two elementary schools, one attended by children from upper middle class, white-collar families and the other attended by middle class, blue-collar families. The school's students are primarily (about 98%) Caucasian. At the time of the study, about 20% of students qualified for free or reduced lunch. Students ($n = 50$) in two (out of five) seventh grade science classes, all taught by the same teacher, were given mobile computing devices to use in science class and to take with them for a little more than half the school year. In this part of the study, we focused on the support mobile computing devices might provide in science learning, both in terms of motivation as well as conceptual understanding.

DATA SOURCES AND ANALYSES

Data collected from all six classes included lesson plans, usage data, work samples, student and teacher interviews, and classroom observations, some of which were videotaped. To answer the first research question, usage data was collected from all students for whom it was available using Rubberneck, a hidden software tool that collects usage data from individual devices. Local transfer of mobile device data to desktop computers sends this data to an off-site server that is accessible through the Internet. Usage data for each student was categorized by application. Because time periods for which usage data was collected varied among students, the aggregated data was then divided by total time of use to yield average use per week for each student. Averages were compared by classes and gender within classes to provide a detailed quantitative portrait of how students used their mobile computing devices both in and outside of class.

Usage data were triangulated with responses from student interviews. Students in all classes were interviewed concerning their use of mobile computing during the final weeks of their classroom experiences. Although the question and interview formats varied somewhat according to age and ability level and between instructional contexts (i.e., laboratory classroom interviews were conducted with individual students as they were working on projects, middle school interviews were conducted with selected students during class time, but separately from class work), all interviews focused on how students used their devices and likes/dislikes related to the equipment. Interviews were recorded on paper or audiotape for qualitative analysis, using constant comparison to detect emergent themes (Glaser, 1978). First, the interview transcripts were triangulated with written notes made regarding the responses to the questions. The results were then reviewed to determine specific themes among comments. Utilizing the established themes as categories, the notes were reviewed a third time and coded according to the categories. Videotaped observations made twice a week of classes in the laboratory classroom were analyzed for evidence of mobile computing use. To answer the second question, student and teacher interview data related to motivation to learn were also analyzed using the constant comparison method. Although students were more implicitly asked about this aspect of the research through questions of likes and dislikes, teacher interview questions were more specific, and included questions such as: Do you think your students' attitudes toward school, motivation to learn, and/or self-efficacy was improved by their use of the mobile computing devices? How? Can you give examples for high, average, and lower achieving students? Student and teacher data were analyzed separately at first, and the results were compared to identify commonalities and differences in response patterns.

Data for the third research question consisted of student work samples collected using PAAM from GoKnow. PAAM transfers all student work to an off-site server whenever individual mobile computing devices are backed up locally. Work was obtained from four students selected in each class as high, medium, and low achieving, and in all but one fourth grade class, for selected special needs students. Work samples were analyzed for conceptual understanding, based on a framework developed by Newmann

(Newmann & Wehlage, 1995; Newmann, Bryk & Nagaoka, 2001), which focuses on evidence of students' use of analytic skills, their depth of conceptual understanding, and their ability to communicate that understanding. (See Table 3.1.) The framework provides rubrics for assessing student work, assigning numeric scores for each of three criteria (a score of 1 being the lowest, 4 the highest, with total scores ranging from 3 to 12). Scores were computed for all selected student work samples, and averaged and compared within and across classes by ability groupings.

Table 3.1 Assessment Criteria for Student Artifacts

Standard	Criteria
Analysis	Measures the extent to which the student demonstrates higher order thinking—student performance demonstrates thinking about the subject matter by organizing, synthesizing, interpreting, hypothesizing, describing patterns, making models or simulations, constructing arguments, inventing procedures
Disciplinary Concepts	Measures the extent to which the student demonstrates use and understanding of specific concepts—student performance demonstrates an understanding of important ideas related to the subject matter that go beyond application of basic concepts by elaborating on definitions, making connections to other concepts within the subject, or to other content areas
Elaborated Communication	Student performance demonstrates a concise, logical, and well-articulated explanation or argument that justifies the student's answer/work—could include diagrams, drawings, or other visual representations—must communicate an accurate, complete and convincing explanation or argument.

Student artifact scores were triangulated with teacher and student interview data, in order to determine whether mobile device usage can enhance student learning processes. Teacher and student data were analyzed separately and then compared to each other as well as the student artifact scores.

Results

Results from this preliminary study of the uses and effects of mobile computing devices are outlined in the sections that follow. They are organized by the research questions.

HOW DO STUDENTS USE MOBILE COMPUTING DEVICES?

All teachers in the study introduced their students to mobile computing, required the use of them for some explicit assignments (see Table 3.2), and encouraged students to use them as needed both inside and outside of class. The teacher at the middle school started out by requiring students to use the devices as much as possible, but a number of equipment issues forced her to make their use an option for the last three months of the school year. Despite the technical issues, most students continued to use their devices. Equipment failure was less of a problem in the laboratory classroom where technical support was constantly at hand:

Table 3.2 Mobile Computing Assignments by Class

Grade	Mobile Computing Usage
7	note-taking, T-charts, Venn diagrams, drawings
6	note-taking, journaling, first draft of autobiography
4	note-taking, journaling
4/3*	note-taking, journaling, worksheet

**classes worked on same unit*

Table 3.2 shows the types of assignments teachers asked students to complete using mobile computing devices. All teachers required their students to use them for taking notes, and teachers in the laboratory classroom also gave journaling and other writing assignments. Interestingly, only the seventh grade science teacher—the teacher with the oldest students—required her students to use drawing programs. Nonetheless, usage data (see Table 3.3) reveals that all students involved in the study used drawing programs and that youngest students used them the most. Students in all classes also made considerable use of personal information management (PIM) applications such as the Date Book, Address Book, and To Do List, as well as the calculator, although such usage was considerably lower and is not shown in Table 3.3. Indeed, the most striking characteristic of the usage data is its variability, both between classes and between individuals, which suggests the ways in which mobile computing was appropriated by individual students and student cultures to personalize learning. Notice for example the significant differences between the two fourth grades and between fourth and third grade students given the exact same assignments.

Table 3.3 Mobile Computing Usage (Minutes/Week) by Class

	Word Processing	PIM Applications	Drawing Programs
Grade 7	40:24	7:12	6:18
Grade 6	1:57:12	2:30	5:48
Grade 4	1:29:12	3:48	1:12
Grade 4*	3:34:42	7:48	17:42
Grade 3*	2:46:24	1:42	1:07:48

**classes worked on same unit*

Table 3.3 also does not show the great variability between individual students within classes. In the sixth grade class, for example, one student used word processing for six hours a week, while students only used it for about one hour on average. A female student in this class spent two hours a week with word processing and another hour using the draw programs, while many students never used the draw programs. Two girls played with the PicChat functions; a few students used the calculator quite a bit while some students never used it; one student spent a good bit of time with Earth and Sun although most students barely looked at this application. Table 3.4 reflects this range of usage across classes, suggesting that at least some students in this study appropriated mobile computing devices for personal use (Roschelle & Pea, 2002).

Table 3.4 Range of Mobile Computing Usage (Minutes/Week) by Class

	Word Processing	Palm Applications	Drawing Programs
Grade 7	0:01:16 to 1:17:00	0:0:00 to 0:28:48	0:00:00 to 0:28:48
Grade 6	0:13:24 to 8:07:48	0:0:00 to 0:17:00	0:00:00 to 0:23:18
Grade 4	0:03:12 to 3:10:36	0:0:00 to 3:10:42	0:00:00 to 0:15:12
Grade 4*	2:09:18 to 7:29:36	0:0:18 to 0:29:42	0:02:06 to 1:58:24
Grade 3*	0:50:18 to 4:48:48	0:0:00 to 0:06:36	0:31:24 to 2:44:54

**classes worked on same unit*

The usage data findings are supported by the student interviews. More than 75% of the students interviewed reported using their mobile devices outside of the classrooms in which they were explicitly assigned—in other classes, at home, on the bus, and in after-school programs. The portability seemed a particularly important factor in their use. For example, when asked to compare mobile computing devices to desktop computers, one student told us "It's kind of like the same thing but it's smaller and easier to do. The computer you can't take with you wherever you go but the [mobile computing device] you can just close it up and take it wherever you go."

Students in the middle school classes reported using their mobile computing devices mostly for taking notes, while elementary students reported using them for a variety of writing activities, noting that they preferred using the devices to writing by hand. Many students also reported that they found them to be most useful for various types of organizational activities (scheduling, creating to-do lists, and outlining ideas). Students also reported enjoying the use of drawing programs and games.

Teachers also reported that students used the mobile computing devices in their classroom, at home, and on the bus to and from the laboratory classroom for writing assignments, journaling, note-taking, drawing, concept maps, spelling lists, test review, and to-do lists. The third and fourth grade teachers who collaborated also commented that the beaming feature (i.e., infrared file transfer from one device to another) was particularly effective for facilitating the peer editing process. Several teachers noted that when mobile computing homework was assigned, all students completed it on time, something that almost never happened with paper and pencil assignments. One suggested that this was as much because using the mobile computing device helped students organize their work as it was a result of increased motivation. Indeed, one seventh grader stated that when using his device "I don't lose homework like with papers." This possibility deserves further exploration.

Table 3.5 compares mobile computing usage across classes by gender. These data show a tendency for girls to use mobile computing devices more than boys. As by far the most frequent use of the devices was for word processing, it may be that this occurred because girls tend to write more than boys, but the result clearly deserves further investigation in light of common findings of the opposite with respect to desktop computers. The gender data also highlight the variability between classroom cultures. Note, for example, the usage among sixth graders; boys in this class used their devices more than girls, suggesting something different happening among at least a group of boys in this class.

Table 3.5 Comparison of Usage (Minutes/Week) by Gender & Special Needs Status

	Male	Female	Regular	Special Needs	All
Grade 7	49:30	87:28	63:04	56:30	61:48
Grade 6	2:39:06	2:03:36	2:21:36	1:09:48	2:12:03
Grade 4	1:15:24	1:53:48	1:51:42	1:07:30	1:38:24
Grade 4*	3:58:18	5:30:54	4:44:24	NA	4:44:24
Grade 3*	3:33:12	4:53:36	4:31:12	3:58:42	4:17:36

**classes worked on same unit*

To summarize, our preliminary findings indicate that the use of mobile computing devices can be beneficial for learning inside and outside the confines of the classroom. This transition of use in and outside of school tends to be seamless, because students are using the same device with the same settings, files, etc., wherever they go. Therefore, learning that may have been taking place already outside of the classroom can be amplified by this technology as well, and should be subject to further study. The data also suggest unique cultures of use evolved within classes and groups within classes (e.g., by gender), indicating higher levels of personal appropriation. In addition, the results indicate that usage tends to be personalized as individual students adapt the use of mobile computing devices to their own needs. Finally, the findings indicate that, at least in this study, mobile computing devices were used most frequently for writing activities (potentially due to the fact that the device used had a built-in keyboard) and that in most cases such use was readily embraced by students. These findings clearly invite further investigation and should inform future research.

DOES THE USE OF MOBILE COMPUTING DEVICES AFFECT STUDENTS' MOTIVATION TO LEARN AND ENGAGEMENT IN LEARNING?

Most teachers interviewed agreed that their students' motivation to learn and engagement in learning activities was improved by their use of mobile computing, which resulted in increased student productivity and improved quality of work. For example, the sixth grade teacher reported that

> Taking the [mobile computing devices] home resulted in everyone's homework always being done, and shortened the time frame for getting work done. Having the [mobile computing devices] also improved the writing of all students.

One of the fourth grade teachers believed that mobile computing devices would be highly engaging in a regular classroom, and observed that "practice makes perfect" when it comes to the writing process, "The one benefit I've noticed is that they do write more with the [mobile computing devices]. And I believe that as much as it occurs with reading, the more you write, the better a writer you become."

This same fourth grade teacher, although noting his students' initial engagement with the devices, also reported that excitement about using them seemed to die off in favor of the more powerful desktop and laptop computers available to them. It should be noted, however, that this class's culminating projects included choices of creating web pages and desktop videos, projects that are both highly motivating and which can only be done on regular computers. The findings here may be an indication that students were making choices with regard to which tools were most appropriate or worked best for particular tasks or projects. This finding is one that warrants further investigation, as making these kinds of choices is one of the pillars on which the success of ubiquitous computing environments for learning rests.

Interviews with students confirm these findings. Students said that they preferred using the mobile devices over writing by hand and that using them for writing assignments made the work "easier" and "more fun." One student noted, for example, that "my writing is poor and the [mobile computing device] makes it easier to read my writing." Students also noted that using mobile computing devices helped them keep their work organized. One student commented, "I don't lose homework like with papers."

Several students commented that they liked being able to share their writing with their friends using the device's beaming capabilities. Although more than a few students noted difficulties and frustrations with the devices, including programs freezing, problems with recharging and hot syncing, losing work, and in a few cases difficulties with the keyboard and the stylus, the majority of these students believed the benefits outweighed these difficulties. Students interviewed particularly liked the fact that they could take their devices everywhere. Mobile computing devices thus enable working on school assignments or exploring personal interests whenever and wherever students are inclined to do so, and seem to be a critical factor in supporting motivation and engagement in learning. It certainly deserves further study.

Videotaped observations of students in the laboratory classroom also provide confirmatory evidence of student engagement in learning when working with mobile computing. Of particular note is their use of the devices for recording data from a variety of experiments undertaken in several of the participating classes. The videotapes show students as engaged in recording data as they are in doing the experiments. Perhaps this is because, as one student noted, the use of mobile computing makes such activities seem more like what "real scientists do." It may also be that the ability to easily carry the devices anywhere, their capacity to collect and store a variety of information, and directly input this into desktop computer applications alleviates much of the drudgery of working with data and supports inquiry learning. As one student commented, "It's really fun. It's nicer than doing it on paper."

In summary, findings show that the use of mobile computing devices can increase student motivation and engagement in learning, especially their motivation to complete written assignments. Findings also indicate that students' motivation to learn and engagement in learning with mobile computing devices may be decreased by equipment problems and/or access to competing technologies. The latter may not actually be a disadvantage, as the availability of a variety of devices for learning will force students to make informed choices about appropriate technology use. Research is needed to further explore these findings.

DOES STUDENTS' USE OF MOBILE COMPUTING DEVICES SUPPORT LEARNING PROCESSES?

Teacher interviews indicate that mobile computing devices have the potential to enhance learning processes, especially with respect to writing. One teacher commented that the use of mobile devices resulted in noticeable improvements in both the peer editing process and the quality of student writing. She stated,

> The biggest change has been in their weekly journals. We have been journaling all year and they have always written them but in using the [mobile computing devices], peer editing takes on so much more meaning when they can beam to someone rather than trading papers. With the [mobile computing devices] they are editing their own writing more and it keeps getting better.

Many teachers also made comments about improvements in spelling and mechanics as a result of more time spent on writing and editing. Perhaps most important, most teachers also noted improvements in the written work of special needs students. One teacher stated, "Having the [mobile computing devices] improved the writing of all students but special education students in particular." Another noted that "the special education students were empowered to write."

Indeed, many of the teachers interviewed commented on ways in which the use of the mobile computing devices seemed to lessen the gap in academic achievement between regular and special needs students. This observation is supported by work samples obtained from the 3–4 targeted students per class in the laboratory classroom, and analyzed for evidence of conceptual understanding (on a scale of 3–12, with 12 being the highest). Average results of these analyses across classes are given in Table 3.6. The results indicated that for the classes in the laboratory classroom special needs students tended to perform on a level similar to medium ability students, while the seventh grade special needs students in science fell somewhere between low and medium ability peers. Analysis of lessons indicates that the overall lower ratings for the seventh grade science students may reflect assignments that did not elicit higher-order thinking, and this may have affected the performance of the special needs students. Nonetheless, the results provide some evidence for positive effects of mobile computing, particularly when supporting the learning of special needs students.

Table 3.6 Comparison of Conceptual Understanding Levels as Evidenced in the Work of Selected Students

	Average conceptual understanding rating for students in laboratory classes	Average conceptual understanding rating for seventh grade science students
High ability	10.0	7.2
Medium ability	9.4	5.5
Low ability	8.5	4.0
Special needs	9.3	4.7

Interviews with students support findings that the use of mobile computing devices may enhance student learning processes. For example, fifteen of the eighteen seventh grade science students interviewed stated that they believed their use of mobile computing helped them in their school work. These students particularly noted their helpful use for taking notes, test review, and doing calculations, while keeping their work on the devices helped them stay more organized.

As previously noted, students in the laboratory classes reported that they preferred using mobile computers over writing things by hand and that using mobile computing for writing assignments made the work "easier" and "more fun." This was even the case for the fourth grade students who preferred the desktops and laptops for higher-end applications such as multimedia presentations, web design, and video editing. The majority of students in these classes also stated that they thought their written work in particular improved as a result of their use of the devices. For example, one student stated, "My writing is poor and the [mobile computing devices] makes it easier to read my writing." Indeed, all students interviewed seemed to view mobile computing devices as a tool that could help them with their school work. This aspect of the use of such devices surely deserves further investigation.

In summary, findings from this preliminary study provide some indication that the use of mobile computing devices can enhance student learning processes, especially when it comes to writing—an activity that the devices used in this study are well suited for, given the availability of a built-in, full-size keyboard. Perhaps more important, the results suggest a lessening of the gap in conceptual understanding levels between regular and special needs students using mobile computing devices, but only when assignments elicit it. Interviews with teachers suggest that the use of mobile computing resulted in greater productivity and improved writing skills among their students. Findings also suggest that mobile computing devices may provide increased support for schoolwork (especially the writing process) and levels of conceptual understanding. These findings surely deserve further investigation and moreover should inform future research.

Conclusions

This preliminary investigation of the use of mobile computing devices shows that elementary and middle school students use them in a variety of ways, principal among these writing, both in and outside of class. The findings suggest both the personalization of learning supported by such devices and their potential usefulness in amplifying learning that may already be happening beyond the classroom. They also suggest that students easily adapt the use of mobile computing devices to their own needs and hint at the influence of classroom cultures on this appropriation. The findings hint at collaborative uses of such devices as well, especially during the editing process. The results of this study further indicate that use of mobile computing devices may increase student motivation to learn and increase their engagement in learning activities, which in turn could lead to an increase in time spent on learning activities and higher quality work.

However, this study has some limitations that need to be considered when interpreting the findings above. For one, as with any technology that is introduced in a learning environment, there is always a novelty effect. Students tend to be more motivated to use a new piece of technology for learning because it is new. Second, the use of the mobile technology was only studied for a relatively short period of time. Further study is needed to determine whether motivation to use and levels of use change over longer periods of time, say three to five years. Third, because some of the data collected is self-reported, there is always the chance of a Hawthorne effect, i.e., participants report what they think the researchers expect to hear or see, not what is actually happening.

On a less positive note, the results indicate that equipment problems can constrain the use of mobile computing devices. These findings suggest that special attention needs to be paid to classroom logistics, equipment maintenance, technical support, and perhaps professional development for teachers using mobile computing options. Future studies should investigate ways of better supporting teachers and classes using such devices (see also Vahey & Crawford, 2002; van 't Hooft, Diaz, & Swan, 2004). Finally, the observation that students have the opportunity to choose a technology tool for a specific task or activity needs closer investigation, as it may provide a clearer insight into how ubiquitous computing environments can be optimized for learning. Technology in itself won't make the difference; it's what students do with it that does.

Author Update

Since we wrote our article in 2005, the field of educational technology has changed dramatically. New tools and new uses for existing technologies seem to appear almost daily. One thing has remained the same, however: While students continue to appropriate digital technologies in their daily lives with relative ease, many teachers and schools continue to struggle with meaningful and effective integration of these same tools in educational contexts. Consequently, while digital technologies have become pervasive in our lives, the same cannot be said for their presence and use in schools. In addition, academic research on the effect of these technologies on teaching and learning is struggling to keep up with the pace.

Our original research questions were simple and broad, but we believe they are still pertinent today: How do students use mobile technologies; does their availability affect student motivation to learn and engagement in learning; and does their use support learning processes? These are big-picture questions, and the kinds of questions that help us to begin understanding how digital technologies may be used to support and amplify student learning, both in and outside of the classroom.

While the specific technology we looked at in 2005 is no longer widely used in classrooms, mobile technologies are, and they promise to grow in importance. Findings from our research concerning the personalization of learning afforded by such devices, their usefulness in extending learning beyond the classroom, and their seeming ability to lessen the gap between regular and special needs students remain relevant. They suggest fruitful avenues of research around today's mobile technologies. The digital tools we work with will change, but their general affordances for teaching and learning stay pretty much the same. It is important that we build on what we know about these. Only then will we be able to help educators prepare students to take on the challenges of the 21st century.

References

Bannasch, S. (1999). The electronic curator: Using a handheld computer at the Exploratorium. *Concord Consortium Newsletter.* Available at www.concord.org/sites/default/files/newsletters/1999/fall/at-concord-fall-1999.pdf

Cole, H., & Stanton, D. (2003). Designing mobile technologies to support co-present collaboration. *Personal and Ubiquitous Computing, 7,* 365–371.

Danesh, A., Inkpen, K., Lau, F., Shu, K., & Booth, K. (2001). Geney: Designing a collaborative activity for the Palm handheld computer. *Proceedings of CHI, Conference on Human Factors in Computing Systems.* Seattle, WA.

Glaser, B. (1978). *Theoretical sensitivity: Advances in the methodology of grounded theory.* Mill Valley, CA: Sociology Press.

Inkpen, K. (2001). Designing handheld technologies for kids. *Proceedings of CHI, Conference on Human Factors in Computing Systems.* Seattle, WA.

Mandryk, R. L., Inkpen, K. M., Bilezkjian, M., Klemmer, S. R., & Landay, J. A. (2001). Supporting children's collaboration across handheld computers. *Proceedings of CHI, Conference on Human Factors in Computing Systems.* Seattle, WA.

Newmann, F. M., Bryk, A. S., & Nagaoka, J. K. (2001). *Authentic intellectual work and standardized tests: conflict or coexistence.* Chicago, IL: Consortium on Chicago School Research.

Newmann, F. M., & Wehlage, G. G. (1995). *Successful school restructuring: A report to the public and educators.* Madison, WI: Document Service, Wisconsin Center for Educational Research.

Roschelle, J. (2003). Unlocking the value of wireless mobile devices. *Journal of Computer Assisted Learning, 19,* 260–272.

Roschelle, J., & Pea, R. (2002) A walk on the WILD side: How wireless handhelds may change computer-supported collaborative learning. *International Journal of Cognition and Technology, 1*(1), 145–272.

Sharples, M. (2000). The design of personal mobile technologies for lifelong learning. *Computers and Education, 34,* 177–193.

Soloway, E., Norris, C., Blumenfeld, P., Fishman, B., Krajcik, J., & Marx, R. (2001). Devices are ready-at-hand. *Communications of the ACM, 44*(6), 15–20.

Staudt, C., & Hsi, S. (1999). Synergy projects and pocket computers. *Concord Consortium Newsletter.* Available at www.concord.org/sites/default/files/newsletters/1999/spring/at-concord-spring-1999.pdf

Tinker, R. (1997). *The whole world in their hands.* Concord Consortium. Retrieved August 10, 2003, from www.ed.gov/Technology/Futures/tinker.html

Tinker, R., & Krajcik, J. (Eds.). (2001). *Portable Technologies: Science Learning in Context.* New York, NY: Kluwer Academic/Plenum Publishers.

U.S. Department of Education (2004). *National Educational Technology Plan.* Washington, DC: Author.

Vahey, P., & Crawford, V. (2002). *Palm Education Pioneers Program: Final evaluation report.* Menlo Park, CA: SRI International.

van 't Hooft, M., Diaz, S., & Swan, K. (2004). Examining the potential of handheld computers: Findings from the Ohio PEP project. *Journal of Educational Computing Research, 30*(4), 295–312.

van 't Hooft, M., & Swan, K. (2004). Special issue on ubiquitous computing: Introduction. *Journal of Educational Computing Research, 30*(4), 275–279.

Weiser, M. (1991). The computer for the 21st century. *Scientific American, 265*(3), 94–95, 98–102.

CHAPTER

4

Large-Scale Research Study on Technology in K–12 Schools: Technology Integration as It Relates to the National Technology Standards

Ann E. Barron | University of South Florida
Kate Kemker | University of South Florida
Christine Harmes | University of South Florida
Kimberly Kalaydjian | University of South Florida

*This article highlights the results of a survey (*n *= 2,156) in one of the largest school districts in the country, focusing on teachers' instructional modes related to technology integration as outlined in the National Educational Technology Standards for Students. Approximately 50% of the teachers who responded to the survey indicated that they were using technology as a classroom communication tool. Smaller percentages were reported for technology integration as a productivity, research, or problem-solving tool. In comparisons across subject areas, statistically significant differences were noted when teachers used computers as a research tool or as a problem-solving/decision-making tool. In both cases, science teachers reported the highest usage, followed by mathematics teachers.*

Expenditures to equip schools with computers and related technology have steadily increased at the national, state, and school levels. The financial investment has resulted in both an improved student-to-computer ratio and increased connectivity to the Internet. Nationwide, the ratio of students per computer has fallen from an average of 10.1 in 1995 to 5.4 in 1999–2000 (Quality Education Data, 2001). The percentage of public schools that have Internet access has increased from 35% (1994) to 99% (2002), and the percentage of public classrooms connected to the Internet has risen from 3% in 1994 to 87% in 2001 (Kleiner & Farris, 2002).

As a result of the significant investments being made in hardware, software, and infrastructure, there is a need for evidence regarding the instructional integration of technology in K–12 classrooms. It is apparent that with the acceleration in the pace of technological innovation and saturation in society, skills such as problem solving, synthesizing information, and communicating via technology are essential for today's students (CEO Forum, 2001).

This study was conducted to determine the extent to which individual teachers in a large school district were using technology as a tool for their students' education. In particular, the research addresses the use of technology as a classroom tool for research, communication, productivity, and problem-solving, as outlined by the National Technology Standards for Students. Analyses include comparisons across grade levels (elementary, middle, and high schools) and subject areas (English, mathematics, science, and social studies). The results of this study can be used to structure inservice training programs, preservice education curricula, and interventions for individual teachers.

Review of the Literature

NATIONAL EDUCATIONAL TECHNOLOGY STANDARDS

Technology standards are not new in the education field. After microcomputers entered schools in the 1970s and 1980s, educators struggled with defining appropriate computer skills for students (Bitter, 1983). At that time, computer literacy was often equated with basic operations and programming. Although several states provided guidelines to benchmark computer literacy at different grade levels, they did not require students to meet such standards in order to graduate (Roblyer, 2000).

In the past few years, a flood of standards has engulfed education. Standards in content areas, such as reading, writing, mathematics, and science, have emerged at the state and national levels. In some cases, these standards are tied to accountability via funding, student advancement, or certification. For example, the Education Commission of the

States estimated that at least 23 states would require students to pass a standard exam to graduate in 2002 (National Center for Policy Analysis, 1999). In addition, President Bush signed the No Child Left Behind Act of 2001 in January 2002. This law requires all states to establish a system of tests to measure students' achievement. In particular, it mandates tests in reading and math for students in grades three through eight, beginning in 2004. In 2005, science testing must begin ("Bush signs education reform law," 2002). The Enhancing Education through Technology Act of 2001, which is Title II, Part D of No Child Left Behind, provides grants for states that meet specific requirements to integrate technology into the curriculum. One of the requirements is that the grant application must include a description addressing "how the State educational agency will ensure ongoing integration of technology into school curricula and instructional strategies in all schools in the State, so that technology will be fully integrated into the curricula and instruction of the schools by December 31, 2006" (Title II, Part D, §2413).

Concurrent with the "standards movement," government officials and educators advocated the need to emphasize technological skills (Trotter, 1997). Rather than focusing on hardware and programming, these skills (often referred to as technological literacy) involved using technology as a tool to communicate, conduct research, and solve problems. Several states took the initiative to set technology benchmarks for various grade levels, and several national organizations undertook the mission of developing national standards for both students and teachers (Bennett, 2000; Roblyer, 2000).

In 1998, the International Society for Technology in Education (ISTE) published their National Educational Technology Standards (NETS) for Students, and, in 2000, published standards for teachers. As of March 2003, 29 states had adopted, adapted, or aligned with the ISTE standards for students, and 30 states were using the ISTE standards for teachers (ISTE, 2003). In some states, such as Alabama and North Carolina, students must pass a computer skills test before graduation. In other states, such as Delaware, Maryland, South Carolina, Tennessee, and Texas, students are required to pass a technology course as a part of their curriculum (Burke, 2001).

Because the ISTE standards serve as the foundation for many state standards, this study was conducted to ascertain the degree to which these guidelines were being addressed in the classroom. NETS for Students provides six areas of technology competencies:

- Basic operations and concepts
- Social, ethical, and human issues
- Technology productivity tools
- Technology communication tools
- Technology research tools
- Technology problem-solving and decision-making tools

The categories provide a framework for linking performance indicators to the standards for grades PK–2, 3–5, 6–8, and 9–12. The intent is that technology be an integral component or tool for learning within the context of academic subject areas (ISTE, 1998).

In the first category, *basic operations and concepts*, students should be able to demonstrate a basic understanding of technology, such as computers, televisions, VCRs, and audio tape players. Performance indicators at various grade levels might include exhibiting proficiency in the use of computer terminology, proper care of the monitor, and selection of a printer.

The second category, *social, ethical, and human issues*, pertains to topics involving the use of technology. A sample performance indicator would include students demonstrating their ability to evaluate media images and to make responsible choices about what they see and hear.

In the third category, *technology productivity tools*, students use various forms of technology to create media such as documents, movies, pictures, and spreadsheets. In addition to using the computer, students demonstrate proper use of an assortment of hardware, such as probes, scanners, and digital cameras to construct their knowledge.

The fourth category, *technology communication tools*, focuses on students' use of media to converse and interact with peers, experts, and other audiences. Students should be able to collaborate, communicate, and interact effectively with a range of audiences for both directed and independent learning.

In the fifth category, *technology research tools*, students use technology as a tool to locate, evaluate, and collect information from a variety of sources. Performance indicators include proficiency in evaluating the accuracy, relevance, appropriateness, comprehensiveness, and bias of online information.

The sixth category, *technology problem-solving and decision-making tools*, involves the use of technology to develop strategies for recognizing and solving problems. Students should be able to identify a problem, determine if technology is useful in solving the problem, and if so, select and implement the appropriate tools.

This study concentrated primarily on categories three through six, the classroom use of technology as a tool for productivity, communication, research, and problem solving.

STUDIES RELATED TO STAGES OF TECHNOLOGY INTEGRATION

Historically, most of the studies related to educational technology have focused on quantifying the numbers of computers or Internet access in classrooms, rather than investigating the manner in which the technology is integrated into the curriculum

(Smerdon et al., 2000). In the 1980s, researchers began to analyze the process of technology integration and attempted to measure how teachers used technology in the classroom. Two important initiatives included the Apple Classrooms of Tomorrow (ACOT) project and the Level of Technology Implementation (LoTi) scale.

Apple Classrooms of Tomorrow

The Apple Classrooms of Tomorrow (ACOT) project began in 1985, and it involved a collaboration among universities, research agencies, Apple Computer, and a cross section of K–12 schools (Sandholtz, Ringstaff, & Dwyer, 1997). Each participating student and teacher received two computers—one for home and one for school. "The intent was to create model, technology-rich learning environments in which teachers and students could use computers on a routine, authentic basis" (Bitter & Pierson, 2002, p. 115).

The ACOT study was primarily a qualitative, longitudinal study, with data collected via classroom observations, student logs, teacher journals, and weekly reports. The project focused on both the process of technology integration and the phases of adoption at the classroom level (Coley, Cradler, & Engel, 1997). Several findings related to the integration of technology emerged from the project. For example, the study found that technology:

- encourages fundamentally different forms of interactions among students and between students and teachers
- engages students systematically in high-order cognitive tasks
- prompts teachers to question old assumptions about instruction and learning. (Dwyer, 1994, p. 8)

The ACOT research also produced an adoption model for the use of technology in the classroom, which is known as the Stages of Instructional Evolution. This model asserted that educators go through five stages of thought and practice when adopting technology:

- *Entry*—Learn the basics of using technology.
- ***Adoption***—Use new technology to support traditional instruction.
- ***Adaptation***—Integrate new technology into traditional classroom practice.
- ***Appropriation***—Focus on cooperative, project-based, and interdisciplinary work, incorporating the technology as needed and as one of many tools.
- ***Invention***—Discover new uses for technology tools. (Apple Computer, Inc., 1995)

The ACOT study served as a foundation for research related to using technology as an integral part of teaching and learning. Linda Roberts of the U.S. Department of Education stated, "The lessons learned provide a rich foundation of experience and knowledge to guide current investments in technology at the local, state, and national level" (as cited in Apple Computer, Inc., 1995, p. 1).

Levels of Technology Implementation

The Levels of Technology Implementation (LoTi) scale was developed by Dr. Christopher Moersch in 1995 to "provide a data-driven approach to staff development and technology planning" (Moersch, 1999, p. 41). Teachers are asked to complete a 50-item questionnaire, indicating their perceptions about how they are using technology in the classroom. The results provide a profile for the teacher across three specific domains—the teacher's level of technology implementation (LoTi), personal computer use (PCU), and current instructional practices (CIP). The LoTi acronym is used in two ways when referring to this scale—to describe the domain of the survey that determines the degree to which the teachers perceive they are using technology, and as the overall score for the instrument that combines the LoTi, PCU, and CIP domains. Based on a teacher's overall LoTi level, recommendations can be made for staff development programs and specific interventions to enable him or her to move to a higher level (LoTi, n.d., Technology Use Profiles section).

A teacher's overall LoTi level corresponds to the LoTi scale, which consists of eight levels ranging from 0 to 6:

- Level 0—Non-use
- Level 1—Awareness
- Level 2—Exploration
- Level 3—Infusion
- Level 4a—Integration (Mechanical)
- Level 4b—Integration (Routine)
- Level 5—Expansion
- Level 6—Refinement

The higher the level, the more the teacher is integrating technology and moving from teacher-centered activities toward learner-centered activities. For example, teachers at Level 1 do not use technology in their classrooms and utilize a teacher-centered curriculum. Teachers at Level 3 use activities that encourage students to draw conclusions from information they find. This approach is more learner-centered and involves a higher level of technology use. At Level 6, teachers utilize a learner-based curriculum, and the technology activities engage students in solving real-life problems (LoTi, n.d., LoTi Breakdown section).

A case study was conducted with the LoTi questionnaire and 120 teachers from the Los Angeles Unified School District (LAUSD). The responses showed that "approximately 49% of the teachers' highest level of instruction achieved a Level 2 classroom use of technology" (Moersch, 1999, p. 42)—meaning they were using technology primarily as extension or enrichment activities, rather than as an integral part of the curriculum. "Approximately 28% of the teachers' highest level corresponded with Level 4 classroom technology use" (Moersch, 1999, p. 42)—meaning that technology was being used as a tool to solve problems and increase students' understanding of concepts. According to the results of the CIP portion of the questionnaire, approximately 39% of the teachers felt that they were not utilizing learner-centered activities; 59% felt that it was somewhat true that they were using learner-centered activities. Based on this study, recommendations were made to the LAUSD. These recommendations included ensuring that all classroom teachers had a working computer and printer in their classrooms, providing assistance to teachers who showed lower levels of technology implementation, and encouraging higher-level teachers to design units that illustrated how they use technology in their curricula (Moersch, 1999).

LARGE-SCALE SURVEYS RELATED TO TECHNOLOGY INTEGRATION

The ACOT and LoTi projects both provide insight into teachers' various stages of technology use and integration, and in many ways set the stage for national standards to emerge. Recently, three large-scale, survey-based studies have been conducted to determine how teachers are using computers in instruction, including research by the National Center for Education Statistics (NCES), the Center for Research and Information Technology and Organizations, and the Consortium on Chicago School Research. Each of these studies included aspects related to the integration of technology, and they provide relevant background information for the current research.

National Center for Education Statistics

In 1999, the National Center for Education Statistics (NCES) administered a short (three-page) survey that investigated teachers' use of computers and the Internet in the classroom (Smerdon et al., 2000). The sample for this survey consisted of 2,019 full-time teachers in the United States—1,016 elementary school teachers and 1,003 secondary/combined school teachers. To derive the sample of teachers, a sampling frame of 78,697 regular public schools was constructed from the 1995–96 NCES Common Core of Data Public School Universe file (Smerdon et al., 2000). A sample of 1,000 schools was selected from the sampling frame after it was stratified by instructional level and school size. "Within the primary strata, schools were also sorted by type of locale (central city, urban fringe, town, rural), geographic region, and percent of students in the school eligible for free or reduced-price school lunch to produce additional implicit stratification" (Smerdon et al., 2000, p. B–4). Each of the 1,000 selected schools was asked to submit the names of all "regular" classroom teachers (full-time teachers who taught in any of grades 1–12, excluding those whose primary teaching assignment was bilingual/English as a second language education, special education, or vocational education). After the teachers' names were submitted, "teacher sampling rates were designed to select at least one but no more than four teachers per school, with an average of slightly more than two teachers per school"—resulting in a total of 2,019 teachers (Smerdon et al., 2000, p. B–5).

The Executive Summary of the NCES survey reported that approximately half of the teachers who had computers or the Internet available in their schools used them for classroom instruction to some extent. The following describe the most common uses of computers:

- 61% reported student assignments that involved word processing or spreadsheets.
- 51% reported assignments that required Internet research.
- 50% used technology in the classroom for practicing drills.
- 50% recounted assignments that focused on using technology to solve problems and analyze data. (Smerdon et al., 2000)

Center for Research and Information Technology and Organizations

A similar study, called Teaching, Learning, and Computing (TLC), was conducted by the Center for Research and Information Technology and Organizations (Becker, 2001). This 1998 study included a 21-page survey of more than 4,000 teachers (grades 4–12). Approximately one-half of the schools in the study were "selected according to size and presence of computer technology, over-sampling larger schools and those with a greater density of various computer technologies" (Becker, 2001, p. 2). The other schools involved in the study were referred to as "purposive samples" and were selected from either "High-End Technology" schools (schools with substantial amounts of computer technology per capita) or "Reform Program" schools (teachers or schools who had been participants in a national or regional program involving major school or instructional reform). "At each sampled school, three to five teachers (3 in elementary, 5 in middle and high schools) were selected with probabilities related to the teacher's reputed use of technology and group projects and emphasis on higher-order thinking" (Becker, 2001, p. 3). In addition, a few teachers were selected by the principal, based on exemplary instructional practice or participation in instructional reform.

The primary results of this study (which relate to technology integration in subject areas) are illustrated in Figure 4.1. This chart is based on the percent of teachers who reported "frequent computer use," which was defined as 20+ uses by a typical student per academic year.

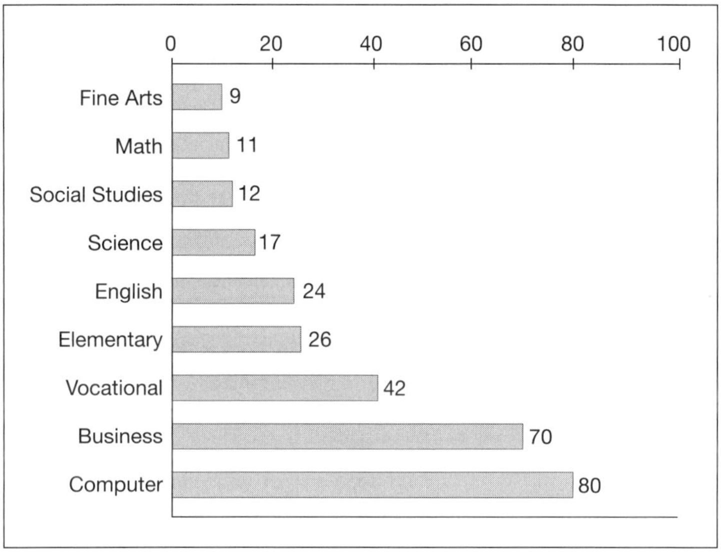

Figure 4.1 Frequent computer use by subject area (expressed as percentage)

Based upon these data, the author concluded that students were most likely to encounter technology in self-contained elementary classes or in technology-related courses in high school (such as computer, business, or vocational settings). "The one area where one might imagine learning to be most impacted by technology—students acquiring information, analyzing ideas, and demonstrating and communicating content understanding in secondary school science, social studies, mathematics, and other academic work—involves computers significantly in only a small minority of secondary school academic classes" (Becker, 2001, p. 4).

Consortium on Chicago School Research

In 2000, the Consortium on Chicago School Research conducted a study to obtain baseline data on the instructional use of computers and the Internet in Chicago public schools (Hart, Allensworth, Lauen, & Gladden, 2002). By including survey questions in conjunction with a biannual survey of teachers and students, the researchers obtained information from 8,572 elementary and 2,642 high school teachers. These surveys represent responses from 434 of the 577 schools in Chicago (representing a 75% participation rate for schools). Students in grades six through ten were also surveyed, with 87,732 responses.

Based on the data, the researchers concluded "the district lags behind the rest of the country in providing teachers and students with adequate access to computers and the Internet" (Hart et al., 2002, p. 1). They also investigated teachers' assignment of technology-related lessons and projects. Based on the responses from the teachers, they categorized teachers' levels of technology integration as follows:

- 6%—***Highly integrated***—Assign basic to moderate tasks on a weekly to daily basis; more complex activities such as demonstration, e-mail, computer programming, and web page creation are assigned anywhere from once or twice a semester to daily.
- 11%—***Integrated***—Assign basic tasks as much as once or twice a week and moderately uncommon tasks, such as analyzing or graphing data and creating presentation, from once or twice a semester or once or twice a month; some occasionally assign using technology for demonstrations or e-mail.
- 24%—***Modestly integrated***—Assign basic tasks once or twice a semester to once or twice a month. Most also assign moderately uncommon tasks up to once or twice a month but do not assign more complex tasks such as demonstrations.
- 31%—***Limited integration***—Assign low-level tasks such as word processing, practice drills, and research on the Internet from once or twice a semester to once or twice a month. Never assign any more complex tasks.
- 29%—***No integration***—Never assign technology to students in their target class. (Hart et al., 2002)

Although there are differences in the selection criteria, survey questions, and findings of the studies conducted by NCES, TLC, and the Chicago Consortium, the studies provide important background information and comparisons for the research outlined in this article.

Method

A large school district in Florida was selected for the study. This district is number 22 on the list of the largest 100 public elementary and secondary school districts in the United

States (Young, 2002). Within the district, there are 113,017 students; approximately 36% of the students are eligible for free and reduced-price lunches (Young, 2002). The district has a technology supervisor at the district level, and technology workshops are offered for teachers on a regular basis.

INSTRUMENTATION

In order to investigate teachers' use of technology in the classroom and to relate that use to the NETS guidelines, a survey was designed and sent to all teachers in the school district. Four domains were selected as focal points of the survey—integration; support; preparation, confidence, and comfort; and attitude toward computer use. This article focuses on aspects related to NETS—the integration domain.

The survey was constructed and reviewed by experts in technology and measurement. A pilot test was conducted with graduate students, including many K–12 teachers. At that point, psychometric information based on the pilot responses and participants' comments was used to guide minor revisions to the survey. The final document consisted of a four-page booklet—the first page was used to collect demographic information and the remaining pages addressed the four domains of investigation.

DATA COLLECTION

After obtaining clearance from the university's Institutional Review Board and the school district, the survey instrument was sent to all teachers in the school district. For each school, a letter addressed to the principal outlined the purpose of the study and requested assistance with the distribution of the individual surveys within the school. Once distributed, each teacher received a letter describing the study and either a paper version of the survey or instructions regarding participation using the web-based version.

To determine which schools received the web versions of the survey, a matched sample of schools was randomly selected. Using information from the Florida Department of Education's website (www.fldoe.org), schools were matched based on grade level, school size, percentage of students receiving free or reduced lunches, non-white representation, and mobility rate. Approximately 20% of the schools were selected to receive the web version (one school of each matched pair was randomly assigned to either the web or paper version). However, schools that were chosen to participate in the web version also received additional paper surveys in the event that individual teachers preferred to respond via paper.

To promote an optimal response rate, both individual and school-based incentives were offered. At the individual level, participation was encouraged by allowing teachers to register for a chance to win a free technology workshop provided by the Florida Center for Instructional Technology. Participants were also informed that the three schools with the highest percentage of teachers responding would win an on-site training session. A website was created so that participants could keep track of the response rates for their school and other participating schools that had responded.

Investigations into potential differences in response rates (paper vs. web) suggested that teachers were more likely to return the survey via paper (39% response rate) than via the web (10% response rate). However, follow-up analyses supported the premise that the web sample and the paper sample were representative of the same general population (Lang, Raver, White, Hogarty, & Kromrey, 2000).

RESPONDENT SAMPLE

The sample of 2,156 respondents represents an overall response rate of 35%, of which 17% were male and 83% were female. These respondents represented a range of educational backgrounds, a variety of disciplines, and a diversity of teaching experience. Sixty-one percent of the respondents held bachelor's degrees, 36% held master's degrees, 2% held specialist or doctoral degrees, and 1% did not fit within these categories. Of the 547 respondents who indicated a core subject area, 33% specialized in English, 28% math, 20% science, and 19% social studies. Fifty-one percent of the respondents taught in elementary school, 26% in middle school, and 23% in high school. Across all three school levels, approximately 61% of the respondents had ten or more years' teaching experience. (See Table 4.1.)

Table 4.1 Years of Teaching Experience: By School Level

	Years of Experience			
School Level	≤1	2–10	11–19	≥20
Elementary	6%	37%	22%	35%
Middle	8%	33%	22%	37%
High	5%	24%	27%	44%

Access to technology was reported both as the availability of a computer lab and the number of computers in the classroom. The average class size was 22, ranging from 1 to 60 students per classroom. More than 61% of the teachers reported access to a computer lab; the remaining 39% did not have access to a lab. The number of computers in the classroom ranged from 0 to 20. (See Table 4.2.)

Table 4.2 Number of Computers in the Classroom

Computers in Classroom	Percentage
0	13%
1	26%
2	21%
3	13%
4	10%
5–9	12%
10–20	5%
Total	**100%**

Results

As mentioned previously, the instrument was divided into logically and practically different sections/domains. Psychometric characteristics related to nonrespondent bias and factor analysis for each section are presented in detail in an article that focuses on the development and validation of the instrument (Hogarty, Lang, & Kromrey, 2003). Cronbach's alpha was calculated for each section of the survey. The analyses are based on classroom teachers' responses that did not contain missing data. Responses from other school personnel (such as guidance counselors) were excluded.

The survey included a section with items directly related to four teaching modes in NETS for Students (using technology as a research tool, communication tool, productivity tool, and problem-solving/decision-making tool). The reliability estimate (Cronbach's alpha) for this set of items was .89 for the paper version and .87 for the web version. Teachers responded on a 5-point frequency scale to items such as those shown in Table 4.3.

Table 4.3 Integration of Computers into the Classroom

Directions: Listed below are teaching modes in which computers may be used. Indicate how often you use computers in each teaching mode. If you feel an item does not apply then circle (NA).	1 = not at all 2 = once a month or less 3 = once a week 4 = several times a week 5 = every day
As a research tool for students	1 2 3 4 5 NA
As a problem-solving/decision-making tool	1 2 3 4 5 NA
As a productivity tool (to create charts, reports, or other products)	1 2 3 4 5 NA
As a communication tool (e.g., e-mail, electronic discussion)	1 2 3 4 5 NA

To simplify the presentation of results, the data were collapsed into two categories for analyses—*Yes* if the technology integration took place at least once a week, and *No* if the frequency was less than once a week. Results were examined for differences by school level and subject area. All tests of statistical significance were conducted at the .05 level.

SCHOOL LEVEL DIFFERENCES

The χ^2 test of independence was used to compare elementary, middle, and high school teachers' integration of computers in the classroom. The proportions, Cramer's V, and probabilities are presented in Table 4.4 and graphically illustrated in Figure 4.2. When teachers used computers for problem solving with their students, a statistically significant difference was observed across the three levels, χ^2 (2, n = 1654) = 15.5317, p = .0004. The proportion of elementary teachers was 29%; middle school teachers, 23%; and high school teachers, 20%. Odds ratios revealed that elementary school teachers were almost twice as likely (1.68) to use computers as a problem-solving or decision-making tool than were high school teachers.

Table 4.4 Integration of Computers in the Classroom by School Level

Use of Technology	Elementary	Middle	High	Cramer's V	Prob.
Problem-Solving Tool	29%	23%	20%	0.10	0.0004
Communication Tool	59%	54%	48%	0.09	0.0008
Productivity Tool	37%	40%	38%	0.02	0.6464
Research Tool	32%	34%	40%	0.07	0.0123

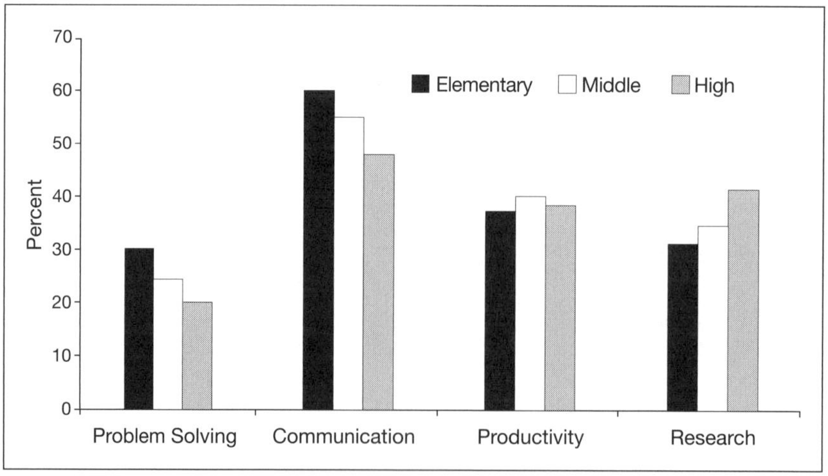

Figure 4.2 Integration of computers in the classroom by school level

Similarly, a statistically significant difference was found among the three levels when teachers used the computer as a communication tool with their students: χ^2 (2, n = 1,671) = 14.3777, p = .0008. The proportion of elementary teachers was 59%; the proportion of middle school teachers 54%; and that of high school teachers 48%. Odds ratios revealed that elementary school teachers were more likely (1.56) to use computers as a communication tool than were high school teachers. Statistical significance was also noted across levels for the use of the computer as a research tool: χ^2 (2, n = 1,668) p = .0123, with the proportion of elementary school teachers at 32%; middle school, 34%; and high school 40%. Statistically significant differences were not found across school levels for computer use as a productivity tool.

SUBJECT AREA DIFFERENCES

The χ^2 test of independence was also used to compare English, math, science, and social studies teachers' integration of computers in the classroom. (See Table 4.5 and Figure 4.3.) In these analyses, only responses from middle and high school teachers were evaluated because the elementary schools did not use subject level differentiation.

Table 4.5 Integration of Computers in the Classroom by Subject Area

Use of Technology	English	Math	Science	Social Studies	Cramer's V	Prob.
Problem-Solving Tool	10%	17%	28%	23%	0.17	0.0066
Communication Tool	49%	49%	59%	54%	0.08	0.4535
Productivity Tool	32%	33%	48%	40%	0.13	0.0617
Research Tool	30%	24%	51%	44%	0.22	0.0001

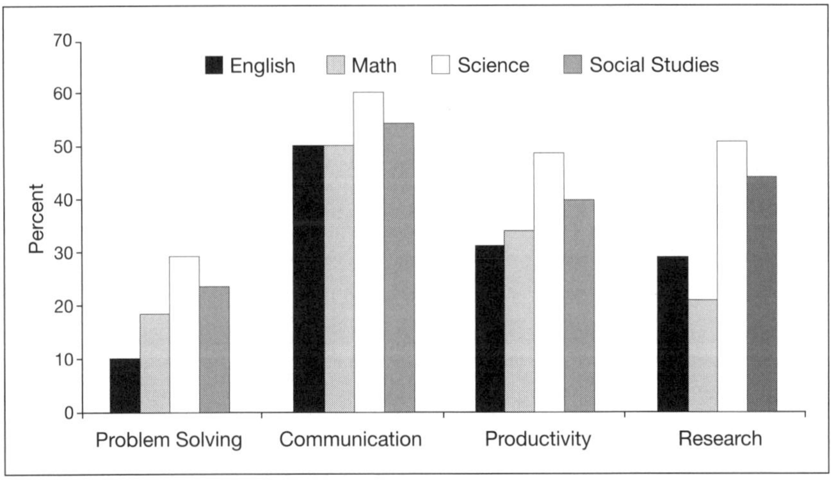

Figure 4.3 Integration of computers in the classroom by subject area

A statistically significant difference was found across subject areas when teachers used computers as a research tool for students, χ^2 (3, n = 413) = 20.3431, p = .0001. The proportion of science teachers was 51%; social studies teachers, 44%; English teachers, 30%; and math teachers, 24%. Science teachers were found to be three times (3.33) as likely as math teachers and twice (2.42) as likely as English teachers to integrate computers as research tools. Similarly, social studies teachers were more than twice (2.52) as likely to use computers as a research tool in the classroom than were math teachers.

A statistically significant difference was also noted across the subject areas when teachers used computers as a problem-solving and decision-making tool with their students, χ^2 (3, n = 409) = 12.2470, p = .0006. The proportion of science teachers was 28%; social studies teachers, 23%; math teachers, 17%; and English teachers, 10%. Science teachers were found three times (3.42) as likely as English teachers, and social studies teachers were more than twice (2.52) as likely as English teachers, to use computers as a problem-solving tool in the classroom.

No statistically significant differences were evidenced between the subject area groups when computers were used as productivity tools or communication tools. In both cases, however, computers were used more in science than in any of the other content areas.

Discussion

Teachers are a key element in addressing the technology standards outlined by the International Society for Technology in Education. This study investigated teachers' integration of technology through the administration and analysis of a survey that was sent to every teacher in a large school district. The response rate was 35% (n = 2,156), and multiple analyses were conducted with the data.

With regard to integration of computers into the classroom, it appears that some components of the NETS for Students guidelines are being addressed in the schools that were surveyed. However, the degree to which the standards are being addressed varies a great deal by school level and subject area, with few of the percentages presented in Tables 4.4 and 4.5 surpassing 50%.

Although the survey items were slightly different in the NCES instrument, the results of this survey indicate a comparable number of teachers using computers in the classroom for research. Instead of using a *frequency of use* scale, the NCES instrument focused on *extent of use*—with values for *large extent, moderate extent, small extent,* and *not at all.* Values for the "Internet research" and "Using technology to solve problems and analyze data" categories were:

Internet research

- 21% Small extent
- 19% Moderate extent
- 12% Large extent
- 51% Total reported in Executive Summary (Does not sum to total due to rounding.)

Solve problems/analyze data

- 23% Small extent
- 19% Moderate extent
- 8% Large extent
- 50% Total reported in Executive Summary (Smerdon et al., 2002)

If one assumes that moderate and large extent (in the NCES study) are roughly equivalent to a frequency of at least once a week (in this study), the numbers are comparable between the two studies—Internet research for NCES = 31%; Internet research for this study = 32% (elementary), 34% (middle), and 40% (high school). Likewise, the percentage of teachers using technology for problem solving in the NCES study (moderate plus large extent) equals 27%; this study reported 29%, 23%, and 20% for elementary, middle, and high school, respectively. Additional integration of technology must take place in this district before all students will have the opportunity to achieve the performance indicators set forth by NETS.

When comparing differences in teachers' integration of computers for various levels (elementary, middle, and high school), odds ratios found that elementary teachers were twice as likely to use computers as a problem-solving tool or communication tool than high school teachers. These results support findings by Becker, Ravitz, and Wong (1999), who found that "elementary teachers are more apt to use computers on a regular basis with their students" (p. 2). This could be because elementary teachers generally have more flexibility in their schedules to integrate innovative approaches. Additional impetus, based on these findings, should be focused on encouraging high school teachers to embrace technology for communication and problem-solving activities.

In the investigation of subject area differences, results indicate that science teachers were three times as likely as math teachers and twice as likely as English teachers to integrate computers as a research tool. Science teachers were also three times as likely as English teachers to use computers as a problem-solving tool. English teachers did not exhibit the largest frequencies in any of the four areas that focused on technology integration and use in the classroom. These results were supported by the Chicago study, which reported mathematics teachers assigning technology at a rate higher than the system average, and English teachers at less than the system average (Hart et al., 2002). However, the results of the current study differ from TLC, which found that "the English teachers (24%) had their students use computers frequently. At the other extreme, only 11 to 17 percent of secondary math, social studies and science teachers frequently assigned computer work…" (Becker et al., 1999, p. 7).

There are several factors that could explain the discrepancy between the results of this study and the 1999 study by Becker et al. The population for this study and the Chicago study included all teachers from a single, large school district. The Becker study included a national sample; however, many of the teachers ($n = 1{,}832$) were "purposively" sampled from high-end technology schools and reform program schools. The remaining teachers ($n = 2{,}251$) "were selected with probabilities related to the teacher's reputed instructional practices and use of technology" (Becker, 2000, p. 8). At each sampled school in the Becker study, only three (elementary) or five (middle and high school) teachers were selected. Purposively sampling technology-savvy teachers may have resulted in the variation of results.

The differences could also be related to the two-year interval between the studies, or they could be related to the structure of the survey questions or the definition of *frequent use*, which the Becker study defined as 20+ uses by a typical student per academic year and this study defined as at least once a week. Further investigations could focus on additional subject area use of technology in the classroom, as well as subject area differences that might exist in teacher preparation and training. Findings could then be used to outline subject-specific training needs (for inservice workshops) and could help structure courses for teacher preparation programs.

LIMITATIONS OF THE STUDY

Some limitations of this study should be noted. First, the study included teachers from only one school district. This district offers inservice technology training and support for teachers through workshops, public television programs, and technology specialists. Surveys of teachers in other states or school districts with different levels of access to technology or various levels of technical support may produce different results.

The fact that the survey results are based on self-reported data is another limitation. One might predict that those teachers who voluntarily responded to the survey were perhaps more interested in computers than those teachers who did not respond. The incentives (technology workshops) may have also served to bias the results toward teachers interested in computer use.

Concluding Remarks

The goal of national and state technology standards is to establish a baseline level of technology competence for all students. "When students are able to choose and use technology tools to help themselves obtain information, analyze, synthesize, and assimilate it, and then present it in an acceptable manner, then technology integration has taken place" (U.S. Department of Education, 2002, p. 79). Large-scale surveys of teachers, such as this one, can provide data to help answer key questions, such as those recently outlined by NCES: "Is technology integrated into the teaching/learning environment?" and "Are technology proficiencies and measures incorporated into teaching and learning standards?" (U.S. Department of Education, 2002, p. 74).

This study provides data that indicate many teachers are implementing technology as a tool for research, communication, productivity, and problem solving; however, the goal of technology integration across all subject areas and grade levels is yet to be reached. The proportion of teachers using computers as a tool in the classroom in this study ranged from 20% (problem-solving tool in high schools) to 59% (communication tool in elementary schools). Across subject areas, the range was 10% (problem-solving tool in English) to 59% (communication tool in science).

The Enhancing Education through Technology Act of 2001 requires that state educational agencies "assist every student in crossing the digital divide by ensuring that every student is technologically literate by the time the student finishes the eighth grade, regardless of the student's race, ethnicity, gender, family income, geographic location, or disability" (No Child Left Behind Act, Title II, Part D, §2402). As this Act takes effect and technology standards are being implemented throughout the nation, measures related to technology integration become crucial. The survey instrument discussed in this article is currently being used in several technology integration research initiatives. For example, several districts throughout Florida have adopted the instrument to gather baseline data or to track progress. In addition, the survey served as a framework for a statewide, web-based study that is currently under way. Copies of the instrument may be obtained from the first author.

Acknowledgments

This research was supported in part by the Florida Center for Instructional Technology at the University of South Florida and the Technology Literacy Challenge Fund for 1999–2000 under Grant 0-12191-9 TLC. The opinions expressed are those of the authors and do not necessarily reflect the views of the Florida Department of Education or the University of South Florida.

Author Update

Technology integration continues to be crucial for K–12 schools. However, a recent report by the National Center for Education Statistics found that only 58% of teachers felt "sufficiently trained to integrate technology into classroom instruction" (Gray & Lewis, 2009, p. 3). Since the publication of this article, the Florida Department of Education (FLDOE) has continued to promote and monitor technology integration throughout Florida.

A key ingredient for effective integration of technology in the classroom is professional development for teachers, administrators, and staff, with a focus on using technology as a tool in the curriculum. The Florida Digital Educators (FDE) initiative is a research-based professional development program focusing on the integration of technology and digital tools across the K–12 curricula. The FDE program includes hands-on training, video-based model lessons, action research, mentoring, and lesson plan development. In addition, the FLDOE supports the development of the Educational Technology Clearinghouse, a directory of the best educational resources on the web (http://etc.usf.edu) and the Technology Integration Matrix, which provides videos that reflect exemplary use of technology in the classroom (http://fcit.usf.edu/matrix/).

To assess teachers' and students' technology literacy, the FLDOE developed the Inventory of Teacher Technology Skills (www.flinnovates.org/itts.htm) and the Student Tool for Technology Literacy (www.flinnovates.org/st2l.htm). Both of these tools are based on the ISTE/NETS standards. They are available throughout Florida, and are used to target technology-related professional development for teachers (Harmes, Barron & Kemker, 2007; Hohlfeld, Ritzhaupt, Barron & Kemker, 2009). The status of technology integration is also monitored annually by the Florida Department of Education through the Technology Resources Survey (www.flinnovates.org/survey/), and trend analyses are conducted to highlight training and curricular needs (Hohlfeld, Ritzhaupt, Barron, & Kemker, 2008; Ritzhaupt, Hohlfeld, Barron, & Kemker, 2008).

References

Apple Computer, Inc. (1995). *Changing the conversation about teaching, learning, and technology: A report on 10 Years of ACOT research*. Cupertino, CA: Apple Computer, Inc. Retrieved from http://imet.csus.edu/imet1/baeza/PDF%20Files/Upload/10yr.pdf

Becker, H. J., Ravitz, J. L., & Wong, Y. T. (1999). *Teacher and teacher-directed student use of computers and software*. Irvine, CA: Center for Research and Information Technology and Organizations, University of California, Irvine & University of Minnesota.

Becker, H. J. (2000). Pedagogical motivations for student computer use that lead to student engagement. *Educational Technology, 40*(5), 5–17.

Becker, H. J. (2001, April). *How are teachers using computers in instruction?* Paper presented at the annual meeting of the American Educational Research Association, Seattle, WA.

Bennett, J. (2000). National educational technology standards: Raising the bar by degrees. *Multimedia Schools, 7*(3), 16–18.

Bitter, G. (1983, June). *A scope and sequence curriculum (K–12) for computer literacy.* Presented at the Symposium on Computer Literacy, Baltimore, MD. (ERIC Document Reproduction Service No. 235 792)

Bitter, G., & Pierson, M. (2002). *Using technology in the classroom* (5th ed.). Boston, MA: Allyn and Bacon.

Burke, J. (2001). *Technology standards for students*. Washington, DC: Office of Educational Research and Improvement.

Bush signs education reform law. (2002, January 9). Cable News Network. Available at http://archives.cnn.com/2002/ALLPOLITICS/01/08/bush.education

CEO Forum. (2001). *School technology and readiness report: Key building blocks for student achievement in the 21st century.* Washington, DC: CEO Forum on Education & Technology.

Coley, R., Cradler, J., & Engel, P. (1997). *Computers and classrooms: The status of technology in U.S. schools*. Princeton, NJ: Educational Testing Service.

Dwyer, D. (1994). Apple classrooms of tomorrow: What we've learned. *Educational Leadership, 51*(7), 4–10.

Gray, L., & Lewis, L. (2009). *Educational technology in public school districts: Fall 2008* (NCES 2010–003). National Center for Education Statistics, Institute of Education Sciences, U.S. Department of Education. Washington, DC.

Hall, G. E., George, A. A., & Rutherford, W. L. (1977). *Measuring stages of concern about the innovation: A manual for use of the SoC questionnaire*. Austin, TX: University of Texas, Research and Development Center for Teacher Education.

Harmes, J. C., Barron, A. E., & Kemker, K. (2007). Development and implementation of an online tool to assess teacher technology skills. In C. Crawford et al. (Eds.), *Proceedings of Society for Information Technology and Teacher Education International Conference 2007* (pp. 802–805). Chesapeake, VA: AACE.

Hart, H. M, Allensworth, E., Lauen, D. L., & Gladden, R. M. (2002). *Educational technology: Availability and use in Chicago's public schools*. Chicago, IL: Consortium on Chicago School Research.

Hogarty, K. Y., Lang, T. R., & Kromrey, J. D. (2003). Another look at technology use in classrooms: The development and validation of an instrument to measure teachers' perceptions. *Educational and Psychological Measurement, 63*(1), 137–160.

Hohlfeld, T. N., Ritzhaupt, A. D., Barron, A. E., & Kemker, K. (2008). Examining the digital divide in K–12 public schools: Four-year trends for supporting ICT literacy in Florida. *Computers & Education, 51*, 1648–1663.

Hohlfeld, T. N., Ritzhaupt, A. D., Barron, A. E., & Kemker, K. (2009, April). *Development and validation of the student tool for technology literacy (ST2L).* Paper presented at the annual meeting of the American Educational Research Association (AERA), April 13–18, 2009, San Diego, CA.

International Society for Technology in Education. (1998). *National educational technology standards for students* [Electronic version]. Available at www.iste.org/standards.aspx

International Society for Technology in Education. (2003). *Use of NETS by state* [Electronic version]. Retrieved from http://cnets.iste.org/docs/States_using_NETS.pdf

Kleiner, A., & Ferris, E. (2002). *Internet access in U.S. public schools and classrooms: 1994–2001.* Washington, DC: US Department of Education, National Center for Education.

Lang, T. R., Raver, R. A., White, J. A., Hogarty, K. Y., & Kromrey, J. D. (2000, November). *Survey data collection strategies: Response differences between web-based and paper-based methods.* Paper presented at the annual meeting of the Florida Education Research Association, Tallahassee, FL.

LoTi (Level of Technology Implementation). (n.d.). Available at http://loticonnection.com/lotilevels.html

Moersch, C. (1999). Assessing current technology use in the classroom: A key to efficient staff development and technology planning. *Learning & Leading with Technology, 26,* 40–49.

National Center for Policy Analysis. (1999). *High stakes testing spreads* [Online document]. Washington, DC: Author. Available at www.ncpa.org/sub/dpd/index.php?Article_ID=11480

No Child Left Behind Act of 2001, Pub. L. No. 107-110, 115 Stat. 1425 (2002).

Quality Education Data. (2001). *Technology purchasing forecast 2000–2001,* (6th ed.). Denver, CO: Quality Education Data.

Ritzhaupt, A. D., Hohlfeld, T. H., Barron, A. E., & Kemker, K. (2008). Trends in technology planning and funding in Florida K–12 schools. *International Journal of Education Policy and Leadership, 3*(8), 1–17.

Roblyer, M. D. (2000). The national educational technology standards (NETS): A review of definitions, implications, and strategies for integrating NETS into K–12 curriculum. *International Journal of Instructional Media, 27*(2), 133–146.

Sandholtz, J., Ringstaff, C., & Dwyer, D. (1997). *Teaching with technology: Creating student-centered classrooms.* New York, NY: Teachers College Press.

Smerdon, B., Cronen, S., Lanahan, L., Anderson, J., Iannotti, N., & Nicholas, A. (2000). *Teachers' tools for the 21st century: A report on teachers' use of technology.* Washington, DC: U.S. Department of Education, National Center for Education Statistics. (NCES 2000-102).

Trotter, A. (1997). Technology counts: Taking technology's measure. *Education Week on the Web.* Retrieved from www.edweek.org/media/ew/tc/archives/TC97full.pdf

U.S. Department of Education, National Center for Education Statistics. (2002, November). *Technology in schools: Suggestions, tools, and guidelines for assessing technology in elementary and secondary education.* Prepared by the Technology in Schools Task Force. Washington, DC: National Forum on Education Statistics. (NCES 2003–313).

Young, B. (2002). *Characteristics of the 100 largest public elementary and secondary school districts in the United States: 2000–01.* Washington, DC: U.S. Department of Education, National Center for Education Statistics.

CHAPTER

5

Implementation and Effects Of One-to-One Computing Initiatives: A Research Synthesis

William R. Penuel | SRI International

There are now a large number of initiatives designed to make laptops with wireless connectivity available to all students in schools. This paper synthesizes findings from research and evaluation studies that analyzed implementation and effects of one-to-one initiatives from a range of countries. Factors related to successful implementation reported in the research include extensive teacher professional development, access to technical support, and positive teacher attitudes toward student technology use. Outcome studies with rigorous designs are few, but those studies that did measure outcomes consistently reported positive effects on technology use, technology literacy, and writing skills.

Introduction

One-to-one computing initiatives that seek to provide laptop computers and Internet access to students for use at home and school are expanding rapidly across the globe. The decreasing costs, combined with the lighter weight of laptops and increasing availability of wireless connectivity, are all making such initiatives more feasible to implement on a broad scale. States such as Maine and Texas, for example, have invested in statewide initiatives to fund access to laptops for secondary school students. Large districts such as Henrico County in Virginia and Cobb County in Georgia are providing laptops and digital content to all middle and high school students. Hundreds of independent, parochial, and individual public schools are also implementing demonstration and large-scale projects that provide one-to-one, 24/7 access to computers and the Internet.

The educational technology research community's collective knowledge about one-to-one initiatives has not to date kept up with the rapid expansion of these initiatives or with their breadth. An earlier 2001 review of laptop initiatives that SRI International researchers conducted under contract with the U.S. Department of Education found just 19 studies that had analyzed outcomes (Penuel et al., 2001). Researchers concluded at that time that there was too little research-based evidence to determine whether such programs were effective, because the overall methodological quality of the studies was weak. Since that review, a number of new one-to-one computing initiatives have begun and have focused on providing wireless access to the Internet. In addition, a number of new studies have been published on the implementation and effects of these initiatives. In this paper, we describe results of a synthesis of research evidence with respect to the following questions:

- What new studies of one-to-one computing initiatives have been conducted, and what has been their focus?
- How are students and teachers using technology in initiatives?
- What new information is available from studies about the conditions necessary for effective implementation?
- Have there been any rigorously-designed outcome studies published on the effectiveness of initiatives? If so, what outcomes have been measured?
- What research is still needed on one-to-one initiatives?

In this paper, we provide a definition of one-to-one computing initiatives and a theoretical framework that elaborates on their potential for improving teaching and learning, as well as likely conditions for successful implementation. We then describe the methodology synthesizing findings from 30 separate studies of one-to-one initiatives. In the results section, we discuss the goals and scale of different initiatives included in the review, describe particular design features and factors that may influence teachers and overall implementation most strongly, and consider evidence of effects shown by the limited number of rigorously designed studies in the field and follow with an analysis of the untapped potential of most one-to-one studies to date. Finally, we consider in the conclusion section what is not yet known but needs to be explored in future studies of one-to-one initiatives.

One-to-One Initiatives: A Definition

There has been widespread interest and investment in initiatives designed to provide each student with a computer to support academic learning for close to ten years now in the United States. The earliest initiatives in the U.S. began appearing in the mid-1990s, and the most visible sponsored initiative at that time was Microsoft's Anytime, Anywhere Learning program (Rockman et al., 1998). As part of this program, scores of schools and districts implemented programs in which students could lease or buy laptop computers that they and their teachers were expected to use in school. In the past five years, Apple Computer, Inc., has become more actively involved in the area, and even though the estimated total cost of ownership of laptop computers remains high (Consortium on School Networking, 2004), whole districts and even states continue to invest in initiatives designed to give every student in particular grade levels a laptop computer.

In practice, the scope and detail of one-to-one initiatives are largely defined by the initiating institutions. Common to most initiatives is the idea that all students have individual access to computers, but program managers have different policies about, for instance, whether students can take computers home and about whether students lease or pay to own their computers. In addition, initiative leaders have adopted a variety of goals for initiatives that are often similar to initiatives in other localities (e.g., improving access to technology resources for all students), but policymakers and program leaders give different emphases to these goals and to the multiplicity of goals they use to convince school boards, foundations, state legislatures, and others to pay for laptop computers (Lemke & Martin, 2003a, 2003b, 2003c, 2003d).

A core set of characteristics shared by a wide number of initiatives, however, coupled with the continued if not growing interest among policymakers and educational leaders in one-to-one initiatives, makes it both possible and important to conduct a review of what is known about their implementation and effectiveness. For purposes of this review, we have chosen three core features common to a wide variety of initiatives as defining characteristics of one-to-one computing in the classroom: (1) providing students with use of portable laptop computers loaded with contemporary productivity software (e.g., word processing tools, spreadsheet tools, etc.), (2) enabling students to access the Internet through schools' wireless networks, and (3) a focus on using laptops to help complete academic tasks such as homework assignments, tests, and presentations.

These characteristics distinguish one-to-one initiatives that are the focus of this review from past efforts aimed at providing each student with his or her own computer. Earlier one-to-one efforts provided students with desktop computers for home use (Chang et al., 1998; Rockman et al., 1995) and with laptops with limited or no capability to access the Internet (e.g., Haynes, 1996; Myers, 1996). An earlier review of the literature (Penuel et al., 2001) included both these types of programs as one-to-one initiatives, but as we argue in the next section, there is a clear need to analyze what we know about the implementation and effectiveness of laptop initiatives in which students have wireless access to the Internet from knowledge of other desktop and portable computers.

Theoretical Framework: Why Wireless One-to-One Computing Matters for Learning and Conditions for Successful Implementation

We drew on two kinds of research to guide our research review: theories of what kinds of learning outcomes are possible with wireless laptop computers and theories of implementation of technological innovations in the classroom. The first area of research helps explain why studying one-to-one initiatives can help us understand the potential of ubiquitous computing in schools and what advantages wirelessly connected computers may have over stand-alone computers. Latter research provides us with insight into both the likely conditions and supports necessary for implementing a technology innovation and the potential barriers to success.

THE POTENTIAL OF WIRELESS LAPTOP COMPUTING FOR STUDENT LEARNING

When they could afford to buy a large number of computers, many schools throughout the 1980s and early 1990s placed them in centrally located laboratories (Means & Olson, 1995). Computer use in labs has been found to be effective at least over the short term (Kulik & Kulik, 1991; Kulik, 1994), but researchers have long argued that for technology to make a powerful difference in student learning, students must be able to use computers more than once or twice a week in a lab at school (Kozma, 1991). Limited access has been cited as a reason why teachers make limited use of technology with students (Adelman et al., 2002; Cuban, 2001; Sheingold & Hadley, 1990). Teachers report that when computers are in labs, they use technology less often for instruction because of the difficulty of scheduling time in the lab and transporting students there (Adelman et al., 2002).

More widespread access to computers makes it possible for students and teachers in schools to transition from occasional, supplemental use of computers for instruction to more frequent, integral use of technology across a multitude of settings (Roschelle & Pea, 2002). Ubiquitous, 24/7 access to computers makes it possible for students to access a wider array of resources to support their learning, to communicate with peers and their teachers, to become fluent in their use of the technological tools of the 21st-century workplace. When students are also able to take computers home, the enhanced access further facilitates students keeping their work organized and makes the computer a more "personal" device (Vahey & Crawford, 2002).

Beyond facilitating more frequent use of technology in class, many argue that providing students with better access to computers can provide students with more equitable access to resources and learning opportunities. Educational leaders have argued that providing students with a computer with Internet access gives everyone the ability to use up-to-date learning resources that before were available only to those who lived close to a library or benefited from school budgets that allowed for regular purchases of new textbooks (Penuel et al., 2001). Early evaluation studies of laptop programs reflected this emphasis on equity; in studies of the Beaufort (South Carolina) Learning with Laptops initiative, for example, researchers examined the extent to which providing laptops narrowed gaps between students of color and White students and between low-income and more advantaged students (see, e.g., Stevenson, 1998, 1999). Further, analyses conducted on some of the first tests of computer proficiency administered by states suggested that home access to computers helped to explain differences in student performance on those tests (North Carolina Department of Public Instruction, 1999). These studies together confirmed both the potential and significance of providing more ubiquitous access to computers to all students.

A number of researchers have also argued that providing students with ubiquitous access to wirelessly connected computers has the potential to transform learning environments and improve student learning outcomes (see Roschelle, Penuel, & Abrahamson, 2004, for a review). When computers are connected in the classroom, for example, the network can facilitate collaborative learning processes that are difficult to coordinate when teachers must be present to ensure that individuals stay on task and group members help each other learn (Zurita & Nussbaum, 2004). Further, graphical displays showing from individual contributions to solving problems (e.g., students creating points on a line for a particular equation) can help illuminate concepts that are otherwise difficult for students to understand and also motivate them to participate more actively in class (Hegedus &

Kaput, 2004; Kaput & Hegedus, 2002; Stroup, 2002). Further, when all students have computers that are connected through a network, students can participate in simulations that allow them to experience complex systems such as patterns of traffic and population dynamics directly (Colella, 2000; Wilensky & Stroup, 2000).

FRAMEWORK FOR ANALYZING CONDITIONS FOR SUCCESSFUL IMPLEMENTATION

Much of the excitement about the potential of providing students with wirelessly connected laptops is tempered by an appreciation for the complexities and difficulties of implementation of educational technologies. All too often, new technological innovations have proven unusable to a wide variety of teachers, whether because schools lack the capacity to implement them well, policies are not congruent with technology use, or the culture of the school is not supportive of technology adoption (Blumenfeld, Fishman, Krajcik, Marx, & Soloway, 2000). Critics of large investments in computers for schools often point out that technologies have been "oversold and underused," and that they have had minimal effects on learning environments (Cuban, 1986, 2001). Past research on implementation of educational technology must serve as a guide to helping interpret the effects (or lack of effects) of providing students with access to laptops, no matter how novel the technology is for classrooms, because the novelty itself poses special challenges for teachers and schools to fully realize the potential of these technologies.

One finding from past research that is likely to influence the implementation of one-to-one initiatives is that teachers' attitudes and beliefs about technology's role in the curriculum can influence how and when teachers integrate computers into their instruction (Becker & Anderson, 2000; Becker, Ravitz, & Wong, 1999; Ertmer, 1999). When teachers do not perceive that expected uses of technology are closely aligned with the curriculum, they use it less often (Sarama, Clements, & Henry, 1998). Other individual teacher characteristics that are associated with technology integration levels include teachers' pedagogical approach (Watson & Tinsley, 1995), their confidence or feelings of preparedness to use technology (National Center for Education Statistics [NCES], 2000; Yarnall, Shechtman, & Penuel, 2006), and their subject-matter expertise (Roschelle, Pea, Hoadley, Gordin, & Means, 2000).

Teachers' beliefs are influenced by the nature and frequency of messages they hear in their environment (Coburn, 2004), and teacher professional development activities are a source of information about how and what to teach; these activities also prepare teachers to use technology effectively. The amount of professional development that teachers have received has been found to be related to teachers' feelings of preparedness to use technology with students (NCES, 2000). Teachers who reported spending nine hours or more in educational technology professional development activities were more likely than teachers who spent less time in such activities to report feeling well- or very well-prepared to use computers and the Internet for instruction.

In addition to the amount of professional development, the form of professional development and its coherence with teachers' standards and curriculum shape the outcomes of professional development experiences. Kanaya, Light, and Culp (2005) found that when teachers perceive professional development activities to be aligned with the content schools expect them to teach and perceive the workshop to be relevant and useful to their teaching, they are more likely to integrate technology into their teaching. In addition, when teachers take on more active roles within professional development for their own learning and for their colleagues' learning, they are more likely to use technology with their students (Frank, Zhao, & Borman, 2004; Riel & Becker, 2000).

The technical infrastructure, including the availability of support for addressing problems as they arise, is also a significant factor in shaping teachers' technology use in the classroom. Difficulties with ensuring adequate resources for purchasing and maintaining hardware and software—including policies that make it difficult to make particular kinds of purchases—can reduce the likelihood that teachers will use technology with students (Blumenfeld et al., 2000). For classrooms using wireless networks, the reliability of the network is frequently an issue and a barrier to widespread use by teachers for instruction (Hill & Reeves, 2004; Tatar, Roschelle, Vahey, & Penuel, 2003). Further, even when access to computers and wireless connectivity is sufficient, perceptions among teachers that there is limited access to timely technical support from school-based or district staff can hinder their integration of technology into the curriculum (Molina, Sussex, & Penuel, 2005).

Methodology Used for the Research Synthesis

In this research synthesis, we sought to identify all high-quality research studies that analyzed implementation or reported outcomes of one-to-one initiatives from English-language journals and websites. We adopted a narrative, rather than meta-analytic approach to synthesizing findings, both because there were so few outcome studies and because the vast majority of studies reported on implementation processes that could better be summarized and synthesized using a narrative approach. In this section, we describe in detail our approach to identifying, selecting, and analyzing studies for the synthesis.

SCOPE OF THE SYNTHESIS

The scope of this synthesis was limited to one-to-one initiatives that used laptop computers with wireless connectivity in K–12 education. We included in our synthesis articles that systematically investigated the implementation of laptop initiatives and/or studied outcomes of laptop initiatives using comparison group designs.

PROCESS FOR FINDING AND SELECTING ARTICLES

We searched English-language peer-reviewed journals, dissertation abstracts, and the web for studies that might be included in the synthesis using a common set of key words. Initially, our search included one-to-one initiatives that used handheld computers or graphing calculators. Researchers downloaded abstracts from all reports or articles found into EndNote, where they recorded essential bibliographic information and a common core of information about how the articles were found.

The initial search yielded 245 articles, of which there were 177 unique articles. Initially, secondary reports of research (those found in magazines such as *Technology and Learning*), meta-analyses, research syntheses, policy documents, curriculum guides, and conference reports were all eliminated from the pool of potential articles for inclusion in the study. After eliminating these, 123 articles remained in the database. Next, we eliminated articles that were outside the intended focus of the study as evidenced by the study abstracts. A total of 68 were eliminated at this point, resulting in 55 articles remaining. Finally, we eliminated articles about handhelds or graphing calculators, leaving 46 articles.

We obtained each of these articles, and researchers produced 2–3 page summaries of key aspects of each study: the goals and design of the one-to-one initiative, nature of the technology used, characteristics of schools in the study, data on implementation, and data on outcomes. A more thorough reading of articles and a subsequent decision to restrict the scope of the synthesis to one-to-one initiatives using laptops with wireless connectivity led us to include a total of 30 articles in the synthesis.

CRITERIA FOR INCLUSION

We included articles in the synthesis that used systematic methods for investigating implementation or outcomes. We applied different criteria for studies we characterize as *implementation studies* and those we describe as *outcome studies. Outcome studies*, to be included, must have employed experimental designs with random assignment or quasi-experimental designs with pre- and posttest data on both treatment and control groups. To be included, *implementation studies* must have employed systematic methods of analysis of implementation data. Examples include statistical analysis of survey data, grounded theory, comparative case study analysis, or ethnographic analysis.

PROCESS FOR SYNTHESIZING RESULTS

Two research team members worked independently to review the 2–3 page summaries, identify a set of recurring themes to highlight in the synthesis, and code individual articles using a spreadsheet to record results of our coding by study. We began with open-coding, beginning by looking at summaries of research reports for potential coding categories within the broad areas of professional development, technical support, teacher beliefs, and student uses of technology for implementation. Once we identified a set of common categories, two coders worked independently to identify whether from study summaries the category was evident within a particular study. We then reviewed and discussed discrepancies on coding to agree on a final code for each study.

Findings from the Synthesis

GOALS AND SCALE OF ONE-TO-ONE INITIATIVES

Beyond providing laptop and Internet access to students, the goals for the one-to-one initiatives included in the research synthesis tend to focus on one or more of four outcomes (Lemke & Martin, 2003a, 2003b, 2003c, 2003d; Zucker, 2004). For some initiatives, the primary focus is on improving academic achievement with the use of technology. For others, the goal is increasing equity of access to digital resources and reducing the digital divide. For still other initiatives, including the statewide initiative in Maine, the goal is increasing the economic competitiveness of the region by preparing its students more effectively for today's technology-saturated workplaces. Finally, some initiatives seek, by introducing ubiquitous access to computers, to effect a transformation in the quality of instruction. Many of the initiatives focused on transforming teaching seek specifically to make instruction more "student-centered," that is, more differentiated, problem- or project-based, and demanding of higher-order thinking skills.

The initiatives also vary widely in their scale. Some initiatives are providing laptop computers with wireless Internet access to tens of thousands of students across a district or an entire state. In still others, schools are experimenting classroom by classroom with introducing laptop computers into instruction. The challenges posed by scale are no doubt different from those posed by small pilot projects. In addition to coordinating professional development and technical support for larger numbers of teachers, large-scale initiatives must address the challenge of ensuring that programs address local teachers' needs and individual schools' goals for improving teaching and learning. Conversely, smaller-scale initiatives often face challenges in finding enough funding to support teachers and the technology; coordinating instruction with laptops when not all students in a school have laptops is an additional challenge.

CLASSROOM USES OF LAPTOPS IN ONE-TO-ONE INITIATIVES

A number of implementation studies have examined how students are using laptops in their classrooms and at home. Across a wide range of studies, students use laptops primarily for writing, taking notes, completing homework assignments, keeping organized, communicating with peers and their teachers, and researching topics on the Internet. (See Table 5.1.) For these tasks, they are using word processing software, web browsers, e-mail clients, and chat programs. Use of software programs designed to teach basic skills appears to be less common, observed in only four of the programs studied by researchers whose work is included in the synthesis (Daitzman, 2003; Davis, Garas, Hopstock, Kellum, & Stephenson, 2005; Mitchell Institute, 2004; Warschauer, Grant, Real, & Rousseau, 2004; Zucker & McGhee, 2005).

Table 5.1 Most Frequently Reported Student Uses of Computers From Studies

Student Use	Number of Studies Reporting
Word processing software	11
Internet browsers (primarily for research)	10
Presentation software	6
Basic skills practice	4
Spreadsheets	3
Multimedia authoring and design	3

The most common uses appear to reflect the fact that the observed students' teachers are in an "adaptation" stage of technology adoption (Sandholtz, Ringstaff, & Dwyer, 1997). In other words, they are adapting traditional teaching strategies to incorporate more adult productivity tools and having students work independently and in small groups, but they have not yet begun to implement widely more student-centered strategies for instruction such as project-based learning. Those students who do engage in more extended projects typically use design and multimedia tools, including presentation software and software for making and editing digital images and movies (Davies, 2004; Davis et al., 2005; Light, McDermott, & Honey, 2002; Mitchell Institute, 2004; Newhouse & Rennie, 2001; Stevenson, 2002; Warschauer et al., 2004; Windschitl & Sahl, 2002). Researchers presented several interesting examples of students' digital products, and some noted that these were particularly compelling to parents and adults in the school community (Light et al., 2002).

HOW TEACHER ATTITUDES AND BELIEFS SHAPE IMPLEMENTATION

Although overall few studies on one-to-one computing initiatives have presented research-based evidence that determines the true effectiveness of the programs, there is evidence that particular program designs and factors affecting teacher attitudes and beliefs influence a program's implementation and success. (See Table 5.2.)

Table 5.2 Most Frequently Cited Ways Teacher Beliefs Influence Implementation

Teacher Belief	Number of Studies Reporting
Perception of adequacy of access to appropriate subject matter content	3
Concern about unauthorized uses of laptops	3
Beliefs about role of computers as a learning tool for student	2
Beliefs about student capabilities for using computers	1

Case studies of teachers in laptop programs have shown that teachers' beliefs about students, the potential role of technology in learning, and the availability of high-quality digital content influence the degree to which they use laptops with students (Lane, 2003; Trimmel & Bachmann, 2004; Windschitl & Sahl, 2002). First, teachers who believe that students are capable of completing complex assignments on their own or in collaboration with peers may be more likely to assign extended projects that require laptop use and allow students to choose the topics for their own research projects. Second, teachers who view technology as a tool with a wide variety of potential applications are more likely to use laptops often with students (Jaillet, 2004; Windschitl & Sahl, 2002). Third, those teachers who believe that there are adequate software and Internet-based resources available to help teach their particular content area may use laptops with students more often than teachers who believe that there are simply not enough high-quality materials available (Lane, 2003; Trimmel & Bachmann, 2004). Conversely, those teachers who are concerned that students will use their laptops for unauthorized purposes, such as playing games or searching the Internet for recreational purposes during class time, are likely to report implementing laptops less often with students in class (Jaillet, 2004; Trimmel & Bachmann, 2004; Zucker & McGhee, 2005).

Particular design features may influence teachers' beliefs in such a way as to make them likely to use laptops in conjunction with student-centered modes of instruction. Project Hiller, a within-school laptop program for high school students, required its teachers to engage in two extended projects with students and to mentor two to three student-driven projects in the school. In their projects, Project Hiller students took on significant and visible roles within the school, including helping teachers with planning lessons that used technology, developing multimedia materials for departmental projects, mentoring younger peers, and producing a newsletter. Many of the teachers reported that their expectations of what their students could do changed after seeing how skilled students were when using multimedia tools. Teachers reported that they then began assigning more complex and challenging work to students (Light et al., 2002).

The researchers who studied Project Hiller found that the number of teachers who reported doing long-term projects lasting more than a week (at least once a year or more) increased from 85% to 95% during the course of the project, as did the number of teachers who use journaling with their students, which rose from 58% to 68%. Analysis of observational data and interviews with Project Hiller teachers, students, and coordinators revealed an increase in the occurrence and quality of informal, project-based, and small group interactions between teachers and students participating in the program (Light et al., 2002).

THE ROLES OF PROFESSIONAL DEVELOPMENT AND TECHNICAL SUPPORT IN FOSTERING IMPLEMENTATION

Several of the implementation studies examined what teachers, students, and administrators believed were critical factors in supporting implementation of laptop programs. In addition, some researchers conducted observations in programs that led them to draw conclusions about what features of programs support or hinder implementation. These studies can provide valuable information to understanding implementation, even though research-based evidence that such factors lead to better student outcomes does not yet exist.

Formal professional development has been a critical component of many large-scale and smaller one-to-one programs, and the features of these activities reported to be important for implementation varied from program to program. (See Table 5.3.) Teacher workshops often focus on providing teachers with skills they need to use the technology themselves, but many reported that what was most critical was a focus on helping teachers integrate technology into their instruction (Davies, 2004; Dinnocenti, 2002; Fairman, 2004; Harris & Smith, 2004; Lane, 2003; Lowther, Ross, & Morrison, 2001). In Maine, content specialists have also been assigned to help teachers with finding digital resources and integrating technology into specific content areas (Silvernail & Harris, 2003). In addition, some programs have assigned staff (either internal to the school or external) to help teachers on an as-needed basis with technology integration (Davies,

2004; Dinnocenti, 2002; Fairman, 2004; Light et al., 2002). A third form of professional development, informal help from colleagues within the school, may be especially important to ensuring implementation success. A number of researchers reported that they observed teachers helping each other with technology problems or engaging in joint curriculum planning, and some have even reported that teachers prefer this form of professional development above others (Davis et al., 2005; Gaynor & Fraser, 2003; Lane, 2003; Silvernail & Harris, 2003; Windschitl & Sahl, 2002).

Table 5.3 Supportive Features of Professional Development Reported in Studies

Student Use	Number of Studies Reporting
Focus on integrating technology into instruction	5
Informal help from colleagues	5
Ongoing access to coaches to help with integration	4
Focus on finding content-rich resources	1

Some of the professional development that is targeted to help teachers become more "student-centered" in their teaching has been especially effective in transforming instruction in laptop classrooms. A good example of such a program is the iNtegrating Technology for inQuiry (NTeQ) model (Morrison, Lowther, & DeMuelle, 1999), which helps teachers develop extended problems and projects that use real-world resources, student collaboration, and computer tools to reach solutions or create final products. The model calls for a full 10 days of professional development for teachers, plus follow-up during the year. Comparison group studies of teachers provided the NTeQ program and then either assigned to a laptop classroom or non-laptop classroom suggest that laptops can facilitate more use of project-based learning and cooperative grouping strategies (Lowther et al., 2001).

In addition to professional development, readily available technical support also appears to be important for laptop programs to succeed. Programs in which teachers report a high degree of reliability for laptops often have both within-building technical support staff devoted to helping with the program and ready access to outside vendors for major problems (Hill & Reeves, 2004). Ensuring that all students' laptops are working makes it less likely that teachers will have to develop two sets of assignments—one for students with laptops and another for students without laptops (Davis et al., 2005; Gaynor & Fraser, 2003; Zucker & McGhee, 2005). Being able to count on the reliability of the school's wireless network is also critical, as students are often using their laptops to access resources available on the web (Hill & Reeves, 2004; Lane, 2003; Light et al., 2002).

Students have played an important role in providing the first line of technical support in several laptop programs. In Maine, for example, student "iTeams" exist in many schools to help troubleshoot routine problems with machines (Silvernail & Harris, 2003; Silvernail & Lane, 2004). In addition, teachers in Maine report that they often turn to students for help with technical problems when they arise in class (Fairman, 2004). In other, smaller-scale laptop programs, students play a similar role in providing technical support, both informally and formally as part of the program design (Dinnocenti, 2002; Light et al., 2002).

Findings from Outcome Studies

Of the studies we identified and reviewed, just four groups of researchers analyzed results from quasi-experimental studies with pretest-posttest designs and comparison groups, and only seven others used comparison groups at all. We summarize findings from each study separately below in narrative form, as each study examined somewhat different outcomes and studied one-to-one programs that cannot be compared easily. The results are most promising in two areas that were identified in an earlier review (Penuel et al., 2001) as showing positive effects for laptops: computer literacy and writing.

Russell, Bebell, and Higgins (2004) compared the advantages for different student-to-computer ratios in classrooms. In a single public school, the school assigned different numbers of laptops to upper elementary grades classrooms to achieve either four-to-one, two-to-one, or one-to-one student-computer ratios. The researchers then observed classrooms and studied how students used computers in the classes and how teachers organized their instruction. The one-to-one classrooms provided several advantages over the two-to-one and four-to-one classrooms. In those classrooms, students used computers more across the curriculum and used them at home for academic purposes. In addition, their images of what is required for writing tasks nearly always included computers. In one-to-one classrooms, instruction was different as well; there was less large-group instruction than in two-to-one and four-to-one classrooms. Research-based evidence from six other comparison group studies that used posttest-only designs also report that students in laptop programs use computers more often and for a wider array of purposes than do students with less ubiquitous access to computers (Jaillet, 2004; Light et al., 2002; Lowther & Ross, 2003; Stevenson, 2002; Trimmel & Bachmann, 2004).

Schaumburg (2001) conducted a quasi-experimental study examining the effects of providing students with laptops on their technology literacy. She studied effects of a program that provided laptops to students in a high school in Germany. She found that the laptop students made greater gains than did comparison group students on a researcher-developed test of their knowledge of hardware and the laptop's operating system, common productivity tools, skill in using the Internet, and knowledge of basic computer security. Other comparison group studies with posttest-only designs reported greater levels of technology literacy among students in laptop programs, using judgments made by researchers on the basis of structured observations of their skill in using computers and the Internet (Lowther & Ross, 2003; Lowther et al., 2001).

We identified four separate studies that reported positive effects of laptop programs on students' writing skills (Gulek & Demirtas, 2005; Light et al., 2002; Lowther & Ross, 2003; Lowther et al., 2001). However, none of these studies used a pretest to determine whether students had actually improved their writing skills over the course of the study. Therefore, although several studies reported positive effects, the research-based evidence that laptop programs can improve writing is somewhat less strong than research-based evidence of effects on technology use and technology literacy.

Discussion and Conclusion

The research studies included in this synthesis provide a basic understanding of how students use laptops and wireless connectivity as part of one-to-one initiatives, and there is some preliminary evidence that providing students with more ubiquitous access to computers gives them more practice in using technology. In contrast to how students use technology in other initiatives that emphasize basic skills development or assessment, in one-to-one initiatives students most often use productivity and design tools in ways that are integrated into other classroom activities and assignments. Students gain practice with using these tools, and as outcome studies document, often improve their technology literacy and skill in using word processing tools to improve their writing skills.

What is less clear from these studies is what the potential is for one-to-one initiatives to improve student achievement in core subjects. Few projects reported using tutorial or practice software in mathematics and reading, subjects that are the central focus of most state accountability tests and systems. One study did examine effects on state achievement test scores (Gulek & Demirtas, 2005), but only results for writing suggest clear positive effects. The expectation that one-to-one initiatives will improve achievement scores bears further investigation, and it is likely that to expect achievement gains, one-to-one initiatives would need to be part of a larger, more comprehensive effort to improve instruction (Light et al., 2002). A number of researchers whose work is included as part of this study have argued that one-to-one initiatives that also provide professional development in how to improve instruction and provide curricular resources tied to content teachers must teach have the best chances of making significant improvements to teaching and learning (see, e.g., Morrison et al., 1999).

The research on implementation synthesized here is largely consistent with past research on educational technology reforms, though it does suggest that peers may pay a particularly important role in supporting implementation for teachers. As other studies have found, when teachers believe that technology can support student learning and offers resources that add value to the curriculum, they are more likely to use it. Similarly, professional development support and technical support are critical for one-to-one initiatives, just as they are for other technology initiatives. The finding that other teachers are particularly important in helping teachers learn how to integrate technology into the classroom, however, has only recently become the focus of systematic research in educational technology (Frank et al., 2004). It is consistent with emerging research on professional development, however, which has found that participating in professional development activities with peers can contribute to its overall effectiveness (Garet, Porter, Desimone, Birman, & Yoon, 2001).

What few studies to date have done is to test specifically the links between hypothesized outcomes for one-to-one initiatives and different implementation measures. In fact, a number of studies in the synthesis did not clearly specify the overall goals of the initiative they were studying. Some did not report on overall usage levels of the computers, and none specifically examined the relationship between usage and outcome measures. Finally, some researchers did not indicate when in the development of the program they conducted their study, making it difficult to know whether some of the implementation findings are primarily an artifact of a program's novelty in a school or district.

Including information about core aspects of the design and implementation of particular one-to-one initiatives in all studies would make research considerably more useful for policymakers and program developers. Policymakers need such information to establish priorities for external funding opportunities and give guidance to programs on the ways they ought to structure professional development opportunities for teachers and provide for technical support. Program developers need such information so that they can begin to identify "best practices" to replicate in their own program designs. Most educational technology innovations combine social, pedagogical, and technological elements, and program designers must constantly adapt and reconfigure these elements as programs evolve (Means & Penuel, 2005).

Different approaches to measuring outcomes are also needed in future evaluation research on one-to-one initiatives to advance research in this area. Several studies that focused more on implementation cited outcomes based on self-report survey data that researchers rarely measured in outcome studies. Half of the studies in this synthesis reported positive effects of laptop programs on student motivation or engagement, but just three attempted to measure it in some way other than by a single self-report item (Lowther & Ross, 2003; Russell et al., 2004; Trimmel & Bachmann, 2004). These researchers measured motivation either by observation or by using previously validated survey scales of achievement motivation. Many laptop programs in this study had as their aim broad goals such as the preparation of students for jobs in the 21st century or improving the economic competitiveness of the region (Jaillet, 2004; Silvernail & Lane, 2004), but these kinds of outcomes are difficult to measure in a one- or two-year evaluation. Similarly, researchers reported that students increased their organizational skills with laptop computers (Lowther et al., 2001; Zucker & McGhee, 2005), and that students gained access to a wider array of up-to-date educational resources as a result of their participation in laptop programs (Dinnocenti, 2002; Gaynor & Fraser, 2003; Lowther et al., 2001; Mitchell Institute, 2004). Both results seem plausible, but there are not many widely accepted measures of organizational skills or of the breadth and quality of materials students can access in school (whether through laptops or textbooks). Unfortunately, the researchers did not attempt to develop scales or measures as part of their evaluation research. Researchers conducting future evaluation studies investigating these potential effects of laptops will have to develop and establish the reliability and validity of a wide variety of outcome measures as part of their research.

The increasing popularity of laptop initiatives with a wide variety of stakeholders in education—policymakers, administrators, teachers, parents, and students—makes the need for sound research-based evidence of effectiveness especially critical at this time. States and district school boards must often choose between funding different compelling kinds of programs for students; data on effectiveness can help inform their decision-making progress. Although they are difficult to conduct, a significant number of experimental and quasi-experimental studies are needed if laptop programs are to provide stronger research-based evidence warranting investments in one-to-one initiatives.

In addition, there will always remain a significant role for research syntheses that periodically review extant research on one-to-one initiatives. Research syntheses can provide policymakers, educators, and researchers with a good idea about what the best evidence is from a range of studies. As scholars who are part of the National Research Council note,

> Rarely does one study produce an unequivocal and durable result; multiple methods, applied over time and tied to evidentiary standards, are essential to establishing a base of scientific knowledge. Formal syntheses of research findings across studies are often necessary to discover, test, and explain the diversity of findings that characterize many fields. (National Research Council, 2002, p. 3)

Acknowledgments

Apple Computer, Inc. funded this research synthesis under contract with SRI International. All findings and opinions expressed herein are the sole responsibility of the author. The author wishes to acknowledge the support of Natalie Nielsen, Jennifer Scott, Benita Kim, Deborah Kim, and Reina Fujii of SRI International for assisting with identifying and reviewing individual studies. In addition, Jeremy Roschelle, Linda Shear, and Sarah Zaner of SRI International, as well as Karen Cator and Linda Roberts of Apple, each provided valuable comments to an earlier version of this paper produced for Apple.

Author Update

Since the publication of this synthesis, schools and districts have continued to invest in one-to-one programs. In the past year, netbooks or ultraportable devices are an increasingly popular choice for districts, because they offer a lower-cost alternative to laptops. In addition, schools are experimenting with achieving one-to-one access through smaller, multipurpose devices, such as iPods and mobile telephones, and through specialized devices such as graphing calculators.

A significant change since 2006 has been in the number of large-scale studies of effectiveness of one-to-one initiatives. An example is the recently concluded Classroom Connectivity in Mathematics and Science study, led by Doug Owens of The Ohio State University. The random assignment study examined the impact of providing professional development and curriculum resources to support teachers' use of the Texas Instruments Navigator system, which connects students' graphing calculators to a classroom network. The study found positive impacts of use on mathematics learning. In the 2006 review, there was no similar study of one-to-one programs using such a rigorous design showing significant gains in a content area other than writing.

Another new development that is likely to affect the future of one-to-one initiatives is the push for open educational resources. Open educational resources are content, tools, and resources that are freely available to educators. In the past, a key challenge for schools and districts has been to identify content for their one-to-one initiatives. As more open educational resources become available for teachers to use and adapt as they wish, lack of content is not likely to be as much of a concern. Educators will face a different challenge in the future: deciding what content will best challenge their students to grow intellectually and to pursue interests and inquiries that only the students themselves can imagine.

References

Adelman, N., Donnelly, M. B., Dove, T., Tiffany-Morales, J., Wayne, A., & Zucker, A. A. (2002). *The integrated studies of educational technology: Professional development and teachers' use of technology.* Menlo Park, CA: SRI International.

Becker, H. J., & Anderson, R. E. (2000). *Subject and teacher objectives for computer-using classes by school socio-economic status.* Irvine, CA, and Minneapolis, MN: Center for Research on Information Technology and Organizations, University of California, Irvine, and University of Minnesota.

Becker, H. J., Ravitz, J., & Wong, Y. (1999). *Teacher and teacher-directed student use of computers and product* (No. 3: Teaching, Learning, and Computation, 1998 National Survey). Irvine, CA: University of California at Irvine.

Blumenfeld, P., Fishman, B. J., Krajcik, J., Marx, R. W., & Soloway, E. (2000). Creating usable innovations in systemic reform: Scaling up technology-embedded project-based science in urban schools. *Educational Psychologist, 35*(3), 149–164.

Chang, H., Henriquez, A., Honey, M., Light, D., Moeller, B., & Ross, N. (1998). *The Union City story: Education reform and technology—students' performance on standardized tests.* New York, NY: Center for Children and Technology.

Coburn, C. E. (2004). Beyond decoupling: Rethinking the relationship between the institutional environment and the classroom. *Sociology of Education, 77*(3), 211–244.

Colella, V. (2000). Participatory simulations: Building collaborative understanding through immersive dynamic modeling. *The Journal of the Learning Sciences, 9*(4), 471–500.

Consortium on School Networking. (2004). *A guide to handheld computing in K–12 education.* Washington, DC: Author.

Cuban, L. (1986). *Teachers and machines: The classroom use of technology since 1920.* New York, NY: Teachers College Press.

Cuban, L. (2001). *Oversold and underused: Computers in the classroom.* Cambridge, MA: Harvard University Press.

Daitzman, P. (2003). *Evaluation of the national model laptop program—technology literacy, a dimension of information literacy: A journey into the global learning community, November 2002–June 2003.* New Haven, CT: East Rock Global Magnet School.

Davies, A. (2004). *Finding proof of learning in a one-to-one computing classroom.* Courtenay, BC: Connections Publishing.

Davis, D., Garas, N., Hopstock, P., Kellum, A., & Stephenson, T. (2005). *Henrico County Public Schools iBook survey report.* Arlington, VA: Development Associates, Inc.

Dinnocenti, S. T. (2002). *Laptop computers in an elementary school: Perspectives on learning environments from students, teachers, administrators, and parents.* Unpublished doctoral dissertation, University of Connecticut, Storrs, CT. UMI Publication Number 3034011.

Ertmer, P. A. (1999). Addressing first- and second-order barriers to change: Strategies for technology integration. *Educational Technology Research and Development, 47*(4), 47–61.

Fairman, J. (2004). *Trading roles: Teachers and students learn with technology.* Orono, ME: Maine Education Policy Research Institute, University of Maine Office.

Frank, K. A., Zhao, Y., & Borman, K. (2004). Social capital and the diffusion of innovations within organizations: Application to the implementation of computer technology in schools. *Sociology of Education, 77*(2), 148–171.

Garet, M. S., Porter, A. C., Desimone, L., Birman, B. F., & Yoon, K. S. (2001). What makes professional development effective?

Results from a national sample of teachers. *American Educational Research Journal, 38*(4), 915–945.

Gaynor, I. W., & Fraser, B. J. (2003). *Online collaborative projects: A journey for two Year 5 technology rich classrooms.* Paper presented at the Western Australian Institute for Educational Research Forum. Retrieved May 5, 2005, from www.waier.org.au/forums/2003/gaynor.html

Gulek, J. C., & Demirtas, H. (2005). Learning with technology: The impact of laptop use on student achievement. *The Journal of Technology, Learning, and Assessment, 3*(2). Available at http://escholarship.bc.edu/jtla/vol3/2/

Harris, W. J., & Smith, L. (2004). *Laptop use by seventh grade students with disabilities: Perceptions of special education teachers.* Orono, ME: Maine Education Policy Research Institute, University of Maine Office.

Haynes, C. (1996). *The effectiveness of using laptop computers with middle school students identified as being inhibited writers.* Unpublished doctoral dissertation, Union Institute, Cincinnati, OH. UMI Publication Number 9630228.

Hegedus, S., & Kaput, J. (2004, September). *An introduction to the profound potential of connected algebra activities: Issues of representation, engagement and pedagogy.* Paper presented at the 28th Conference of the International Group for the Psychology of Mathematics Education, Bergen, Norway. Available at www.eric.ed.gov

Hill, J., & Reeves, T. (2004). *Change takes time: The promise of ubiquitous computing in schools. A report of a four year evaluation of the laptop initiative at Athens Academy.* Athens, GA: University of Georgia.

Jaillet, A. (2004). What is happening with portable computers in schools? *Journal of Science Education and Technology, 13*(1), 115–128.

Kanaya, T., Light, D., & Culp, K. M. (2005). Factors influencing outcomes from a technology-focused professional development program. *Journal of Research on Technology in Education, 37*(3), 313–329.

Kaput, J., & Hegedus, S. (2002). *Exploiting classroom connectivity by aggregating student constructions to create new learning opportunities.* Paper presented at the 26th Conference of the International Group for the Psychology of Mathematics Education, Norwich, UK. Available at www.kaputcenter.umassd.edu/downloads/simcalc/cc1/library/kaputhegeduspme2002.pdf

Kozma, R. B. (1991). Learning with media. *Review of Educational Research, 61*, 179–212.

Kulik, C.-L. C., & Kulik, J. A. (1991). Effectiveness of computer-based instruction: An updated analysis. *Computers in Human Behavior, 7*, 75–94.

Kulik, J. A. (1994). Meta-analytic studies of findings on computer-based instruction. In E. L. Baker & H. F. O'Neill, Jr. (Eds.), *Technology assessment in education and training* (pp. 9–33). Hillsdale, NJ: Lawrence Erlbaum.

Lane, D. M. M. (2003). *The Maine Learning Technology Initiative impact on students and learning.* Portland, ME: Center for Education Policy, Applied Research, and Evaluation, University of Southern Maine.

Lemke, C., & Martin, C. (2003a). *One-to-one computing in Indiana: A state profile.* Culver City, CA: Metiri Group.

Lemke, C., & Martin, C. (2003b). *One-to-one computing in Maine: A state profile.* Culver City, CA: Metiri Group.

Lemke, C., & Martin, C. (2003c). *One-to-one computing in Michigan: A state profile.* Culver City, CA: Metiri Group.

Lemke, C., & Martin, C. (2003d). *One-to-one computing in Virginia: A state profile.* Culver City, CA: Metiri Group.

Light, D., McDermott, M., & Honey, M. (2002). *Project Hiller: The impact of ubiquitous portable technology on an urban school.* New York, NY: Center for Children and Technology, Education Development Center.

Lowther, D. L., & Ross, S. M. (2003, April). *When each one has one: The influences on teaching strategies and student achievement of using laptops in the classroom.* Paper presented at the Annual Meeting of the American Educational Research Association, Chicago, IL. Available at www.eric.ed.gov

Lowther, D. L., Ross, S. M., & Morrison, G. R. (2001, July). *Evaluation of a laptop program: Successes and recommendations.* Paper presented at the National Education Computing Conference, Chicago, IL. Available at www.eric.ed.gov

Means, B., & Olson, K. (1995). *Technology's role in education reform: Findings from a national study of innovating schools.* Menlo Park, CA: SRI International.

Means, B., & Penuel, W. R. (2005). Research to support scaling up technology-based educational innovations. In C. Dede, J. P. Honan, & L. C. Peters (Eds.), *Scaling up success: Lessons from technology-based educational improvement* (pp. 176–197). San Francisco, CA: Jossey-Bass.

Mitchell Institute. (2004). *One-to-one laptops in a high school environment: Piscataquis Community High School study final report.* Portland, ME: Great Maine Schools Project, George J. Mitchell Scholarship Research Institute.

Molina, A., Sussex, W., & Penuel, W. R. (2005). *Training Wheels evaluation report.* Menlo Park, CA: SRI International.

Morrison, G. R., Lowther, D., & DeMuelle, L. (1999). *Integrating computer technology into the classroom.* Englewood Cliffs, NJ: Merrill/Prentice Hall.

Myers, J. L. (1996). *The influence of a take-home computer program on mathematics achievement and attitudes of Title I elementary school children.* Unpublished doctoral dissertation, University of Georgia, Athens, GA. UMI Publication Number 9636476.

National Center for Education Statistics. (2000). *Teachers' tools for the 21st century: A report on teachers' use of technology.* Washington, DC: U.S. Department of Education.

National Research Council. (2002). *Scientific research in education.* Washington, DC: National Academy Press.

Newhouse, C. P., & Rennie, L. (2001). A longitudinal study of the use of student-owned portable computers in a secondary school. *Computers & Education, 36*(3), 223–243.

North Carolina Department of Public Instruction. (1999). *1997-98 report of student performance: North Carolina Tests of Computer Skills.* Raleigh, NC: North Carolina Department of Public Instruction.

Penuel, W. R., Kim, D. Y., Michalchik, V., Lewis, S., Means, B., Murphy, B., et al. (2001). *Using technology to enhance connections between home and school: A research synthesis.* Menlo Park, CA: SRI International.

Riel, M., & Becker, H. J. (2000, April). *The beliefs, practices, and computer use of teacher leaders.* Paper presented at the Annual Meeting of the American Educational Research Association, New Orleans.

Rockman, S., Chessler, M., & Walker, L. (1998). *Powerful tools for schooling: Second year study of the laptop program.* San Francisco, CA: Authors.

Rockman, S., & Sloan, K. R. (1995). *Assessing the growth: The Buddy Project evaluation, 1994–95.* San Francisco, CA: Authors.

Roschelle, J., & Pea, R. D. (2002). A walk on the WILD side: How wireless handhelds may change computer-supported collaborative learning. *International Journal of Cognition and Technology, 1*(1), 145–168.

Roschelle, J., Pea, R. D., Hoadley, C. M., Gordin, D. G., & Means, B. (2000). Changing how and what children learn in school with computer-based technologies. *The Future of Children, 10*(2), 76–101.

Roschelle, J., Penuel, W. R., & Abrahamson, A. L. (2004). The networked classroom. *Educational Leadership, 61*(5), 50–54.

Russell, M., Bebell, D., & Higgins, J. (2004). *Laptop learning: A comparison of teaching and learning in upper elementary classrooms equipped with shared carts of laptops and permanent one-to-one laptops*. Boston, MA: Technology and Assessment Study Collaborative, Boston College.

Sandholtz, J., Ringstaff, C., & Dwyer, D. (1997). *Teaching with technology: Creating student-centered classrooms*. New York, NY: Teachers College Press.

Sarama, J., Clements, D. H., & Henry, J. J. (1998). Network of influences in an implementation of a mathematics curriculum innovation. *International Journal of Computers for Mathematical Learning, 3*(2), 113–148.

Schaumburg, H. (2001, June). *Fostering girls' computer literacy through laptop learning*. Paper presented at the National Educational Computing Conference, Chicago, IL.

Sheingold, K., & Hadley, M. (1990). *Accomplished teachers: Integrating computers into classroom practice*. New York, NY: Center for Technology in Education, Bank Street College of Education.

Silvernail, D. L., & Harris, W. J. (2003). *The Maine Learning Technology Initiative teacher, student, and school perspectives: Mid-year evaluation report*. Portland, ME: Maine Education Policy Research Institute, University of Southern Maine.

Silvernail, D. L., & Lane, D. M. M. (2004). *The impact of Maine's one-to-one laptop program on middle school teachers and students: Phase one summary evidence*. Portland, ME: Maine Education Policy Research Institute, University of Southern Maine.

Stevenson, K. R. (1998). *Evaluation report—Year 2: Middle School Laptop Program, Beaufort County School District*. Beaufort, SC: Beaufort County School District.

Stevenson, K. R. (1999). *Evaluation report—Year 3: Middle School Laptop Program, Beaufort County School District*. Beaufort, SC: Beaufort County School District.

Stevenson, K. R. (2002). *Evaluation report—Year 2: High school laptop computer program* (Final Report, for school year 2001/2002). Liverpool: Liverpool Central School District, New York.

Stroup, W. M. (2002, September). *Instantiating seeing mathematics structuring the social sphere (MS3): Updating generative teaching and learning for networked mathematics and science classrooms*. Paper presented at the First International Conference on Wireless and Mobile Technologies in Education, Vaxjo, Sweden.

Tatar, D., Roschelle, J., Vahey, P., & Penuel, W. R. (2003). Handhelds go to school. *IEEE Computer, 36*(9), 30–37.

Trimmel, M., & Bachmann, J. (2004). Cognitive, social, motivational and health aspects of students in laptop classrooms. *Journal of Computer Assisted Learning, 20*(2), 151–158.

Vahey, P., & Crawford, V. (2002). *Palm Education Pioneers program: Final evaluation*. Menlo Park, CA: SRI International.

Warschauer, M., Grant, D., Real, G. D., & Rousseau, M. (2004). Promoting academic literacy with technology: Successful laptop programs in K–12 schools. *System, 32*(I4), 525–538.

Watson, D. M., & Tinsley, D. M. (Eds.). (1995). *Integrating information technology into education*. London, UK: Chapman and Hall.

Wilensky, U., & Stroup, W. M. (2000). Networked gridlock: Students enacting complex dynamic phenomena with the HubNet architecture. In B. Fishman & S. O'Connor-Divelbiss (Eds.), *Fourth international conference of the learning sciences* (pp. 282–289). Mahwah, NJ: Lawrence Erlbaum.

Windschitl, M., & Sahl, K. (2002). Tracing teachers' use of technology in a laptop computer school: The interplay of teacher beliefs, social dynamics, and institutional culture. *American Educational Research Journal, 39*(1), 165–205.

Yarnall, L., Shechtman, N., & Penuel, W. R. (2006). Using handheld computers to support improved classroom assessment in science: Results from a field trial. *Journal of Science Education and Technology, 15*(2), 142–158.

Zucker, A. A. (2004). Developing a research agenda for ubiquitous computing in schools. *Journal of Educational Computing Research, 30*(4), 371–386.

Zucker, A. A., & McGhee, R. (2005). *A study of one-to-one computer use in mathematics and science instruction at the secondary level in Henrico County Public Schools.* Arlington, VA: SRI International.

Zurita, G., & Nussbaum, M. (2004). Computer supported collaborative learning using wirelessly connected handheld computers. *Computers and Education, 42,* 289–314.

CHAPTER

6

The Influence of Teachers' Technology Use on Instructional Practices

Glenda C. Rakes | The University of Tennessee—Martin

Valerie S. Fields | Louisiana Campus Compact

Karee E. Cox | The University of Memphis

This study investigated the relationship between technology use and skills and the use of constructivist instructional practices among teachers in rural schools. Teachers in this study responded to Moersch's instrument, the Levels of Technology Implementation (LoTi). The LoTi was administered to the fourth and eighth grade teachers in 11 school districts to determine if levels of classroom technology use and personal computer use predicted the use of constructivist instructional practices. Results indicate that there is a significant, positive relationship between both levels of classroom technology use and personal computer use and the use of constructivist instructional practices, with personal computer use being the strongest predictor.

Introduction

Educators struggle with the problem of overcoming the inertia of instructional practices in the traditional classroom (Trimble, 2003). In these traditional classrooms, students are typically not provided with whole, dynamic learning experiences, but rather with limited, arbitrary activities. Schools frequently teach information from the various disciplines without providing adequate contextual support with opportunities for students to apply what they are taught. "The resulting inauthenticity of classroom activity makes it difficult for children to see how school learning applies to their lives" (Perchman, 1992, p. 33).

Brooks (2004) believes that there is a lack of focus on higher-order thinking skills because of an emphasis on standardized testing. She refers to such testing as single-event measures of accountability, which serve as a substitute for preparing students for the many different worlds beyond school classrooms. "Like agriculture, education has replaced natural processes with artificial ones. Over time, these artificial practices have become common" (p. 9).

This lack of attention to authentic experiences in education is particularly troubling when considering opportunities for children in poor, underfunded, often rural areas of the United States. Research indicates nationwide low performance in many subject areas (Bracey, 2002; Collins & Dewees, 2001; Riley, 2002). Riley's (2002) research further indicates that some geographic areas, particularly rural areas, are reporting low performance and that the achievement gap is persistent and intrinsically linked to the fact that millions of the nation's children still live in poverty.

Children in rural schools frequently do not have the same level of access to resources and experiences as children who live in suburban and urban areas. Beeson and Strange (2003) report that 43% of the nation's public schools are in rural communities or small towns of fewer than 25,000 people, and 31% of the nation's children attend these schools. Poverty is the largest persistent challenge rural schools face. Per capita income, salaries, computer use in the classrooms, school administrative costs, and transportation are among the top challenges for rural schools (Beeson & Strange, 2003).

Another serious problem plaguing rural schools is difficulty in hiring and retaining qualified teachers. Ingersoll (2004) examined data regarding staffing issues in high-poverty schools in both rural and urban areas. He concluded that factors tied to the characteristics and conditions of these schools are behind the teacher shortage in these schools. One of the main reasons for high turnover rates in these schools is the fact that teachers in high-poverty schools are frequently paid less than teachers in other types of schools. Other significant factors related to staffing problems in these schools are related to inadequate administrative support, excessive intrusions on teaching time, student discipline problems, and limited faculty input in decisions related to the schools.

Constructivism and Learning

One way of increasing authenticity in the classroom is through the use of constructivist teaching methods (Voss & Post, 1988; Wenglinsky, 2004; White & Frederiksen, 1998). Constructivism is a learning theory that proposes learners create their own understanding as they combine what they already believe to be true based on a blend of past experiences with new experiences (Richardson, 1997). Constructivism as a philosophy of learning can be traced primarily to the work of John Dewey (1916) and Jean Piaget (1973). Vygotsky's work (1978) also contributed to the movement toward constructivism. Throughout most of the early to middle part of the 20th century, theories of learning shifted from a behaviorist orientation based on observable phenomenon to a cognitive orientation in the 1970s that emphasized internal cognitive processing. By the 1980s, a shift toward constructivism became evident. The perception that learning is an internal learner process continues to grow.

Dewey (1916) believed that learning was based on activity. Knowledge could only emerge from a context in which ideas were drawn out of circumstances that had meaning to the learner. He believed that the learning context must be a social context in which students work together to build knowledge. Piaget's view (1973) of learning was based on his view of child development. He believed that understanding is based on discovery and active involvement. Vygotsky (1978) believed that children should be encouraged to link concepts and derive their own ideas from those introduced to them. He developed a social learning perspective through which children learn through interaction with others.

Over the past several decades, both educators and policymakers have argued whether schools should emphasize facts or critical thinking skills. Much of this debate has not been based on empirical data. Wenglinsky (2004), using data from the National Assessment of Educational Progress (NAEP), concluded that a clear pattern emerges from these data. Even though students must learn facts and basic skills, the data suggest that emphasis on advanced reasoning skills promotes higher student performance.

The use of constructivist pedagogical models promotes this meaningful type of learning process, a process in which learning helps students make sense of new information experienced in authentic problems by integrating the new information with previously constructed knowledge (von Glasersfeld, 1981). Authentic problems or actions are ill-structured complex problems analogous to those students face in everyday experience and will face in their future professions. In the learning process, these problems help learners organize their learning and facilitate growth in reasoning and problem-solving skills (Voss & Post, 1988; White & Frederiksen, 1998).

The philosophy of constructivism is not new to education, but the ways in which it is applied to education are still evolving. One relatively new tool that can play a vital role in the use of constructivist teaching practices is technology-enhanced instruction.

Technology and Constructivism

One of the first and most vocal proponents of the use of technology to promote this type of meaningful learning was Seymour Papert (1980, 1994) who believed that computers could provide powerful tools for learning. He also noted that schools frequently ignored the broad capacities computers have for instructional support, isolating them from the learning process rather than integrating them into all areas of the curriculum.

When constructivism is used effectively, teachers incorporate the ideas of students to prepare the lessons that they will teach in their classrooms. Teachers are beginning to use technology as a tool to promote students' ability to reason and solve authentic problems. "Teachers use existing technology to transform classrooms into dynamic centers of purposeful and experiential learning that intuitively move students from awareness to authentic action" (Moersch, 1998, p. 53). The appropriate use of technology can reinforce higher cognitive skill development and complex thinking skills such as problem solving, reasoning, decision making, and scientific inquiry (Moersch, 1999).

When teachers thoroughly integrate technology into the classroom, constructivist learning environments can evolve. A constructivist learning environment (Reeves, 1998) is a place in which learners work together and support each other as they use a variety of tools and information resources in their guided pursuit of learning goals and problem-solving activities. Constructivist learning environments frequently encompass many different applications of media and technology (Becker & Ravitz, 1999; Middleton & Murray, 1999; Rakes, Flowers, Casey, & Santana, 1999). Such environments create active classrooms that combine the tools of constructivism with communication and visualization tools that enable communication and collaboration among learners in a sociocultural context. Increased student achievement can result because of the synergy created through dynamic interactions (Dwyer, 1994; Sandholtz, Ringstaff, & Dwyer, 1997).

In a ten-year study of how the routine use of technology by teachers and students affected student learning, the Apple Classroom of Tomorrow (ACOT) project studied five classrooms throughout the United States (Dwyer, 1994; Sandholtz, Ringstaff, & Dwyer, 1997). Researchers provided each classroom with a wide variety of technology tools, training for teachers, and a coordinator at each school to provide technology assistance. The project's primary purpose was to investigate how routine use of computers and technology influence teaching and learning.

The analysis of data from the evaluation of the ACOT project was based on a database of more than 20,000 entries. Researchers saw technology "profoundly disturb the inertia of traditional classrooms" (Dwyer, p. 7). Researchers saw an increase in the use of constructivist teaching strategies with the use of technology in the classroom, observations also supported by research from Rakes et al. (1999) and Becker and Ravitz (1999). Teachers encouraged cooperative learning and collaborative efforts as they used more complex tasks and materials in their instruction along with more performance-based evaluation.

There is a need for further research on the link between teachers' technology use and classroom instructional practices. In spite of the apparent commitment to technology of some schools, it appears that many teachers use computers to support their current traditional teaching practices rather than as a tool to promote more innovative, constructivist practices (Cuban, 2001). Much of the current teacher technology training programs and other uses of technology-related funds may not be delivering the desired result: a positive effect on student learning. For example, Doherty and Orlofsky (2001) studied 500 students in grades 7–12. As part of this research, investigators asked students how their teachers used computers for learning. The survey revealed that most students said their teachers do not use computers in sophisticated ways. If teachers are not provided the useful support needed to integrate computers into the overall framework of the classroom, it is unlikely that their students will use computers in ways that will improve learning (Fuller, 2000).

In order for technology to positively affect teaching methods—and therefore student learning—teachers must possess the technology-related skills needed to use technology and must actively use these tools in their classrooms (Iding, Crosby, & Speitel, 2002). In order to encourage these behaviors, teachers need appropriate, research-based training; opportunities to practice these skills; access to technology tools; and support, both in terms of encouragement from school administrators (Dawson & Rakes, 2003) and technical support (Fuller, 2000). Teachers and students cannot use computers that do not work. Increasing technology use can create a vehicle through which educators can address teaching and learning opportunities for all students. The need for these opportunities is especially apparent in poor rural areas of the United States.

Research Questions

The present study explores whether teacher use of technology, both in the classroom and for personal use, relates to the use of constructivist teaching practices and addresses four specific research questions.

> ***Research Question 1:*** What are the predominate teacher levels on the Level of Technology Implementation, Personal Computer Use, and Current Instructional Practices scales?
>
> ***Research Question 2:*** Is there a relationship between teachers' Current Instructional Practices scores and teachers' Level of Technology Implementation scores?

Research Question 3: Is there a relationship between teachers' Current Instructional Practices scores and teachers' Personal Computer Use scores?

Research Question 4: Is there a relationship between teachers' Current Instructional Practices scores and teachers' scores on both the Levels of Technology Implementation and Personal Computer Use scales?

Population

The purposive sample for this study comprised 186 fourth and eighth grade teachers from 36 elementary schools, 17 middle/junior high schools, and 13 high schools from 11 rural school districts in a southern state. The 11 districts were chosen from those designated by the Delta Rural Systemic Initiative.

The purpose of this federal program was to bring about reform in delta communities in three southern states. These school districts also received a federally funded Technology Literacy Challenge grant that provided equipment and professional development for teachers in the use of technology. The total provided for equipment was $10,931,503. Each district was provided about 300 hours of professional development for teachers. The equipment and training had been in place for a year prior to collection of the survey data.

Only school districts that served populations that consisted of 20% or more families whose incomes were below the poverty line were included in this study. The schools included in the sample included similar minority as well as free- and reduced-lunch populations. In the sample schools, the percent of free and reduced lunches ranged from 54% to 91%. From the total purposive sample of 186 teachers, 123 volunteered to participate. Seventy-one fourth grade teachers and 52 eighth grade teachers participated in the study; those grades were chosen because the state's "high stakes testing" is done at those two grade levels.

Methodology

Teachers in the study responded to a fifty-item instrument, the Level of Technology Implementation (LoTi). The LoTi was administered to the fourth and eighth grade teachers to determine if their level of classroom technology use and personal computer use predicted their Current Instructional Practices. The instrument generated a profile for each participant in three domains: Level of Technology Implementation (LoTi), Personal Computer Use (PCU), and Current Instructional Practices (CIP).

INSTRUMENTATION

The Levels of Technology Implementation (LoTi): A Guide for Measuring Classroom Technology Use was initially tested in August of 1997 and in June of 1998. Moersch (1995, 1998) determined reliability by using Cronbach's Alpha, which showed a reliability measure of .74 for the LoTi, .81 for Personal Computer Use, and .73 for Current Instructional Practices. (People interested in using the instrument must register in order to see the entire instrument. Information concerning all details related to the instrument can be found at www.loticonnection.com.)

Levels of Technology Implementation

The LoTi instrument measures the teacher's level of classroom technology implementation ranging from 0 (non-use) to 6 (refinement) as described in Table 6.1.

Table 6.1 Levels of Technology Implementation Summary

Level	Description
0 Non-Use	There is no visible evidence of computer access or instructional use of computers in the classroom.
1 Awareness	Available classroom computer(s) are used primarily for teacher productivity (e.g., e-mail, word processing, grading programs).
2 Exploration	Student technology projects (e.g., designing web pages, research via the Internet, creating multimedia presentations) focus on the content under investigation.
3 Infusion	Tool-based applications (e.g., graphing, concept-mapping) are primarily used by students for analyzing data, making inferences, and drawing conclusions.
4a Integration (Mechanical)	The use of outside resources and/or interventions aid the teacher in developing challenging learning experiences using available classroom computers.
4b Integration (Routine)	Teachers can readily design learning experiences with no outside assistance that empower students to identify and solve authentic problems using technology.
5 Expansion	Teachers actively use technology and information from outside entities to expand student experiences directed at problem solving, issues resolution, and student action.
6 Refinement	Computers provide a seamless and almost transparent medium for information queries, problem solving, and/or product development.

The Levels of Technology Implementation (LoTi) scale measures authentic classroom technology use in seven categories with responses to statements of 1–2 indicating "Not True of Me Now," 3–5 "Somewhat True of Me," and 6–7 "Very True of Me Now."

Current Instructional Practices

The Current Instructional Practices (CIP) scale measures teachers' classroom practices relating to a subject-matter versus a learner-based curriculum approach based on eight elements as described in Table 6.2.

Table 6.2 Current Instructional Practices Summary

Level of Intensity	Description
0	One or more questions were not applicable to the respondent.
1	Instructional practices are subject-matter based; strategies lean toward lectures and/or teacher-lead presentations; student evaluation is traditional.
2	The participant supports instructional practices consistent with a subject-matter based approach to teaching and learning, but not at the same level of intensity or commitment as Level 3. Teaching strategies tend to lean toward lectures and/or teacher-led presentations.
3	Teacher still uses a subject-matter approach, but also supports the use of student-directed projects that provide opportunities for students to determine the "look and feel" of a final product based on specific content standards.
4	Teacher may feel comfortable supporting or implementing either a subject-matter or learning-based approach. Learning activities are diversified and based mostly on student questions, the teacher serves more as a facilitator, student-projects are primarily student-directed, and alternative assessment strategies are used.
5	Instructional practices tend to lean more toward a learner-based approach. The essential content embedded in the standards emerges based on what students "need to know" as they attempt to research and solve issues of importance to them using critical thinking and problem-solving skills.
6	The teacher at this level of intensity supports instructional practices consistent with a learner-based approach, but not at the same level of intensity or commitment as Level 7.
7	Instructional practices align exclusively with a learner-based approach. The essential content embedded in the standards emerges based on students "need to know" as they attempt to research and solve issues of importance to them using critical thinking and problem-solving skills. Learning activities and teaching strategies are diversified and driven by student questions. Assessment includes performance-based, journals, peer reviews, self-reflections.

The Current Instructional Practices (CIP) scale measures teachers' current classroom practices relating to a subject-matter versus a learner-based curriculum approach based on eight intensity levels with responses to statements consisting of 1–2 indicating "Not True of Me Now," 3–5 "Somewhat True of Me," and 6–7 "Very True of Me Now."

Personal Computer Use

The Personal Computer Use (PCU) scale measures the skill and comfort level of teachers when using technology for personal use based on eight intensity levels as described in Table 6.3.

Table 6.3 Personal Computer Use Summary

Level of Intensity	Description
0	The participant does not feel comfortable or have the skill level to use computers for personal use. Participants rely more on the use of overhead projectors, chalkboards, and/or paper/pencil activities than using computers for conveying information or classroom management tasks.
1	The participant demonstrates little skill level. Participants may have a general awareness of various technology-related tools such as word processors, spreadsheets, or the Internet, but generally are not using them.
2	The participant demonstrates little to moderate skill level. Participants may occasionally browse the Internet, use e-mail, or use a word processor program, yet may not have the confidence or feel comfortable troubleshooting simple "technology" problems or glitches as they arise. At school, their use of computers may be limited to a grade book or attendance program.
3	The participant demonstrates moderate skill. Participants may begin to become "regular" users of selected applications such as the Internet, e-mail, or a word processor program. They may also feel comfortable troubleshooting simple "technology" problems, but rely on mostly technology support staff or others to assist them with any troubleshooting issues.
4	The participant demonstrates moderate to high skill. Participants commonly use a broader range of software applications including multimedia (e.g., PowerPoint, HyperStudio), simple database applications, and spreadsheets. They typically are able to troubleshoot simple hardware and/or peripheral problems without assistance from technology support staff.
5	The participant demonstrates high skill level. Participants are commonly able to use the computer to create their own web pages, produce sophisticated multimedia products, and/or effortlessly use common productivity applications (e.g., FileMaker Pro, Excel), desktop publishing software, and web-based tools. They are also able to troubleshoot most hardware and/or peripheral problems without assistance from technology support staff.
6	The participant demonstrates high to extremely high skill level. Participants are sophisticated in the use of most multimedia, web-based, desktop publishing, and web-based applications. They typically serve as "troubleshooters" for others in need of assistance and sometimes seek certification for achieving selected technology-related skills.
7	The participant is an expert computer user, troubleshooter, and/or technology mentor. They typically are involved in training others on any technology-related task and are usually involved in selected support groups from around the world that allow them access to answers for all technology-based inquiries they may have.

The Personal Computer Use (PCU) scale measures the teacher's comfort and skill level with computers based on eight intensity levels with responses to statements of 1–2 indicating "Not True of Me Now," 3–5 "Somewhat True of Me," and 6–7 "Very True of Me Now."

LIMITATIONS

Results of this study should be interpreted in view of the following limitations.

1. The questionnaire did not consider the complexity of software applications used at the school sites or the frequency of their use.
2. The sample is restricted to fourth and eighth grade teachers in 11 poor, rural school districts in a southern state.
3. The study explored relationships among variables; therefore, the analysis cannot establish cause and effect relationships.
4. There may exist unexamined factors affecting the relationship between technology use by teachers and their instructional practices that are not accounted for in the methodology.
5. All information in the survey is self-reported data. The information provided was based exclusively on the perceptions of the participants.

Results and Discussion

RESEARCH QUESTION 1

What are the predominate teacher levels on the Level of Technology Implementation, Personal Computer Use, and Current Instructional Practice scales?

Levels of Technology Implementation Results Summary

For this sample, the predominate level is 0 (Non-Use). A Level 0 implies technology-based tools (e.g., computers) are either (1) completely unavailable in the classroom, (2) not easily accessible by the classroom teacher, or (3) there is a lack of time to pursue electronic technology implementation. Existing technology is predominately text-based (e.g., ditto sheets, chalkboard, overhead projector).

Figure 6.1 displays the LoTi profile and approximates the degree to which each respondent is either supporting or implementing the instructional uses of technology in a classroom setting. Based on their responses, 35.1% of the respondents' highest level corresponded with Level 0 (Non-Use). This indicates participants perceive a lack of access to or time to use technology. The percent of the population for the remaining levels include Level 1 at 11.2%, Level 2 at 18.7%, Level 3 at 13.2%, Level 4a at 20.1%, and Level 4b at 0.7%. None of the teachers in the sample scored at the highest levels of Expansion (Level 5) or Refinement (Level 6).

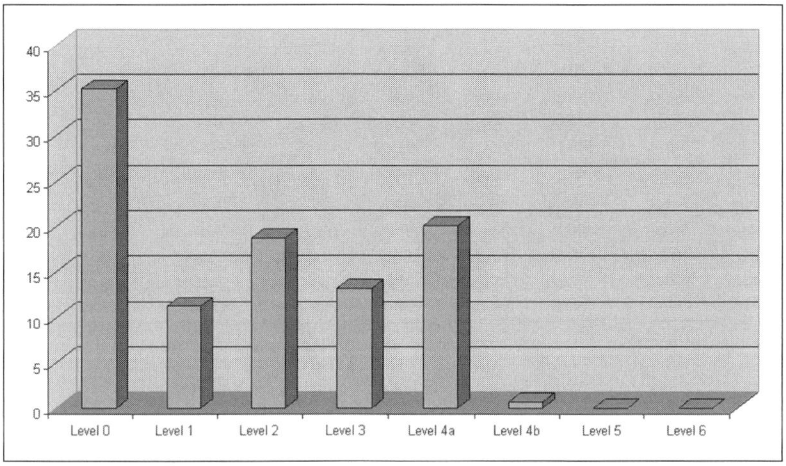

Figure 6.1 Levels of technology implementation

This represents an alarmingly high number of teachers who express a lack of technology use given the amount of technology training and equipment provided for these poor, rural school districts. Despite substantial grant-funded infusions of money for training and equipment, teachers in this sample still perceived their ability to use technology as extremely limited, whether because of lack of access to equipment or lack of time to use technology.

Personal Computer Use Results Summary

The predominate intensity level for this sample is 3, indicating moderate skill levels. Figure 6.2 displays the Personal Computer Use (PCU) results that address each respondent's comfort and proficiency level with computer use (troubleshooting simple hardware problems, using multimedia applications) at home or in the workplace). Level 0 (0.9%) indicates that the respondents do not feel comfortable or have the skill level to use computers for personal use. Level 1 (8.3%) indicates little skill levels. Level 2 (20.4%) indicates little to moderate skill levels. Level 3 (22.2%) indicates moderate skill levels. Level 4 (20.4%) indicates moderate to high skill levels. Level 5 (15.7%) indicates high skill levels. Level 6 (10.2%) indicates high to extremely high skill levels. Level 7 (1.9%) indicates the respondents are expert computer users and/or technology mentors.

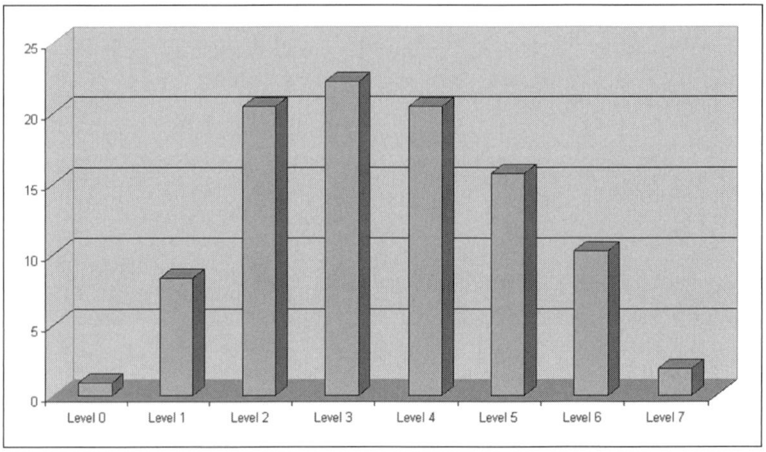

Figure 6.2 Personal computer use

Only slightly more than one-fourth (27.8%) of the respondents scored in the highest three skill levels (5, 6, and 7). Again, these results are disappointing coming from a population that was targeted for technology training and equipment. The levels of teacher skill and comfort levels with computers were lower than expected.

Current Instructional Practices Results Summary

The predominate intensity level for the CIP for this sample is 4. Figure 6.3 displays the Current Instructional Practices (CIP), which addresses the respondents' support for or implementation of instructional practices consistent with a constructivist, learner-based curriculum design (i.e., learning materials determined by the problem areas under investigation, multiple assessment strategies integrated authentically throughout the curriculum, teacher as co-learner/facilitator, focus on learner-based questions).

For the CIP scale, responses at Level 0 (0.9%) indicate that one or more questions were not applicable to the participants. Level 1 (2.8%) responses indicate that instructional practices are subject based. Level 2 (8.3%) responses indicate a level similar to Level 1, but with more intensity. Level 3 (25.7%) responses indicate that the participants use a subject-matter approach, but also support the use of student-directed projects. Level 4 (26.6%) responses indicate that the respondents may feel comfortable supporting or implementing either a subject-matter or learning-based approach. Level 5 (23.9%) responses indicate that the participants' instructional practices tend to lean more toward a learner-based approach. Level 6 (10.1%) responses indicate that the participants are similar to those at Level 7, but with less intensity. Level 7 (1.8%) responses indicate that the participants' instructional practices align exclusively with a learner-based approach.

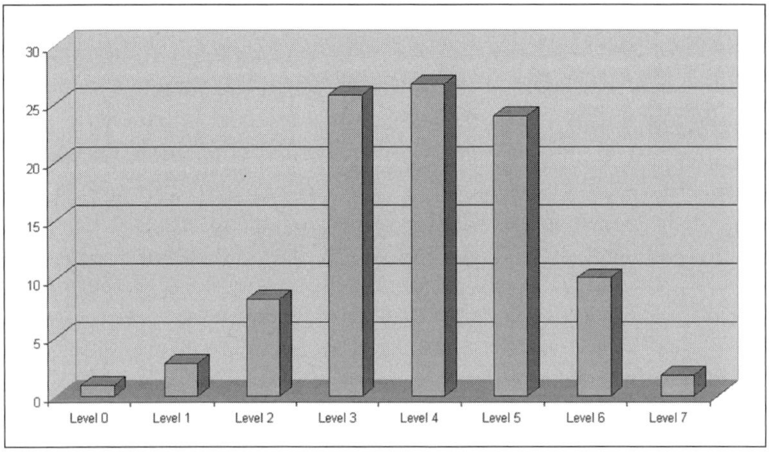

Figure 6.3 Current instructional practices

These results were more encouraging than expected, with more than half of the respondents describing the use of constructivist teaching practices to at least a moderate degree.

RESEARCH QUESTION 2

Is there a relationship between teachers' Current Instructional Practices scores and teachers' Level of Technology Implementation scores?

In order to examine the relationship between the score on the Current Instructional Practices scale and the scores on the Level of Technology scale, the data were analyzed using multiple regression with Current Instructional Practices scores entered as the dependent variable and the Level of Technology Integration scores entered as the independent or predictor variable.

Results of standard multiple regression, in which all variables were entered into the predictive equation, revealed an R^2 of .16, $F = 23.07$, $p < .001$, and indicates there was a significant linear relationship between the criterion variable (CIP) and the predictor variable (LoTi). About 16% of the variance in the Current Instructional Practices scores can be accounted for by the LoTi score. Results indicate that R^2 is very poor (.16) and the predictive value of the Level of Technology Integration score is likely to be unacceptable.

The bivariate correlation (2-tailed) between CIP and LoTi is .40 ($p < .01$). The positive, moderate correlation between CIP and LoTi indicates that teachers who scored higher on the LoTi scored higher on the Current Instructional Practices scale. Based on results of research by Becker and Ravitz (1999) and Middleton and Murray (1999), it was expected that the positive relationship between the Levels of Technology Implementation and Current Instructional Practices would be stronger. Becker and Ravitz found that teachers who used various computer technologies in the classroom, particularly student-centered, Internet-based teaching activities, are more likely than other teachers to demonstrate changes associated with constructivist reforms. In this particular population, the positive relationship exists, but does not provide sufficient predictive power. This may be an additional indication that the technology-related training provided to these teachers did not provide a strong enough link between technology tools and their curriculum as indicated in the LoTi results for these teachers.

RESEARCH QUESTION 3

Is there a relationship between teachers' Current Instructional Practices scores and teachers' Personal Computer Use scores?

In order to examine the relationship between the scores on the Current Instructional Practices scale and the scores on the Personal Computer Use scale, the data were analyzed using multiple regression with Current Instructional Practices scores entered as the dependent variable and the Personal Computer Use scores entered as the independent or predictor variable.

Results of standard multiple regression, in which all variables were entered into the predictive equation, revealed an R^2 of .25, $F = 22.83$, $p < .001$ indicate there was a significant linear relationship between the criterion variable (CIP) and the predictor variable (LoTi). About 25% of the variance in the Current Instructional Practices scores can be accounted for by the Personal Computer Use score. Results indicate that the Current Instructional Practices score can be predicted by the Personal Computer Use score. In this case, R^2 is weak, but interpretable.

The bivariate correlation (2-tailed) between CIP and PCU is .51 ($p < .01$). The positive, moderate correlation between CIP and PCU indicates that teachers who scored higher on the PCU have higher scores on the Current Instructional Practices scale.

These results are similar to findings by Rakes et al. (1999). Teachers' strong, basic technology skill levels appear to provide teachers with a comfort level with computers needed to support constructivist teaching practices. In this regard, the basic technology skills training provided these teachers appears to have been somewhat successful with a segment of the population.

RESEARCH QUESTION 4

Is there a relationship between teachers' Current Instructional Practices and teachers' scores on both the Levels of Technology Implementation and Personal Computer Use scales?

In order to examine the relationship between the score on the Current Instructional Practices and the scores on both the Level of Technology Implementation scale and Personal Computer Use scales, the data were analyzed using multiple regression with Current Instructional Practices scores entered as the dependent variable and the Level of Technology Implementation and Personal Computer Use scores entered as the independent or predictor variables.

Results of standard multiple regression, in which all variables were entered into the predictive equation, revealed an R^2 of .28, $F = 23.84$, $p < .001$, and indicate there was a significant linear relationship between the criterion variable (CIP) and the set of predictor variables. Results indicate that the Current Instructional Practices score can be predicted by both the Level of Technology Implementation score and the Personal Computer Use scores. About 28% of the variance in the Current Instructional Practices scores can be accounted for by both the LoTi and the PCU scores. In this case, R^2 is weak, but interpretable. The sample multiple correlation coefficient was .53. The positive, moderate correlations between both LoTi and PCU and CIP indicate that teachers who scored higher on both the LoTi and PCU have higher levels of Current Instructional Practices. Both predictors, Levels of Technology Implementation and Personal Computer Use, contributed to a slightly better prediction of Current Instructional Practices scores. This result confirms Moersch's (1999) assertion that appropriate use of technology can reinforce higher cognitive skill development and complex thinking skills as promoted through the use of constructivist teaching practices.

Future Research

One challenge for future research is to discover more specific ways computer-based technologies influence the classroom practices of teachers. What other factors may act in conjunction with technology use that encourage constructivist practices? How do preexisting teacher attitudes toward technology affect their use of technology in the classroom? How do preexisting teacher attitudes toward constructivism affect their use of these teachings? How do various types of training affect constructivist teaching practices? How does the availability of technology resources contribute to constructivist teaching practices? What types of technology training best facilitates the change from traditional to constructivist teaching methods?

McKenzie (2001) laments the fact that many school districts have put the proverbial cart before the horse in planning for the use of technology with a less than desirable return on the investment. There continues to be much emphasis on the purchase and installation of equipment without sufficient funding for staff development.

> This challenge should be about using new tools to help students master the key concepts and skills embedded in the science, social studies, art and other curriculum standards. It is not so much about PowerPointing, spreadsheeting or word processing. The focus should be on teaching and learning strategies that make a difference in daily practice—on activities translating into stronger student performance. (¶10)

The results of the current study confirm that teachers who have solid basic skills and comfort levels with technology and those who use computer technologies in their classrooms are more likely to use constructivist teaching practices. Given the current emphasis on producing students with high levels of thinking skills, any tools that can encourage the use of constructivist classroom practices and encourage the development of thinking skills in students should be considered important for all teachers and students. Promoting higher achievement in efficient ways of using computer technologies, particularly in underfunded schools, is worthy of further investigation.

The ultimate goal of research on the use of technology as a tool for constructivist teaching practices is to verify a link between classroom technology use, constructivist instructional practices, and improved student achievement. Future research should specifically explore the effect of technology use in constructivist classrooms on student performance.

As demonstrated in this study's teacher population, the availability of computers and training do not necessarily result in the widespread use of technology. Perhaps one key to understanding this lack of action on the part of many teachers lies in the future analysis of teacher beliefs regarding the effectiveness of technology as an instructional tool. Pajares (1992) suggested that "Beliefs are far more influential than knowledge in determining how individuals organize and define tasks and problems and are stronger predictors of behavior" (p. 311). Teacher beliefs concerning their personal ability to effectively use technology and their beliefs regarding the potential effect on student achievement is quite possibly a significant factor in determining what actually happens in the classroom.

Author Update

This study was a continuation of research by the authors concerning the influence of technology training on K–12 teachers. This article was sparked by interest in the effects of an influx of resources into a rural school environment. Many have been concerned that, in particular, rural school students with fewer resources may become part of the "digital divide" that could contribute to more hardships for these students in the future.

Educators have long expressed the belief that, if used properly, technology can be an essential part of increasing student achievement and can better prepare them for careers in the digital age. But in order for this to occur, teachers must use technology effectively in their classrooms. Well-designed, curriculum-specific training is essential. Education policymakers have invested large sums of money into equipment and training, expecting measurable learning returns on the investment. At the time of the publication of this article, the United States Department of Education reported over $1 billion in federal funding designed to prepare teachers to effectively integrate technology into K–12 classrooms.

The schools involved in this study received an infusion of funds for technology equipment and teacher training from a federal grant during the year prior to data collection. Although some positive trends emerged from the funding efforts, the results of this study confirmed the results of continuing research: investing money in school technology does not always equal desired results. For example, about one-third of the teachers in this study reported that they simply did not use the available technology. Data from the National Center for Education Statistics (NCES) and other researchers continue to report a lack of evidence that the availability of resources and training has had a significant impact on student achievement.

Hopefully, any shift from teacher-centered to student-centered instructional models will create an environment in which teachers can more effectively use the technology tools available. The authors continue to investigate the influence of technology training in the context of teachers' learner-centered beliefs.

References

Becker, H. J., & Ravitz, J. (1999). The influence of computer and Internet use on teachers' pedagogical practices and perceptions. *Journal of Research on Computers in Education. 31*(4), 356–379.

Beeson, E., & Strange, M. (2003, February). *Why rural matters 2003: The continuing need for every state to take action on rural education. A report of the Rural School and Community Trust Policy Program* [Online]. Available at www.ruraledu.org/articles.php?id=2138

Bracey, G. W. (2002). Raising achievement of at-risk students or not. *Phi Delta Kappan, 83*(6), 431–432.

Brooks, J. G. (2004). To see beyond the lesson. *Educational Leadership, 62*(1), 8–12.

Collins, T., & Dewees, S. (2001). Challenge and promise: Technology in the classroom. *Southern Rural Development Center, 18*, 1–6.

Cuban, L. (2001). *Oversold and underused: Computers in the classroom.* Cambridge, MA: Harvard University Press.

Dawson, C. & Rakes, G. C. (2003). The influence of principals' technology training on the integration of technology into schools. *Journal of Research on Technology in Education, 36*(1), 29–49.

Dewey, J. (1916). *Democracy and education: An introduction to the philosophy of education.* New York, NY: Free Press.

Doherty, K. M., & Orlofsky, G. F. (2001). Student survey says: Schools are probably not using educational technology as wisely or effectively as they could. *Education Week, 20*(35), 45–48.

Dwyer, D. C. (1994). Apple classrooms of tomorrow: What we've learned. *Educational Leadership, 52*, 4–10.

Fuller, H. L. (2000). First teach their teachers: Technology support and computer use in academic subjects. *Journal of Research on Computing in Education, 32*(4), 511–535.

Iding, M., Crosby, M. E., & Speitel, T. (2002). Teachers and technology: Beliefs and practices. *International Journal of Instructional Media, 29*(2), 153–171.

Ingersoll, R. M. (2004). *Why do high-poverty schools have difficulty staffing their classrooms with qualified teachers? (Report prepared for Renewing Our Schools, Securing Our Future—A National Task Force on Public Education).* Washington, DC: The Center for American Progress and the Institute for America's Future. Available at www.americanprogress.org/issues/2004/11/b252682.html

McKenzie, J. (2001). How teachers learn technology best. *From Now On, 10*(6). Retrieved December 14, 2005, from www.fno.org/mar01/howlearn.html

Middleton, B. M., & Murray, R. K. (1999). The impact of instructional technology on student academic achievement in reading and mathematics. *International Journal of Instructional Media, 26*(1), 109–116.

Moersch, C. (1995). Levels of technology implementation (LoTi): A framework for measuring classroom technology use. *Learning & Leading with Technology, 23*(3), 40–42.

Moersch, C. (1998). Enhancing students' thinking skills. *Learning & Leading with Technology, 25*(6), 50–53.

Moersch, C. (1999). Assessing current technology use in the classroom: A key to efficient staff development and technology planning. *Learning & Leading with Technology, 26*(8), 40–49.

Pajares, M. F. (1992). Teachers' beliefs and educational research: Cleaning up a messy construct. *Review of Educational Research, 62*(3), 307–332.

Papert, S. (1980). *Mindstorms: Children, computers and powerful ideas.* New York, NY: Harper Collins.

Papert, S. (1994). *The children's machine: Rethinking school in the age of the computer.* New York, NY: Basic Books.

Perchman, E. M. (1992). Child as meaning maker: The organizing theme for professional practice schools. In M. Levine (Ed.), *Professional practice schools* (pp. 25–62). New York, NY: Teachers College Press.

Piaget, J. (1973). *To understand is to invent.* New York, NY: Grossman.

Rakes, G. C., Flowers, B. F., Casey, H. B, & Santana, R. (1999). An analysis of instructional technology use and constructivist behaviors in K–12 teachers. *International Journal of Educational Technology, 1*(2). Available at www.ascilite.org.au/ajet/ijet/v1n2/rakes

Reeves, T. (1998, February). *The impact of media and technology in schools. A research report prepared for the Bertelsmann Foundation.* Available at http://it.coe.uga.edu/~treeves/edit6900/BertelsmannReeves98.pdf

Richardson, V. (1997). Constructivist teaching and teacher education: Theory and practice. In V. Richardson (Ed.), *Constructivist teacher education: Building a world of new understandings* (pp. 3–14). Washington, DC: Falmer Press.

Riley, R. W. (2002). Education reform through standards and partnerships, 1993–2000. *Phi Delta Kappan, 83*(9), 700–707.

Sandholtz, J. H., Ringstaff, C., & Dwyer, D. C. (1997). *Teaching with technology: Creating student-centered classrooms.* New York, NY: Teachers College.

Trimble, S. (2003). Between reform and improvement in the classroom. *Principal Leadership, 4*(1), 35–39.

von Glasersfeld, E. (1981). The concepts of adoption and viability in a radical constructivist theory of knowledge. In I. E. Sigel, D. M. Broinsky, & R. M. Golinkoff (Eds.), *New directions in Piagetian theory and practice* (pp. 87–95). Hillsdale, NJ: Lawrence Erlbaum.

Voss, J. F., & Post, T. A. (1988). On the solving of ill-structured problems. In M. T. H. Chi, R. Glaser, & M. J. Farr (Eds.), *The nature of expertise* (pp. 261–285). Hillsdale, NJ: Lawrence Erlbaum.

Vygotsky, L. S. (1978). *Mind in society: The development of higher psychological processes.* Cambridge, MA: Harvard University Press.

Wenglinsky, H. (2004). Facts or critical thinking skills? What NAEP results say. *Educational Leadership, 62*(1), 32–35.

White, B. Y., & Frederiksen, J. R. (1998). Inquiry, modeling, and metacognition: Making science accessible to all students. *Cognition and Instruction, 16*(1), 3–18.

CHAPTER

7

Teacher Concerns During Initial Implementation of a One-to-One Laptop Initiative at the Middle School Level

Loretta Donovan | California State University, Fullerton
Kendall Hartley | University of Nevada, Las Vegas
Neal Strudler | University of Nevada, Las Vegas

Many schools are initiating projects that place laptop computers into the hands of each student and teacher in the school. These projects entail a great deal of planning and investment by all involved. The teachers in these schools are faced with significant challenges as they prepare for teaching in classrooms where every student has a computer. Using the Concerns-Based Adoption Model of change, this study investigated the concerns of teachers in the early stages of a one-to-one laptop initiative. The results of the study indicate that teachers fall into two relatively well-defined categories in terms of their concerns regarding the innovation. The majority of teachers have genuine concerns about how the introduction of laptop computers into the school environment will impact them personally. A lesser number have concerns about how they will be able to best use the laptops to meet the needs of the students. Implications for professional development include differentiating training based on teacher concerns, ensuring teachers have a voice in the process and are well-informed of decisions pertaining to the adoption, and implementation of the innovation.

Introduction

At a time of nationwide emphasis on school improvement, the role of educational technology continues to be a much-debated topic at the school, district, state, and national levels. While some would argue that the introduction of technology into schools changed education, others would suggest that the appearance of the classroom changed, but many of the activities remain the same (Cuban, 2002; Richardson & Placier, 2001; Sandholtz, Ringstaff & Dwyer, 1997; Tyack, & Cuban, 2000).

One-to-one laptop programs are being initiated with ever increasing frequency in K–12 schools in the United States and abroad. These represent significant investments that necessitate substantial evaluation of the rationale, goals, and outcomes of each initiative. A number of these initiatives have been reported upon and have provided useful information regarding goals and outcome data such as student achievement, attendance, and attitudes (see, for example, Anderson & Dexter, 2003; Lowther, Ross, & Morrison, 2003; Silvernail & Lane, 2004). However, we know from prior research on innovation adoption that successful implementation is deeply rooted in an understanding of the concerns of the individuals delivering the innovation (Hall & Hord, 2001). The purpose of this study was to examine one-to-one computing access in the middle school setting from the perspective of those being asked to change.

Review of Literature

After five years of examining the impact of technology in education, the CEO forum formulated the *School Technology and Readiness Report* (2001). Key findings included: (a) technology can enhance student achievement in many ways; (b) the impact of technology is greatest when integrated into a curriculum that has clear, measurable objectives; (c) assessment is often not aligned with curriculum, nor is it measuring 21st-century skills; and (d) strategies to measure and improve technology integration in education are few and far between (CEO Forum, 2001). These recommendations were echoed by the Partnership for 21st Century Skills (2002). The partnership believes that educators and educational agencies must stress teaching and learning 21st-century content, skills, and assessments. The introduction of computers into the teaching and learning experience is in many ways acting as a catalyst for educational change toward a more 21st-century learning environment.

ONE-TO-ONE COMPUTING ACCESS

The one-to-one computer access movement began in the 1980s with the Apple Classrooms of Tomorrow (ACOT) project. ACOT was the first large-scale initiative providing one-to-one access to students and teachers in the K–12 setting. By preparing ACOT project classrooms for digital teaching and learning, the project sought to not only examine, but to promote a changing educational context (Sandholtz, Ringstaff, & Dwyer, 1997).

The Instructional Evolution Model that resulted from the ACOT study is particularly relevant to the current study. Based on results of the ACOT study, Sandholtz, Ringstaff, and Dwyer (1997) proposed that innovation adoption is a process in which teachers will gradually change their teaching based on changing comfort levels with the technology. In a review of literature on one-to-one computing, Penuel (2006) reported that in the majority of studies of laptop implementation, teachers are in the adaptation stage in which they are adapting their existing teacher-centered practices to allow for the integration of the laptops into the learning experience of the students. Additionally, studies of professional development for one-to-one computing initiatives (Rockman et al., 2000; Sandholtz, Ringstaff, & Dwyer, 1997; Silvernail & Lane, 2004; Windschitl & Sahl, 2002; Yang, 2002) reported that staff development must match the current needs of the teachers. In other words, the teacher's current level (or stage) should be a primary consideration when designing and delivering staff development opportunities.

One-to-one computing access initiatives have evolved with the changing technology and aim to implement more portable versions of computers into the learning environment. The Microsoft Anytime, Anywhere Learning (AAL) initiative was a large-scale example of this type of one-to-one access providing students and teachers with laptop computers. In 1996, like the ACOT project, Microsoft's AAL initiative helped to establish a foundation and starting point for future one-to-one computing programs.

Reported findings from three years of AAL research by an independent evaluation team included enthusiasm for teaching and learning with technology, improved writing skills across all grade levels, a progression of increasingly authentic and purposeful uses and access to technology, and relevant to this study, a gradual shift toward constructivist pedagogies (Rockman et al., 1997; 1998; 2000).

One-to-one initiatives continue to be implemented across the United States with initial research findings and anecdotal evidence suggesting improved student achievement and overall satisfaction with teaching and learning with laptops. In 2002, Henrico County Public Schools (Virginia) embarked on the largest one-to-one initiative in the United States and provided over 25,000 laptops to teachers and students in grades 6–12. Students and teachers were reported as using the laptops in all subject areas for a variety of reasons. In addition, teachers, students, and families considered the laptops to be a positive addition to the teaching and learning experience with improved student-teacher and school-home interaction, increased student self-directed learning, and enhanced student motivation to learn (Zucker & McGhee, 2005).

In examining existing research on one-to-one laptop initiatives, Apple (2005) reported similar results across many studies. This report compared the impact of different levels of computer access on student outcomes. Benefits of one-to-one access over student-computer ratios of 2:1 and 4:1 included students using computers for a greater variety of purposes and subject areas, improved student writing skill, and enhanced student technology literacy (Apple, 2005). These findings are further echoed by Penuel (2006) in his examination of 30 articles in which laptop computers and wireless Internet access were the focus. Penuel reported that laptop initiatives in the United States and abroad have cited meeting the goal of preparing students for 21st-century citizenship, enhancing computer literacy, and showing positive effects on student writing as support for program implementations.

As the literature reporting positive outcomes of one-to-one computing initiatives continues to become available, a greater influx of this form of educational change will likely result. In order for one-to-one laptop initiatives to be sustained, however, it is crucial that change facilitators are aware of teacher concerns. What often happens is that teachers who are going through the change process are rarely consulted on the usefulness of the innovation, yet they are expected to adopt it with open arms (Richardson & Placier, 2001; Tyack & Cuban, 2000).

Purpose of Study

The purpose of this study was to determine teacher concerns during the introduction of a one-to-one computing access initiative in the middle school setting. More specifically, the question guiding this study was: *What are teacher concerns during initial implementation of a one-to-one laptop initiative at the middle school level?*

Results of this study can be used by K–12 teachers, school administrators, teacher educators, and professional developers to gain a better understanding of potential challenges faced during initial adoption of a one-to-one laptop program. Additionally, results of this study may be useful to professional developers to align content and delivery of professional development with teacher concerns.

Theoretical Framework

This study is grounded in a theoretical framework of educational change. Wiersma (1991) suggested that "conditions under which research is conducted and data obtained within and across studies must be incorporated into a meaningful whole" (p. 19). As a theoretical framework, change theory informs the guiding question of this study. Scholars such as Rogers (2003) have provided invaluable descriptions of the change processes and constructs. Others such as Fullan have provided insight into how these concepts affect educational settings (2001). Additionally, Hall and associates developed a change model that is well suited to address the questions posed here (Hall & Hord, 2001). More specifically, the Concerns-Based Adoption Model (CBAM) provides a theoretical framework as well as the tools with which the study was conducted. Using the CBAM in the current study enabled the research to focus on the key players in the change process—the teachers.

CBAM is unique because it considers change from the perspective of those implementing the innovations (Heck, Stiegelbauer, Hall, & Loucks, 1981). In particular, this study examined the impact of a changing educational context on the teachers. The CBAM model and diagnostic tools will be more completely described in the following section.

Method

PARTICIPANTS AND SETTING

The context of this study is unique for a one-to-one computing initiative. The school site, an urban middle school in the Southwestern United States, was one of several GEAR UP (Gaining Early Awareness and Readiness for Undergraduate Programs) schools in the school district, but the only one at which students were given laptop computers. As part of the GEAR UP involvement, the school received funding for a one-to-one laptop initiative that included funds for teacher training, encouraging parent involvement, and developing more student-centered learning activities through the integration of technology into teaching and learning. Students at the school were reported by teachers and administrators as having little motivation to attend college but having aspirations to work in the service or labor industry. In addition to the students who were the focus of GEAR UP, the school hosted an International Baccalaureate Magnet Program. The students enrolled in the magnet program were not from the surrounding area and were higher achieving and more professional in their attitude toward their education. Nonetheless, the school population was considered at risk in that 84% of students were eligible for free or reduced lunch and a large percentage (55%) of the student population were English language learners.

Class sizes were in alignment with the overall school district ranging between 25 and 28 students in each class. One of the school's goals was to provide an environment of enhanced technology integration to support the preparation of students for the 21st century. All classrooms within the school had Internet access, each classroom had at least one desktop computer, and every teacher had a laptop computer.

Participants for this study were 17 seventh grade teachers (out of a possible 20 who taught core subjects and were in the laptop program) and two building-level administrators. The teacher participants taught the core subjects of history, math, language, reading, and science, with several of them teaching in the magnet program as well as the mainstream program. Participants for this study were included on a volunteer basis.

RESEARCH TOOLS

The Concerns-Based Adoption Model provides a research-supported framework to evaluate the concerns of teachers in the early stages of participating in a one-to-one laptop implementation (Hall & Hord, 2001). In particular, principles of change unique to the CBAM relevant to this study include the premise that the individuals within the school are the primary units of change, and teacher attitudes, beliefs, and values influence the change process.

CONCERNS-BASED ADOPTION MODEL

The CBAM is a change model in which relationships between users and the resource system of an innovation can be examined. For this study, the resource system consisted of the GEAR UP federal grant program and the school district administration. The users were the teachers and students at the middle school site being studied. School administration can be considered change facilitators, and as the study evolved, the researcher came to be viewed by the teachers as a change facilitator. The three diagnostic tools of the CBAM user system are the Stages of Concern (SoC), Levels of Use (LoU), and Innovation Configurations (IC). This study was one of several conducted at the school site using the CBAM. In addition to this study, an Innovation Configuration was developed. The SoC dimension of the CBAM is most relevant to this study as it focuses on change during initial innovation adoption from the perspective of the individuals involved in the change, and can be used as a tool for continued examination of the innovation adoption.

The SoC dimension utilizes three data collection tools to identify individual and group concerns about an innovation. Concerns were identified through informal interviews, open-ended concerns statements, and Stages of Concern questionnaires (Hall & Hord, 2001). Once collected, concerns data are represented by seven stages of concern within four levels—unrelated, self, task, and impact (Table 7.1).

Table 7.1 Stages of Concern

Level	Stage of Concern	Description
Unrelated	Awareness	Just beginning to think about the innovation but not concerned about it at all
Self	Informational	Interested, but not concerned beyond curiosity about features of the innovation
	Personal	Concerned about own role in innovation adoption and how it will impact them as an individual
Task	Management	Concerned about how they are using the innovation, how best to find and use resources and how much time and effort is being put into the innovation
Impact	Consequence	Concerned about how the innovation is impacting others (e.g., students and community)
	Collaboration	Concerned about sharing impact of innovation with others in local and global community
	Refocusing	Concerned about modifying or replacing the innovation

Adapted from Hall and Hord's (2001) work

The *Unrelated* level consists of only one stage, Awareness, in which the individual has no concerns about the innovation. At the opposite end of the continuum, the *Impact* level has three stages and sees the individual progressing from being less concerned about the innovation's impact on them as an individual and being more global in their concerns. Between these levels are the *Self* and *Task* levels. Individuals at the *Self* level (Informational and Personal stages) of concern have not necessarily fully adopted the innovation. Individuals at a *Task* level (Management stage) may be asking themselves about ways to best organize their time to allow for innovation use (Hall & Hord, 2001). Additionally, the individual in a Management stage may have concerns about taking full advantage of resources and materials that are associated with the innovation. In the case of this study, teachers at this stage may be concerned about having enough time to fully explore the potential of using laptop computers to best meet the learning needs of the students.

Three tools were employed for identifying concerns during innovation adoption in this study.

STAGES OF CONCERN QUESTIONNAIRE (SoCQ)

The SoCQ is a self-report survey developed by Hall and his associates to understand the feelings and perceptions about change from the individuals involved in the change process. The SoCQ has been tested for reliability (test/retest reliability range from .65–.68) and validity (alpha-coefficients range from .64–.83) (Hall & Hord, 2001). The SoCQ is not focused on the internal factors of the innovation, but is more personal and seeks to determine the concerns of the individual user. Questions directly relate to the stages of concern. For the purpose of this study, the SoCQ was used to determine both individual and group concerns of teachers involved in the initial phase of a one-to-one laptop initiative.

The format of the questionnaire is a series of statements to which the participant responds to the relevance of the statement to them at that time (see Appendix 7.A). Participants respond by selecting the degree of relevance on an 8-point scale: 0 indicates irrelevant, 1—*not true of me now*, through to 7—*very true of me now*. Statements that participants respond to vary from *I am not concerned about the innovation* to *I would like to discuss the possibility of using the innovation*. In addition to the 35 Likert-scale type items, the SoCQ used for this study included open-ended questions.

OPEN-ENDED QUESTIONS

The open-ended questions of the SoCQ ask the innovation adopter to use complete sentences to describe or share any other concerns they may have at this time (Hall & Hord, 2001). Where the Likert-scale items are used to create individual concerns profiles, responses to the open-ended questions contribute to the creation of a group concerns profile (Hall & Hord, 2001). Data from the open-ended questions are used to exemplify group concerns by painting a verbal picture of concerns. As recommended by Hall (personal communication, May 5, 2004) the open-ended questions were adapted from the example provided by Hall and Hord (2001). The resulting open-ended questions were: (1) *What other concerns if any do you have at this time?* and (2) *Briefly describe your job function.*

ONE-LEGGED INTERVIEWS

One-legged interviews are a diagnostic tool of the CBAM for assessing concerns in an informal and non-intimidating manner. The premise of a one-legged interview is that it occurs at an unspecified time and is often little more than a "how's it going?" question. The one-legged interview got its name from the image of two people with only one leg planted on the ground as they pass each other in a corridor or other public space (Hall

& Hord, 2001). There is no formal question format and transcripts of interviews are recorded as notes by the change facilitator. Advantages of one-legged interviews include the unobtrusive nature of the research tool and the establishment of a relationship in which the change facilitator can show support for the innovation adopter (Hall & Hord, 2001). For this study, the one-legged interviews were informal conversations during and after observations conducted for the Innovation Configuration study (Donovan, 2005) in which the lead researcher simply chatted with the teachers. For example, "How's your week been?" was a common conversation starter to which teacher participants often began to share some of the challenges or tribulations they had experienced with the laptops over the past few days. Analysis of one-legged interviews follows similar format for analysis of open-ended questions in that patterns are identified and quotes extrapolated. The patterns are then used to add support to the group concerns profiles in the form of examples of specific concerns.

PROCEDURE

Data collection for this study was conducted in two stages. The first stage included the collection of the primary data source for the study, the SoCQ and open-ended questions. The second stage consisted of the informal one-legged interviews conducted throughout the school year.

Stage One: SoCQ and Open-Ended Questions

The SoCQ was administered as an integral part of a teacher training session relative to the laptop initiative. Initial administration was in June 2004 at a paid training for currently employed 7th grade teachers. A second administration was conducted in August 2004 for teachers hired over the summer or those unable to attend the June training.

The survey was administered by one of the researchers during the first day of the paid training. The same procedure was followed at both administrations and will be addressed as one. Teachers attending the trainings were the teachers of the core subjects (history, math, language, reading, and science) only. Teachers of computer literacy, physical education, special education, library, and foreign language did not attend the trainings and were not participants in this study. Some of the teachers involved in the laptop initiative were unable to attend either training and did not complete the survey. The survey was administered such that participants did not need to identify themselves other than if they chose to in the open-ended question asking them to briefly describe their job function. The researcher was introduced as being affiliated with the local university and the survey was handed to teachers with no time limit set for completion.

The researcher remained in the room while teachers completed surveys, and surveys were handed to the researcher upon completion. Teachers took approximately 15 minutes to complete the survey. Administration of the surveys for the school administrators was less formal and entailed the researcher handing the survey to the participants and asking them to complete it. Administrator surveys were not completed immediately, and were collected during a follow-up visit to the school.

Stage Two: One-Legged Interviews

One-legged interviews, as the name implies, were conducted on an impromptu basis by one of the researchers. It should be noted that the current study was one of several concurrent studies at the middle school centering on the laptop initiative, and the researcher was considered a *familiar face* by the teachers. One-legged interviews were more informal conversations about what was going on in the classroom and what the teacher's week had been like. For the administration, one-legged interviews were less frequent and usually began with a question relating to "How's everything going?" In addition to one-legged interviews conducted at the school site, the researcher was a faculty member of the university at which several of the participants were Master of Education students, so other one-legged interviews were conducted on the university campus. These interviews were usually brief yet often had a more "academic" tone.

DATA ANALYSIS

Data for this study were analyzed following the guidelines and recommendations for evaluating concerns (Hall, George, & Rutherford, 1998; Hall & Hord, 2001). First, individual data were entered into a spreadsheet program with participants as columns and survey questions as rows. Second, because each question relates to a specific stage

Table 7.2 Excerpt from Data Analysis Program

Stage of Concern	Participant's raw score for each stage of concern		
	Part. A	Part. B	Part. C
0	5	5	11
1	13	9	21
2	14	8	29
3	16	10	31
4	18	15	24
5	22	7	12
6	15	4	8

of concern, individual participant's raw data were converted to stage of concern data, and total "points" from the Likert scale items added. For example, questions 3, 12, 21, 23, and 30 all related to Stage 0 Awareness concerns, and questions 2, 9, 20, 22, and 31 all related to Stage 6 Refocusing concerns. Table 7.2 is an excerpt from the spreadsheet program used during data analysis. In this excerpt, there are three participants (A, B, C). Rows represent participant's totaled score for each stage. For example, participant A has a total raw score of five in Stage 0 Awareness and a total raw score of 22 in Stage 5 Collaboration.

The next step in developing concerns profiles was to convert raw scores to percentages. A quick scoring table developed by Parker and Griffith (Hall, George et al., 1998, p. 97) was used to convert raw scores to percentages and these data were also entered into the spreadsheet. Table 7.3 shows the above participant's raw scores converted into percentages. Finally, using the charting feature of the Excel program, individual concerns profile graphs were created, using the stage of concern for the *x*-axis and the percent of concern for the *y*-axis. Additionally, a teacher group profile, an administrator group profile, and a whole group profile were created using the same procedure but using an average of the group's percentage concern data.

Table 7.3 Sample Raw Scores Converted into Percentages

Stage of Concern	Participant's percentage score for each stage of concern		
	Part. A	Part. B	Part. C
0	53	53	84
1	51	40	75
2	55	35	92
3	60	34	98
4	24	16	48
5	55	9	19
6	42	6	17

Results

A total of 17 seventh grade teachers and two school administrators completed the SoCQ. Two of the teacher SoCQs could not be included in the data analysis because they did not complete the entire survey, omitting a "back side" of the two double-sided pages. Results will be reported in two sections: teacher concerns group profile and administrator concerns profiles.

TEACHER CONCERNS GROUP PROFILE

Teacher concerns group profile represents the concerns of the teachers as a group and not as individuals. The group profile for teachers was examined in two ways. First, individual profiles were examined to determine where individual teachers' most intense concerns were. This was determined by recording the highest peaks on the individual concerns graphs. The highest peak represents the most intense concerns of the teacher and does not mean they do not also have other concerns.

Figures 7.1 and 7.2 represent individual concerns profiles for two of the teacher participants in this study. These graphs are representative of the two most commonly occurring profiles. Figure 7.1 shows an individual with high Personal concerns (Stage 2) and low Consequence concerns (Stage 4). Figure 7.2 also represents concerns of an individual with high Personal concerns (Stage 2) and low Consequence concerns (Stage 4); however, what is interesting about the teacher concerns represented in Figure 7.2 is that this teacher also has relatively high level Collaboration concerns (Stage 5).

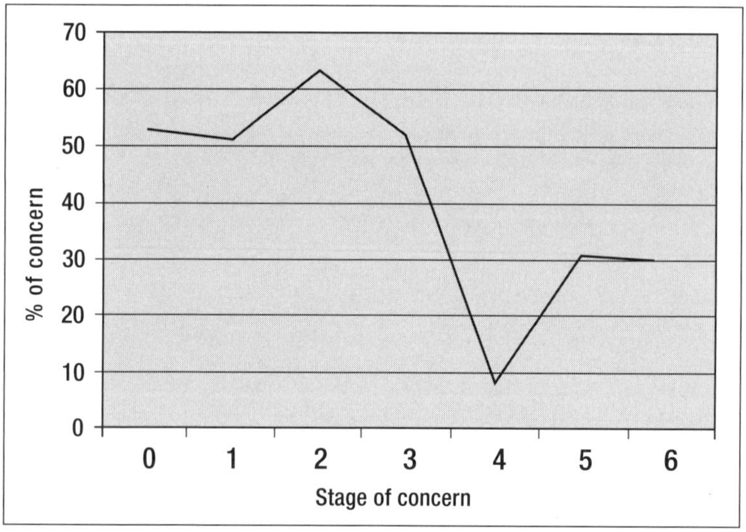

Figure 7.1 High level Personal, low level Consequence individual concern profile

Table 7.4 shows the percentage of teacher participants whose concerns peaked at each of the different stages. Of the 17 teachers, more than half (52%) of them had intense Self concerns at the Personal stage. An additional 18% had high Task level Management stage concerns and 23% had intense Impact Level, Consequence stage concerns. From Table 7.4, it is evident that as a population or group, teacher participants in this study cluster around having high intensity Stage 2 Personal concerns.

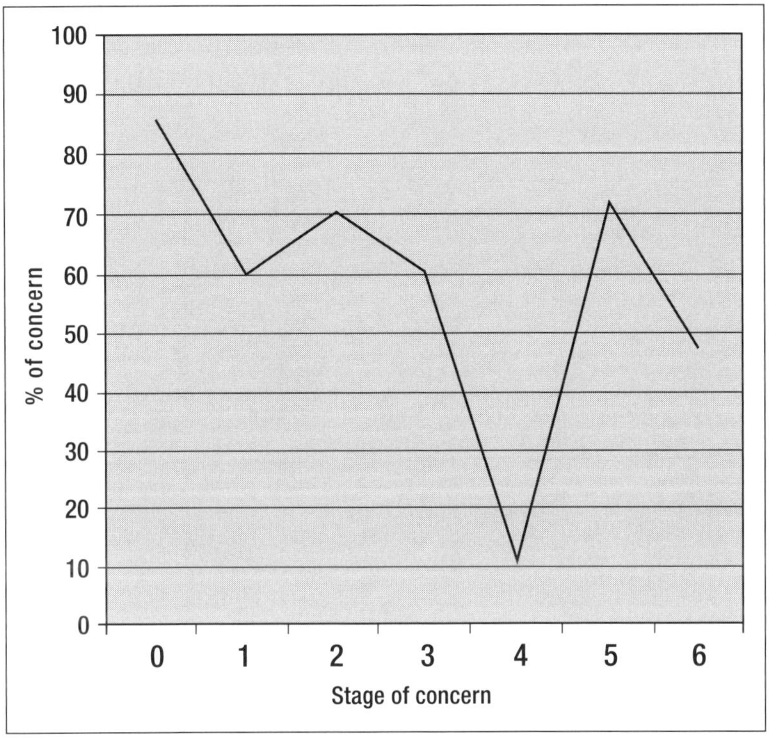

Figure 7.2 High level Awareness, Personal and Collaboration, low level Consequence individual concern profile

Table 7.4 Teacher Population Concerns Clusters

Level (Stage of Concern)	% of Teachers
Awareness	0
Self (1—Informational)	0
Self (2—Personal)	52
Task (3—Management)	18
Impact (4—Consequence)	5
Impact (5—Collaboration)	23
Impact (6—Refocusing)	5

Teacher concerns can be more fully explored by examining the group concerns profile. Figure 7.3 represents the teacher group concerns profile. Unlike Table 7.4 in which only the *most intense* concerns were represented, the group concerns profile represents the overall concerns at all levels as averaged across all participants. Concerns for the group peak at Stage 2 Personal concerns, and have a distinct valley at Stage 4 Consequence concerns.

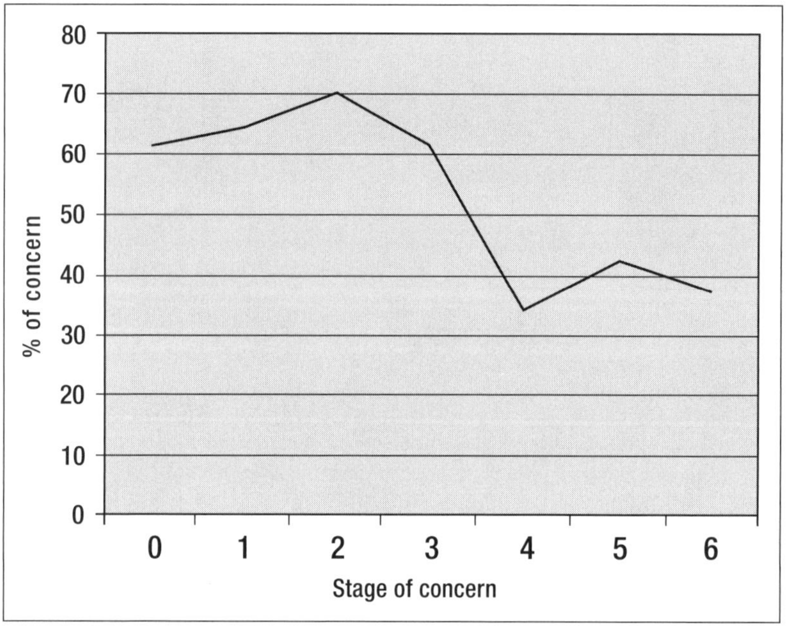

Figure 7.3 Teacher Group Concerns profile

Group personal concerns can be even further understood by looking at data from one-legged interviews and answers to the open-ended questions. One-legged interview and open-ended statement comments confirmed teacher concerns at the Self level Personal stage (Stage 2). Comments such as the following are representative of many teachers' Personal concerns about the innovation adoption:

> I'm worried about teaching with the laptops because I don't really know what to do
>
> You can come and observe me but not today because I'm still working on my plans
>
> I'm concerned with being able to cover all course requirements while being bogged down with the laptops
>
> Teaching our students all the ins and outs of the applications

Other teachers' concerns represented Task level Management stage (Stage 3) concerns. Comments from open-ended questions and interviews illustrate these concerns:

> It bothers me that I can't grade assignments and make comments on them and then send them back to the students

> It bothers me that I can't use the laptop for attendance because I love the laptop but we have to take attendance on the desktop computer

> It bothers me that I can't use the projector with the student laptops

In summary, teacher concerns during the initial stage of the one-to-one laptop initiative were predominantly about the impact the introduction of laptops has on them as an individual in that they are concerned how it may impact their time, planning, and instructional practices. A smaller percentage of teachers had concerns about how to best use the laptops to promote learning, routines, and teacher effectiveness and how to collaborate with others about the program.

ADMINISTRATOR GROUP CONCERNS PROFILE

Two administrators comprise the administrator group. Administrator A had been involved in the laptop program since the planning stage and Administrator B was new to the school the year this study was conducted. Because the two administrators were at contrastingly different stages of concern they will be addressed as individual concerns profiles rather than as a group. Figure 7.4 shows Administrator A's concern profile.

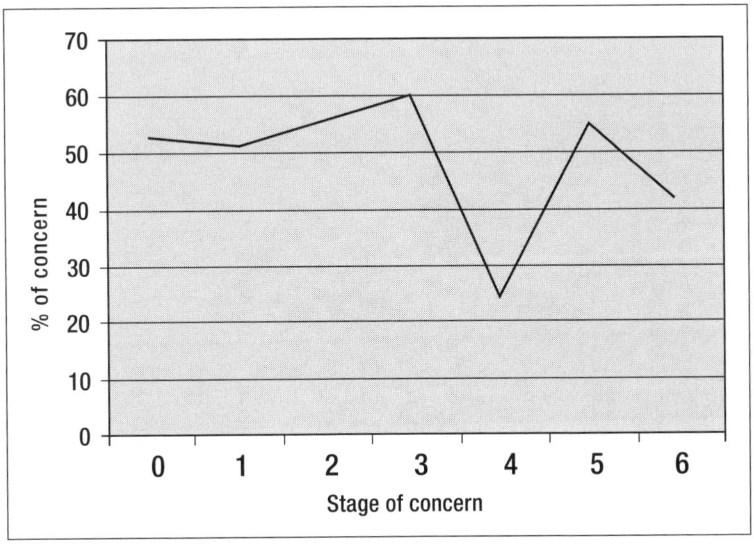

Figure 7.4 Administrator A's Concerns profile

Concerns of Administrator A peak at both Management and again at Collaboration. Administrator A's biggest concern as described in the open-ended statement was "to be certain that teachers are trained properly for the implementation of the program in grade 7." Additionally, Administrator A expressed concerns during one-legged interviews about sustaining the program for the future and making sure things ran smoothly.

Figure 7.5 shows Administrator B's concern profile. Administrator B has highest Awareness concerns (Stage 0) and a small peak at the Management level (Stage 3). Open-ended statements for the administrator refer to concerns about maintaining the one-to-one laptop program and ensuring the decision to invest money and modify teaching loads would be reflected in the success of the program. It is also worth noting that while Administrator B was supportive of the project, the relatively high level of Awareness concerns are in part a consequence of this being a project that was started before her arrival.

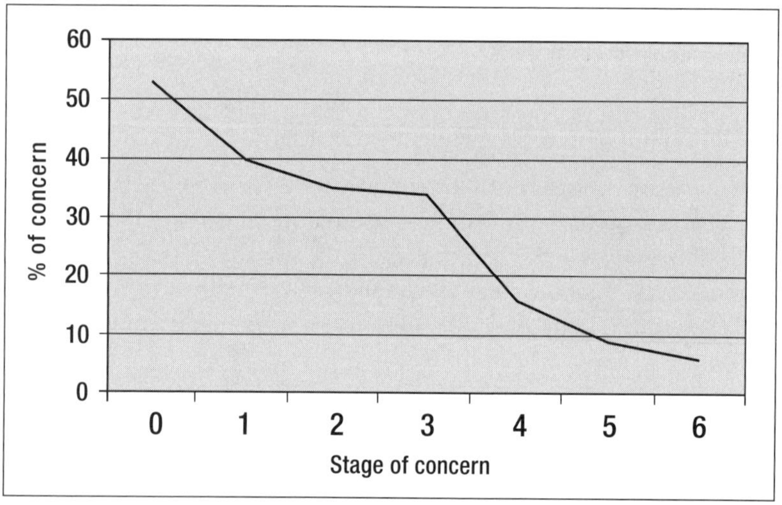

Figure 7.5 Administrator B's Concerns profile

Discussion

OVERVIEW

This study examined teacher and administrator concerns during the initial phase of a one-to-one laptop initiative at an urban at-risk middle school in the Southwestern United States. Stages of Concern can be examined by level or by stage. Teacher concerns in this study were at many levels; however, concerns were primarily at the *Self* or *Task* level. Self concerns were at the Personal stage (Stage 2) and Task concerns were at the Management stage (Stage 3). As a group, teacher concerns were predominantly about the innovations' impact on them as individuals; however, a smaller percentage of teachers were concerned about the best way to utilize the laptops for maximum teacher effectiveness.

Although teachers at this school were involved in the laptop initiative by choice (some teachers even requested a change in assignment to be involved), their concerns of involvement in the laptop initiative were genuine. High level Self concerns are typical of teachers anticipating educational change (Hall & Hord, 2001; Newhouse, 2001). Teachers' concerns in the Self stage were reflected by their hesitation to allow the researcher to observe them, their admissions of not feeling comfortable with the laptops for instructional purposes, and their struggle with how to integrate the laptops into their teaching routines.

Results of this study will be discussed by examining concerns profiles, followed by a more detailed discussion of the impact of this study on professional development and program continuation plans at the school. Finally, recommendations for future one-to-one initiatives will be made, and limitations of this study will be addressed.

It was evident in this study that change is a process that is initially discomforting. Teachers' concerns centered on readying themselves for the challenge of teaching in the one-to-one environment, yet when considered in relation to the concerns of the two administrators, we can see stages of concern along the continuum. Administrator B, who was the newest to the school and the initiative, exhibited high Awareness concerns indicating a deep desire to learn as much about the program as possible. The teachers whose concerns were predominantly at the Self level (Personal stage) were further along the continuum because they had been involved in the program for longer than Administrator B, yet not long enough to be fully comfortable with it. Note that several of the teachers had been involved in the pilot program the previous semester and/or were somewhat comfortable with technology as they were pursuing masters degrees in educational technology.

At the beginning of any school year, teachers have concerns about being fully prepared to teach the incoming students. When the introduction of an innovation is added to that, it is not surprising that their concerns are at a Personal stage. High level Informational and Personal concerns could be considered an indicator that teachers had not started or were barely using an innovation (James, Lamb, Householder, & Bailey, 2000). Observations throughout the first year of the laptop initiative (in the concurrent study) revealed that several teachers rarely used the laptops for teaching and learning, once again confirming their concerns about being proficient with the innovation. It was apparent in interviews that teachers did not feel proficient with the technology to integrate it in innovative ways.

These teachers more frequently used the technology for functions they were personally comfortable with such as word processing and searching the Internet. Similarly, if an innovation was being fully implemented, concerns would be at a Management stage (James et al., 2000). Not surprisingly, teachers who expressed Management concerns in the one-legged interviews and through open-ended statements were observed to be those teachers making the greatest effort to incorporate the one-to-one computer access into the daily routines, lesson plans, and student activities. These same teachers were the ones completing master's degrees at the university and one teacher who was identified through interview to be clearly constructivist in philosophy and pedagogy.

Teachers in this study were uncomfortable as they attempted to blend their traditional pedagogies with the requirements for teaching in the one-to-one environment. Some of the teachers' biggest concerns were in relation to planning and meeting curricular goals. This can be interpreted as an indication that they were uncomfortable with the prospect of modifying their existing practices and making accommodations for teaching in a one-to-one environment. Observations conducted in the concurrent study confirmed this interpretation as teachers were observed primarily using laptops for word processing and other teacher-centered curriculum activities.

The concerns of the administration are also significant. Administrator B was primarily concerned with gaining a greater understanding of the laptop program. The Awareness and Informational concerns of Administrator B are consistent with one who is currently peripheral to the innovation adoption and joined the school after the program had been initiated (Hall & Hord, 2001). Administrator A, who had been involved with the program since its inception, was concerned about management of the innovation but also had high level Impact concerns indicating a desire to share the effect of the one-to-one initiative with the immediate and distant community. Concerns of Administrator A were also reflected in comments about making sure there was adequate training for teachers and comments about concern for sustaining the program in the future. Additionally, Administrator A was very involved in the coordination of rollout sessions in which students got their laptops and, as time passed, in coordinating the repair and recall of student laptops.

IMPLICATIONS

This study provided a great deal of useful information regarding the teacher concerns in initial adoption and implementation of a one-to-one laptop initiative. The implications have relevance for those considering a one-to-one laptop initiative as well as other innovations. Based upon the findings in this study, three recommendations are offered below. These recommendations are viewed by the researchers as necessary points of emphasis for anyone engaging in similar innovation adoptions.

ALIGNMENT OF PROFESSIONAL DEVELOPMENT AND TEACHER CONCERNS

This study found that teachers asked to integrate one-to-one computer access into their classrooms have genuine concerns on different levels. Many of these concerns stem from the teachers' comfort level with the technology and its role in their teaching. It is an important consideration when planning professional development to be aware of teacher concerns. Training and development should be related to teacher concerns if training is going to be meaningful and innovation adoption sustained (Hall & Hord, 2001). Professional development should be in alignment with the stage of concern if innovation adoption is going to be sustained (Dobbs, 2005). Effective professional development should be relevant and meaningful. Professional developers can focus on meaningful content by addressing teacher concerns. As a result of this study, differentiated professional development was recommended to school administration. For example, for the teachers who were concerned about how to integrate technology and meet curriculum standards, the recommendation was put forth that the professional development team focus on promoting student tasks involving technology rather than more complex concepts such as online communication or electronic submission of assignments. Specific recommendations included training on programs and applications as well as general management strategies for one-to-one computing environments. For teachers with management concerns who were worried about taking full advantage of the technology for teaching and learning, it was recommended that professional development focus on moving ahead with student-centered technology integration, such as having students create multimedia projects. Additionally, ongoing training on technology management utilizing electronic communication, online quizzes, and general networking could be provided. This more advanced level of professional development would be overwhelming and intimidating to novices. For those with personal concerns, this may act more as an inhibitor to effective use of laptops for learning. In addition, it was recommended that training be differentiated based on the specific student population being served (e.g., magnet cohort, classes where 1:1 was not 100% due to students not consistently bringing laptops). As the one-to-one initiative continues, it is recommended that teacher concerns be re-evaluated to not only track changing teacher concerns, but to ensure that professional development continues to be in alignment with concerns.

The professional development recommendations for the school evaluated in this study are worth addressing as the profiles described are likely consistent with other schools in the initial stages of an innovation adoption. Recommended actions for this school take into account the two profiles that were frequently observed as their needs are different. Another approach would utilize those at more advanced stages working with others through mentoring or sharing activities. However, this particular school already has a team approach to much of the planning process and thus this was not necessary.

GIVE TEACHERS A VOICE IN INNOVATION ADOPTION

Too often, teachers who are going through the change process are not consulted on the usefulness of the innovation yet are expected to adopt it with open arms (Richardson & Placier, 2001; Tyack & Cuban, 2000). By acknowledging teacher concerns, change facilitators can support teachers throughout the change process. At a time when teachers are being asked to do more and more to meet state and national standards and concerns such as the No Child Left Behind (NCLB) act requirements, many efforts at innovation adoption are met with resistance.

It is critical that when asked to adopt an innovation teachers feel important and involved. Many teachers at this school shared in one-legged interviews that their attitude toward the laptop program though initially positive waned over time due to factors such as student attitude and uncertainty of the continuation of the program. Teachers' comments illustrate their concerns of not being informed of the program's continuing status. Teachers had concerns about investing large amounts of time into developing new curriculum to only find that next year they would have to go back to a non-laptop environment. It was recommended as a result of this and other concurrent studies at the school site that the program continue and the teachers be kept informed of all decisions involving the laptop initiative. Other concerns centered on dealing with student apathy toward having laptops "ready" for learning. Students were aware of the consequences for breaking the laptop to the extent that at times this served as an inhibitor to bringing the laptop to school, yet students did not see any consequence for not including laptop preparedness as integral to learning readiness (Donovan, Hartley & Strudler, 2004). It was therefore recommended that teacher concerns about student apathy toward bringing laptops to class be addressed in a program-wide consequence system.

UNDERSTANDING THAT CHANGE IS A PROCESS

While the results of this study indicate that there are significant levels of Self concerns, the data merely provide a snapshot. Simply stated, we are living in a period of significant flux in education. A greater understanding of the change process by all participants should increase the likelihood that projects such as this will be effectively implemented and continued. It was recommended to the administration of this school that they do not get disheartened by the concerns of the teachers during this early phase of the program, but that they continue to monitor such concerns so they can continue to address them. Teacher buy-in is crucial for sustained innovation implementation (Hall & Hord, 2001) and by acknowledging and addressing feelings of discomfort and teacher concerns through professional development and support, change facilitators can better ensure sustainability of innovations. The results of this study are consistent with concerns that are found in other innovations that are in the early stages. By sharing this type of information with the users, the change facilitator can help those involved see the innovation adoption and implementation as a developmental process rather than an event.

LIMITATIONS OF CURRENT STUDY

All studies have limitations and this study is no exception. Limitations of this study lie in participants, setting, and research findings. This study was conducted in a unique setting in that the middle school is in an extremely large school district. More importantly, the selected school site is included in a GEAR UP grant initiative to prepare students from low-income families for college. The student population at this school was considered by their teachers to be less motivated in general when compared to other 7th grade students. This may have affected teacher concerns about the sustainability and viability of the one-to-one initiative. Similarly, teachers expressed concerns about general school climate in addition to concerns about one-to-one laptop implementation. The number of participants in this study was not extensive and as a result may not be transferable to larger populations. Finally, this study examined teacher concerns during initial implementation of a one-to-one laptop initiative. It does not represent concerns that may have changed as a result of continued implementation.

Conclusion

Twenty years have passed since the Apple Classrooms of Tomorrow project first introduced computers to teachers and students on a large scale. Advancements in technology and cost reductions have only recently made such initiatives possible for wide implementation. This rapid increase necessitates an extensive and reasoned evaluation of the one-to-one computing projects (Penuel, 2006). These evaluations should leverage what we know about innovation adoption and utilize the research tools available to gauge not only student outcomes but also process and implementation variables.

The results of this study are largely consistent with previous research in the areas of innovation adoption and more specifically one-to-one computing projects. In terms of innovation adoption in general, participants' concerns were largely personal in nature as noted by Hall and Hord (2001) and Newhouse (2001). Similarly, previous studies on one-to-one computing initiatives reported significant teacher concerns related to how their teaching will need to be adapted to effectively utilize the computers (Penuel 2006).

This study has also contributed to an understanding of the critical connection between technology integration and teacher practice. In essence, teachers whose classrooms are more traditional are being asked to adopt two innovations—the one-to-one computing environment and a more student-centered classroom. Rockman and associates noted the gradual shift toward constructivism in the AAL research (1997, 1998, 2000). Zucker (2005) reported that students' self-directed learning increased and the ACOT studies described how the teacher practices were changed (Sandholtz, Ringstaff, & Dwyer, 1997). Prior research implies that the use of technology in some way encourages this shift toward more student-centered or constructivist classrooms. In other words, the technology *causes* the shift. An alternative explanation is that the introduction of a one-to-one computing initiative *requires* a shift toward student-centered practices.

This study provides some insights from the one-legged interviews—particularly with teachers exhibiting more pronounced Self level concerns. The teachers' comments often indicate that they are struggling with how they can accommodate a teacher-centered classroom that is populated with student-centered tools. One route the teachers can take is best described by Cuban's (2002) classroom observations that the technology can be added but the learning activities will more or less remain the same. Findings from the current study, however, suggest that focusing on teachers' concerns will likely contribute to more effective professional development and ultimately support changes in teachers' practice in one-to-one computing environments.

Author Update

Our research on concerns of teachers who are in the initial stages of implementing a one-to-one laptop initiative in the middle school still holds relevance now. What we found in our study was that the majority of teachers were concerned about how being part of the one-to-one initiative would impact them personally (time, extra effort, teaching routines). A smaller group of teachers was less personally concerned and more concerned about how they could best use the laptops to enhance student learning and teacher effectiveness.

Although specific to the implementation of a one-to-one laptop initiative, the findings of our study have bearing with nearly any technology innovation adoption. With the continued interest in putting laptops in the hands of students, the increase in interactive whiteboards and student response systems in schools, and the surge of educational applications for smartphones and handhelds, teachers who are being asked (or expected) to implement these technologies into their classrooms will have concerns. Identification and consideration of teacher concerns about innovation adoption will affect success and sustainability (Dobbs, 2005; Hall & Hord, 2006). Further, we know from professional development literature that the alignment between professional development and innovation implementation is not definitive (Bradshaw, 2002), that teachers need to feel individually supported (Levin & Wadmany, 2008; Sugar, 2005), and need *just in time* support (Chen, 2008). Identifying data regarding participants' concerns during initial stages of innovation adoption would allow for these issues to be addressed.

The conclusions in this study were based upon data that included extensive classroom observations, stakeholder interviews (formal and informal), and survey data. As a result, one of the lasting contributions of this work is how a comprehensive understanding of the context of an innovation can provide information critical to sustainability and effectiveness.

References

Anderson, R. E., & Dexter, S. (2003). *Mantua Elementary: A basic school powered by technology.* Available at http://edtechcases.info/schools/mantua/Mantua%20Elementary.pdf

Apple Computing Inc. (1995). *Changing the conversation about teaching, learning, and technology.* Available at http://imet.csus.edu/imet1/baeza/PDF%20Files/Upload/10yr.pdf

Apple Computing Inc. (2005). *Research: What it says about 1 to 1 learning.* Retrieved January 29, 2006, from: www.ubiqcomputing.org/Apple_1-to-1_Research.pdf

Bradshaw, L. K. (2002). Technology for teaching and learning: Strategies for staff development and follow-up support. *Journal of Technology and Teacher Education, 10*(1), 131–150.

CEO Forum (2001). *School technology and readiness report.* Retrieved November 28, 2004, from www.ceoforum.org/reports.html

Chen, C. (2008). Why do teachers not practice what they believe regarding technology integration? *The Journal of Educational Research, 102*, 65–75.

Cuban, L. (2002). *Oversold and Underused: Computers in the Classroom.* Cambridge, MA: Harvard University Press.

Dobbs, R. L. (2005). An experimental study of the impact of training on faculty concerns. *Journal of Industrial Technology, 21*(1). Available at http://atmae.org/jit/Articles/dobbs010605.pdf

Donovan, L. (2005). *Exploring relationships between configurations of laptop use and student off-task behavior.* Unpublished doctoral dissertation, University of Nevada, Las Vegas.

Donovan, L., Hartley, K., & Strudler, N. (2004). *The impact of one-to-one computing on 7th grade teachers and students at Roy Martin Middle School.* Unpublished evaluation.

Fullan, M. (2001). *The new meaning of educational change* (3rd ed.). New York, NY: Teachers College Press.

Hall, G. E., George, A. A., & Rutherford, W. L. (1998). *Measuring stages of concern about the innovation: A manual for use of the SoC questionnaire.* Austin, TX: Southwest Educational Development Laboratory.

Hall, G. E., & Hord, S. M. (2001). *Implementing change: Patterns, principles, and potholes.* Boston, MA: Allyn and Bacon.

Hall, G. E., & Hord, S. M. (2006). *Implementing change: Patterns, principles, and potholes.* (2nd ed.). Boston, MA: Allyn and Bacon.

Heck, S., Stiegelbauer, S. M., Hall, G. E., & Loucks, S. F. (1981). *Measuring innovation configurations: Procedures and application.* Austin, TX: Southwest Educational Development Laboratory.

James, R. K., Lamb, C. E., Householder, D. L., & Bailey, M. A. (2000). Integrating science, mathematics, and technology in middle school technology-rich environments: A study of implementation and change. *School Science and Mathematics, 100*(1), 27–35.

Levin, T., & Wadmany, R. (2008). Teachers' views on factors affecting effective integration of information technology in the classroom: developmental scenery. *Journal of Technology and Teacher Education, 16*, 233–263.

Lowther, D. L., Ross, S. M., & Morrison, G. M. (2003). When each one has one: The influences on teaching strategies and student achievement of using laptops in the classroom. *Educational Technology Research and Development* 5(3), 23–44.

Newhouse, C. P. (2001). Applying the concerns-based adoption model to research on computers in classrooms. *Journal of Research on Technology in Education, 33*(5).

Partnership for 21st Century Skills (2002). *Learning for the 21st century*. Available at www.p21.org/images/stories/otherdocs/p21up_Report.pdf

Penuel, W. R. (2006). Implementation effects of one-to-one computing initiatives: A research synthesis. *Journal of Research on Technology in Education, 38*(3), 329–348.

Richardson, V., & Placier, P. (2001) Teacher change. In V. Richardson (Ed.), *Handbook of research on teaching* (4th ed., pp. 905–947). Washington, DC: American Educational Research Association.

Rockman et al. (1997). *Report of a laptop pilot program*. Available at www.rockman.com/projects/126.micro.aal/yr1_report.pdf

Rockman et al. (1998). *Powerful tools for schooling: Second year study of the laptop program*. Available at www.rockman.com/projects/126.micro.aal/yr2_report.pdf

Rockman et al. (2000). *A more complex picture: Laptop use and impact in the context of changing home and school access*. Available at www.rockman.com/projects/126.micro.aal/yr3_report.pdf

Rogers, E. M. (2003). *Diffusion of innovations* (5th ed.). New York, NY: Free Press.

Sandholtz, J. H., Ringstaff, C., & Dwyer, D. C. (1997). *Teaching with technology: Creating student-centered classrooms*. New York, NY: Teachers College Press.

Silvernail, D. L. & Lane, D. M. (2004). *The impact of Maine's one-to-one laptop program on middle school teachers and students*. (Research Report #1). University of Southern Maine, Maine Education Policy Research Institute.

Sugar, W. (2005). Instructional technologist as a coach: Impact of a situated professional development program on teachers' technology use. *Journal of Technology and Teacher Education, 13*, 447–571.

Tyack, D. & Cuban, L. (2000). Teaching by machine. In Jossey-Bass (Ed.), *Technology and Learning* (pp. 247–254). San Francisco, CA: Jossey-Bass.

Wiersma W. (1991). *Research methods in education: An introduction* (5th ed.). Boston, MA: Allyn and Bacon.

Windschitl, M., & Sahl, K. (2002). Tracing teachers' use of technology in a laptop computer school: The interplay of teacher beliefs, social dynamics, and institutional culture. *American Educational Research Journal, 39*(1), 165–205.

Yang, C. (2002, June). Integration of laptops into a K–12 learning environment: A Case study of a science teacher in the middle school. *World Conference on Educational Multimedia and Telecommunications, 2002*(1), 2097–2102. Retrieved September 2, 2004, from http://dl.aace.org/10530

Zucker, A. A., & McGhee, R. (2005). *A study of one-to-one computer use in mathematics and science instruction at the secondary level in Henrico county public schools*. Menlo Park, CA: SRI International. Retrieved January 23, 2006, from http://ubiqcomputing.org/FinalReport.pdf

APPENDIX

7.A

Stages of Concern Questionnaire

The purpose of this questionnaire is to determine the concerns teachers and staff at XXXXXX Middle School have about being part of the Apple Laptop Program. The items in this questionnaire were developed from typical responses of school and college teachers who have been part of educational change and ranged from no knowledge about new technologies to many years of experience with the technology. At this stage, some of the items may be of little relevance or irrelevant to you.

For items that are completely irrelevant, circle 0. other items will represent those concerns you do have, in varying degrees of intensity, and should be marked higher on the scale—1 being not true of me now to 7 being very true of me now.

For example:

This statement is very true of me at this time.	0 1 2 3 4 5 6 [7]
This statement is somewhat true of me now.	0 1 2 3 [4] 5 6 7
This statement is not at all true of me at this time.	0 [1] 2 3 4 5 6 7
This statement is irrelevant to me.	[0] 1 2 3 4 5 6 7

Please respond to items in terms of your *present concerns* or how you feel about being part of the laptop program at XXXXXX Middle School. The results of this questionnaire will be used in the evaluation of the program. Thank you for your time.

0	Irrelevant	3–4	Somewhat true of me now
1–2	Not true of me now	5–7	Very true of me now

1.	I am concerned about students' attitude toward the laptop program.	0 1 2 3 4 5 6 7
2.	I know of some other approaches that might work better.	0 1 2 3 4 5 6 7
3.	I don't even know about the laptop program.	0 1 2 3 4 5 6 7
4.	I am concerned about not having enough time to organize myself each day.	0 1 2 3 4 5 6 7
5.	I would like to help other faculty in their use of the laptops.	0 1 2 3 4 5 6 7
6.	I have very limited knowledge about the laptop program.	0 1 2 3 4 5 6 7
7.	I would like to know the effect of the laptop program on my professional status.	0 1 2 3 4 5 6 7

Continued

0	Irrelevant	3–4	Somewhat true of me now
1–2	Not true of me now	5–7	Very true of me now

8.	I am concerned about conflict between my interests and my responsibilities.	0 1 2 3 4 5 6 7
9.	I am concerned about revising my use of the laptop.	0 1 2 3 4 5 6 7
10.	I would like to develop working relationships with both our faculty and outside faculty involved in a laptop program.	0 1 2 3 4 5 6 7
11.	I am concerned about how the laptop program affects students.	0 1 2 3 4 5 6 7
12.	I am not concerned about the laptop program.	0 1 2 3 4 5 6 7
13.	I would like to know who will make the decisions in the laptop program.	0 1 2 3 4 5 6 7
14.	I would like to discuss the possibility of using the laptops.	0 1 2 3 4 5 6 7
15.	I would like to know what resources are available for the laptop program.	0 1 2 3 4 5 6 7
16.	I am concerned about my inability to manage all the laptop program requires.	0 1 2 3 4 5 6 7
17.	I would like to know how my teaching or administration is supposed to change.	0 1 2 3 4 5 6 7
18.	I would like to familiarize other departments or persons with the progress of the laptop program.	0 1 2 3 4 5 6 7
19.	I am concerned about evaluating my impact on students.	0 1 2 3 4 5 6 7
20.	I would like to revise the laptop program's instructional approach.	0 1 2 3 4 5 6 7
21.	I am completely occupied with other things.	0 1 2 3 4 5 6 7
22.	I would like to modify our use of the laptops based on the students' experiences.	0 1 2 3 4 5 6 7
23.	Although I don't know about the laptop program, I am concerned about other things in the area.	0 1 2 3 4 5 6 7
24.	I would like to excite my students about their part in the laptop program.	0 1 2 3 4 5 6 7
25.	I am concerned about my time spent working with nonacademic problems related to the laptops.	0 1 2 3 4 5 6 7
26.	I would like to know what the use of laptops will require in the immediate future.	0 1 2 3 4 5 6 7
27.	I would like to coordinate my efforts with others to maximize the laptop program's effects.	0 1 2 3 4 5 6 7
28.	I would like to have more information on time and energy commitments required by the laptop program.	0 1 2 3 4 5 6 7
29.	I would like to know what other faculty are doing in this area.	0 1 2 3 4 5 6 7
30.	At this time, I am not interested in learning about the laptop program.	0 1 2 3 4 5 6 7
31.	I would like to determine how to supplement, enhance, or replace the laptop program.	0 1 2 3 4 5 6 7
32.	I would like to use feedback from students to change the laptop program.	0 1 2 3 4 5 6 7
33.	I would like to know how my role will change when I am using the laptops.	0 1 2 3 4 5 6 7

Continued

0	Irrelevant	3–4	Somewhat true of me now
1–2	Not true of me now	5–7	Very true of me now

34. Coordination of tasks and people is taking too much of my time. 0 1 2 3 4 5 6 7

35. I would like to know how the laptop program is better than what we now have. 0 1 2 3 4 5 6 7

36. What other concerns, if any, do you have at this time? (please describe them using complete sentences)

37. Briefly describe your job function.

CHAPTER

8

Web-Based Learning: How Task Scaffolding and Website Design Support Knowledge Acquisition

S. Kim MacGregor | Louisiana State University

Yiping Lou | Louisiana State University

Using WebQuests for inquiry-based learning represents a higher-order use of technology requiring students to exercise information seeking, analyzing, and synthesizing strategies. This research was designed to obtain a better understanding of how to enhance the pedagogical effectiveness of WebQuests and of how students interact with the various features inherent to informational websites. A major objective was to examine the effect of providing instructional scaffolds to support fifth grade students' WebQuesting experiences. The findings indicated that concept mapping templates coordinated with the research tasks enhanced students' free recall and application of acquired knowledge. The importance of site design features, especially discourse quality, multimedia elements, and navigational systems, are discussed with respect to students' ability to locate, extract, and apply information.

Introduction

Classrooms have been provided with increasingly easier access to the Internet and teachers are challenged to create meaningful web-based learning activities for their students. The WebQuest, an approach to organizing Internet-based learning tasks for students (Dodge, 1995), frequently is utilized as an instructional activity in the elementary school curriculum. Major components of the WebQuest protocol include a topic description, a list of relevant web resources, and a set of task requirements and processes. Teachers, busy managing their classrooms and attending to learner needs, seek a balance between providing structure and encouraging the development of self-regulated learning skills. The purpose of this research project was to learn how task activities should be structured to provide an appropriate level of scaffolding and how to select web resources to support WebQuest learning experiences.

INTERNET-BASED LEARNING: HOPES AND CAUTIONS

With the rich array of resources such as up-to-date digital libraries, primary source documents, museum exhibits, and multimedia presentations about events, topics, and processes available on the Internet, educators have been optimistic about the value of exposing students to web-based resources (McArthur & Lewis, 1998). For example, exposure to current, authentic information uniquely available through websites can provide students with environments that support inquiry-based and constructivist learning (Oliver, 2000), improve student-test performance, and develop broader forms of social, cultural, and intellectual capacity (Guile, 1998). A recent large-scale study in California, however, found that there was no impact of having access to the Internet in the schools on student achievement scores (Trotter, 2002). The results of the study suggest that mere exposure to Internet resources is not sufficient to improve student learning. Lack of an evidential base of measured student performance has been noted by other researchers (Reynolds, Treharne, & Tripp, 2003). Although one may argue that standardized test scores are not good measures for these kinds of higher-order skills, decades of research on instructional technology suggest that quality instructional design of learning tasks and learning environments is necessary for improving student learning (Clark, 1983, 2003; Jonassen, 2002).

A major issue related to student use of hypermedia oriented websites is their ability to navigate through the site, finding the information needed to solve problems and complete tasks. Previous research indicates that students' ability to use hypermedia organized information systems are influenced by factors such as prior knowledge and self-regulation strategies (MacGregor, 1999). Although many students are savvy enough to "surf" the Internet, they may lack the strategies necessary to efficiently and effectively negotiate the reams of available information.

WEBQUEST

With its six major components, including introduction, task, resources, processes, evaluation, and conclusion, the WebQuest model was created by Dodge (1995) and his colleague Tom March (1998) as a framework for teachers to structure student-centered learning using Internet resources. In the introduction, the topic is usually launched with some interesting background information and a challenging authentic problem. Then a general description of the assigned task is presented in the task section. A set of websites that students can explore to complete the task are provided in the resource section or embedded in the process section, which provides detailed step-by-step procedures that students should follow to complete the task. The evaluation component describes the evaluation criteria, usually in the format of a rubric, that will be used to assess the students' work. Conclusion brings closure to the quest, reminds the learners about what they've learned, and encourages them to extend the experience into other domains.

Since its creation, the WebQuest model has been embraced by many educators, and numerous WebQuests have been created by inservice and preservice teachers for all grade levels (Dodge, 1998–2004). However, there is very little in the way of empirical research on the effects of WebQuests on student learning and on elements that make an effective WebQuest (Dodge, 2003). A search of "WebQuest" in the ERIC database located 49 articles published since 1995. Most were about why WebQuests should have an effect on student learning and/or how to design WebQuests. A few articles (e.g., Lipscomb, 2003) describing classroom use of WebQuests indicated that students often found the learning activities interesting and fun. Lipscomb, however, also found that the activities before and after student Internet research were very important in guiding the students. King (2003) conducted an empirical study investigating preservice teachers' self efficacy and outcome expectancies related to using WebQuests as a strategy to develop inquiry skills among elementary students. Contrary to her expectation, the group of preservice teachers who implemented their designed quests in actual classrooms had lower outcome expectancies than the group of preservice teachers who did not implement their designed quests.

The above results may be unexpected, but not surprising. A similar finding was observed in an exploratory study the authors conducted with two classes of preservice teachers, who designed and tried out their WebQuests with elementary age children (Lou & MacGregor, 2001). The pairs of preservice teachers designed their WebQuests specifically for the children they knew and carefully followed the design guidelines as suggested by Dodge (1998–2004). Before the tryout, most of the preservice teachers were confident that their designed WebQuests were perfect. During the implementation, students found that their assistance was needed by the children more frequently than they expected. In their post-implementation journals, many of them commented about this experience and felt that they needed to design their WebQuests more carefully and provide more supporting activities and materials. These preliminary research studies indicate that WebQuest implementation may be more difficult than designers expected.

ROLE OF SCAFFOLDS IN RESOURCE-BASED LEARNING

Resource-based learning differs from traditional instruction in a number of ways (Hill & Hannafin, 2001). Traditional instruction is didactic, focusing on known learning goals using predetermined, well-organized resources and directed learning activities. In traditional instruction, students look to the teacher for what to learn, how to learn it, and whether sufficient learning has taken place. The most common way for students to learn about a topic is to listen to a lecture, read the textbook, and complete the corresponding assignment. In this type of learning, there's no need for the learner to look for additional resources or to evaluate whether the resources are relevant and sufficient for the given assignment. Traditional instruction is often criticized for being too structured and for developing learner compliance rather than critical thinking and self-regulated learning skills that are highly needed in today's fast-changing information world.

Different from traditional instruction, resource-based learning such as a WebQuest is often learner-centered, focusing on open-ended learning goals using a variety of authentic resources that are not specifically designed for completing the specific tasks. A resource does not teach as a textbook often does, but "provides candidate information to be engaged and interpreted" (Hill & Hannafin, 2001, p. 5). In resource-based learning, especially on the web, there is an abundance of resources within easy clicks of a computer mouse. However, unlike refereed books and journals in a library, anyone can publish on the web without being reviewed or approved by experts or following any standards in designing the website homepage (Nielsen & Tahir, 2002) or information architecture (Morville & Rosenfeld, 2002). Thus, in web resource-based learning, learners are confronted with the need to quickly and critically evaluate both the credibility and content relevance of a website for a given task (Case, 2003). They have to interpret and synthesize a variety of resources that may not be well organized and designed for the assigned task. These needs call for new skills in managing complex information, higher-order cognitive processes (Naidu & Bernath, 2002), and sufficient metacognitive awareness and self-regulated learning skills (Hill & Hanaffin, 2001). Because most of our current learners are accustomed to didactic instruction and directed learning, they often feel insecure and uncomfortable and are unable to learn effectively in such learning environments (Case, 2003).

Resource-based learning has great potential to improve the development of higher-order cognitive skills, critical thinking, and problem-solving skills that the fast-paced information age demands; however, in order for it to work, students need support and scaffolding in developing the requisite skills (Hill & Hannafin, 2001). This research project focused on investigating the use of a conceptual scaffold in the form of a concept map template in guiding the learners and the design features of websites that students used in getting relevant information for completing their WebQuest tasks.

METHOD

An exploratory pilot project was first conducted to determine the effect of providing an explicit set of procedures that directed fourth grade students' research while completing a WebQuest. The instructional goal of the WebQuest was for students to identify important features (e.g., government, recreation, weather, education) of their community and to create a brochure that depicted positive and interesting features of that community. One group of students (n = 12) was provided with the WebQuest goal and was given guidelines for the criteria that must be met for creating the brochure. The other group of students (n = 12) was provided with the same basics, but was given an explicit set of directions that identified what information should be included and how that information should be organized.

To ensure that the students in each of the groups had comparable levels of language arts ability and prior knowledge about their community, their recent scores on the Iowa Test of Basic Skills were obtained and a pretest of community knowledge was administered. A comparison of the pretest scores of the two groups revealed that they had similar levels of language arts achievement and prior knowledge about their community. At the end of the last session, the community knowledge assessment was re-administered and the brochures created by the students were scored according to a rubric that included criteria related to the number of different ideas that were expressed, the use of organizational features such as headings and subheadings, the depth of information that was provided, evidence of style and personality, balance in the use of text and graphics, and coherence and consistency in the presentation. Field notes were recorded while students were engaged in the process of searching the Internet, collecting information, and creating the brochure.

A comparison of the performance of the two groups revealed that the students who were given the explicit procedures acquired more community knowledge and created higher quality brochures. Additionally, observations revealed that these students spent more time assimilating information within sections of the website, whereas the students in the other group were more likely to surf the site and navigate out to external links that were not necessarily related to the task at hand. It was also noted that, although the set of procedures provided some direction, a number of the students disregarded some or all of the procedures that were listed. Observations also revealed that many students had difficulty with orientation and navigation within the websites they visited, making it necessary for an adult to facilitate the navigation process. In analyzing instances where students had successful and unsuccessful searches, it was apparent that site design features affected the search process and outcome. As a result of these findings, it was determined that providing students with explicit procedures facilitates WebQuest activities and supports the acquisition of knowledge. However, though these procedures were helpful, they were not sufficient in maximizing the knowledge students obtained from their searches. To continue investigating how to design WebQuests to enhance their pedagogical effectiveness, the current study was planned.

DESIGN OF THE STUDY

This mixed method research was conducted with two fifth grade classes (26 students in each class) taught by the same teacher in an elementary school. The students were not the same children who participated in the pilot project. The objectives were to examine: (1) the effects of providing students with a concept mapping template on their free recall of information and their production of an informational multimedia slide show, (2) how students perceived the usefulness of the websites accessed, and (3) the relationships among task procedures, resources, and student performance.

DATA SOURCES

Students' prior knowledge of the topic was assessed using a 12-item multiple-choice pretest about topics related to endangered species. Questions about the reasons for endangerment and solutions to the problem were included. Students' knowledge acquisition during and after participating in the project was measured by three assessment approaches:

- A study guide that contained nine items to which the students were directed to find relevant information. The guide was scored such that the student received one point for each item for which they obtained correct and relevant information.
- A free recall protocol where the students were requested to write down "What I Learned" was administered after the students completed their study guide and data collection activities. Students received one point for each item of correct information that they wrote down.
- Multimedia slide shows were created by the students and were scored by a rubric (Table 8.1) assessing creativity, content, and organization.

Table 8.1 Rubric for Scoring Multimedia Slide Shows

Criteria	Rating
Creativity	
Use of multimedia elements [0 = not present; 1 = present]	
Creative strength (e.g., use of humor, unusual perspectives, emotional expression, fantasy, movement, richness of imagery) [0 = not present;1 = present]	
Content Presentation	
Description	
Habitat	
Threats (i.e., causes of endangerment)	
Solution (e.g., how to help)	
Additional appropriate information (e.g., diet, life span)	
[Each of these was rated: 0 = no accurate information; 1 = accurate statement; 2 = multiple accurate statements]	
Content Organization	
Organization of content ideas (e.g., each idea has subtitle or is on a separate screen [0 = no organizational elements; 3 = some organizational features; 5 = extensive organizational features]	
Total Score	

Students' perceptions of the quality of the primary website they used were measured in two ways:

- An attitude scale designed as a semantic differential consisting of six adjective pairs (boring-interesting, meaningless-meaningful, important-unimportant, informative-uninformative, disorganized-organized, easy-difficult) with five intervals was administered to the students. The target object was the website the students selected as most important for researching their topic.
- Observations and individual conversations with students where they were prompted to do "talk alouds" while they visited their sites.

Information provided by the students during the individual conversations and their responses to the semantic differential were considered in the development of a rubric to assess the design of websites. The students' responses to the semantic differential attitude scale were used to identify desirable and undesirable websites. During the individual observations and conversations conducted by the researchers while students navigated these sites, student comments relevant to the site features were transcribed. A constant comparative analysis (Glaser, 1978) of the transcribed data revealed five categories of the site design that influenced students' perceptions of website quality. The rubric (Table 8.2) was utilized to evaluate the sites for: ease of navigation, the degree to which relevant information was present, amount and usefulness of visual and audio support, discourse quality, and general appearance. Two scorers, using the website evaluation rubric, rated the sites from which each student acquired the most information. An inter-rater reliability (determined by percentage of agreement of individual scores) of at least 90% was attained through practice ratings. A similar comparison of the ratings made on a random selection of site evaluations verified the reliability.

Table 8.2 Rubric for Evaluation of Websites

Features	Rating
Navigation	
Links are well organized and easy to use (e.g., information is no more than one click away) [0 = not present, 1 = present]	
Locators that let you know where you are (e.g., clear section indicators, image captions) [0 = not present, 1 = present]	
Content Presentation	
The site offers sufficient information related to the needs of the assignment [1: one category..., 4: four or more categories]	
Multimedia	
Still graphics [0 = not present; 1 = present]	
Video clips [0 = not present; 1 = present]	
Sound effects [0 = not present; 1 = present]	
Quality of multimedia (e.g., clarity, relevance to text) [1 = limited relevance, poor clarity; 3 = moderate relevance; 5 = high relevance, extends knowledge of topic]	
Quantity of multimedia (% of screen space) [0 = none; 1 = 1% to 25%; 2 = 25% to 50%; 3 = >50%	
Discourse Features	
Readability [1 = long sentence/paragraph/sections and difficult (i.e., adult) vocabulary; 2 = either long sentence/paragraph/section and some difficult vocabulary; 3 = short sentences and 5th grade vocabulary]	
The content is clearly organized (e.g., box, labels, headings, subheadings, lists with bullets, etc.) [1 = limited use of organizational features; 2 = moderate use; 3 = extensive use]	
Total Score	

PROCEDURES

Students completed the WebQuest activities in their science classroom over a period of three weeks during their daily, one-hour science block. The classroom was set up with clusters of six desks arranged in a table layout. A mobile laboratory was available for the project and each student was given a laptop computer to access the Internet and for using Microsoft PowerPoint to create their multimedia slide shows. These students had average to high levels of computer and information literacy skills and worked independently and collaboratively to complete the WebQuest tasks.

A WebQuest on endangered species was designed by the authors to coordinate with the fifth grade science curriculum. Students were provided an introduction to the WebQuest through some motivational activities that included a video tape related to the topic and a newspaper article reporting the work of a local scientist. The primary objectives were for each student to (a) select an endangered species, (b) gather information on that species using Internet resources, and (c) create a multimedia slide show that could be used to teach the topic to second grade students in their school.

The procedures included several steps. First, students were directed to collect information using the study guide that required them to record specific types of information about their endangered species (e.g., habitat, description, reasons for endangered status). Although explicit directions for collecting information were found to be beneficial in the pilot project, it was determined that they were not sufficient. Therefore, the study guide was required. Addresses for topic-related websites were provided, but students were not restricted to these sites. Second, students were required to design their slide show presentation for second grade students. A random selection of half the students in each class was provided with a concept mapping template. The template provided a framework that specified how the learner was to make connections from the information they acquired with their study guide to the major relevant concepts (e.g., characteristics of their species, habitat issues, and how these factors contributed to the causes of endangerment). The concept mapping template was then used as a design mechanism for their slide show presentation. The other half of the students were requested to select and organize the information that they collected with their study guide in their own way to create a storyboard for their slide show. After the students completed the design of their slide show, the free recall "What I Learned" assessment was administered. Subsequently, students were directed to use their designs to create their slide show presentations.

Students were observed and field notes documented their website interactions as they searched for information. Additionally, the researchers met with each student individually at a computer station, and asked them to revisit their favorite site. During this individual observation session, the students were prompted to identify and talk about the design features that facilitated and/or impeded their search for relevant information.

While they were engaged in reviewing this website they were requested to respond to the semantic differential scale.

Results

The data were analyzed using both quantitative and qualitative strategies. Statistical analyses were implemented to test for significance of the quantitative findings and constant comparative analyses were used to find patterns and themes in the observational field notes and conversations with students. The data from only one of the classes were used in the statistical analyses because a more complete set of data was available from this class.

TASK SCAFFOLDING

To determine whether providing students with a concept mapping scaffold for organizing their newly acquired knowledge influenced their learning, a comparison between the students who used the scaffold and those who did not was made. To ensure that the groups were comparable, t-tests were conducted to compare their levels of prior knowledge and their performance on the study guide that was completed before the concept map was used. The results of a t-test comparing mean scores on the test of prior knowledge for the concept map group ($M = 6.44$, $SD = 1.81$) and the no-scaffold group ($M = 5.82$, $SD = 2.04$) revealed no significant difference between the groups. Likewise, the results of a t-test comparing the mean scores on the information collected on their study guides for the concept map group ($M = 8.33$, $SD = 2.24$) and the no-scaffold group ($M = 7.88$, $SD = 2.09$) revealed no significant difference.

Preliminary analyses on the dependent variables indicated that the four measures (free recall and creativity, content, and organization of the slide show) were highly correlated. With the exception of the correlation between free recall and creativity ($r = .08$) and creativity and the amount of content included in the slide show presentation ($r = .37$), the other correlations were significant: free recall with content ($r = .56$, $p < .01$), free recall with organization ($r = .45$, $p < .05$), creativity with organization ($r = .50$, $p < .02$), and content with organization ($r = .80$, $p < .01$). Therefore, a one-way MANOVA by the concept map condition was conducted. A significant Wilks' Lambda (Λ) = 4.81, $F(4,17) = 4.58$, $p < .01$, was obtained for the use of the concept map scaffold. Follow-up ANOVAs revealed specific effects for each of the dependent variables. A significant difference between the groups for their scores on their "What I Learned" free recall assessment was found, $F(1,20) = 9.20$, $p < .01$. A similar pattern emerged for the differences between the groups for both the content of their slide show presentation ($F(1,20) = 15.93$, $p < .001$) and the organization of that content ($F(1,20) = 6.84$, $p < .02$). There was no difference in the level of creativity represented by students in the two groups, which makes sense given that the treatment was not designed to enhance creativeness. Descriptive statistics for the dependent variables are presented in Table 8.3. The significant effects of the intervention have important implications for planning instruction of this type. It appears that providing scaffolding for the students in the form of a concept mapping template helps them to extract information from websites and then to be able to remember, present, and organize that information.

Table 8.3 Mean Scores on Student Measures of Performance by Task Scaffold

Scaffold		What I Learned	Multimedia Slide Show Creativity	Content	Organization
None	Mean	4.53	2.47	4.87	2.54
(*n* = 13)	SD	(1.42)	(0.99)	(2.59)	(1.13)
Concept	Mean	6.22	2.86	7.71	3.67
Map (*n* = 9)	SD	(2.22)	(0.90)	(1.89)	(1.00)

SITE DESIGN FEATURES

Observation and Interviews. Discourse quality, mentioned most frequently by students, was composed of elements of writing style, readability level, and text organization. The students indicated a preference for expository text that was written concisely, clearly, and at a simple readability level. One student commented, "This website gave a lot of information, but the words could be easier." The concern with wordiness was expressed by another student: "It had a lot of words and it was hard to find the information." A preference was expressed for sites where there was ample use of subtitles and short segments of corresponding text. Observations of students while they searched for information revealed that, in general, they scrolled through the site looking for relevant headings, and once a heading was located, skimmed the text to find specific information. Students repeatedly noted their preferences for "bold headings and short paragraphs." In a few cases students chose sites where the information was written in the context of a story narration and they expressed a keen interest in this kind of format.

Interestingly, students expressed a dislike for menus with links that required them to leave the main page and navigate to other sections. One child went to a site that had navigation buttons across the top of the screen providing connections to the corresponding information. After clicking on one button that went to another page, the child left that website and moved to another. When queried about this action, she said, "It's too hard to find what I need." Another student who was working on a site with very simple navigation paths said, "This site isn't hard because you don't have to click on things to find the information … it 's all on one page." A possible explanation for this preference at this developmental level is that it may be more cognitively demanding to maintain the conceptual connections when navigation to new space is required.

The aesthetic appearance of the web page also contributed to students' perceptions of the site usability. Text enclosed in boxes and "fast fact" ways of presenting information were identified as functional features. One student expressed her fondness for the use of borders in saying that "The side chart in the boxes was perfect. It showed what I needed." The use of color backgrounds for text boxes was repeatedly mentioned as appealing. Multimedia features were important to students as they searched for information relevant to their task. "I like the fact that there is a picture of an animal and then a sentence" illustrated the importance of graphic support. An appreciation for maps was expressed: "I liked the map that shows where they live." One student noted the importance of audio clips, "It was very interesting because I found the sound and how they (the animal) communicate." Movie clips, when available, were enthusiastically accessed and one student stated that it was important because "it shows movement and what my animal does." Students didn't settle for sites that were lacking the desired features, and moved rapidly from site to site seeking ones which they believed would provide them the most information quickly.

Rubric-Based Rating of the Sites. The most highly rated sites were those containing screens on which the information was clearly organized (e.g., using borders, subtitles, short paragraphs, or proper white space), had simple, if any, menus, and contained graphics (e.g., charts, tables, photographs) and other multimedia elements such as sound and videos. The lowest rated sites used few, if any, of the desired screen design features, and data from the semantic differential scale indicated that students considered these sites to be disorganized, boring, uninformative, difficult, and meaningless. Table 8.4 provides a summary of the features that characterized sites receiving both low and high ratings.

RELATIONSHIP BETWEEN TASK PROCEDURES, RESOURCES, AND STUDENT PERFORMANCE

Bivariate correlations were conducted to test the degree of relationships between the instructional variables, the web resource features, student perceptions, and the student performance measures, including the study guide, free recall, and multimedia slide show.

A significant correlation ($r = .7$, $p < .001$), determined from the website evaluation rubric, was found for the relationship between the content rating of the website and the amount of information gathered for the study guide. Total website quality was significantly correlated with the students' scores on the "What I Learned" free recall assessment ($r = .45$,

Table 8.4 Characteristics of High- and Low-Rated Websites

	High Rating	Low Rating
Discourse	Concise sentences Vocabulary at grade level or lower Headings	Long sentences/paragraphs Complex vocabulary Minimal headings
Content	High relevance to task objectives Breadth of coverage	Limited relevance to task Depth of coverage
Navigation	Limited use of menus Information that is accessible with only one click Site and section locators	Layers of menus and submenus
General Appearance	Borders around text Color fill in text boxes Lots of "white" space	Web page covered with text Busy space
Multimedia	Still graphics providing explication of textual elements Audio features Video clips demonstrating concepts Clarity	Irrelevance to text Poor clarity

$p < .05$), indicating that site design features are significantly related to how much a student learns from a particular site. A significant correlation was found between the students' scores on the study guide and their scores on the "What I Learned" free recall posttest ($r = .38$, $p < .05$), suggesting that the amount of information extracted from the resource sites and recorded on the study guide had a positive influence on how much students learned as measured by the free recall posttest. This finding underscores the importance of the study guide as a means of supporting student learning. Visual features, including video clips and still graphics, were identified as desirable for providing information that supported or enriched the textual information and this was corroborated by a significant correlation ($r = .65$, $p < .01$) between the rating of the multimedia for the sites and the score students received on their study guide. There also was a significant correlation between certain elements of the website and the quality and relevance of the content the students produced in their multimedia slide shows. The quality of the multimedia features offered at the site ($r = .56$, $p < .01$) and the relevance and clarity of the content ($r = .59$, $p < .01$) were associated with higher quality presentations.

The correlations between students' perceptions of the websites, measured by the semantic differential scale, and their study guide score ($r = .34$, $p < .05$) was significant. This may suggest that their perception of the website was related to how much information the students were able to extract from the sites and how helpful it was to them in completing

WebQuest tasks. The websites that supported higher levels of knowledge acquisition were judged by the students to be more organized, interesting, informative, meaningful, and were easier to use. Students' awareness of the usefulness of the websites that they visited may demonstrate that this particular group of students had a fairly high level of information literacy.

Conclusions

Using WebQuests for inquiry-based learning represents a higher-order use of technology. It requires students to analyze and synthesize information and exercise information-seeking strategies that represent higher levels of cognition than simple knowledge acquisition. Identifying strategies that help the learner to be savvy about how to select sites, extract relevant information from those sites, and then synthesize that information in meaningful ways is an important endeavor to educators at all levels. Prior research indicates that although WebQuests were promising, results of their implementation often were not as good as designers expected.

Hill and Hannafin (2001) suggested four types of scaffolds: conceptual, metacognitive, procedural, and strategic that may be used to support resource-based learning. Conceptual scaffolds may include outlines and concept maps that assist the learner in deciding what to consider or to prioritize what is important. Metacognitive scaffolds may include a simple reminder to reflect on the goal or a problem-solving model, which help learners assess what they know and what to do as they learn. Procedural scaffolds may include procedures, site navigation maps, textual charts, and graphic representations that help the learner access and use resources while reducing the cognitive load in the mechanics of procedures and navigation. Strategic scaffolds may include suggestions for alternative approaches to engaging a task that help the learner develop alternative perspective or ways in solving a problem.

The findings of this study revealed that conceptual scaffolds in the form of a study guide and a concept mapping template supported students as they were engaged in learner-centered resource-based learning. Providing a study guide that identified what information to extract and a concept map that provided cues for organizing and synthesizing their information were helpful in keeping students on task and facilitated higher-order learning. The concept map template was effective in guiding students' synthesizing and organizing the information they gathered for their target purpose and audience.

The results of this study also revealed that in web resource-based inquiry learning, it is important for teachers to be cognizant of the design features within a site and understand how they facilitate student use in achieving learning objectives. Design features that provided support for the students included appropriate discourse readability, high content relevance, easy navigation, user-friendly screen design, and informative multimedia. These findings were consistent with research on reading comprehension on the Internet (Coiro, 2003) and design principles in computer-based instruction (Clark & Mayer, 2002). Due to different features such as hypertext, multimedia, and interactivity, learning from Internet-based resources places different demands on the learner than traditional text-based, linear resources. Learning is facilitated when multimedia elements such as graphics provide illustration of the concepts, readability is appropriate for the target learners, and when screen design is appealing and easy to read and navigate.

Nielsen and his colleagues conducted extensive usability studies of both corporate websites (Nielsen & Tahir, 2002) and children's websites (Gilutz & Nielsen, 2002). Based on these studies, they developed comprehensive usability guidelines for designing and evaluating corporate home pages and websites for children. Although many guidelines for corporate websites focus on the commercial value of design features, several common usability problems were experienced by both adults and children in their studies and were also noted by the fifth grade students in this study. These included unclear site focus and complex navigation structure. When visiting a site, both adults and children want to know quickly what the focus of the site is and whether they can get the information they are seeking from the site. With respect to graphics, the fifth grade students were similar to the adults in Nielsen and Tahir (2002) in their view that graphics should add value to the content. The students also noted that they liked clustered texts with subheadings and textboxes in helping them identify and focus on the most important content. According to Hill and Hannafin (2001), these navigational usability features of websites may be considered procedural scaffolds. They reduce cognitive load and help learners focus on their tasks.

RECOMMENDATIONS FOR FUTURE RESEARCH

This research study was conducted using a science WebQuest with two classes of fifth grade students. The results may be limited to the characteristics of the study, especially the characteristics of the students. More research is needed to replicate the study in different subject areas and at different grade levels. It is possible that different types of scaffolds may be needed for different types of learning tasks and for students at different grade levels. Similarly, it is possible that younger or older students with different levels of metacognitive skills and experiences with the Internet may have different perceptions of what constitutes the most supportive site design features.

The results of this study indicate that multimedia elements that illustrate textual information were positively associated with student acquisition of knowledge from the sites they visited. During the WebQuest activities, the authors also noticed that students were often pleased and excited when they found interesting media elements such as the recorded sounds and video clips of the endangered species they were researching. A future study may examine both the motivational appeal and cognitive support of multimedia elements in Internet resource-based inquiry learning. It is also possible that different types of media may be needed for different types of content discourse and learning tasks.

Author Update

Inquiry-based learning is an instructional approach based on the belief that it provides students with the opportunity to develop and apply higher-order cognitive skills and in the process become life-long learners. However, research reveals that learners may encounter a variety of difficulties when engaged in inquiry-based learning. WebQuesting, an instructional innovation designed to support the learning process, is grounded in the theory of inquiry-based and student-driven approaches to learning. Although questions have been raised about the effectiveness of using WebQuests for inquiry-based learning, our research provided insights about factors that influenced their successful use by elementary school students. Student strategies in gathering and organizing information are critical in determining the path they take to address a learning task. Both task support and the design of websites accessed by the students were found to be significant factors in facilitating learning. Cognitive scaffolding, a task support in the form of concept mapping, afforded learners increased capacity to engage in the necessary learning processes. Concept mapping can be used to provide learners with a tool that has the potential to reduce cognitive overload and disorientation. Currently, there is research in the field of artificial intelligence aimed toward the development of personal concept maps that connect the learner's prior and desired knowledge to allow for optimizing the learning process. WebQuests continue to be a popular technology-enhanced instructional strategy utilized in K–12 and higher education classrooms. Despite the repeated call for further investigation, rigorous research on the impacts and factors affecting its success remains scanty. Of the few empirical studies conducted, most of the findings related to student perceptions were positive, but few have investigated the factors that optimize learning outcomes. Future research should investigate how to structure learning tasks and design cognitive scaffolds that support inquiry-based learning in Internet environments.

References

Case, R. (2003). Making critical thinking an integral part of electronic research. *School Libraries in Canada, 22*(4), 13–16.

Clark, E. R. (1983). Reconsidering research on learning from media. *Review of Educational Research, 53*(4), 445–459.

Clark, E. R. (2003). Research on web-based learning: A half-full glass. In R. Bruning, C. A. Horn, & L. M. PytlikZillig (Eds.), *Web-based learning: What do we know? Where do we go?* (pp. 1–22). Greenwich, CT: Information Publishing.

Clark, R. C. & Mayer, R. E. (2002). *E-learning and the science of instruction: Proven guidelines for consumers and designers of multimedia learning.* Hoboken, NJ: Jossey-Bass.

Coiro, J. (2003). Reading comprehension on the Internet: Expanding our understanding of reading comprehension to encompass new literacies. *Reading Teacher, 56*(5), 458–464.

Dodge, B. (1995). Some thoughts about WebQuests. *The Distance Educator, 1*(3), 12–15.

Dodge, B. (2003). *WebQuest research chat transcript.* Retrieved November 5th, 2003, from http://webquest.sdsu.edu/tappedin-031112.html

Dodge, B. J. (1998–2004). *The WebQuest page.* Retrieved October 15, 2003, from http://webquest.org

Gilutz, S., & Nielsen, J. (2002). Usability of websites for children: 70 design guidelines based on usability studies with kids. Retrieved July 3, 2004, from www.nngroup.com/reports/kids/

Glaser, B. (1978). *Theoretical sensitivity: Advances in the methodology of grounded theory.* Mill Valley, CA: Sociology Press.

Guile, D. (1998). *Information and communication technology and education.* London, UK: University of London Press.

Hill, J., & Hannafin, M. (2001). Teaching and learning in digital environments: The resurgence of resource-based learning. *Educational Technology Research and Development, 49*(3), 37–52.

Jonassen, D. (2002). Learning to solve problems online. In C. Vrasidas & G. V. Glass (Eds.), *Distance education and distributed learning* (pp. 75–98). Greenwich, CT: Information Age Publishing.

King, K. P. (2003). *The WebQuest as a means of enhancing computer efficacy.* (ERIC Document Reproduction Service No. ED474439)

Lipscomb, G. (2003). "I guess it was pretty fun": Using WebQuests in the middle school classroom. *Clearing House, 76* (3), 52–55.

Lou, Y., & MacGregor, K. (2001). *Learning with Internet resources: Task structure and group collaboration.* Paper presented at the 12th International Conference of Society for Information Technology and Teacher Education, March, Orlando, FL.

MacGregor, S. K. (1999). Hypermedia navigation profiles: Cognitive characteristics and information processing strategies. *Journal of Educational Computing Research, 20*(2), 189–206.

March, T. (1998). *Why WebQuesting: An introduction.* Available at http://tommarch.com/writings/intro_wq.php

McArthur, D., & Lewis, M. (1998). *Untangling the web: Applications of the internet and other information technologies to higher learning.* Santa Monica, CA: Rand.

Morville, P., & Rosenfeld, L. (2002). Information architecture for the World Wide Web, 2nd ed. Cambridge, MA: O'Reilly Publishing.

Naidu, S., & Bernath, U. (2002, July). *Training the trainers in the essentials of online learning.* Paper presented at the 2nd Pan-Commonwealth Forum on Open Learning, Durban, South Africa.

Nielsen, J., & Tahir, M. (2002). *Homepage usability: 50 websites deconstructed.* Indianapolis, IN: New Riders.

Oliver, K. (2000). Methods for developing constructivist learning on the web. *Educational Technology, 40*(6), 5–16.

Reynolds, D., Treharne, D., & Tripp, H. (2003). ICT—the hopes and the reality. *British Journal of Educational Technology, 34*(2), 151–167.

Trotter, A. (2002, September 4). Internet access has no impact. Education Week. Available at www.edweek.org/ew/articles/2002/09/04/01internet.h22.html?qs=Internet+access+has+no+impact (subscription required)

CHAPTER

9

The Effect of Web-Based Question Prompts on Scaffolding Knowledge Integration and Ill-Structured Problem Solving

Ching-Huei Chen | National Changhua University of Education, Taiwan
Amy C. Bradshaw | University of Oklahoma

This study examined the effects of question prompts, knowledge integration prompts, and problem-solving prompts embedded in a web-based learning environment in scaffolding preservice teachers' conceptual understanding and problem solving in an ill-structured domain. A mixed-method study was employed to investigate the outcomes of students' conceptual knowledge and ill-structured problem solving. The quantitative results indicated that students who received knowledge integration prompts had significantly higher scores in overall problem-solving performance, but the same was not true for prompts focused on conceptual knowledge. Further, the qualitative findings revealed the positive effects of knowledge integration prompts in facilitating students to make intentional efforts to identify and explain major concepts and their relationships that are necessary for solving the ill-structured problem. This study has implications for designing curricula in ill-defined domains that seek to integrate and promote the application of educational principles to real-world problems.

Introduction

An important characteristic of experts is their extensive, well-organized knowledge in their disciplines, which allows them to flexibly and efficiently retrieve relevant knowledge (Bransford, Brown, & Cocking, 2000). Experts also have cognitive frameworks that support problem analysis and guide retrieval and application of past experiences to solve new problems (Beck, McKeown, & Grommell, 1989; Ericsson & Staszewski, 1989; Glaser & Chi, 1988; Hasselbring, Goin, & Bransford, 1987; Simon, 1980). However, novices do not possess such integrative knowledge frameworks, which leads to a tendency toward oversimplifying the complexity of the new knowledge, generating vague relationships between prior and new knowledge, and processing information superficially and mindlessly (Feltovich, Spiro, Coulson, & Feltovich, 1996; Pressley et al., 1992). Yet in previous research, novices' deficiencies in problem solving have been attributed to limitations in both domain and metacognitive knowledge (Brown, 1987).

Many researchers have emphasized that knowledge integration is an important process in students' science learning because it engages students to monitor, actively reflect, evaluate, and modify their own knowledge (e.g., Davis & Linn, 2000; Linn & Hsi, 2000). Due to the lack of recent empirical studies focused on ill-structured problem solving in social science domains, it is critical for the researchers to build a theoretical framework on the earlier literature from cognitive science perspectives. From the few investigations on the effectiveness of knowledge integration from previous research in supporting conceptual knowledge and ill-structured problem solving in the social sciences, we believed that scaffolding strategies targeted at knowledge integration and problem solving could support students' cognitive and metacognitive skills. In this study, we specifically examined the effects of two types of question prompts, namely knowledge integration prompts and problem-solving prompts, to scaffold students' conceptual knowledge and problem-solving processes in an ill-defined domain. The curriculum context used for this study was educational measurement because it represented authentic and real-world problems in the practice and research of education. A web-based learning environment was created that provided the information students needed within the discipline as well as learning scenarios to engage them in authentic problem-solving activities and guide their learning process through scaffolding (Hannafin, Land, & Oliver, 1999; Jonassen, 1999).

Theoretical Framework

KNOWLEDGE INTEGRATION

Learning is an active process by which students construct their own knowledge in light of their existing knowledge and through a process of generation, integration, and transformation of their experiential world (Gao, Baylor, & Shen, 2005). Unfortunately, students often hold multiple conflicting views before learning new information and create their repertoire of views without reflecting on their existing knowledge. Students' existing knowledge serves as an interpretative framework for knowledge integration because new knowledge is filtered through existing knowledge. Consequently, students' existing knowledge plays an important role in understanding new information. Understanding also goes hand-in-hand with the construction of an integrated conceptual framework (Hewitt, 2002). For this reason, promoting an integrated conceptual framework that furthers understanding should be explicitly taught.

Thus, Linn and her colleagues (2000) sought to design an instructional aid that promoted a more integrated student understanding of complex science concepts and processes. The Web-based Inquiry Science Environment (WISE) is one of the curriculum projects they created to help students develop more cohesive, coherent, and thoughtful accounts of scientific phenomena (Linn, Clark, & Slotta, 2003). WISE was guided by an instructional framework called scaffolded knowledge integration framework (SKI), derived from substantive and extensive research such as that on cognitive apprenticeships (Collins, Brown, & Newman, 1989). Significantly, a scaffolded knowledge integration framework requires students to reflect on their deliberately developed repertoire of models for complex phenomena, and to work toward expanding, refining, reconciling, and linking these models (Bell, 2002; Linn, 1995). In an intervention study, Davis and Linn (2000) found that students who were encouraged to monitor their learning progress and identify new connections among ideas showed greater integrated understanding of the science phenomena compared to students who only devoted their attention to the inquiry process. Apparently, students who only focus on inquiry without a theoretical base are less likely to develop a robust conceptual understanding than students who compared ideas, distinguished cases, identified the links and connections among notions, sought evidence to resolve uncertainty, and sorted out valid relationships, thus improving their knowledge integration (Davis & Linn, 2000).

Likewise, Scardamalia and Bereiter (2003) indicated that we need to prepare for student learning as knowledge building. In a computer-based learning environment called Computer-Supported Intentional Learning Environments (CSILE), students were encouraged to clarify problem statements, develop theories, state difficulties in understanding certain issues, and summarize what they have learned; thus, students actively build their own knowledge bases (Scardamalia & Bereiter, 1996). Associations developed exclusively within the context of new material were less effective for knowledge building than those developed between new material and prior understanding. They concluded that instruction should support students' knowledge to be integrated, as opposed to disjointed and static.

As indicated, the features of a scaffolded knowledge integration instructional framework recognize students' weaknesses by critically examining their own thoughts and the evidence bearing on them in both their informal thinking about everyday topics and their thinking within formal academic studies (Linn, 2005). The framework has been examined and implemented in science inquiry learning contexts, in which students were constantly asked to reflect to help them monitor thoughts and construct a coherent and robust conceptual understanding (Linn & Hsi, 2000), which is also called metacognition.

ILL-STRUCTURED PROBLEM SOLVING

In contrast to well-structured problems commonly encountered in educational settings, ill-structured problems are the kinds of problems that students face routinely in everyday life (Jonassen, 2002). Ill-structured problems have vague and less-defined goals and unstated constraint information (Voss, Wolfe, Lawrence, & Eagle, 1991). These problems have no right or wrong concepts, rules, and principles for arriving at the solution and possess multiple solutions or may not have any definite solution at all (Butler & Thomas, 1999). As a result, experts and novices also approach these problems differently (Bransford, Brown, & Cocking, 2000). The components and processes in experts and novices' ill-structured problem solving are discussed below.

The primary predictor of successful problem solving is domain knowledge (Murphy & Alexander, 2002). How much solvers know about a domain is important to understanding the problem and generating solutions. However, ill-structured problems cannot be solved simply by finding the information and following a constrained set of rules. In fact, that domain knowledge must be well-integrated in order to support ill-structured problem solving. Such "integratedness" also is described as structural knowledge. Structural knowledge is the knowledge of integrating domain knowledge into useful procedural knowledge for solving domain problems (Jonassen, Beissner, & Yacci, 1993). In a study conducted in the Soviet Union, Voss and his associates (1986) found that the domain knowledge possessed by novices seemed to consist of bits and pieces of information that were not integrated and that ultimately impaired their problem-solving processes. A series of additional investigations on expert and novice problem solving also indicated that experts were better problem solvers because their representations acquire more integrated domain knowledge of the problem and that helps them to construct a meaningful internal representation that can be manipulated (Wineburg, 1998). In brief, domain knowledge is not enough to solve ill-structured problems; it must be integrated as structural knowledge to enable problem representation and solve ill-structured problems.

In addition to representational and selection complexities, ill-structured problems have no clear solutions and demand that problem solvers consider alternative goals as well as handle competing goals. This requires problem solvers to control and monitor the selection and execution of a solution process. In other words, they have to use metacognitive skills such as self-awareness of cognitive knowledge and self-regulation of cognitive processes and strategies during problem solving (Brown, 1987). King (1991) examined the effectiveness of self-questioning as a metacognitive strategy on students' reading comprehension. She found that self-questioning promotes internal dialogue for systematically analyzing problem information and regulating execution of cognitive strategies (King, 1991). Likewise, Delclos and Harrington (1991) found that students who monitored their own problem-solving processes tended to use more metacognitive strategies for completing the task. In sum, successful problem solvers use self-questioning and monitoring to gain access to and guide execution of strategies and to regulate use of strategies and problem-solving performance (Lin, 2001). Although well-structured and ill-structured problems share similarities in some respects, ill-structured problems often require solvers to go beyond what is represented in the problem statement and consider alternatives using more metacognitive skills. Ge and Land (2004) synthesized past studies and created a model for ill-structured problem solving, including four processes: (a) representing problem(s), (b) generating and selecting solutions, (c) making justifications, and (d) monitoring and evaluating goals and solutions.

QUESTION PROMPTS AS SCAFFOLDING STRATEGIES

Merely presenting information generally will not cause students to develop accurate and integrative knowledge that fosters the understanding of pragmatic principle(s) and dynamic stances toward new knowledge. Therefore, intentional instructional supports should be made to elicit such knowledge-building processes (Scardamalia & Bereiter, 1994). Students need to be prompted to think about new material in such a way that they transform the material, thus constructing new knowledge. Question prompts as instructional supports have been found to effectively promote students' knowledge integration. For instance, the studies of King and Rosenshine (1993), King (1994), and Davis and Linn (2000) used prompts to engage students in knowledge integration that furthered their knowledge acquisition. In a similar manner, merely asking students to solve problems without providing necessary instructional supports appears to decrease the possibility of accomplishing the ill-structured problem-solving process. Ge and Land (2003) investigated the use of question prompts in facilitating students' ill-structured problem solving and found that students who were prompted by questions made increased deliberate efforts to identify and seek relevant information in the problem.

Different question prompts may serve different needs and purposes for students. Recently, researchers have started to investigate in depth different types of questions that promote students' cognition and metacognition. For example, Davis (2003) examined science students' reflection productivity through what she labeled as "generic" and "directed" prompts. "Generic" prompts entailed having students to simply stop and think, whereas directed prompts were more elaborate, providing students with hints or directions for reflective thinking. She found that the "generic" prompts promoted more productive reflective thinking than did the "directed" prompts. Therefore, prompt types make a difference. While researchers in science contexts have begun to pay attention to different types of question prompts, it also is important to focus attention on the research in social science contexts.

Despite the justification for the use of question prompts to facilitate knowledge integration in science learning, the relationship between different types of questioning strategies and social science has not been sufficiently studied. Davis and Linn (2000) studied the effects of guided questions on metacognitive skills, knowledge integration, and problem solving. However, in Davis and Linn's (2000) study, the problems were situated in science and the subjects were eighth graders. Ge and Land (2003) provided a list of questions that were mapped to ill-structured problem-solving processes to guide undergraduate students in completing ill-structured problem-solving tasks in information science and technology. Although Ge and Land (2003) found that question prompts had positive effect on students' ill-structured problem solving, their study did not examine the students' prior knowledge aside from self-reports on prior problem-solving experience across different conditions. The students' self-reports might be a questionable measurement of what students knew. Further, Ge, Chen, and Davis (2005) called for future research to compare the effects of different question prompts on students' conceptual knowledge and ill-structured problem solving.

Purpose of the Study

The purpose of this study was to investigate the effects of (a) knowledge integration prompts, (b) problem-solving prompts, and (c) both knowledge integration and problem-solving prompts on scaffolding students' conceptual knowledge and problem-solving processes in an ill-structured task. The problem-solving outcomes and processes investigated were (a) problem representation, (b) developing and evaluating solutions, and (c) monitoring and justifying a plan of action (Ge & Land, 2004).

The knowledge integration prompts in this study referred to a set of questions that prompted students to connect ideas, compare ideas, seek uncertainty evidence, transfer ideas, and summarize valid relationships. They also were intended to direct students' attention to explain and understand how, why, and what. The problem-solving prompts in this study were a set of questions with specific procedures for problem solving.

The study examined the following questions:

1. Does the use of knowledge integration prompts only, problem-solving prompts only, or the combination of knowledge integration and problem-solving prompts have an effect on students' knowledge acquisition and problem-solving outcomes in the domain of educational measurement in the web-based learning environment?

2. How does the use of different question prompts influence students' conceptual knowledge and ill-structured problem solving?

Methodology

A mixed-method study was employed to investigate two research questions. The use of quantitative and qualitative methods helped the researcher to examine the results from different data sources and expand the scope and breadth of the study. The experimental study, designed to answer research question 1, was conducted to measure students' conceptual knowledge and problem-solving outcomes in an ill-structured task. The qualitative study consisting of an analysis of students' ill-structured problem-solving reports and follow-up interviews added depth and anecdotal evidence to findings from quantitative measures.

PARTICIPANTS

Participants in the experimental design were 51 undergraduate students (32 female and 19 male) recruited from three class sections of an introductory course in the Department of Educational Psychology at a south central U.S. university. Of these, 15 also participated in the follow-up interview. Most of the students were sophomores and juniors. About 70% had taken at least one educational psychology class and 47% had not yet taken an educational measurement class.

The Experimental Study

DESIGN AND PROCEDURES

Four versions of web-based learning environments were created. A database was developed so that participants' responses could be saved and retrieved. The 51 participants were assigned to one of four web-based learning environment study conditions: a) knowledge integration (KI) (n = 13), b) problem solving (PS) (n = 14), c) the combination of knowledge prompts and problem-solving prompts (KP) (n = 13), and d) control condition (Control) (n = 11). Following the pretest, the participants were directed to read a set of instructional passages about educational measurement, particularly reliability and validity, and then solve an ill-structured problem in the discipline. The participants in the KI and KP conditions were provided with and required to respond to a series of knowledge integration prompts after the presentation of the instructional passages. Their completed responses would be submitted, saved to the database, and displayed later. The participants in the PS and Control conditions simply read through the instructional passages. During the ill-structured problem solving, only the participants in the PS and KP conditions were provided with and required to respond to a series of problem-solving prompts after the presentation of the case study. Again, their completed responses were submitted, saved to the database, and displayed on the next screen, where the participants could copy and paste their prior responses to be organized and edited into final solution reports. The participants in the KI and KP conditions could also retrieve their responses from the knowledge integration prompts. After solving the problem, the participants completed a posttest before exiting the study.

MATERIALS

Prompt Types. Knowledge integration prompts were adapted from King (1994) and Linn (1995) studies, which addressed critiquing, interpreting, and explaining key concepts. For example, "Explain why reliability and validity are important," and "Go beyond what was covered in the instructional passages, summarize the purpose and the meaning of reliability and validity." Problem-solving prompts were generated to be parallel with the ill-structured problem-solving processes proposed by Ge and Land (2004), for example, "What facts from this case suggest a problem?", "Why is it occurring?", and "What specific strategies do you want to suggest to the teacher to help him solve the problems that you have identified?"

Pre/Posttests. A 19-item test about reliability and validity in educational measurement was developed to assess students' conceptual knowledge of the instructional passages provided. The test was evaluated by the instructors of measurement and evaluation courses to validate that the items were adequately and appropriately represented. The test included three major items: terminology (seven items), comprehension (seven items), and application (five items) tests. The test had a split-half internal consistency .65 reliability coefficient.

Ill-Structured Problem. The problem was generated from a real-world educational measurement problem with embedded reliability and validity principles. A rubric was developed to assess students' problem-solving outcomes on the ill-structured problem. Students' problem-solving outcomes were scored numerically based on their performances on (a) problem representation, (b) developing and justifying solution(s), and (c) monitoring and evaluating a plan of action. These coding schemes were chosen because they serve as indicators for the processes in solving ill-structured tasks (Ge & Land, 2004). Instructors from the educational psychology department and experts in research on ill-structured problem solving also validated the rubric. Before grading, two raters reached a conceptual consensus on how to interpret the scoring rubrics through discussion and examples. Any discrepancies of assigned values were discussed among raters. Consequently, a high consensus was reached. A split-half internal consistency procedure was performed and found that the scoring rubric had .87 reliability coefficient.

DATA ANALYSES

Quantitative data was analyzed first, followed by qualitative data. Multivariate analysis of variance (MANOVA) was conducted to examine the effects of different types of prompts on students' conceptual knowledge and ill-structured problem-solving outcomes. MANOVA was used for this study because it allows researchers to include multiple dependent variables and evaluate whether the means on a set of dependent variables vary across levels of factors (Green & Salkind, 2003). Wilks's Lambda (Λ) ($\alpha = .05$) was used in interpreting the multivariate test results. As shown by the results from the Levene's Test, the assumption of equal variance was met at the .05 alpha level, and thus met the MANOVA testing assumption that the residual errors follow a multivariate normal distribution in the population.

The Qualitative Study

PROCEDURES AND MATERIALS

All 51 participants' problem-solving reports were retrieved from the database by the first author. Different from the rubric that was developed to score quantitatively, the researcher coded each report individually in how participants defined and identified the concepts in their problem-solving reports. Following the completion of the experimental study, participants were selected based on their willingness to take part in audiotaped interviews.

DATA ANALYSES

The analysis process involved reading and jotting marginal notes on the transcripts, identifying emerging patterns into categories, and drawing conclusions. For example, the first author read through each student's problem-solving report and highlighted the places where he or she identified key concepts and their relationships. Highlighted places were used to examine the participants' conceptual knowledge in the context of question prompts or no prompts. The next procedure was to organize and display the emerging patterns so that comparison could be made across different conditions. The analyses of problem-solving reports and follow-up interviews added reliability to the findings along with member checks for validity and the use of multiple coders for inter-rater reliability (Bogdan & Biklen, 1998).

Results

QUANTITATIVE OUTCOMES

Multivariate analysis of variance (MANOVA) was employed to answer research question 1, "Does the use of knowledge integration prompts only, problem-solving prompts only, or the combination of knowledge integration and problem-solving prompts have an effect on students' conceptual knowledge and problem-solving outcomes in the domain of educational measurement in the web-based learning environment?" The results of MANOVA on the effect of students' conceptual knowledge did not reveal significant differences among conditions, Wilks's Lambda (Λ) = .80, $F(6, 92) = 1.80$, $p > .05$, $\eta^2 = .11$, observed power = .65. Table 9.1 shows means and standard deviations for the conceptual knowledge posttests by groups.

Although there was no significant main effect on students' conceptual knowledge among groups, we found that there was a significant main effect on ill-structured problem solving, Wilk's Lambda (Λ) = .50, $F(9, 110) = 4.0$, $p = .000$. The multivariate η^2 based on Cohen (1988) was quite strong, .21, and observed power also was considerably high, .97. Further, a univariate test of between-subjects effects revealed significant effects in two of the three problem-solving processes, i.e., developing and justifying solutions, $F(3, 47) = 3.38$, $p = .026$, $\eta^2 = .18$, observed power .73, and monitoring and evaluating a plan of action, $F(3, 47) = 6.50$, $p = .001$, $\eta^2 = .29$, observed power .96. Table 9.2 shows means and standard deviations for the four conditions. The result indicated that the knowledge integration group had the highest mean scores on developing and justifying solution(s) (M = 4.57, SD = 2.50), and monitoring and evaluating a plan of action (M = 4.85, SD = 1.99) of all the groups. Follow-up post hoc comparison indicated significant differences between the KI and Control groups resided on developing/evaluating solutions and monitoring/evaluating a plan of action.

Table 9.1 Means and Standard Deviations for the Conceptual Knowledge by Question Prompt Types

	Condition	*N*	*Mean*	*Std. Deviation*
Pretest	KI	13	6.92	2.18
	PS	14	6.79	2.33
	KP	13	8.08	1.89
	Control	11	7.46	2.12
Posttest	KI	13	11.08	2.60
	PS	14	9.43	1.95
	KP	13	10.69	2.43
	Control	11	9.00	2.45

Note: The possible ranges of scores for pre/posttests are 0–19.

Table 9.2 Means and Standard Deviations of Dependent Variables by Treatment Group

	Treatment Group											
	Knowledge integration (KI)			Problem solving (PS)			Knowledge integration and problem solving (KP)			Control		
DVs	*N*	*M*	*SD*	*N*	*M*	*SD*	*N*	*M*	*SD*	*N*	*M*	*SD*
Problem representation	13	5.08	1.94	14	5.64	2.82	13	5.08	2.53	11	3.36	1.91
Developing solutions	13	4.57	2.50	14	4.07	1.90	13	4.50	2.93	11	1.64	1.69
Monitoring and evaluating a plan of action	13	4.85	1.99	14	3.00	1.92	13	2.63	2.64	11	1.18	1.25

Note: The possible ranges of scores for problem representation are 0–7; developing solutions are 0–6; monitoring and evaluating a plan of action are 0–6.

QUALITATIVE FINDINGS

The participants' problem-solving performance in different conditions were examined qualitatively to supplement the quantitative findings. Below is a brief report of students' conceptual knowledge and ill-structured problem solving on the effects of different question prompts.

Analysis of the participants' ill-structured problem-solving reports produced the following two findings. First, the participants who received knowledge integration prompts made intentional efforts to identify major concepts and their relationships that are necessary for solving the ill-structured problem. For example, "Validity refers to the appropriateness of the interpretation of the results of an assessment procedure for a given group of individuals, not to the procedure itself;" "the project was not valid as well when appropriateness of interpretation of assessment result…;"and "the purpose of reliability is to ensure that the tests that are given are consistent and do not vary in their form of results…" On the other hand, participants who did not receive knowledge integration prompts appeared to identify the concepts vaguely and ambiguously, and they also failed to draw clear connections and relationships among concepts. Examples from students' problem-solving reports indicate that they used the concepts' reliability and validity interchangeably and showed misconceptions of what the concepts mean: "A reliable and valid rubric will yield more accurate content assessment;" "if there were a clear set of criteria there could be more reliability since…;" and "…you might want to compare students' grades to another to check validity."

Second, the participants who received problem-solving prompts appeared to make efforts to construct solutions and explicitly provide arguments for subsequent implementation. Those prompts also directed the participants' attention to seek alternative solutions they might have overlooked. For example, "Perhaps you can find another way to assess students, like have them sit in groups to work on things. However, make the projects individually based and grade each student individually upon completion of the project." And another student said, "I suggest the teacher give objectives to the students so they know exactly what they are being evaluated on and can work toward that goal." Comparing groups that received problem-solving prompts with those that received knowledge integration prompts, the researcher found that problem-solving prompts did not suffice to help the participants to retrieve constructed schema, which required participants to rely heavily on their limited working memory capacities to negotiate meanings.

Lastly, the follow-up interviews also were analyzed to provide in-depth insights. The participants who received knowledge integration prompts said that those prompts helped them think about different aspects and the relationship of things. Those prompts also served as an "organizer" to understanding concepts and problem solving, and activated reflective thinking to draw attention to important elements, and also organized and transferred concepts as they applied in real-world situations. The participants who received only problem-solving prompts mentioned that the problem seemed vague at first and, despite the prompts, they still had to spend time to pull the information together, relying more on their knowledge of the concepts than on problem-solving process. One student mentioned, "I think they helped more in the problem-solving skill than the actual understanding of the concepts." The problem-solving prompts seemed to help students focus on some of the important problems in the case studies, analyze the specific problem in-depth, and break down the problems into sub-problems.

Discussion

Although the quantitative results did not show a significant difference between students who received knowledge integration prompts and those who did not with regard to conceptual knowledge, the qualitative results indicated that these students felt that they developed a better integrated understanding of educational measurement despite the challenges they faced learning this topic. When the students were prompted to proceed with the knowledge integration process, they abandoned single knowledge elements for multiple knowledge elements, so that new or stronger connections were fostered through engagement with this web-based learning environment. By the end, these students were more likely to explain their reasoning with a well-integrated answer than with a less connected answer. Clearly, compared to instruction without scaffoldings, providing scaffoldings was more beneficial. In many cognitive situations with instructional goals such as learning a new unit of domain knowledge, knowledge integration prompts may be more useful than problem-solving prompts when asking students to engage in connecting, summarizing, and reflecting. Problem-solving prompts, on the other hand, focus students' attention only on the problem-solving processes, and may not always correspond as well to students' understandings.

In the present study, problem-solving prompts did not have a positive effect on solving the ill-structured problem. This finding contradicted Ge and Land's (2003) study, in which problem-solving prompts had effects on students' ill-structured problem solving processes such as problem representation, developing and justifying solutions, and monitoring and evaluating a plan of action. In the qualitative analyses of students' problem-solving reports and follow-up interviews, it was found that these prompts directed students to construct solutions and argumentations for subsequent implementation. However, the absence of integrative knowledge structures caused them to overlook a broader range of solutions.

The scaffoldings of both knowledge integration prompts and problem-solving prompts did not have the increased positive results over the single scaffolding as we would expect. The knowledge integration prompts used in this study were developed to help students identify weakness in their knowledge (Linn, 1995). The problem-solving prompts were to guide students' attention to perform like experts in the problem-solving processes (Ge & Land, 2004). However, other research shows that when students cannot interpret specific prompts, they may flounder or dismiss the purposes of all those prompts (Davis, 2003; Ge, Chen, & Davis, 2005). Further, when students are not in control of their learning, they may experience fatigue that could greatly impact the overall performance. The use of question prompts as scaffolding should be used with caution and consideration of students' prior knowledge and experiences. Excessive question prompts may cause a certain degree of cognitive overload, as seems indicated by the lower scores of participants with both knowledge integration and problem-solving prompts. The design strategy of combining different types of prompts should be carefully evaluated in order to provide more explicit opportunities to help students apply concepts to real-world problems. A recent research endeavor looking at adaptive scaffolding by a human tutor provides new perspectives on how we can better diagnose students' level of understanding (Azevedo, Cromley, & Seibert, 2004; Azevedo, Cromley, Winters, Moos, & Greene, 2005).

Implications

The study has practical implications for web-based instruction, where question prompts embedded in web-based learning environments can challenge students' knowledge integration and support complex learning tasks. Web-based learning has considerable promise in the development and facilitation of students' understanding. This study yields several implications for designing such an environment to support the development of cognitive skills and models of understanding.

First, in order to support cognitive development effectively, a system is needed to facilitate intentional reflection and retention. Such a mechanism will raise students' awareness of the gaps and detect biases in their knowledge bases. Therefore, the web-based cognitive modeling system should structure opportunities for intentional reflection.

Second, in order to engage students in meaningful learning, the system should provide real-world problems to help students reconcile the application of knowledge. Students often experience difficulty connecting educational theories with real-world problems;

therefore, utilizing question prompts to act as a mediator for the instructor role will enable the linking system to activate students' knowledge application.

Last, but not least, it may be useful to provide feedback or features that structure opportunities for students to interact with experts and their peers. Distance learning is characterized by the separation between instructors and the students, whether by temporal or spatial distance. The cognitive advantage of incorporating a system that includes knowledge integration and problem-solving prompts into distance education is that viewing materials from multiple perspectives can increase cognitive flexibility and interconnections as well as giving opportunities to share and become involved with the learning community.

Recommendations for Future Research

This study urges further validation on the assessment of knowledge integration. Multiple assessment sources should help define and better represent knowledge integration. Possible multiple assessment sources should be investigated. Accordingly, it may be beneficial to examine and adapt methods used in other fields to understand knowledge integration better. For instance, a group of researchers used benchmarking as one of the techniques to assess the process of knowledge integration (Lee, Husic, Liu, & Hofstetter, 2006). A mixed initiative assessment that includes humans and computers has been widely discussed and implemented in real scaffolding classroom settings (e.g., Zimmerman, 2005). This dynamic assessment evaluates transitions in knowledge representations and performance while learners are in the process of solving problems, rather than after they have completed a problem, which is critical for providing valid interpretations of students' performance. A further investigation on the use of computers to assess and capture students' learning progress needs to be explored and discussed.

Another avenue for future research is how knowledge is integrated through the use of other scaffolding techniques, such as cooperative groups and expert modeling (Lajoie, 2005). Peer learning is assumed to promote sharing and the development of understanding. This study indicates that interaction and feedback loops may be useful in facilitating better knowledge integration. The web-based learning environment developed for use in this study was specifically designed to promote knowledge integration and problem solving through different types of question prompts. From a design perspective, it would be useful to know whether other tools had a greater impact on students' knowledge integration than the question prompts (Chen & Ge, 2006). Knowing this might lead to more generalizable design principles for designing better knowledge integration environments. Research on this question would likely involve conducting interviews with students specifically regarding the use of tools, collecting pre-post analyses of knowledge integration, tracking students' progress (e.g., time logs of overall frequency of use as well as frequency of specific tool use), and increasing numbers of participants in the treatment and control groups to provide additional valuable information.

Author Update

The design of web-based cognitive modeling systems has emphasized the importance of stimulating students' cognitive and metacognitive thinking through external scaffoldings. Web-based question prompts, one of the most frequently used scaffoldings, are found to help students' knowledge building and to elicit meaningful cognitive engagement, such as integrating cognitive schema and constructing cogent arguments. While studies have consistently pointed to the advantages of the use of question prompts in promoting effective and productive problem solving, different question prompts induce different cognitive and metacognitive functions in the problem-solving process. Therefore, question prompts may not be equally effective for all individuals or every learning task. It is necessary to further examine the effect of different question prompts on students' learning in different contexts.

Question prompts have been applied widely in the context of computer-mediated communication (CMC), as they provide students with clearly-structured tasks to foster effective group interaction and collaboration. Encouraging or requiring students in groups to respond to questions that encourage social negotiation and informal reasoning can enhance the quality and effectiveness of group discussion and interaction. Increasing attention is being paid to the motivational aspect of learning as it serves to mediate learners' outcomes and performance. Although scaffolds that purposively promote meaningful cognitive engagement may have a stronger impact, instructors should also be aware of individuals' motivational preference differences, as they may moderate how a learner chooses to exert effort or mindful use of question prompts. One of our previous studies (Chen & Bradshaw, 2007) suggests the design of question prompts should be adaptive, rather than one size fits all, and map onto each student's zone of proximal development so that better scaffolds and supports are provided for knowledge acquisition and deeper understanding. Adaptive question prompts also can promote meaningful cognitive engagement that consists of specific cognitive activities such as deliberate planning and monitoring as learners encounter academic tasks.

References

Azevedo, R., Cromley, J. G., & Seibert, D. (2004). Does adaptive scaffolding facilitate students' ability to regulate their learning with hypermedia. *Contemporary Educational Psychology, 29*, 344–370.

Azevedo, R., Cromley, J. G., Winters, F. I., Moos, D. C., & Greene, J. A. (2005). Adaptive human scaffolding facilitates adolescents' self-regulated learning with hypermedia. *Instructional Science, 33*, 381–412.

Beck, I. L., McKeown, M. G., & Grommell, E. W. (1989). Learning from social studies texts. *Cognition and Instruction, 6*, 99–158.

Bell, P. (2002). Using argument map representations to make thinking visible for individuals and groups. In T. Koschmann, R. Hall, & N. Miyake (Eds.), *CSCL 2: Carrying forward the conversation* (Vol. 2, pp. 449–505). Mahwah, NJ: Lawrence Erlbaum.

Bogdan, R. C., & Biklen, S. K. (1998). *Qualitative research for education: An introduction to theory and methods.* Needham Heights, MA: Allyn & Bacon.

Bransford, J. D., Brown, A. L., & Cocking, R. R. (2000). *How people learn: Brain, mind, experience, and school.* Washington, DC: National Academy Press.

Brown, A. L. (1987). Metacognition, executive control, self-regulation, and other more mysterious mechanisms. In F. Weinert, R. Kluwe (Eds.), *Metacognition, motivation, and understanding* (pp. 65–116). Hillsdale, NJ: Lawrence Erlbaum.

Butler, D. L., & Thomas, K. M. (1999). Preliminary study of the effectiveness of some heuristics used to generate solutions to ill-structured problems. *Psychological Reports, 84*, 817–827.

Chen, C.-H., & Bradshaw, A. (2007). The effect of web-based question prompts on scaffolding knowledge integration and ill-structured problem solving. *Journal of Research on Technology in Education, 39*(4), 359–375.

Chen, C.-H., & Ge, X. (2006). The design of a web-based cognitive modeling system to support ill-structured problem solving. *British Journal of Educational Technology, 37*(2), 299–302.

Cohen, J. (1988). *Statistical power analysis for the behavioral sciences* (2nd ed.). New York, NY: Routledge Academic.

Collins, A., Brown, J. S., & Newman, S. E. (1989). Cognitive apprenticeship: Teaching the crafts of reading, writing, and mathematics. In L. B. Resnick (Ed.), *Knowing, learning, and instruction: Essays in honor of Robert Glaser* (pp. 453–494). Hillsdale, NJ: Lawrence Erlbaum.

Davis, E. A. (2003). Prompting middle school science students for productive reflection: Generic and directed prompts. *The Journal of Learning Sciences, 12*(1), 91–142.

Davis, E. A., & Linn, M. C. (2000). Scaffolding students' knowledge integration: Prompts for reflection in KIE. *International Journal of Science Education, 22*(8), 819–837.

Delclos, V., & Harrington, C. (1991). Effects of strategy monitoring and proactive instruction on children's problem-based performance. *Journal of Educational Psychology, 83*, 35–42.

Ericsson, K. A., & Staszewski, J. J. (1989). Skilled memory and expertise: Mechanisms of exceptional performance. In D. Klahr & K. Kotovsky (Eds.), *Complex information processing: The impact of Herbert A. Simon* (pp. 281–299). Hillsdale, NJ: Erlbaum.

Feltovich, P. J., Spiro, R. J., Coulson, R. L., & Feltovich, J. (1996). Collaboration within and among minds: Mastering complexity, individually and in groups. In T. Koschmann (Ed.), *CSCL: Theory and practice of an emerging paradigm* (pp. 25–44). Mahwah, NJ: Lawrence Erlbaum.

Gao, H., Baylor, A. L., & Shen, E. (2005). Designer support for online collaboration and knowledge construction. *Educational Technology & Society, 8*(1), 69–79.

Ge, X., Chen, C.-H., & Davis, K. (2005). Scaffolding novice instructional designers' problem solving processes using question prompts in a web-based learning environment. *Journal of Educational Computing Research, 33*(2), 219–248.

Ge, X., & Land, S. M. (2003). Scaffolding students' problem-solving processes in an ill-structured task using question prompts and peer interactions. *Educational Technology Research and Development, 51*(1), 21–38.

Ge, X., & Land, S. M. (2004). A conceptual framework for scaffolding ill-structured problem-solving processes using question prompts and peer interactions. *Educational Technology Research and Development, 52*(2), 5–22.

Glaser, R., & Chi, M. T. H. (1988). Introduction: What is it to be an expert? In M. T. H. Chi, R. Glaser, & M. J. Farr (Eds.), *The nature of expertise* (pp. xv–xxi). Hillsdale, NJ: Lawrence Erlbaum.

Green, S. B., & Salkind, N. J. (2003). *Using SPSS for Windows and Macintosh: Analyzing and understanding data*. Upper Saddle River, NJ: Prentice Hall.

Hannafin, M., Land, S., & Oliver, K. (1999). Open learning environments: foundations, methods, and models. In C. Reigeluth (Ed.), *Instructional design theories and models* (pp. 115–140). Mahwah, NJ: Lawrence Erlbaum.

Hasselbring, T. S., Goin, L., & Bransford, J. D. (1987). Effective mathematics instruction: Developing automaticity. *Teaching Exceptional Children, 19*(3), 30–33.

Hewitt, J. (2002). From a focus on tasks to a focus on understanding: The cultural transformation of a Toronto classroom. In T. Koschmann, R. Hall, & N. Miyake, (Eds.), *CSCL2: Carrying forward the conversation* (Vol. 2, pp. 11–41). Mahwah, NJ: Lawrence Erlbaum.

Jonassen, D. H. (1999). Designing constructivist learning environments. In C. M. Reigeluth (Ed.), *Instructional design theories and models: A new paradigm of instructional theory* (Vol. 2, pp. 215–239). Mahwah, NJ: Lawrence Erlbaum.

Jonassen, D. H. (2002). Engaging and supporting problem solving in online learning. *Quarterly Review of Distance Education, 3*(1), 1–13.

Jonassen, D. H., Beissner, K., & Yacci, M. (1993). *Structural knowledge: Techniques for representing, conveying, and acquiring structural knowledge*. Hillsdale, NJ: Lawrence Erlbaum.

King, A. (1991). Effects of training in strategic questioning on children's problem-solving performance. *Journal of Educational Psychology, 83*(3), 307–317.

King, A. (1994). Guiding knowledge construction in the classroom: Effects of teaching children how to question and how to explain. *American Educational Research Journal, 31*(2), 338–368.

King, A., & Rosenshine, B. (1993). Effects of guided cooperative questioning on children's knowledge construction. *Journal of Experimental Education, 61*(2), 127–148.

Lajoie, S. (2005). Extending the scaffolding metaphor. *Instructional Science, 33*(5–6), 541–557.

Lee, S. H., Husic, F., Liu, L., & Hofstetter, C. (2006). Assessing knowledge integration in technology enhanced learning in science. Retrieved July 20, 2006, from www.telscenter.org/research/research%20update/AERA2005/LeehusicLiuhofstetter.pdf

Lin, X. (2001). Designing metacognitive activities. *Educational Technology Research & Development, 49*, 23–40.

Linn, M. C. (1992). The computer as learning partner: Can computer tools teach science? In K. Sheingold, L. G. Roberts, & S. M. Malcom (Eds.), *This year in school science 1991: Technology for teaching and learning* (pp. 31–69). Washington, DC: American Association for the Advancement of Science.

Linn, M. C. (1995). Designing computer learning environments for engineering and computer science: The scaffolded knowledge integration framework. *Journal of Science Education and Technology, 4*(2), 103–126.

Linn, M. C. (2005). WISE design for lifelong learning—Pivotal cases. In P. Gärdenfors & P. Johansson (Eds.), *Cognition, education and communication technology.* Mahwah, NJ: Lawrence Erlbaum.

Linn, M. C., Clark, D., & Slotta, J. D. (2003). WISE design for knowledge integration. *Science Education, 87,* 517–538.

Linn, M. C., & Hsi, S. (2000). *Computers, teachers, peers: Science learning partners.* Mahwah, NJ: Lawrence Erlbaum.

Murphy, P. K., & Alexander, P. A. (2002). What counts? The predictive powers of subject-matter knowledge, strategic processing, and interest in domain-specific performance. *The Journal of Experimental Education, 70,* 197–214.

Pressley, M., Wood, E., Woloshyn, V. E., Martin, V., King, A., & Menke, D. (1992). Encouraging mindful use of prior knowledge: Attempting to construct explanatory answers facilitates learning. *Educational Psychologist, 27*(1), 91–109.

Scardamalia, M., & Bereiter, C. (1994). Computer support for knowledge-building communities. *The Journal of the Learning Sciences, 3,* 265–283.

Scardamalia, M., & Bereiter, C. (1996). Computer support for knowledge-building communities. In T. Koschmann (Ed.), *CSCL: Theory and practice of an emerging paradigm* (pp. 249–268). Mahwah, NJ: Lawrence Erlbaum.

Scardamalia, M., & Bereiter, C. (2003). Knowledge building. In J. W. Guthrie (Ed.), *Encyclopedia of education* (2nd ed., pp. 1370–1373). New York, NY: Macmillan Reference Library.

Simon, H. A. (1980). Problem solving and education. In D. T. Tuma & R. Reif (Eds.), *Problem solving and education: Issues in teaching and research* (pp. 81–96). Hillsdale, NJ: Lawrence Erlbaum.

Voss, J. F., Blais, J., Means, M. L., & Greene, T. R. (1986). Informal reasoning and subject matter knowledge in the solving of economics problems by naive and novice individuals. *Cognition and Instruction, 3,* 269–302.

Voss, J. F., Wolfe, C. R., Lawrence, J. A., & Eagle, R. A. (1991). From representation to decision: An analysis of problem solving in international relations. In R. J. Sternberg & P. Frensch (Eds.), *Complex problem solving: Principles and mechanisms* (pp. 119–158). Hillsdale, NJ: Lawrence Erlbaum.

Wineburg, S. (1998). Reading Abraham Lincoln: An expert-expert study in the interpretation of historical texts. *Cognitive Science, 22,* 319–346.

Zimmerman, T. D. (2005). *Prompting knowledge integration of scientific principles and environment stewardship: Assessing an issue-based approach to teaching evolution and marine conservation.* Unpublished doctoral dissertation. University of California, Berkeley, CA.

CHAPTER

10

Effects of Multimedia Software on Achievement of Middle School Students in an American History Class

Karla V. Kingsley | University of New Mexico

Randall Boone | University of Nevada, Las Vegas

This study investigated social studies achievement as a result of utilizing a multimedia-based American history software program (Ignite! Early American History, 2003) to augment textbook and lecture materials for seventh grade middle school history students in an ethnically and linguistically diverse urban school district. The instructional software used was an interactive multimedia program designed to teach middle school students through video, song, animation, text, and other media to develop critical-thinking skills while acquiring knowledge of required content strands (Ignite! Learning, 2003). Teacher and student activities, pretest and posttest scores, and instructional methods for experimental and control conditions were documented in order to provide a comprehensive understanding of the results.

Introduction and Purpose of the Study

While there is a significant body of literature that discusses technology integration in schools and classrooms, there remains a dearth of data-based research specifically addressing the issue of the effectiveness of different types of educational software in relation to student achievement outcomes (Crosier, Cobb, & Wilson, 2002; Mills, 2001; Williams, Boone, & Kingsley, 2004). The National Research Council (2002) and others (Campbell, 1969; Cook, 2001) found repeatedly that although most educational software is commercially produced, "Those with commercial interests are not expected by educators, policy makers or the public to use research to support what they sell" (National Research Council, 2002, p. 96). Consequently, the National Research Council (NRC) explained, "Educators are unlikely to draw on scientific knowledge to improve their practices in any meaningful way" (p. 96). The current culture of high-stakes testing in the United States, with its focus on high expectations and accountability, has sparked renewed interest in identifying effective educational interventions, including computer assisted instruction, that increase student achievement. This investigation adds to the small body of studies utilizing a rigorous, scientifically based research methodology, as defined by the Institute of Education Sciences (IES), to examine student outcomes as a result of a technology intervention within a school setting (Poggi, 2003).

INTERACTIVE MEDIA FOCUS

The term *multimedia* describes any system that combines two or more media into a single product or presentation, such as a software program or a web page. Although interactive multimedia capabilities are constantly evolving and have become very popular among educators in recent years, the body of research on interactive multimedia as an instructional approach is not yet extensive (Alessi & Trollip, 2001; Lockard & Abrams, 2004). According to Mayer (2003), a multimedia instructional message is "a presentation consisting of words and pictures that is designed to foster meaningful learning. Thus, there are two parts to the definition: (a) the presentation contains words and pictures, and (b) the presentation is designed to foster meaningful learning" (p. 128).

Mayer (2003) and others (Brouwer, Muller, & Rietdijk, 2007; Thompson, 2007) have emphasized the unique contributions multimedia brings to the learning experience. There are data to support the assertion that multimedia capabilities are unique because both sensory stimulation and user navigation in interactive multimedia (IMM) parallel students' natural ways of learning (Bagui, 1998; Gibbs, Graves, & Bernas, 2001). Roblyer (1999) asserted that the multiple channels through which multimedia communicates to the learner seem to be the source of its benefits. The sound, images, animation, and interactivity in electronic books have also been shown to increase motivation and comprehension scores as compared to students' reading of printed texts

(Greenlee-Moore & Smith, 1996; Labbo, 2002). According to some researchers (Becker, 2000; Mayer, 2003; Moreno, 2006), interactive multimedia is one of the best technologies to help students learn. Although claims such as this one elicit varying responses among scholars and educators, some research appears to indicate that IMM can indeed provide learning benefits (Hancock, Knezek, & Christensen, 2007).

Media-focused research. Much multimedia research has focused on the specific media employed for instruction. Clark and Mayer (2003) provided a list of several research-based principles for instructional multimedia that focused on media type. For example, their *multimedia* principle discussed the use of text with accompanying graphics as opposed to text alone. Similarly, their *contiguity* principle looked at the proximity and placement of a graphic to its corresponding text. And while much of this research is based on design principles that focus on cognitive processing, especially cognitive load theory (Brünken, Plass, & Leutner, 2003; Mayer, 2005; Moreno & Valdez, 2005; van Merriënboer & Sweller, 2005), priority remains centered on the media elements.

SUPPORTIVE RESOURCE FOCUS

While the instructional modalities of the software used in this study included the expected multimedia components, text remained the predominant vehicle for instruction. Text was incorporated into alternate contexts such as maps, matching problems, text-documented illustrations, document facsimiles, timelines, concurrent text with spoken audio, and karaoke-style song lyrics. With electronic *text transformations* (e.g., timelines, document facsimiles) composing the bulk of the content of the software used in this study, the Clark and Mayer (2003) media-focused theoretical construct prevalent in much previous research did not provide a satisfactory framework for consideration of this software as it was implemented. Rather, a typology of supportive resources developed by Anderson-Inman and Horney (1998, 2007) that describe how the process of reading can be made easier or more educational (Horney & Anderson-Inman, 1999) provided the framework for a functional matrix of the educational resources in the software.

Several of these text transformations closely resembled well-documented instructional strategies (e.g., advance organizers, graphic organizers, visual displays such as timelines, and mnemonic devices) from research into adapting challenging textbooks for students experiencing difficulty in reading (Boone & Higgins, 2005; Higgins & Boone, 2001; Higgins, Boone, & Lovitt, 2002). The overwhelming reliance on text for content delivery in this software suggested an instructional design relying more on a concept of supported electronic text (Anderson-Inman & Horney, 2007) than the traditional media interactions often associated with multimedia.

Typology of resources. A recently revised description of the Anderson-Inman and Horney (2007) typology of resources for supported electronic text included 11 resource types: presentational, navigational, translational, explanatory, illustrative, summarizing, enrichment, instructional, notational, collaborative, and evaluational. Anderson-Inman and Horney stated that the advantage of a typology that does not "focus on what media is being used to modify or enhance the electronic text, but rather what function the supportive resources play in the reading process" (p. 153) is its usefulness for "teachers, students, and parents … to think critically about the modifications, enhancements, and additions they encounter when selecting or reading electronic versions of assigned texts" (p. 154).

Supported electronic text. Overlaying this framework on the supportive resources from the American history software used in this research, a clearer design for instruction emerged. Resources from the Anderson-Inman and Horney (2007) typology that matched the resources provided by the software used in the intervention included the following:

1. Customizable content (Presentational resource)
2. Links to resources and related documents and media (Navigational resource)
3. Alternate versions of content (Translational resource)
4. Descriptions and clarifications of content (Explanatory resource)
5. Visual representations of content (Illustrative resource)
6. Questions and testing (Evaluational resource)

Based on an analysis of the software used in this research, in relation to the two conceptual frameworks discussed (e.g., media focused vs. supportive resource), a construct of supported electronic text emerged to best describe the intervention used in this study. The research, therefore, focused on typical outcome measures associated with content area reading and related learning strategies (Higgins, Boone, & Lovitt, 2002; Readence & Moore, 1992). Indeed, the questioning format utilized in the pretest/posttest phases of this study has been emphasized as a formal and codified reading and comprehension assessment for almost 100 years (Readence & Moore, 1992).

TEACHING HISTORY AND SOCIAL STUDIES

Many of the difficulties students face in content area learning stem from mismatches between the teachers' instructional approaches and students' strategies for cognitive intake and processing of the material presented (Boone & Higgins, 2007; Chapin & Messick, 1999; Higgins, Boone, & Lovitt, 2002). These mismatches, along with disparate levels of literacy development for students within the same grade level, combine to create formidable challenges for the teaching of subject areas where student interest is already low. Mounting evidence suggests that students generally find history and social studies dull and unimportant, that they have difficulty understanding their textbooks, and that overall, they remember very little of what they learned (Ciborowski, 2005; Stetson & Williams, 2005; White, 1999). In fact, social studies and history are rated by middle school students as two of the least favorite subjects in the curriculum (Higgins, Boone, & Lovitt, 2002; Lounsbury, 1988; Shaughnessy & Haladyna, 1985), with only English receiving more negative reviews about the teaching of its content.

TECHNOLOGY-SUPPORTED SOCIAL STUDIES LEARNING

Educational technology and interactive multimedia play an increasingly vital role in efforts to move social studies from the rote memorization of dates and information toward a more student-centered, hands-on, authentic learning experience (Bitter & Pierson, 2005; Trinkle & Merriman, 2000). And despite movements within the discipline to promote student computer use to facilitate reflective inquiry, decision making, and problem solving (Evans, 2004; National Council for the Social Studies, 1994), social studies education for the most part continues to focus on traditional, teacher-directed, lecture-and-textbook-based approaches and activities (Diem, 2000; Friedman & Hicks, 2006; White, 1999).

The research base on the effectiveness of technology as an instructional component for teaching social studies is quite limited (Cantu, 2000). Nonetheless, there are data indicating that when integrated effectively, multimedia technology can support history and social studies learning by promoting student-centered instruction, increasing learner motivation, and extending and deepening understandings of historic and civic concepts (Molebash, 2002). Some studies have reported modest positive outcomes for several groups of students who used computer-adapted tutorial programs for the practice of social studies skills (Twyman & Tindal, 2006). In two research studies conducted a full decade apart, Higgins, Boone, and Lovitt (1996) found that hypermedia study guides resulted in positive gains for ninth grade social studies students with regard to recall, comprehension, and attitudes, while Boon et al. (2006) reported similar results in their investigation of high school students' use of technology-enhanced cognitive organizers.

Method

This study investigated social studies achievement as a result of utilizing a multimedia-based, American history software program to augment textbook and lecture materials for seventh grade middle school history students. Student pretest and posttest scores on a multiple-choice assessment instrument served as the primary data source in this quasi-experimental research design.

THE EARLY AMERICAN HISTORY SOFTWARE

The early American history software used in this study was an online middle school curriculum designed to help students learn the content and skills specified by state and national academic standards in a student-centered, multimedia-rich manner appealing to a wide variety of learning styles and interests (Ignite! Learning, 2003). The software was a type of computer-aided instruction (CAI) that blended networked multimedia technologies for content delivery with tools to aid teachers in tracking student progress and designing individualized instruction based on the program's assessments. The program itself was web browser-based, but self-contained in that it prevented access to the Internet and World Wide Web while the program was running. The software contained 15 units that combined multiple modalities to meet the learning objectives in each unit. The researchers had no relationship with the software company that produced the history program used in the study. A software license was purchased by the school district on a one-year trial basis, during which the district technology coordinator requested that the researchers evaluate the software. The company provided online and on-site technical assistance for the district technology coordinator, classroom teachers, and researchers for the duration of the trial period.

RESEARCH DESIGN

This study sought to examine the correlation between multimedia software use and student outcome scores, specifically whether use of the American history software would significantly raise student achievement scores on a criterion-referenced, standards-based test. Analyses of data from 184 student test scores utilized descriptive and inferential statistical procedures to interpret the outcome-oriented test results. Pretest and posttest scores for students in control and experimental groups were compared using a two-tailed t-test with unequal variance. A two-tailed t-test with unequal variance was implemented because it was unclear at the time of comparison which direction mean test scores would shift and because a two-tailed t-test is more sensitive to changes than a one-tailed t-test.

The study aligned with the criteria for methodology, data collection, analysis, and description for scientifically based research as explicated in the No Child Left Behind Act (NCLB, 2002). Professional literature on NCLB's criteria for scientifically based research (Margolin & Buchler, 2004; NCLB, 2002; Poggi, 2003; U.S. Department of Education, 2005) guided the methodology, with Dawson's (2004) framework providing the overarching criteria for scientifically based research, which included:

1. Empirical methods are used to carry out the research, which is conducted in a systematic and consistent manner, with keen attention to detail.

2. Data collection and analysis are rigorously conducted to ensure that the data are collected, analyzed, and interpreted correctly.

3. Measurements or observational methods that provide scientifically valid and reliable measurements across many different measurement points and observations are used.

4. The studies employ experimental or quasi-experimental methodology to optimize the researchers' ability to answer the questions under investigation.

5. Enough data and description should be provided so that future researchers can attempt to replicate the findings by conducting a study using the same methods and instruments. (p. 5)

PARTICIPANTS

Students. Subjects were seventh grade students enrolled in public middle schools in a large urban school district in the southwestern United States. Students in eight separate sections of seventh grade history, taught by four different teachers in three different middle schools participated in the study. The experimental group of students received treatment (i.e., use of the Ignite! program) in addition to textbook- and lecture-based instruction for all units of early American history study. The control group received textbook and lecture instruction only but did not use the Ignite! program. During both instructional conditions, the same teacher administered textbook- and lecture-based instruction in presenting the same information to both groups of students. The overall sample size was 184 pretests and posttests, obtained from an experimental group comprised of 93 students, and a control group comprising 91 students.

Teachers. Four female teachers participated in the study. The teachers worked at three different middle schools, collectively teaching American history to a total of 637 seventh grade students each day. Each participating teacher taught an experimental group (one full class) of students in which the American history software was used as an instructional supplement, as well as a control group (a different class) in which the software was not used. This ensured that both control and experimental group students had the same teacher, helping to reduce the chance of sampling bias. The average age of the teachers was 35 years, with an average of 9.5 years of teaching experience. Descriptive information about the participating teachers (names are pseudonyms) is shown in Table 10.1. Table 10.2 provides information about the schools participating in the study (names are pseudonyms).

Table 10.1 Descriptive Data for Participating Teachers (all are pseudonyms)

Teacher Name	Middle School	Age	Years Teaching	Highest Degree
Romero	Samuels	30	5	B.A.
Gage	Hawthorne	55	26	M.A.
Smith	Hawthorne	31	7	M.A.
Brown	Jackson	24	0	B.A.

Table 10.2 Middle School Student Demographic Info (all are pseudonyms)

Teacher Name	Middle School	% of LEP Students	% of IEP Students	% Eligible for Free or Reduced Lunch
Romero	Samuels	22.5	11.2	61.8
Gage	Hawthorne	17.5	12.0	48.6
Smith	Hawthorne	17.5	12.0	48.6
Brown	Jackson	6.7	12.2	31.7

Setting. The study was conducted in a large, rapidly growing school district in the Southwest, in which approximately 40.4% of seventh grade students qualified to receive free or reduced lunch, 14.92% of seventh graders were non-English proficient or had limited English proficiency, and 11.1% received special education services under an individualized education program (IEP). The district's student population was approximately 14% African American, 33.4% Hispanic, and 43.9% Caucasian. However, two of the three schools included in this study had a higher than average rate of seventh graders eligible to receive free or reduced lunch: 50.7% and 61.8%, with minority populations of 61.6% and 56.2% respectively. The schools that participated in the study were geographically distributed throughout the district, with every effort made to select equivalent teachers and students for the treatment and control groups who were representative of the district's typical student population.

Eligibility for school participation. In selecting the sites for the study, participation was limited to schools with adequate technology infrastructure, computer facilities, and interested teachers. This decision was made after reviewing findings from a pilot study (Kingsley, 2003) to determine potential difficulties and problems associated with implementing the program in schools on a larger scale. Results from the pilot study indicated that schools lacking high-speed, high-capacity server and networking capabilities were frequently plagued with server and workstation crashes, software freezes, very slow response time, and/or inability for students to run all of the media segments contained in the program. As random selection of participating schools was not possible, the decision was made to follow Stake's (2000) heuristic that in some cases, the opportunity to learn from a site should take priority over concern for its typicality of an entire population.

Teacher training. At the start of the school year, all participating teachers attended mandatory introductory training that provided an overview of the American history software and familiarized the teachers with available content and media options. In the training session teachers learned how to construct assignments, select assessments, create new sections for classes using the program, create student logins and passwords, and locate and use the multimedia options.

At the start of the school year, the teachers conducted an orientation session to show students in the experimental groups how to log in to the program and set their passwords and demonstrated the program's content options and navigational aids. At that time, the students were given teacher-facilitated, hands-on time to familiarize themselves with login procedures and with the program's interface, functionality, and media choices prior to commencement of actual instruction. Additionally, all students in the experimental and control groups received an overview of the history textbook to be used in the course, an outline of the seventh grade history curriculum, and a syllabus for the entire history course.

DATA COLLECTION

Procdure. Prior to using the American history software, each participating teacher designated one of her classes to be a treatment group, and another, similar class as a control group of students. In all cases, the treatment and control classes were inclusive, homogeneous, general education seventh grade history classes to which students had been assigned independently of teacher or researcher oversight or influence. The overall sample size was 184 pretests and posttests, obtained from an experimental group comprising 93 students, and a control group comprising 91 students. Every effort was made to select groups that would be as similar as possible; however, the use of intact classrooms often results in Non-Equivalent Group Design (NEGD). NEGD, a common feature of social and educational research, is particularly susceptible to internal validity and selection maturation threats, which require further statistical analyses (Hancock, Knezek, & Christensen, 2007). Two additional reliability tests for internal consistency (e.g., Split-Half Correlation and Cronbach's Alpha) were conducted to support and validate the findings of this study.

Instructional Conditions. The experimental group of students received treatment (i.e., use of the American history software) in addition to textbook and lecture-based instruction for all units of study. The control group received textbook and lecture instruction but did not use the American history software. During both instructional conditions, the same teacher administered textbook and lecture-based instruction in presenting the same information to both groups of students.

With the treatment group students, teachers reserved a minimum of 20% of the instructional time, or approximately one day per week, for use of the American history software. Regular textbook instruction consisted of using either *The American Journey* (Appleby, Brinkley & McPherson, 2003), or *The American Nation* (Davidson, Castillo, & Stoff, 2002). Both district-approved books were similar in content, scope, and sequence of information. The textbooks included graphic organizers and other visual aids, such as timelines, photographs and illustrations, and political maps, as well as vocabulary lists, chapter outlines, and chapter summaries. Teachers supplemented book-based instruction with online and offline auxiliary activities provided by the textbook publishers, as well as with their own materials, worksheets, and selected websites. No other instructional software programs were used for history instruction during the study. As specified by district policy, students had a copy of their history textbook at home, and each classroom had another set for student use at school. Students were unable to access the American history software from home. In both the experimental and control groups, the curriculum requirements were identical and were based on the state history standards scope and sequence.

The procedure for both instructional groups from pretest to posttest conditions lasted approximately seven months. Classes consisted of 50-minute block periods encompassing daily review, learning objectives, presentation of new information, and in some cases independent practice. On days the software was used by students in the experimental groups, class sessions consisted of students navigating through the assigned lesson in any order and at their own pace, provided that they viewed all of the media contained in the assigned module. After viewing the media pieces for the assignment, students completed a Topic Review: a six-item multiple-choice assessment built into each lesson. Scores from the Topic Reviews were not used for the current study; rather, they served as an instructional focal point for students while they used the program. In each 50-minute class period where the software was used, students were able to complete one full lesson and its accompanying Topic Review. Upon completion of the early American history portion of the history course, student participants were given the 50-item posttest to measure their knowledge and recall of major concepts related to the period of American history from 1492 to 1877 (i.e., the period of Reconstruction).

Instrument. Because the quizzes and topic reviews contained in the software were closely tied to that specific content, they were not used as a measure of achievement for the study. Rather, an independent, criterion-referenced pretest was administered to all participating students at the onset of the seventh grade school year. Material on the pretest consisted of knowledge required to master the seventh grade history curriculum as outlined by state standards. The full pretest instrument consisted of 50 multiple-choice questions based on the state's scope and sequence history standards. An identical posttest was administered at the conclusion of the seven-month instructional period.

The multiple-choice pretest-posttest instrument included questions drawn from a test bank of 4,500 questions accompanying *The American Journey* (Appleby, Brinkley & McPherson, 2003) history textbook, as well as questions contributed by several history teachers in the participating middle schools. Because multiple-choice tests tend to focus on basic facts and are not always good measures of higher level cognitive processing (Becker, 1992), some multiple-choice questions on the pretest and posttest were adjusted slightly to facilitate problem solving, decision making, and/or higher order thinking skills related to the concepts covered in the history knowledge being tested. The pretest-posttest instrument was compiled by three researchers with experience in designing and conducting education research and evaluation who were familiar with this research project. Reliability checks on the instrument were conducted independently by the test designers, and discrepancies were discussed and assessed to obtain 100% agreement. In addition, due to the identification of NEGD in this study, two additional post hoc reliability tests for measuring internal consistency were performed on this instrument. The first test, a Split-Half Correlation, randomly divides all the instrument items into two sets and measures the correlation between the total scores for each randomly divided half of the questions, which resulted in a high internal validity score ($\alpha = .99$) that greatly exceeds the acceptable standard, $\alpha > 0.90$. The second, Cronbach's Alpha, which tends to be a more stringent test, revealed high reliability for the control ($\alpha = .98$) and experimental groups ($\alpha = .99$), as well as the comparison of all groups using the pretest analysis ($\alpha = .98$). The instrument's concurrent validity with questions from the test bank of questions drawn from the district-approved textbook *The American Journey* was checked and obtained a high validity coefficient (.87). The instrument was examined and approved by the district technology coordinator, the district social studies coordinator, and two of the most experienced participating history teachers for content validity to ensure high correlation with the scope and sequence of American history content as specified in the state curriculum standards. It was then pilot tested with a small sample of doctoral students before the study began.

USE OF THE AMERICAN HISTORY SOFTWARE

Throughout this study, qualitative data were collected to document the degree of fidelity with which the history software was used by all participating teachers and students. Weekly classroom observations were augmented by conversations and informal interviews with the teachers throughout the seven-month investigation period. Transcripts from observations and teacher interviews revealed that each of the participating teachers used the program for the equivalent of one class period per week throughout the period of investigation.

Students used the history software in a computer lab where they had access to their own computers and were free to work through the assigned modules at their own pace. On occasion, the history classes were usurped by another group of students who needed to use the computer lab. In these cases the teachers requested an extra day the following week in order to recoup the missed lab time. On a few occasions when the computer lab was occupied on their assigned lab day, the teachers used the American history software as a teacher-directed, whole-class instructional tool. In these rare cases, the teacher led a discussion of the materials and showed the media pieces to the students on a large projection screen in the class, while students took notes or completed an outline of the material covered. However, the vast majority of time spent using the American history software was weekly time in the computer lab with students engaged one-to-one with the program on a computer, setting their own pace and using the media pieces in any order they preferred.

DATA ANALYSIS

Descriptive and inferential statistics, including mean, standard deviation, and two-tailed t-tests, were used on the pretest and posttest scores for students in the experimental and control groups. Statistical analyses were conducted using the Statistical Product and Service Solutions (SPSS) software to determine the significance of variables related to the research question. According to Valdez (2004), educational researchers, especially those who have conducted meta-analyses, agree that when used appropriately, technology can improve education in the effect-size range of between 0.30 and 0.40 (Kulik, 2002). Cohen (1977) classified effect sizes of around 0.2 as small, around 0.5 as moderate, and around 0.8 as large (p. 1). In order to obtain a power rating of .80 with an effect size of .50 (moderate effect), there needed to be at least 50 students in each of the control and treatment groups, assuming use of a two-tailed test with an alpha of .025 (Gay & Airasian, 2000). With sample numbers of more than 50 for each group, it was possible to measure lesser effects. Two-tailed t-tests were used because it was unknown whether effects from using the American history software would be positive or negative.

Results

This investigation examined whether there was a statistically significant difference between pretest and posttest achievement scores for students who used the American history software compared to students who did not use the program. Using the computer software program Statistical Product and Service Solutions (SPSS), descriptive and inferential statistics were compiled from the pretest and posttest scores of students in control and experimental groups. The mean scores of control and experimental groups on pretests and posttests were calculated, then compared using a two-tailed t-test with unequal variance.

Pretest

For students in the pretest control group ($n = 91$), the average number of correct answers was 33.60 out of 50 total questions with a standard deviation of 5.30, while the average number of correct answers for all students in the pretest experimental group ($n = 93$) was 30.95 out of 50 total questions, with a standard deviation of 6.12. In other words, students in the control group had a 67.2% pretest average for correct answers, while students in the experimental group had a pretest average of 61.9% for correct answers.

Posttest

At the end of the instructional period being studied, the average number of correct answers for students in the posttest control group ($n = 91$) was 36.66 out of a total of 50 questions with a standard deviation of 5.58, the equivalent of 73.32% correct, while the average number of correct answers for students in the posttest experimental group ($n = 93$) was 37.04 of 50 total questions with a standard deviation of 5.51, the equivalent of 74.07% correct.

The mean posttest scores indicated that students who used American history software, as well as those who did not use it, both increased their test scores from pretest to posttest conditions. These data describe the classic "selection-maturation threat" potential of any NEGD project, in which improvement was observed in both the "non-equal" experimental and control groups. However, examination of the percentage increase between pretest control and pretest experimental groups to posttest control and posttest experimental group revealed that students in the control group increased their mean test scores an average of 6.1%, while students in the experimental group increased their mean test scores an average of 12.2%, or approximately twice as much. This difference in mean test scores was statistically significant. Moreover, although the reliability measures (i.e., Split-Half, Cronbach's Alpha) demonstrated reliability for all groups for the pretest–posttest reliability was significantly reduced ($\alpha = 0.48$), providing further evidence that suggests the experimental treatment was sufficient to significantly alter the outcomes measured by this instrument.

The significance level associated with the difference in test score results between the control and experimental groups was less than 0.01%. The question less confidently answered was the likelihood of attribution of the treatment to the 12.2% mean test score increase for students in the experimental group versus the 6.1% mean test score increase for students in the control group.

Discussion

This section addresses the research question: Was there a significant difference between pretest and posttest achievement scores for students who used the American history software as compared to students who did not use the program? Results indicated statistically significant positive effects on overall achievement scores for students who used the American history software. Mean test scores for students who used the software improved by 12.2% and an average of 6.09 more correct answers from pretest to posttest, while mean scores for control group students improved by 6.1%, an average of 3.06 more correct answers from pretest to posttest. The significance level in a statistical study is the risk associated with not being 100% confident that what was observed in an experiment or quasi-experiment was due to the treatment or what was being tested. In this case the treatment was student usage of the American history software program. Since the impact of all other potential factors on the differences observed between outcomes of treatment and control groups cannot be eliminated confidently, some level of probability (i.e., the p value) is assigned and reported. On a two-tailed t-test of unequal variance, a very high level of significance was found, $p = 0.0000000337623$, where p represents the probability that the increase in mean test scores was attributable to something other than use of the American history software. The data suggest that the difference in outcome scores for students in the experimental group was likely due to their use of the American history software.

In addition to reporting outcomes and probability levels for errors, studies conducted in consonance with the No Child Left Behind (2002) definition for scientifically based research must also report the effect size and statistical power of a study. Statistical power is related to the variance: the smaller the variation relative to each group (e.g., between the experimental and control groups), the larger a sample size must be in order to obtain a high power rating. The power of a statistical hypothesis test measures the test's ability to reject the null hypothesis when it is actually false—that is, to make a correct decision (Hinkle, Wiersma, & Jurs, 1998). Obviously, the higher the power rating, the more reliable the statistical test. The maximum power a test can have is 1, and the minimum is 0. Ideally, researchers would strive to have a high power or a number close to 1. In this study, for the control group of students the power was 0.965, and for the experimental group the power was 1.00. In other words, there was a 96.5% statistical likelihood that the two-tailed t-test was able to detect the effects for the control group of students, and a 100% chance that it was able to detect the effects for the experimental group. Consequently, it can be asserted that the results of the two-tailed t-test on both the control and experimental groups yielded valid, reliable results. Overall, results of this quasi-experiment suggest a strong link between use of a technology-enhanced intervention and higher outcome achievement scores for this group of middle school learners.

LIMITATIONS OF THE STUDY

Because participants in this study were not randomly selected but were instead part of a cohort, the generalizability of the results to similar student populations is considered lower than if the sampling process had been completely random. The non-experimental group design (NEGD) of this study precludes the drawing of causal inferences. Generalizability may also be limited by the fact that all of the participating teachers were female.

IMPLICATIONS AND FUTURE RESEARCH

This study was designed and conducted in consonance with criteria specified in the No Child Left Behind Act's (2002) definition of scientifically based research. With instructional technology playing an increasingly central role in all academic areas, more research, and more effective approaches are needed to document student achievement related to computer-based training and educational programs (Bull, Knezek, Roblyer, Schrum, & Thompson, 2005; U.S. Department of Education, 2005). This study adds to the body of scientifically based research literature on student achievement directly linked to the use of educational software. Bull et al. describe the compelling need for this sort of research by stating "[t]o date there have been no documented systemic increases in student achievement and learning directly attributable to technological innovation" (p. 218). They add, "[t]here is no area in which well-conceived and effectively implemented research could be of greater value than in the area of [educational] technological innovation" (p. 218). The current study responds to calls for accountability from scholars, policymakers, and educators at all levels for rigorous evidence indicating whether technology investments can truly support student learning (Jones et al., 2004–2005) in educational settings. Furthermore, this study adds to the very limited body of research on the effectiveness of technology as a component for teaching social studies (Cantu, 2000; Diem, 2000).

Results of this study suggest several potential directions for further exploration. One possible avenue for investigation addresses concerns that a major shortcoming of scholarly literature on the efficacy of technology in education is that the research varies tremendously in methodology, sampling, and focus. Researchers (Kirkpatrick & Cuban, 1998; Waxman, Lin & Michko, 2003) have documented studies with large variations in sampling, such as differences in student grade levels, socioeconomic classes, and aptitudes. The current study employed a quasi-experimental methodology that implemented all NCLB criteria for scientifically based research, including a disparate sampling of teachers and students from the school district, and a strong emphasis on using the instructional intervention with fidelity. An experimental research design employing in-depth qualitative and quantitative data analyses would provide greater insight into the causal factors surrounding the differences in student achievement, while also providing information related to the processes teachers use to integrate new technology into their existing curriculum.

In the current study, the data suggest that use of a software program affected student achievement scores on a standards-based, multiple-choice test; however, many questions about the effects of educational software on student learning remain unanswered. Another possible direction for further research would be to investigate gains in student achievement if the program were to be used with students for more than the 20% of instructional time implemented in this study. For instance, students who did not use the software showed an average mean test score increase of around 6%, while those who used the program had mean test score increases of about 12%, or twice as much. It would be interesting to investigate what might happen if software usage were increased to 25%, or even to 50% of instructional time. Would students continue to show gains on standardized assessments, or would a point of diminishing returns be reached?

Final directions for further investigation include exploring whether test score increases attributed to use of the history software would be enough to truly make a difference in whether students pass their seventh grade history courses (i.e., practical significance vs. statistical significance) and whether knowledge gained from use of the software transfers to more complex learning tasks outside the context of a standardized written examination.

Author Update

This research was set squarely in the midst of the first decade of No Child Left Behind. With the national educational narrative focusing more directly on student outcomes and with those outcomes linked to the effectiveness of practices implemented in schools, we set out to anchor this research in a school-based setting that could realistically support the technology-based intervention without removing it from the day-to-day milieu of a typical urban middle school. Likewise, the study served to invigorate our interest in the myriad challenges and problematic circumstances encountered while conducting school-based empirical research that is largely grounded in classical (quantitative) measures of knowledge and learning (Schuman, 2004). Success in the classroom environment was viewed as different from, but equally as important as, validation of an effective instructional design implemented in a more clinical setting. Holding on to our school-based theme, we chose a fully developed and commercially available product to study. This is a departure from much published research in our field but fits nicely within a "use-inspired" basic research model (Stokes, 1997), contending that the gap between basic and applied research exists as a continuum, with many overlapping questions to be investigated. And while many caveats might be raised for considering either school-based empirical research or a study utilizing commercial educational materials, we believe the results of this study successfully informed questions of both applied and basic research foci in this particular area.

References

Alessi, S. M., & Trollip, S. R. (2001). *Multimedia for learning: Methods and development* (3rd ed.). Boston, MA: Allyn & Bacon.

Anderson-Inman, L., & Horney, M. (1998). Transforming text for at-risk readers. In D. Reinking, L. D. Labbo, M. C. McKenna, & R. D. Kieffer (Eds.), *Handbook of literacy and technology: Transformations in a post-typographic world* (pp. 15–43). Mahwah, NJ: Lawrence Erlbaum.

Anderson-Inman, L., & Horney, M. (2007). Supported etext: Assistive technology through text transformations. *Reading Research Quarterly, 42*(1), 153–160.

Appleby, J., Brinkley, A., & McPherson, J. M. (2003). *The American journey.* New York, NY: Glencoe McGraw-Hill.

Bagui, S. (1998). Reasons for increased learning using multimedia. *Journal of Educational Multimedia and Hypermedia, 7*(1), 3–18.

Becker, H. J. (1992). Integrated learning systems and their alternatives: Problems and cautions. *Educational Technology, 32*, 51–57.

Becker, H. J. (2000). Findings from the Teaching, Learning, and Computing survey: Is Larry Cuban right? *Education Policy Analysis Archives 8*(51). Available at http://epaa.asu.edu/ojs/article/view/442

Bitter, G. G., & Pierson, M. E. (2005). *Using Technology in the Classroom* (6th ed.). Boston, MA: Pearson Education.

Boon, R. T., Burke, M., Fore, C., & Spencer, V. (2006). The impact of cognitive organizers and technology-based practices on student success in secondary social studies classrooms. *Journal of Special Education Technology, 21*(1), 5–15.

Boone, R., & Higgins, K. (2005). Designing digital materials for students with disabilities. In D. Edyburn, K. Higgins, & R. Boone (Eds.), *Handbook of special education technology research and practice* (pp. 481–492). Whitefish Bay, WI: Knowledge by Design.

Boone, R., & Higgins, K. (2007). The role of instructional design in assistive technology research and development. *Reading Research Quarterly, 42*(1), 135–140.

Brouwer, N., Muller, G., & Rietdijk, H. (2007). Educational designing with MicroWorlds. *Journal of Technology and Teacher Education, 15*(4), 439–462.

Brünken, R., Plass, J., & Leutner, D. (2003). Direct measurement of cognitive load. *Educational Psychologist, 38*(1), 53–61.

Bull, G., Knezek, G., Roblyer, M. D., Schrum, L., & Thompson, A. (2005). A proactive approach to a research agenda for educational technology. *Journal of Research on Technology in Education, 37*, 217–220.

Campbell, D. T. (1969). Reforms as experiments. *American Psychologist, 24*, 409–429.

Cantu, D. A. (2000). Technology integration in pre-service history teacher education. *Journal of the Association for History and Computing, 3*(2). Available at http://quod.lib.umich.edu/cgi/p/pod/dod-idx?c=jahc;idno=3310410.0003.210

Chapin, J. R., & Messick, R. G. (1999). *Elementary Social Studies* (4th ed.). New York, NY: Longman.

Ciborowski, J. (2005). Textbooks and the students who can't read them. In G. Moss (Ed.), *Critical reading in the content areas* (pp. 206–216). Dubuque, IA: McGraw-Hill/Dushkin.

Clark, R. C., & Mayer, R. (Eds.). (2003). *E-learning and the science of instruction: Proven guidelines for consumers and designers of multimedia learning.* San Francisco, CA: Pfeiffer.

Cohen, J. (1977). *Statistical Power Analysis for the Behavioral Sciences* (2nd ed.). New York, NY: Academic Press.

Cook, J. (2001). Bridging the gap between empirical data on open-ended tutorial interactions and computational models.

International Journal of Artificial Intelligence in Education, 12(1), 85–99.

Crosier, J., Cobb, S., & Wilson, J. (2002). Key lessons for the design and integration of virtual environments in secondary science. *Computers & Education, 38*, 77–94.

Davidson, J. W., Castillo, P., & Stoff, M. B. (2002). *The American Nation*. Upper Saddle River, NJ: Prentice Hall.

Dawson, M. (2004). NCREL Quick Key No. 7: A foundation for understanding and evaluating scientifically based research. *Educational Technology News, 4*(1), 5. Naperville, IL: North Central Regional Educational Laboratory.

Diem, R. A. (2000). Can it make a difference? Technology and the social studies. *Theory & Research in Social Education, 28*(4), 493–501.

Evans, R. W. (2004). *The social studies wars: What should we teach the children?* New York, NY: Teachers College Press.

Friedman, A. M., & Hicks, D. (2006). Guest editorial: The state of the field: Technology, social studies, and teacher education. *Contemporary Issues in Technology in Teacher Education, 6*, 246–258.

Gay, L. R., & Airasian, P. (2000). *Educational research: Competencies for analysis and application* (6th ed.). Upper Saddle River, NJ: Prentice Hall.

Gibbs, W., Graves, P., & Bernas, R. (2001). Educational guidelines for multimedia courseware. *Journal of Research on Technology and Education, 34*(1), 2–18.

Greenlee-Moore, M. E., & Smith, L. L. (1996). Interactive computer software: The effects on young children's reading achievement. *Reading Psychology, 17*(1), 43–64.

Hancock, R., Knezek, G., & Christensen, R. (2007). Cross-validating measures of technology integration: A first step toward examining potential relationships between technology integration and student achievement. *Journal of Computing in Teacher Education, 24*(1), 15–21.

Higgins, K., & Boone, R. (2001). Adapting instruction for children with disabilities. In L. W. Searfoss & J. E. Readence (Eds.), *Helping children learn to read: Creating a classroom literacy environment* (4th ed. pp. 330–365). Boston, MA: Allyn and Bacon.

Higgins, K., Boone, R., & Lovitt, T. (1996). Hypertext support for remedial students and students with learning disabilities. *Journal of Learning Disabilities, 29*(4), 402–412.

Higgins, K., Boone, R., & Lovitt, T. C. (2002). Adapting challenging textbooks to improve content area learning. In G. Stoner, M. R. Shinn, & H. Walker (Eds.), *Interventions for achievement and behavior problems* (2nd ed., pp. 755–790). Silver Spring, MD: National Association for School Psychologists.

Hinkle, D. E., Wiersma, W., & Jurs, S. G. (1998). *Applied Statistics for the Behavioral Sciences* (4th ed.). Boston, MA: Houghton Mifflin Company.

Horney, M., & Anderson-Inman, L. (1999). Supported text in electronic reading environments. *Reading and Writing Quarterly, 15*(2), 127–168.

Ignite! Early American History. (2003). [Computer software]. Austin, TX: Ignite! Learning.

Ignite! Learning. (2003). *Teaching students in the ways they learn best: The Ignite! method of instructional design*. Retrieved January 22, 2005, from www.ignitelearning.com/methodology.shtml

Jones, J. D., Staats, W. D., Bowling, N., Bickel, R. D., Cunningham, M. L., & Cadle, C., (2004–2005). An evaluation of the Merit Reading Software Program in the Calhoun County (WV) Middle/High School. *Journal of Research on Technology in Education, 37*(2), 177–195.

Kingsley, K. V. (2003). *Evaluating the viability of the Ignite! Early America History program in middle schools: A pilot study*. Unpublished manuscript, University of Nevada, Las Vegas.

Kirkpatrick, H., & Cuban, L. (1998). Computers make kids smarter—right? *Technos Quarterly, 7*(2). Available at www.ait.net/technos/tq_07/2cuban.php

Kulik, J. A. (2002). *School mathematics and science programs benefit from instructional technology* (InfoBrief). Washington, DC: National Science Foundation. Available at www.nsf.gov/statistics/infbrief/nsf03301/

Labbo, L. (2002). Computers, kids, and comprehension: Instructional practices that make a difference. In C. C. Block, L. B. Gambrell, & M. Pressley, (Eds.), *Improving comprehension instruction: Rethinking research, theory, and classroom practice* (pp. 275–289). San Francisco, CA: Jossey-Bass.

Lockard, J., & Abrams, P. D. (2004). *Computers for twenty-first century educators* (6th ed.). Boston, MA: Allyn & Bacon.

Lounsbury, J. (1988). Middle-level social studies: Points to ponder. *Social Education, 52*(2), 116–118.

Margolin, J., & Buchler, B. (2004). *Critical Issue: Using scientifically based research to guide educational decisions.* Naperville, IL: North Central Regional Educational Laboratory. Retrieved on January 10, 2005, from www.ncrel.org/sdrs/areas/issues/envrnmnt/go/go900.htm

Mayer, R. E. (2003). The promise of multimedia learning: Using the same instructional design methods across different media. *Learning and Instruction, 13*, 125–139.

Mayer, R. E. (2005). Introduction to multimedia learning. In R. E. Mayer (Ed.), *The Cambridge handbook of multimedia learning* (pp. 1–18). New York, NY: Cambridge University Press.

Mills, R. J. (2001). Analyzing instructional software using a computer-tracking system. *Information Technology, Learning, and Performance Journal, 19*(1), 21–30.

Molebash, P. E. (2002). Constructivism meets technology integration: The CUFA technology guidelines in an elementary social studies methods course. *Theory and Research on Social Education, 30*(3), 429–455.

Moreno, R. (2006). Learning with high tech and multimedia environments. *Current Directions, 15*, 63–67.

Moreno, R., & Valdez, A. (2005). Cognitive load and learning effects of having students organize pictures and words in multimedia environments: The role of student interactivity and feedback. *Educational Technology Research & Development, 53*(3), 35–45.

National Council for the Social Studies. (1994). *Expectations of excellence: Curriculum Standards for Social Studies.* Washington, DC: Author.

National Research Council. (2002). *Scientific research in education.* Washington, DC: National Academy Press.

No Child Left Behind Act of 2001, Pub. L. No. 107–110, 115 Stat. 1425. (2002). Retrieved December 1, 2007, from www.ed.gov/policy/elsec/leg/esea02/index.html

Poggi, S. (2003). *Wake-up call: Facing the challenge to use scientifically based research in schools.* Naperville, IL: North Central Regional Educational Laboratory. Retrieved January 10, 2005, from www.ncrel.org/info/nlp/lpsp03/index.html

Readence, J. E., & Moore, D. W. (1992). Why questions? A historical perspective on standardized reading comprehension tests. In E. K. Dishner, T. W. Bean, J. E. Readence, & D. W. Moore (Eds.), *Reading in the content areas* (3rd ed., pp. 390–398). Dubuque, IA: Kendall/Hunt Publishing Company.

Roblyer, M. D. (1999). Our multimedia future: Recent research on multimedia's impact on education. *Learning & Leading with Technology, 26*(6), 51–54.

Schuman, D. (2004). American Schools, *American Teachers: Issues and Perspectives.* Boston, MA: Pearson.

Shaughnessy, J. M., & Haladyna, T. M. (1985). *Research on student attitudes toward social studies. Social Education, 49*, 692–695.

Stake, R. (2000). Case studies. In N. K. Denzin & Y. S. Lincoln (Eds.) *Handbook of qualitative research* (2nd ed., pp. 435–454). Thousand Oaks, CA: Sage.

Stetson, E., & Williams, R. (2005). Learning from social studies textbooks: Why some students succeed and others fail. In G. Moss (Ed.), *Critical reading in the content areas* (pp. 135–142). Dubuque, IA: McGraw-Hill/ Dushkin.

Stokes, D. E. (1997). *Pasteur's Quadrant–Basic Science and Technological Innovation.* Washington, DC: Brookings Institution Press.

Thompson, A. (2007). Scientifically based research: Establishing a research agenda for the technology and teacher education community. *Journal of Research on Technology in Education, 37*(4), 331–338.

Trinkle, D. A., & Merriman, S. A. (2000). *The history highway 2000: A guide to Internet resources* (2nd ed.). Armonk, NY: M.E. Sharpe.

Twyman, T., & Tindal, G. (2006). Using a computer-adapted, conceptually based history text to increase comprehension and problem-solving skills of students with disabilities. *Journal of Special Education Technology, 21*(2), 5–16.

U.S. Department of Education. (2005). *Toward a new golden age in American education: How the Internet, the law and today's students are revolutionizing expectations.* Washington, DC: Office of Educational Technology.

Valdez, G. (2004). *Critical issue: Technology leadership: Enhancing positive educational change.* Naperville, IL: North Central Regional Educational Laboratory. Retrieved January 3, 2006, from www.ncrel.org/sdrs/areas/issues/educatrs/leadrshp/le700.htm

van Merriënboer, J. G., & Sweller, J. (2005). Cognitive load theory and complex learning systems: Recent developments and future directions. *Educational Psychology Review, 17*(2), 147–177.

Waxman, H. C., Lin, M., & Michko, G. M. (2003). *A meta-analysis of the effectiveness of teaching and learning with technology on student outcomes.* Naperville, IL: Learning Point Associates.

White, C. W. (1999). *Transforming Social Studies Education: A Critical Perspective.* Springfield, IL: Charles C. Thomas.

Williams, D. W, Boone, R., & Kingsley, K. V. (2004). Teacher beliefs about educational software: A Delphi study. *Journal of Research on Technology in Education, 36*(3), 213–230.

CHAPTER

11

The Effect of Electronic Scaffolding for Technology Integration on Perceived Task Effort and Confidence of Primary Student Teachers

Charoula Angeli | University of Cyprus
Nicos Valanides | University of Cyprus

Forty-one primary student teachers were divided into two groups and were instructed how to integrate certain Information and Communication Technology (ICT) tools in learning activities. Only one group was guided to use Filamentality, a fill-in-the-blank interactive website, and to organize Internet information in a Hotlist and a Scrapbook. Questionnaires were administered to collect data related to students' perceived task effort (PTE) as a result of integrating ICT in the learning environment, and their confidence levels in using ICT tools, while their initial attitudes toward ICT and its integration in the classroom were taken into consideration. The results indicated that Filamentality effectively scaffolded particular aspects of ICT integration in learning and instruction, and significantly reduced learners' amount of PTE, but there was not always a significant effect on learners' self-reported confidence levels.

Introduction

Cognitive theorists unanimously agree that the capacity of working memory is severely limited in the amount of information that can be processed. This means that the amount of information presented to learners, the difficulty of the material, and the format in which the material is presented are factors that may inhibit or assist learners in cognitively processing the information (Baddeley, 1986, 1999; Chandler & Sweller, 1996; Mayer, 2001). In technology-enhanced environments, Information and Communication Technology (ICT; the term ICT is broadly used to include the Internet, the World Wide Web, and all computer-based technologies) is a tool with certain affordances that is used to present information to students and a tool that students can use to complete learning tasks. The notion of affordances is based on the concept of "tool mediation" that stems from Vygotsky's work (Cole & Engestrom, 1993). In the context of ICT, the concept of "tool" embraces both symbolic objects, such as language and mathematics, and physical objects, such as computers and associated software (Gibson, 1982). Thus, affordances are function-oriented properties that relate to properties intentionally designed into the object, or to properties that can be creatively attributed to the object in certain situations. Basically, affordances describe applications, limitations, and/or implications that relate to how a tool can be used. Technological tools that are employed in the learning environment may facilitate or inhibit students' cognitive engagement in the learning process, depending on their affordances (Gibson, 1982).

For these reasons, the concepts of cognitive load and Perceived Task Effort (PTE) seem to be highly relevant to and important for the task of integrating ICT tools in an educational context. Cognitive load theory views the limitations of working memory to be an impediment to learning and attempts to improve the quality of instructional design by considering the role and limitations of working memory (Sweller, 1994). If the amount of cognitive load exceeds learners' mental resources, then learning will be impeded. Thus, when cognitive load is high, efforts should be directed toward instructional design manipulations for lowering cognitive load, so that it falls to a level within the bounds of learners' mental resources. PTE is closely related to cognitive load, and, as it is operationalized in this paper, represents the level of effort a learner estimates that he or she expended over a period of time in order to complete an assigned task (Locke, Shaw, Saari, & Latham, 1981; Mohr & Bitner, 1995). Whereas cognitive load is measured in terms of the mental effort a learner perceives at *an instance in time* as he or she is still learning, PTE is measured *in retrospect* as the learner estimates it after the completion of a task. The bottom line is that both the cognitive load and the PTE need to be considered when designing ICT-enhanced learning activities.

According to Chandler and Sweller (1996), the use of ICT tools creates an additional cognitive load related to the tools to be learned. If learners are not experienced users of ICT, then ICT integration will make considerable demands on learners' cognitive processing activities. Several other researchers (de Jong et al., 1999) define the total cognitive load imposed in an ICT-enhanced learning environment in terms of (a) subject matter difficulty (is the subject matter easy or difficult?), (b) ICT usage (is working with the ICT tools easy or difficult?), and (c) instructional use of ICT (do ICT tools make the learning task easier or more difficult?). Thus, three different sources of PTE are also present in a learning situation corresponding to each one of the defined sources of cognitive load.

Of interest to the issues of cognitive load and PTE is the Internet as a tool that a teacher can use to locate useful information and use it in the design of instructional activities. Jonassen (2000a) argues that the World Wide Web (web) has so many interesting topics to explore that it is easy for learners to lose awareness of where they are in cyberspace. Hence, even though the web offers individuals a wealth of information that can be used to support the curriculum, they often become frustrated with the quantity of resources and the time needed to actually identify the best websites to use in learning (International Society for Technology in Education, 2002). Similarly, when individuals use the web as a tool of inquiry, they may experience a heavy cognitive load, because they may become overwhelmed by the vast amount of information they need to assimilate, or even accommodate, in their knowledge schemata. These individuals are expected to report high PTE after completing the task.

Research and theory on learning also emphasize the relationships between attitudinal and knowledge components, and the fundamental role played by attitudes and perceptions in facilitating ICT literacy, which entails a "collection of skills, knowledge, understanding, values, and relationships" (Watt, 1980, p. 3) that allow a person to deal effectively with ICT. In other words, dealing effectively with ICT relates not only to knowledge about the affordances of ICT, but also to individuals' attitudes and perceptions regarding ICT tools. Attitudes and perceptions act as a filter through which all learning occurs (Marzano, 1992), and are considered as a constituent part of learners' "self-esteem" that oversees all other systems (Markus & Ruvulo, 1990). Thus, learners continually filter their behaviors through their self-belief system to the extent that they even attempt to modify the "outside world" and make it more consistent with the "inside world" (Glaser, 1981).

From this perspective, researchers have studied several factors that seem to play an important role in affecting how individuals use ICT. These factors include not only ICT knowledge and the amount and nature of prior ICT experience, but also ICT-related attitudes and learners' beliefs in the ability to work successfully with ICT tools (self-confidence or self-efficacy) (Levine & Donitsa-Schmidt, 1998; Liaw, 2002; Murphy, Coover, & Owen, 1989). Attitudes and beliefs are also considered as predictors of behaviors and behavioral intentions that are linked to self-confidence. Beliefs about an object usually lead to attitudes toward it, and, in turn, attitudes lead to behavioral intentions regarding the object, which affect actual behaviors toward the object. Finally, there is a feedback loop where behavioral experience modifies preexisting beliefs about the object. In terms of ICT use, attitudes toward ICT affect users' intentions or desire to use ICT. Intentions in turn affect actual ICT usage or experience, which modifies beliefs and consequent behaviors or behavioral intentions (future desire) and self-confidence or self-efficacy in employing ICT in learning.

In this study, we intended to manage the amount of cognitive load and PTE by integrating (or not integrating) ICT tools in the learning environment for management of the cognitive load and PTE related to ICT that may adversely affect learners' processing capacity. For example, there exist several web-based tools, such as Filamentality (www.kn.pacbell.com/wired/fil), that can be incorporated into the learning environment to help manage the additional cognitive load and PTE that are caused by searching the web. Thus, we hypothesized that the task of designing instructional activities using materials from the web can be optimally managed by integrating Filamentality in the learning environment. This does not imply that Filamentality, or other ICT tools, will make the task easier, but that it may help learners manage the cognitive load and their PTE related to the ICT tools more efficiently and effectively, and, consequently, it may influence their confidence in using ICT tools. A successful attempt to lower the cognitive load will have implications on learners' PTE and may result in more successful performance. Such a performance will positively affect learners' confidence levels in employing similar tools and strategies in new learning situations. Learners' initial attitudes toward ICT and its integration in the classroom may also have implications on learners' behaviors and behavioral intentions, such as their PTE and confidence levels.

Thus, the study was undertaken to examine whether integrating, or not integrating, Filamentality in a science education method course would affect primary student teachers' PTE (as a result of the perceived difficulty) in learning with these tools and learners' perceived confidence levels in employing them for new learning. Specifically, the study set out to provide answers to the question: Does learning with certain ICT tools, such as Filamentality, affect learners' self-reported PTE and self-reported confidence levels in using ICT tools, after adjusting for the effects of their initial attitudes?

Methodology

THE CONTEXT OF THE STUDY

Forty-one primary student teachers, who were enrolled in a science education method course, participated in the study. Prior to taking this course, students completed two basic computing courses in which they learned Word, Excel, PowerPoint, Internet, and HyperStudio skills. The objective of these courses was mainly to raise students' skill proficiency level. The science education method course was designed around three major objectives: (a) to familiarize students with current trends in science teaching, (b) to capitalize on the interrelationships among science, ICT, and society, and (c) to integrate ICT tools for designing and developing interactive instructional activities. The instructor of the course (second author) in collaboration with an expert in instructional technology (first author) jointly redesigned the course in an attempt to integrate ICT tools in certain instructional situations.

FILAMENTALITY AND HYPERSTUDIO

Filamentality is a fill-in-the-blank interactive website that assists learners in defining a topic and guides them through searching the web and collecting appropriate websites. Thereafter, it assists with turning these online resources into different types of learning activities. The creators of Filamentality saw the process of learning and teaching with Filamentality as a three-step process, namely, gathering and analyzing input (i.e., different types of online resources), transformation of input (i.e., through different strategies and activities), and production, during which learners' investigations can be published on the web (Chylinski, 1999). In essence, Filamentality provides electronic scaffolding through a simple template design, which offers the capability of organizing online information, and, thereafter, creating one or more of five types of activities, such as Hotlists, Scrapbooks, Treasure Hunts, Samplers, and WebQuests.

Of interest to this study were the activities Hotlist and Scrapbook. A Hotlist is a web page with links to text-based materials for a topic that are organized meaningfully into categories. According to the International Society for Technology in Education (2002), this focuses the search and minimizes the time needed to locate relevant information. A Scrapbook is a web page with links to a variety of media, such as images, sound, video clips, and virtual reality tours as these relate to a topic. Learners can use a Hotlist to read about a topic, and, thereafter, a Scrapbook to explore aspects of the topic they feel are important.

The process of creating an activity in Filamentality begins with the registration of a new topic. As it is shown in Figure 11.1, the registration procedure requires the title of the activity, the creator's name, and a password. The next step, shown in Figure 11.2, is to add Internet links to the activity. Filamentality provides users with direct access to the most well known search engines to help with the identification of appropriate links.

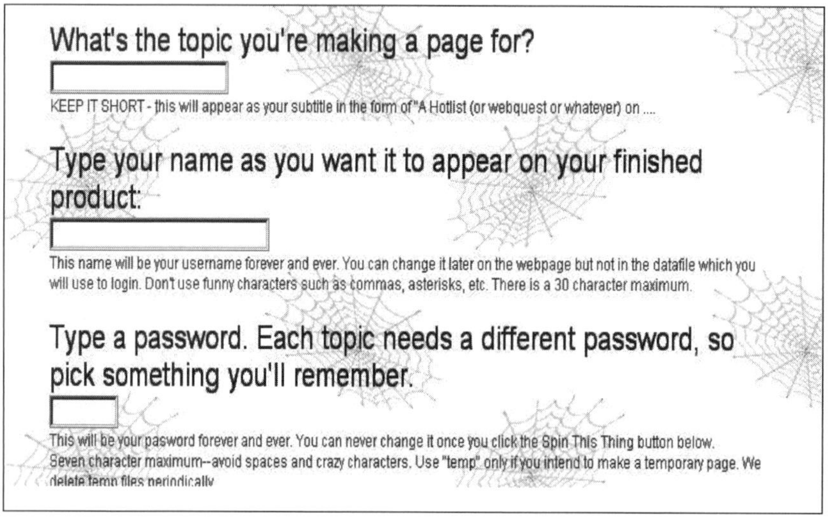
What's the topic you're making a page for?
KEEP IT SHORT - this will appear as your subtitle in the form of "A Hotlist (or webquest or whatever) on ....
Type your name as you want it to appear on your finished product:
This name will be your username forever and ever. You can change it later on the webpage but not in the datafile which you will use to login. Don't use funny characters such as commas, asterisks, etc. There is a 30 character maximum.
Type a password. Each topic needs a different password, so pick something you'll remember.
This will be your pasword forever and ever. You can never change it once you click the Spin This Thing button below.
Seven character maximum--avoid spaces and crazy characters. Use "temp" only if you intend to make a temporary page. We

Figure 11.1 Defining a topic in Filamentality

Once the links are collected and their URLs are recorded in the template, the user chooses one of five possible instructional templates, corresponding to Hotlists, Scrapbooks, Treasure Hunts, Samplers, and WebQuests, to fill in. Then, Filamentality prompts the user with questions and task descriptions that need to be filled in appropriately. At the end, the activity can be published on the Internet with a click of the mouse, and the URL of the published website is displayed on the screen.

In summary, Filamentality enables a user to create a web page, to selectively record the results of a search of resources available on the Internet, to meaningfully organize them into categories, and, thereafter, to use these resources to create instructional activities. The resources found in a Hotlist and a multimedia Scrapbook can be downloaded, for example, into a HyperStudio stack and manipulated accordingly by the learner. HyperStudio is a well-known multimedia-authoring tool that is widely used by teachers and students to communicate ideas in multimedia form by bringing together text, sound, graphics, and video.

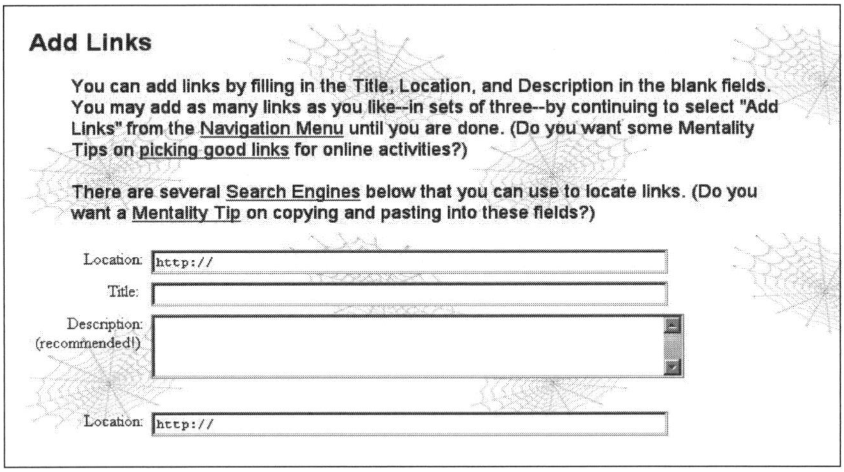
Add Links
You can add links by filling in the Title, Location, and Description in the blank fields. You may add as many links as you like--in sets of three--by continuing to select "Add Links" from the Navigation Menu until you are done. (Do you want some Mentality Tips on picking good links for online activities?)
There are several Search Engines below that you can use to locate links. (Do you want a Mentality Tip on copying and pasting into these fields?)
Location: http://
Title:
Description: (recommended!)
Location: http://

Figure 11.2 Adding links in Filamentality

RESEARCH PROCEDURES

Over the course of the semester, participants attended lectures and laboratory meetings. For the 13 two-hour lectures, students met as a group, whereas for laboratory meetings, they were randomly divided into two groups. Each group had 13 90-minute laboratory meetings. Laboratory work included experiments, ICT training, and design of ICT-enhanced lessons. Students' lab performances were assessed based on performances on a design and development project, which required each student to: (a) select a different topic from the elementary science curriculum, (b) identify and evaluate websites suitable for teaching this topic, (c) use materials found on the web to develop a HyperStudio stack, and (d) integrate computer-based activities in an 80-minute ICT-enhanced science lesson for ages 7–12 to be taught in a real classroom setting in conjunction with other planned activities. Students were guided to design their lessons based on principles of learning theories that place the learner at the center of the learning process as the constructor of knowledge.

Of the 13 90-minute laboratory meetings, seven meetings were devoted to ICT training. Three kinds of ICT training sessions for each group were administered: (a) HyperStudio training, (b) Internet training, and (c) design of ICT-enhanced activities. Even though students had been previously taught how to use both HyperStudio and the Internet, they felt they needed further instruction about how to use and integrate them in a lesson plan. For these reasons, each group of students had two workshops about HyperStudio and its added value in the teaching and learning process, three workshops about the

Internet, and two workshops on how to design ICT-enhanced lesson plans. The first author conducted all ICT training sessions for both groups, while the second author conducted the remaining sessions of the course.

Internet training differed between the two groups. The control group learned about how to employ different strategies to effectively search the web, and which engines were most appropriate for locating different kinds of information, such as images, video clips, sounds, animations, etc. These students also studied how to evaluate web-based resources using different criteria, such as (a) accuracy, (b) depth, (c) breadth, and (d) relevance to students' lives.

Students in the Filamentality group had the same basic Internet training as students in the control group, but they also learned how to use Filamentality. In their lab sessions, students were taught how to create a Hotlist about a topic they themselves selected from the elementary science curriculum, using the Filamentality tool. The lab instructor also explained the minor differences between a Hotlist and a Scrapbook, and assisted students with the creation of a Scrapbook about the same topic. Thus, students in the Filamentality group received instruction relevant to learning how to organize the results of their searches with Filamentality and how to create instructional activities using Filamentality. Students in the Filamentality group were encouraged to use Filamentality regularly, and students in both groups were encouraged to consult with the course instructors regarding the design of their ICT-enhanced lessons for elementary school children.

INSTRUMENTS

At the beginning of the semester, a questionnaire was used to measure students' attitudes toward ICT and its integration in the classroom. The questionnaire consisted of 12 questions presented in Table 11.1, with a Likert-type scale from 1 to 5 (disagree a lot, disagree, neutral, agree, agree a lot). At the end of the semester, students were given two additional questionnaires. One questionnaire was used to measure different aspects of students' PTE. A Likert-type scale from 1 to 5 (very small, small, neither small nor large, large, and very large PTE) was used. There were two forms of this questionnaire, one for each group. The PTE for the control group was measured in terms of (a) the PTE to use HyperStudio, (b) the PTE to use the Internet and collect quality information for their projects, and (c) the PTE to design instructional activities using HyperStudio (instructional use of HyperStudio). Similarly, the PTE for the Filamentality group was measured in terms of (a) the PTE to use HyperStudio, (b) the PTE to use the Internet, collect quality information for their projects, and organize the information using Filamentality in a Hotlist and a Scrapbook for later use with their HyperStudio stacks, and (c) the PTE to design instructional activities using HyperStudio (instructional use of HyperStudio). The difference between the two groups was that only the Filamentality group was deliberately instructed and guided to use Filamentality and organize the information in a Hotlist and a Scrapbook. The aspect of PTE related to subject matter difficulty was not measured, because students chose a topic of their liking, and thus probably a topic they understood best. In addition, at the end of the PTE questionnaire there was an open-ended question asking students to describe their experiences in learning with the tools, and, in particular, how the tools helped them to carry out their task and what difficulties they encountered.

The other questionnaire that was administered at the end of the semester was given to both groups of students and measured their self-reported confidence levels in using specific ICT tools in a classroom for instructional purposes. The questionnaire included six questions, presented in Table 11.3, and a Likert-type scale from 1 to 5 (disagree a lot, disagree, neutral, agree, agree a lot) was also used. These questions examined the extent to which learners felt confident in teaching their own students how to use HyperStudio and the web, and how confident they felt in integrating these tools in teaching and learning.

Results

Table 11.1 shows the frequencies of students' responses to the 12-item attitude questionnaire. There were no statistically significant differences between the two laboratory groups in terms of their responses to the attitude questionnaire. Thus, the results were collapsed over the two groups and attitude was not considered as a covariate in the subsequent analyses. The split-half correlation method, with the Spearman-Brown correction, gave a reliability estimate of .86.

Table 11.1 Students' Initial Attitudes about ICT ($n = 41$)

Item	Disagree a lot %	Disagree %	Neutral %	Agree %	Agree a lot %
1. I feel comfortable learning the new technologies	2.4	9.8	9.8	39.0	39.0
2. Using the computer constitutes a skill that students must learn	0.0	0.0	0.0	17.1	82.9
3. The computer imposes stress on me, because, if anything goes wrong, I wouldn't know what to do	19.5	53.7	12.2	9.8	4.9
4. I feel comfortable with my abilities to be able to learn how to use the computer	2.4	9.8	4.9	58.5	24.4
5. The use of computers in education makes me skeptical	9.8	24.4	9.8	46.3	9.8
6. The use of computers in education makes me enthusiastic	0.0	2.4	7.3	53.7	36.6
7. The use of computers in education interests me	0.0	2.4	0.0	51.2	46.3
8. The use of computers in education scares me	26.8	41.5	14.6	14.6	2.4
9. Computers confuse me	34.1	48.8	7.3	9.8	0.0
10. I don't think computers will be valuable in my profession	82.9	14.6	0.0	0.0	2.4
11. I enjoy learning how to use the new technologies	0.0	2.4	12.2	39.0	46.3
12. Whatever the computer can do, I can do it equally well with another way	7.3	68.3	22.0	2.4	0.0

The results in Table 11.1 show that the majority of students felt the need for employing new technologies in the learning environment, felt comfortable in learning how to use new technologies, and were rather enthusiastic to learn how to integrate ICT in their teaching, although there were students who expressed some skepticism. In general, there was an overall positive attitude and a positive momentum toward ICT integration. Of course, even though ICT-related attitudes seem to play an important role in how ICT is used in teaching and learning (Levine & Donitsa-Schmidt, 1998), research has also shown that positive attitudes alone are not always good indicators of preservice teachers' eventual use of ICT in the classroom (Wild, 1996). Preservice teachers, for example, may have positive attitudes about ICT integration without realizing how difficult the task can be, or how much effort they may need to invest to successfully complete the task. Thus, despite preservice teachers' initial positive disposition toward ICT integration, they may still find the task of integrating ICT in the classroom difficult once they realize what it really entails.

Table 11.2 shows descriptive statistics on each aspect of students' PTE. Students in the control group reported a higher PTE on all aspects of the dependent variable, namely, (a) difficulty of HyperStudio, (b) use of the Internet, and (c) instructional use of HyperStudio.

Table 11.2 Descriptive Statistics of Students' Perceived Task Effort (PTE) (n = 41)

Aspects of PTE	Group	*M*	*SD*	*n*
Difficulty of HyperStudio	Control group	2.71	.78	21
	Filamentality group	2.35	.67	20
Use of Internet	Control group	3.29	1.00	21
	Filamentality group	2.35	.75	20
Instructional use of HyperStudio	Control group	3.81	.68	21
	Filamentality group	3.25	.97	20
Total PTE	Control group	9.81	1.75	21
	Filamentality group	7.95	1.64	20

A multivariate ANOVA, using the three ratings of PTE and the total PTE as the dependent variables, was subsequently conducted. The results indicated that the ratings on the total PTE between the two groups were statistically significant, $F = 12.314, p = .001$. The ratings on use of the Internet and instructional use of HyperStudio were also statistically significant, $F = 11.344, p = .002$, and $F = 4.634, p = .038$, respectively, but the ratings on HyperStudio difficulty were not statistically significant between the two groups, $F = 2.545, p = .119$.

These findings indicate that students who were instructed to employ Filamentality in their work reported lower PTE related to the use of the Internet, design of instructional activities using HyperStudio, and total PTE. The findings signify that Filamentality produced a facilitating effect in searching the Internet and organizing the information in a Hotlist and a Scrapbook, and in carrying out the design task. Interestingly enough, the PTE related to the difficulty of HyperStudio was not significantly different between the two groups, but the PTE related to the design of instructional activities using HyperStudio was significant. The results seem to indicate that the lower total PTE for the Filamentality group was attributed to a facilitating effect directly related to Filamentality.

A qualitative analysis (Lincoln & Guba, 1985; Merriam, 1988) of students' answers to the open-ended question at the end of the PTE questionnaire was subsequently performed. In qualitative analysis, the process of data analysis is recursive and dynamic, and aims at identifying emerging themes or categories (Merriam, 1988). The qualitative analysis of students' answers led to the identification of two emerging themes. First, the 20 students in the Filamentality group agreed that the amount of PTE was much lower than what it would have been without using Filamentality. They explained that Filamentality was easy to use and enabled them to organize the results of their searches into categories. Therefore, it was easy to access the information when they needed it to design instructional activities using HyperStudio. Second, the 21 students in the control group stated that they faced difficulties in integrating not only the Internet but also HyperStudio in their design activities. Specifically, students in the control group stated that they felt frustrated integrating materials from the web in their HyperStudio stacks. Although they invested a tremendous amount of time searching the web, they failed to organize the results of their searches electronically, and thus they spent extra time searching for them again when they actually needed to use them in their HyperStudio stacks.

Descriptive statistics of students' self-reported (subjective) confidence levels are shown in Table 11.3. The results in Table 11.3 indicate that students in the Filamentality group tended to have higher confidence levels in almost every item of the questionnaire. A multivariate ANOVA, using the self-reported confidence levels on each item of the questionnaire and the total subjective confidence level as the dependent variables, was subsequently conducted.

Table 11.3 Descriptive Statistics of Students' Perceived Confidence Levels ($n = 40$)

Aspects of Confidence	Group	*M*	*SD*	*n*
1. I feel confident in designing ICT-enhanced activities for my students	Control Filamentality	3.76 3.74	.70 .87	21 19
2. I feel confident in integrating computers in my classroom practices	Control Filamentality	4.05 4.11	.74 .66	21 19
3. I feel confident in utilizing HyperStudio for instructional purposes with my students	Control Filamentality	3.33 3.89	.91 .81	21 19
4. I feel confident in teaching my students how to use different search engines to efficiently search for information on the World Wide Web	Control Filamentality	4.00 4.32	.71 .48	21 19
5. I feel confident in teaching my students how to utilize HyperStudio in their projects	Control Filamentality	3.38 4.00	.92 .82	21 19
6. I feel confident in using the World Wide Web in my classroom	Control Filamentality	4.10 4.32	.54 .67	21 19
Total	Control Filamentality	22.62 24.37	2.48 3.39	21 19

Note: One student was not present when the questionnaire was administered.

The results indicate that the students who were instructed to employ Filamentality reported significantly higher confidence levels related to only item 3, $F(1, 38) = 4.198$, $p = .047$, and item 5, $F(1, 38) = 5.017$, $p = .031$. The existing significant differences were related to students' perceived confidence in utilizing HyperStudio for instructional purposes and their perceived confidence in teaching their own students to utilize HyperStudio in their projects. Nevertheless, students in the two groups felt equally confident in designing ICT-enhanced activities for their students, integrating computers in classroom practices, teaching their students how to use different search engines, and using the web in the classroom. The existing significant differences and other non-significant differences did not, however, add up to significant differences between the two groups in terms of their cumulative subjective confidence levels.

Discussion and Implications

In this study, two groups of primary student teachers were provided with opportunities for how to design ICT-enhanced learning, but only one group was intentionally instructed to use electronic scaffolding with the Filamentality tool. The purpose was to investigate whether Filamentality could affect primary student teachers' PTE and confidence levels, after controlling for the effects of the differences in their initial attitudes toward ICT and its integration in the classroom. The results showed that students in both the control and the Filamentality groups had positive attitudes toward ICT and its integration in the classroom, and that there were no significant differences between the two groups in terms of their attitudes. Woodrow (1994) emphasized that positive attitudes are necessary but may be insufficient to instigate ICT-related behavior. Based on our results, we cannot provide any further insights related to the relative importance of attitudes toward ICT utilization.

The results indicate, however, that students who used Filamentality experienced, in general, a significantly lower PTE in completing their design task than those who completed the task without Filamentality. Filamentality served as a cognitive tool that helped students to effectively organize their thinking and facilitated fast retrieval and use of information when students needed to use it at a later time. However, the differences were restricted to the use of the Internet and the design of instructional activities using HyperStudio and not to the difficulty of using HyperStudio per se. The findings seem to suggest that adding tools to the learning environment, such as Filamentality, does not necessarily raise the PTE and may even lower it. More importantly, the results indicate that students' PTE was not linked with technical skills, but rather with designing learning activities with ICT and integrating ICT in the classroom.

Nonetheless, the results of the study do not paint a clear picture in terms of the differences between the two groups related to their self-confidence in employing ICT tools in teaching and learning. There was, however, evidence suggesting that when students perceived a lower PTE, their self-reported confidence in integrating ICT in learning was higher than those students who reported a higher PTE. For example, students in the Filamentality group reported significantly higher confidence levels only in terms of utilizing HyperStudio or teaching their future students how to utilize HyperStudio for instructional purposes in their projects, and not in terms of just using the tools. Thus, the findings did not show any significant differences for items strongly linked with technical skills, such as using the Internet or the web, or for items linked with a general perception of feeling competent in integrating ICT in instruction, such as designing technology-enhanced activities or integrating computers in classroom practices.

The cumulative evidence seems to suggest that engaging student teachers as designers of ICT-enhanced learning in a methods course can affect their perceived confidence levels about their future uses of ICT for instructional purposes. Jonassen (2000b) argues that when learners use ICT tools as designers they engage in "intellectual partnership" with them for "accessing information, interpreting and organizing their personal knowledge, and representing what they know to others" (p. 2). From this perspective, ICT tools, in and of themselves, are not so important, but the kinds of activities that they afford become crucial. The effects, of course, greatly depend on the mindful engagement of learners with the tools. "Effects *with* technology can redefine and enhance performance as students work in partnership with intelligent technologies—those that undertake a significant part of the cognitive processing that otherwise would have to be managed by the person" (Salomon, Perkins, & Globerson, 1991, p. 8).

The human partnership with ICT tools, such as Filamentality, usually entails a complementary division of labor, as tools with their powerful facilities assume part of the intellectual burden of information processing that shortcut the cognitive effort to produce a result. It seems that the electronic prompts provided by Filamentality would not be so successful if, for example, they were provided on paper, because Filamentality not only provided electronic prompts, but it also shared the intellectual burden of organizing and retrieving online resources. Thus, the electronic scaffolding provided by Filamentality liberated the learners to engage in cognitive activities that would, under different conditions, be out of their reach. It becomes rather obvious that once we couple technologies with people, then the technological component may decrease the intellectual share of the human partner, and any outcome should be treated as the joint product of person and ICT tools that become partners in what is called "distributed intelligence" (Pea, 1989).

In conclusion, the findings of this study indicate that ICT integration in teacher education programs should be carefully planned to ensure that student teachers' PTE decreases and confidence levels increase. Thus, it is crucial to carefully select appropriate ICT tools, so that students do not experience a high PTE related to the difficulty and instructional use of these tools. Similarly, we need to keep looking for ways to make our students feel confident about integrating ICT in their teaching practices, as it is a prerequisite for students to accept ICT as a powerful learning tool (Greenberg, Raphael, Keller, & Tobias, 1998; Zammit, 1992) and as an intellectual partner. Such partnerships are considered "joint cognitive systems" (Dalal & Kasper, 1994), where systems—not individuals alone—carry out intellectual tasks. Our results clearly relate to the changes in performance that learners display while employing ICT tools, such as Filamentality and HyperStudio, or the effects when working *with* ICT tools. Nonetheless, the limitations of the present study (i.e., a small experiment, small sample, and small duration of the intervention) restrict the generalizability of the results and suggest that more robust research designs and coordinated research efforts are needed to systematically investigate the impact of ICT tools on human thinking, learning, and performance.

Author Update

The view of computers as cognitive tools or intellectual partners represents a non-trivial departure from traditional approaches to using computers in schools. It reflects a distinction between computers as media of conveyance and knowledge dissemination or acquisition, and computers as tools for facilitating critical thinking, problem solving, and higher-order thinking. In this article we examine factors that may facilitate or inhibit students' cognitive performance with cognitive tools. Specifically, we investigated whether integrating Filamentality in a science education methods course would affect preservice teachers' perceived task effort during a design task. The results indicated that students who used Filamentality experienced a significantly lower perceived task effort in completing their design task than those who did not use it. Filamentality served as a cognitive tool that facilitated fast retrieval, organization, and use of information. Thus, the research findings suggest that the electronic scaffolds afforded by Filamentality assumed part of the intellectual burden of organizing and retrieving online resources, and clearly relate to the changes in performance that learners show when employing or working with ICT tools to accomplish a task. The significance of this paper is important as it provides evidence showing that the question that is often asked by practitioners, namely, "Is learning with computers effective?" cannot be answered with a simple yes or no, because the intricacies of the specific context (i.e., task, learners' characteristics, tool characteristics, etc.) need to be carefully examined so that an informed interpretation of the empirical results can be derived.

References

Baddeley, A. D. (1986). *Working memory.* Oxford, UK: Oxford University Press.

Baddeley, A. D. (1999). *Human memory.* Boston, MA: Allyn & Bacon.

Chandler, P., & Sweller, J. (1991). Cognitive load theory and the format of instruction. *Cognition and Instruction, 8,* 293–332.

Chandler, P., & Sweller, J. (1996). Cognitive load while learning to use a computer program. *Applied Cognitive Psychology, 10,* 151–170.

Chylinski, R. (1999, October). Filamentality: Producing internet-based activities. Paper presented at 12th ELICOS Association Educational Conference, Adelaide, Australia.

Cole, M., & Engestrom, Y. (1993). A cultural–historical approach to distributed intelligence. In G. Salomon (Ed.), *Distributed cognitions: Psychological and educational considerations* (pp. 1–46). New York, NY: Cambridge University Press.

Dalal, K. P., & Kasper, G. M. (1994). The design of joint cognitive systems: Effect of cognitive coupling on performance. *International Journal of Human-Computer Studies, 40,* 677–702.

de Jong, T., Martin, E., Zamarro, J.-M., Esquembre, F., Swaak, J., & van Jooligen, W. R. (1999). The integration of computer simulation and learning support: An example from the physics domain of collisions. *Journal of Research in Science Teaching, 36*(5), 597–615.

Gibson, J. J. (1982). *Reasons for realism: Selected essays of J. Gibson.* Hillsdale, NJ: Lawrence Erlbaum.

Glaser, W. (1981). *Stations of the mind.* New York, NY: Harper & Row.

Greenberg, R., Raphael, J., Keller, J., & Tobias, S. (1998). Teaching high school science using image processing: A case study of implementation of computer technology. *Journal of Research in Science Teaching, 35*(3), 297–327.

International Society for Technology in Education. (2002). *National Educational Technology Standards for Teachers: Preparing teachers to use technology.* Eugene, OR: Author.

Jonassen, D. H. (2000a). *Computers as mindtools for schools: Engaging critical thinking* (2nd ed.). Upper Saddle River, NJ: Prentice-Hall.

Jonassen, D. H. (2000b). Technology as cognitive tools: Learners as designers [6 pages]. Retrieved from http://it.coe.uga.edu/itforum/paper1/paper.html

Levine, T., & Donitsa-Schmidt, S. (1998). Computer use, confidence, attitudes, and knowledge: A causal analysis. *Computers in Human Behavior, 14*(1), 125–146.

Liaw, S. S. (2002). Understanding user perceptions of worldwide web environments. *Journal of Computer Assisted Learning, 18,* 137–148.

Lincoln, Y., & Guba, E. G. (1985). *Naturalistic inquiry.* Newbury Park, CA: Sage.

Locke, E., Shaw, K. N., Saari, L. M., & Latham, G. P. (1981). Goal setting and task performance. *Psychological Bulletin, 90,* 169–181.

Markus, H., & Ruvulo, A. (1990). "Possible selves." Personalized representation of goals. In L. Pervin (Ed.), *Goal concepts in psychology* (pp. 211–241). Hillsdale, NJ: Lawrence Erlbaum.

Marzano, R. J. (1992). *A different kind of classroom: Teaching with dimensions of learning.* Alexandria, VA: ASCD.

Mayer, R. E. (2001). *Multimedia learning.* New York, NY: Cambridge University Press.

Merriam, S. B. (1988). *Case study research in education: A qualitative approach.* San Francisco, CA: Jossey-Bass.

Mohr, L. A., & Bitner, M. J. (1995). The role of employee effort in satisfaction with service transactions. *Journal of Business Research, 32,* 239–252.

Murphy, C. A., Coover, D., & Owen, S. V. (1989). Development and validity of the computer self-efficacy scale. *Educational and Psychological Measurement, 49*, 893–899.

Pea, R. D. (1989, June). Distributed intelligence and education. Paper presented at the annual meeting of the Social Science Research Council on Computers and Learning, British Virgin Islands.

Salomon, G., Perkins, D. N., & Globerson, T. (1991). Partners in cognition: Extending human intelligence with intelligent technologies. *Educational Researcher, 20*(3), 2–9.

Sweller, J. (1994). Cognitive load theory, learning difficulty, and instructional design. *Learning and Instruction, 4*, 295–312.

Watt, D. H. (1980). Computer literacy: What should schools be doing about it? *Classroom Computer News, 1*(2), 1–26.

Wild, M. (1996). Technology refusal: Rationalizing the future of student and beginning teachers to use computers. *British Journal of Educational Technology, 27*(2), 134–143.

Woodrow, J. E. J. (1994). The development of computer-related attitudes of secondary students. *Journal of Educational Computing Research, 11*, 307–338.

Zammit, S. A. (1992). Factors facilitating or hindering the use of computers in schools. *Educational Researcher, 34*(1), 57.

CHAPTER

12

Technology and Education Change: Focus on Student Learning

Barbara Means | SRI International

This study examined technology implementation practices associated with student learning gains. Interviews and observations were conducted with staff at schools where teachers using reading or mathematics software with their students attained above-average achievement gains and at schools where software-using teachers had below-average gains. The findings highlight the importance of school practices in the areas of principal support and teacher collaboration around software use and of teacher practices concerning classroom management and use of software-generated student performance data. The issues of instructional coherence and competition for instructional time are highlighted as challenges to software implementation.

Observers of technology use in schools and classrooms have long noted the relatively modest use of educational technology within most schools and classrooms (Cuban, 2001). As the lives of students and teachers outside of school have evolved to include more and more use of technology, the situation presents a paradox. Despite decades of national, state, and local promotion of educational uses of technology, classroom practice in most schools has changed little from that of the mid-20th century. Recent large-scale national surveys of teacher practices with technology found an increase in teacher use of technology as a productivity tool supporting their own work between 2005 and 2007 but no increase in the level of teacher-assignment of technology-based learning activities for students during the same time period (Bakia, Means, Gallagher, Chen, & Jones, 2009). Teachers and students use technology more frequently outside of school than they do during class time.

Although many teachers certainly are using today's technologies in innovative ways, they remain the exception rather than the rule. In terms of Moore's (1999) innovation adoption model, few learning technologies have managed to "cross the chasm" from adoption by technology enthusiasts and visionaries to acceptance by the vast majority of teachers, who are pragmatists and conservatives.

Technology adoption and implementation require not just funding resources but also ongoing effort. The premise underlying this paper is that teachers' and school systems' fundamental priorities concern student learning outcomes. Most educators will expend the effort needed to integrate technology into instruction when, and only when, they are convinced that there will be significant payoffs in terms of student learning outcomes. Hence, to make technology an agent of education change, the field needs to understand the kinds of learning outcomes that technology can enhance and the circumstances under which that enhancement will be realized in practice. Sound guidance on how to implement technology in ways that produce student learning gains is integral to efforts to use technology as a lever for education change.

As illustrated in Tables 12.1 and 12.2, an extensive literature on "best practices" in technology implementation does exist. The first column in Table 12.1 lists common recommendations for school-level practices in support of instructional uses of technology.

The first column of Table 12.2 lists commonly recommended teachers' classroom practices with respect to technology implementation.

Table 12.1 Recommended School-Level Instructional Technology Practices

Implementation Recommendation	Recommended by	Prior Research Support for Practice: Correlation with Technology Use	Prior Research Support for Practice: Correlation with Learning Outcomes	Prior Research Support for Practice: Controlled Studies on Technology Use
Schoolwide Coherence				
Technology use integrated with a consistent school-wide instructional vision	Barnett (2001) Means & Olson (1995) OTA (1995)	Means & Olson (1995)		
Technology aligned with local curriculum	Barnett (2001) Ertmer (1999) Sarama et al. (1998) Sweet et al. (2004)			
Principal demonstration of support for technology integration	Brand (1997) Coley et al. (1997) OTA (1995)	Mann et al. (1998) O'Dwyer et al. (2004, 2005) Zhao et al. (2002)		
Teacher Training				
Teachers trained on concepts of student-centered teaching and technology integration	Barnett (2001)	Becker (1994, 2000) Mann et al. (1998) O'Dwyer et al. (2004, 2005) Zhao et al. (2002)	eMINTS (2003) Wenglinsky (1998)	
Teachers trained on implementation of the specific software/innovation	EETI vendors	Becker (1994) Mann et al. (1998) U.S. Department of Education (2000)	Mann et al. (1998)	
Professional development is ongoing, not one-time (e.g., mentoring or coaching)	Brand (1997) Jones et al. (1995) OTA (1995)	Adelman et al. (2002) Becker (1994) U.S. Department of Education (2000)	Cole, Simkins, & Penuel (2002)	
Professional development involves teachers in designing technology-supported learning activities/resources		Martin et al. (2003) Yamagata-Lynch (2003)		
Technology Access				
Computers/Internet accessible in regular classrooms	Barnett (2001) Mann et al. (1998) OTA (1995)	Becker (2000)	Mann et al. (1998)	
Adequate access to technology for all students	Barnett (2001)	O'Dwyer et al. (2004, 2005)		

Continued

Table 12.1, *Continued*

Implementation Recommendation	Recommended by	Prior Research Support for Practice		
		Correlation with Technology Use	Correlation with Learning Outcomes	Controlled Studies on Technology Use
Support for Technology Use				
Technical support available at the school	Barnett (2001) Sweet et al. (2004)	Becker (1994) Hill & Reeves (2004) Zhao et al. (2002)	Cole, Simkins, & Penuel (2002)	
Teachers collaborate around technology use	Brand (1997)	Becker (2000) Frank, Zhao, & Borman (2004) Means & Olson (1995) Zhao et al. (2002)		

Table 12.2 Recommended Classroom-Level Instructional Technology Practices

Recommendation (1)	Recommended by (2)	Prior Research Support for Practice		
		Correlation with Technology Use (3)	Correlation with Learning Outcomes (4)	Controlled Studies on Learning Outcomes (5)
Integration of technology with learning goals and offline learning activities		Becker (1994) Means & Olson (1995)	Wenglinsky (1998)	
Technology used frequently	Van Dusen & Worthen (1995)		Mann et al. (1998) Wenglinsky (1998)	
Teacher present and facilitates learning when technology is used		Sandholtz et al. (1997)		Powell et al. (2003)
Teacher reviews software reports				Powell et al. (2003)
Efficient routines established for shifting in and out of technology use (classroom management)	Coley et al. (1997)	OTA (1995)		
Low student-to-computer ratio in classroom	Barnett (2001) Glennan & Melmed (1996) OTA (1995)	O'Dwyer et al. (2004, 2005)	Cavalier & Klein (1998)	

These tables also show that, in most cases, the basis for recommending the implementation practices is expert opinion or a correlation between the practice and the observed extent of technology use. Only a handful of articles document a correlation between an implementation practice and student learning outcomes. Very few studies with a rigorous, controlled design have examined the effects of one of the recommended technology implementation practices on student learning outcomes. A formal search of the ERIC and PsychInfo databases to identify empirical studies using a control group design (either experimental or quasi-experimental) was conducted in support of a large research study (Dynarski et al., 2007) sponsored by the Institute of Education Sciences. Only a single published study meeting these criteria (Powell, Aeby, & Carpenter-Aeby, 2003) was identified through this search. Subsequent work with the technology implementation research uncovered a quasi-experimental study (Cole, Simkins, & Penuel, 2002) that found student learning benefits associated with teachers' receipt of support from school-based technology integration specialists skilled in the design of project-based learning activities involving student use of multimedia technology. Powell, Aeby, and Carpenter-Aeby (2003) found that teacher presence during use of instructional software and teacher review of software reports of student performance on the software produced greater student learning. Hence, we are urging schools and teachers to implement technology with little or no empirically based guidance on how to do so in ways that enhance student learning.

An implication of the discussion above is that technology implementation practices need to be investigated in conjunction with studies of technology effects on student learning. Unfortunately, few large-scale studies have measured both effects of technology on student learning and technology implementation practices. A prominent exception is the congressionally mandated national experiment on the Effectiveness of Educational Technology Interventions (EETI), which examined the effects of reading software for students in grades 1 and 4 and of mathematics software for students in Grade 6 and algebra classes (Dynarski et al., 2007). EETI found that, on average, the effect size for using reading or mathematics software was not statistically different from 0 at any of the four grade levels included in the study. Within each grade level and product, the classes using the software did better than those that did not at some schools, whereas the classes using their conventional approaches did better than those using the software at other schools. The only significant relationships between effect sizes and software implementation variables found in this study were larger effects in classes with more students per computer in Grade 1 (contrary to a common recommendation for technology implementation) and a relationship between effect size and the amount of time students spent using the reading software in Grade 4 (Dynarski et al., 2007).

In contrast, a study of a large urban district's implementation of the Waterford early reading software by Hansen, Llosa, and Slayton (2004) found that the amount of time students spent with the software was not correlated with measures of student learning. A randomized control trial of Accelerated Reader conducted by Nunnery, Ross, and McDonald (2006) found no relationship between the study's quality of implementation index and student achievement growth. In short, despite the existence and extensive dissemination of conventional wisdom concerning how technology should be implemented, the evidence base for recommending particular practices is neither deep nor internally consistent.

The research reported here was conducted with a subset of the EETI school sample to provide insights for those responsible for implementing reading and mathematics software by providing a closer look at school and classroom implementation practices. This study contrasts practices in schools whose students had above-average achievement gains in their first year of software use as part of the EETI study with those of schools where treatment classes had below-average gains. This correlational analysis used implementation data from the EETI study as well as data from a set of follow-up interviews and observations conducted with staff at 13 schools continuing to use the software they had implemented the prior year as part of the EETI study.

This study focused on two central questions:

- What classroom-level practices are associated with higher achievement gains in classrooms using reading or math software?
- What school-level practices are associated with higher achievement gains in classrooms using reading or math software?

To explore issues of software implementation, analysts identified those EETI schools where software-using teachers' students experienced above-average achievement gains and those whose students had below-average gains in the first year of the EETI software effectiveness study. Identification of the schools for case studies was based on information made available from the Effectiveness of Educational Technology Interventions (EETI) study (Dynarski et al., 2007). From these two school subsamples, 14 schools were selected for follow-up—7 in the above-average group and 7 in the below-average group. The 14 selected schools were using seven different software products (four reading products and three mathematics products) and included an above-average- and a below-average-gain school for each product. For each product, researchers looked for a high-gain school with a positive effect size and above-average use of the software for which a low-gain school matched on student demographic variables could be identified. For each product, schools were selected to be as similar as possible except for their differing levels of student gains.

The 14 schools selected for case study were contacted in April 2006 to ascertain whether they would be willing to participate in this follow-up data collection by completing phone interviews or hosting a site visit. All of the schools initially agreed to participate, but one of the low-gain schools subsequently dropped out of the data collection, resulting in a follow-up sample of 13 schools, as shown in Table 12.3.

Table 12.3 Characteristics of High- and Low-Gain Schools in the Follow-Up Sample

Variable	High-Gain Schools ($n = 7$)	Low-Gain Schools ($n = 6$)
Teacher experience level (years)	8.8	12.7
Teacher certification (percent)	79	83
Urban schools (percent)	71	50
Free/reduced-price lunch (percent)	57	56
African American (percent)	32	36
Hispanic (percent)	16	31
Special education (percent)	10*	3
Student-to-teacher ratio	18.0	16.0
Pretest score (standardized)	-0.14	0.21
Gain score	0.77*	-0.70

** Significant at $p < .05$.*

By virtue of the selection process, the two groups of schools differed in average class standardized achievement gain (0.77 for the high-gain group versus -0.70 for the low-gain group). As intended, they were very similar in terms of variables related to their staff and student populations. The proportions of students eligible for free or reduced-price lunch, for example, were 57% and 56% in high- and low-gain schools, respectively.

The schools in the case study sample were using seven software products—four reading products and three mathematics products. Table 12.4 shows the number of classrooms using each product and the instructional features of those products, as judged by instructional design experts on the research team. (The coding team developed a set of instructional features, such as incorporation of practice opportunities, on which all software products could be judged. Two coders independently reviewed products, retaining feature categories for which intercoder agreement was 80 percent or better.)

Table 12.4 Instructional Features of Case Study Software Products

Product Type/ Code	No. Case Study Classes Using	Learning Opportunities		Individualization									Types Feedback to Teachers			Types Feedback to Students					
				Automatic			Teacher Input			Student Input						Immediate		Mastery		Diagnostic	
		Tutorial	Practice	T	P	A	T	P	A	T	P	A	Student Mastery	Learning Paths	Class Performance	P	A	P	A	P	A
Grade 1 Reading A	5	Many	Many	●	●	●	●	●	●		●		●	●	●	●		●	●	●	
Grade 1 Reading B	5	Many	Many	●	●		●	●	●				●		●	●	●		●	●	●
Grade 4 Reading A	4	Some	Many	●	●	●		●	●	●	●		●	●	●	●			●	●	
Grade 4 Reading B	2	Some	Many	●	●	●		●	●		●		●	●	●	●		●	●		
Grade 6 Pre-Algebra A	4	Many	Many	●	●	●	●	●	●	●	●	●	●	●	●	●				●	
Algebra A	4	Few	Many		●	●		●	●	●	●		●	●	●	●		●			
Algebra B	3	Many	Many	●	●	●	●	●	●	●	●	●	●	●	●	●				●	

Source: Staff review.

Key: T = Tutorial mode; P = Practice mode; A = Assessment mode

Definitions:

Immediate feedback: Learner is told whether response is correct immediately after completing module.
Mastery feedback: Learner is informed of number correct and whether or not a skil or concept has been acquired after completing a sequence of items.
Diagnostic feedback: Learner receives hints or other information concerning probable source of error.

Method

One pair of schools (a high- and a low-gain school both using the same product) at each grade level was designated for a site visit, which would involve interviews with the principal or other school leader and the school technology coordinator (if there was one), as well as with each teacher who had participated in the treatment condition in the EETI study. Site visits also involved observing each teacher twice—once while using the software with students and once while teaching the relevant subject (math or reading) without the software. In some cases, this protocol had to be modified for elementary reading because the implementation model for the product was to have a portion of the students working independently on computers, whereas another portion worked with the teacher in a small group during all reading instruction. For follow-up schools that did not receive a site visit, researchers conducted phone interviews with the principal, technology coordinator, and teachers using the same interview protocols employed on the site visits. They used the same interview protocols for high-gain and low-gain schools, and site visitors did not inform interviewers of the school's categorization as high or low gain.

Analysts blind to the level of gains a school or teacher had experienced during their first year of software use coded the data obtained through interviews and observations for descriptions of school practices (such as principal support), classroom practices (actions undertaken by individual teachers), conditions (demographic variables and other characteristics existing prior to software implementation), and perceived outcomes. Data coding began with two analysts independently coding each paragraph of the data forms for two schools. Interrater agreement for the independent coding was greater than 75%. A single analyst conducted the remaining coding. The coded data was entered into a qualitative analysis software database (ATLAS.ti) to facilitate identification of examples of particular practices and analysis of differences between high- and low-gain schools in terms of both teachers' classroom practices and schoolwide supports for software implementation.

Results

The differences the analysts identified between high- and low-gain schools are reported below for teachers' classroom practices as they use the software and for schoolwide supports for software implementation.

TEACHER IMPLEMENTATION PRACTICES

Level of Software Use

Teachers participating in the EETI software effectiveness study received training on use of the software, which included specification of the amount of time they should give students on the software each week. Software vendors' recommendations for weekly use of their products ranged from 75 to 135 minutes. When each teacher's reported use was compared to the usage recommended for the product in that class, the proportion of teachers meeting or exceeding vendor usage specifications in high-gain schools, at 64%, was not significantly different from that in low-gain schools (50%). The average weekly number of minutes teachers reported in high- and low-gain schools was roughly equivalent (119 and 102 minutes, respectively). Teacher reports indicated that the great majority of teachers were making a good-faith effort to have their students spend a significant amount of time with the software, and thus it is possible that level of use would be more strongly associated with achievement in implementations where usage levels varied more widely.

Although the amount of time that teachers reported having their students use the software was not associated with student gains in the case study sample (or in three of four grades for the EETI sample as a whole), there was a significant relationship between student gains and the point in the school year when classes started software use. On average, teachers in the high-gain case study schools started software implementation 4.5 weeks after school started, whereas teachers in low-gain schools did not begin until 7.7 weeks into the school year. The later start in low-gain schools did not appear to decrease the total number of hours the average student received on the software, as logged by the six software products from which such records could be obtained. The average annual software exposure was 23.1 hours for students in high-gain schools and 23.3 for students in low-gain schools. It may be that the speed with which a school ramped up for software implementation was influenced by other factors that can also influence technology implementation, such as the quality of the school's technology infrastructure and support, or the school's overall management efficiency.

Classroom Management

In interviews, teachers talked about the need to develop classroom routines for moving onto and off the software. A number of the teachers said that students needed to learn how to execute this transition and log on and off the software independently for the class to run smoothly. When asked what advice they would give another teacher using the software for the first time, teachers were more likely to provide recommendations on classroom management than on any other topic.

For those teachers who were observed in the act of teaching, all of the teachers in high-gain schools were rated as effective in terms of classroom management compared to just 17% of observed teachers in low-gain schools. Classroom management quality was judged on the basis of the proportion of time the class spent in learning and instruction, as opposed to moving around, preparing materials, or student disruptions. Thus, effective classroom management routines for software use appear to be important. In observed classrooms, effective classroom management appeared to allow greater focus on the instructional activities of the software rather than the logistics of its use. Ironically, this aspect of implementation is seldom mentioned in the literature on educational technology "best practices."

Facilitation During Software Use

Software vendors recommend that the regular classroom teacher be present while their students use instructional software. In addition to managing classroom behavior and activity flow, teachers also provide more or less substantive support for students' learning during periods when they are using the software. Software products are typically designed so that students can use them independently, but technology advocates often make the case that by engaging all students in learning independently, the software provides the opportunity for teachers to interact one-on-one with those students needing the most help.

Nearly all of the case study teachers (25 of 27) reported being present in the room while their students used the software. Observed teachers varied, however, in the amount of substantive support they provided for students' learning during software use. Some of the case study teachers were observed rotating through the room of software-using students, identifying students who were experiencing difficulty and working with them one-on-one. For example, in one sixth grade mathematics class using software in a computer lab, the teacher circulated around the room, interacting not only with students who raised their hands but also with students she observed to be progressing slowly (Means et al., 2006):

> The teacher helped one student who asked, "When you have a + and – sign, which do you keep?"
>
> "Think about what the sign needs to be to get you to +2x," the teacher said as she directed the student's attention to what he had written on a piece of scrap paper. "Think about that. That gets you to –2x + x.... There you go, look at that! Good."
>
> The student responded, "Right, right, thank you," and the teacher moved on to another student who had looked up for help.

In a sixth grade mathematics classroom at another school, the teacher was in the room as students worked with the software but spent about half of the class period on activities such as grading homework and talking on the phone that did not support students' work with the software.

The observed quality of teacher facilitation was measured for only the six teachers in the follow-up sample who could be observed teaching with the software during the school site visits, and two-thirds of the observed teachers in both high- and low-gain schools engaged in facilitation of learning in the software sessions the researchers watched.

Articulation and Integration of Instruction With and Without Software

Coordination of learning done through the software with instruction in the same topic that does not involve software emerged as an issue in interviews with the case-study teachers. None of the classes did all of their reading or mathematics learning through software. Five of the seven software products in this study were designed as supplements to regular instruction rather than as the core reading or mathematics curriculum. Even in classrooms using a mathematics product intended as the core curriculum, the product included offline as well as technology-based activities and materials. For products intended as supplements, the software was not a component of the core curriculum, and therefore teachers were using software produced by one vendor and a textbook or other set of core-curriculum instructional materials from another source. This situation raised several challenges for the teacher. First, the teacher must coordinate the topics across the two sets of instructional materials. Most of the software products allow teachers flexibility in sequencing software modules so that the use of software on a given topic or skill can be fit into a logical place in the core curriculum. Although quite feasible, this effort does take time. Teachers at some of the case-study schools reported that they had not worked through the software themselves or compared its coverage to that of their core curriculum to identify areas of overlap prior to implementing the software with their students. In some cases, teachers were aware that they could change the sequence of the software modules to match what they were doing in class, but had not done so. As one teacher said, "A lot of times we just let it [the software] roll the kids into the next level."

Other teachers did take the time to become familiar with the software and think about how to articulate the software modules with classroom activities. A high school algebra teacher, for example, chose the software modules her students would use each week based on what she would be teaching in the classroom. In addition to instances of adapting the sequence of software activities to match what was happening in the core curriculum, there were also instances of teachers adapting what they did in class on the basis of insights gained from observing students working with the software.

This observation from a first grade class implementing reading software illustrates the way in which students' software-based activity can influence a teacher's core instruction (Means et al., 2006):

> The first grade teacher began by reviewing the vowels. In her interview, the teacher said she did this because she had heard one of the students singing an "a-e-i-o-u" song from the software during lunch. She said that she often listened to students humming to themselves or singing songs from the software and used that as an indication of where they were in the software and where their skills might need reinforcing.

A second issue related to integrating software use and other instruction is the way that concepts or procedures are presented. This appeared to be particularly troublesome in mathematics, when different terminology and different procedures for handling problems of the same type were likely to be conveyed in the textbook and in the software. Mathematics teachers at one school found this discrepancy to be so confusing to their students during the first year of using the software that they decided not to teach the same topic with the textbook and the software in close temporal proximity in the second year, reasoning that students would be less confused by the representation of something in the software if they had had time to forget how it was presented in the text.

Analysts coded teachers' observed practices as their students were using software (where available) for evidence that the teachers were helping students integrate ideas and representations covered by instruction with and without software so that students could make connections between what they learned through the two modalities. Unless there was evidence of a lack of implementation of non-software components, those teachers who used a core curriculum product with both computer-based and non-computer-based material were coded as having integrated software use and other instruction. A high school algebra class provided an example of a teacher bringing content from the software into her classroom instruction (Means et al., 2006):

> The high school algebra class returned from the computer lab and sat down in rows of desk chairs facing the blackboard. At 2:55 p.m. the class began with the teacher saying, "Some of you were looking at this in the computer lab." She then began talking about simplifying rational expressions and went through some problems on the board.

We also observed examples of teachers referring to what the students had experienced in class as the students were working with software in the computer lab, as illustrated by the observation below from a middle school mathematics class (Means et al., 2006):

> As students worked with the math software in the computer lab, their teacher looked for students with raised hands or puzzled looks and provided individual assistance. The students were working with problems calling for them to do arithmetic operations with combinations of positive and negative integers. After noting that several of the students were struggling, the teacher addressed the class as a whole: "Remember when you add integers, use those algebra tiles we talked about in class. Red was for positive numbers and blue for negative numbers." (The software uses a number line depiction rather than algebra tiles, but it also uses red for negative numbers and blue for positive numbers.)

There were too few observations of software use during the follow-up study to support firm conclusions, but teachers' responses to interview items about integration of software-based and other instruction did suggest a relationship between integration and gains. Eighty-six percent of teachers in high-gain schools said that they had done this kind of integration, compared to 77% of teachers in low-gain schools.

Those teachers who actively facilitate their students' work with software are in a position to adapt their non-technology-based instruction by drawing on insights gained from interactions with the software. The software in essence provides the teacher with formative assessments, which research suggests can improve learning if the teacher uses them to guide future instruction (Black & Wiliam, 1998). Some of the case study teachers described this kind of practice. An algebra teacher, for example, reported that she finds that helping students individually while they are using the software is a good way of gauging their understanding and identifying areas to reteach. She said that students "who won't ask questions in the classroom will ask in the computer lab because they don't feel so much on the spot." She described her practice of taking the questions that students asked in the computer lab back into the classroom and reteaching concepts as needed.

Use of Software Data to Inform Instruction

Software vendors have long urged teachers to run the automated reports provided by their products and review them on a regular basis. Typically, these reports provide data on individual student progress through and mastery of the various software skill modules, as well as summary-level information for the class as a whole. Although the vendors' recommendation is rooted in concerns over teachers' support for software use and the desire to make sure the software is used appropriately, this practice appears to have broader benefit. Teachers at the high-gain schools in the follow-up sample reported doing frequent review of the student performance reports the software generates. Seventy-eight percent of the teachers in high-gain schools said they looked at software reports for all their students once a week or more, compared to 17% of teachers in low-gain schools. Thus, use of software-generated data reports was one of the largest differences between high-gain and low-gain implementations. Although it may be that achievement-oriented teachers implement many useful practices in addition to looking at data, our qualitative data are consistent with the hypothesis that the use of student performance information generated by software products helps teachers target their instruction to the things that students need to learn. Two examples illustrate teachers' use of the detailed student progress reports generated by software systems (Means et al., 2006):

> A fourth grade teacher reported that she looked at the software student performance reports on a monthly basis to monitor student progress and check what students were working on. She used the results of one report to group students during the core reading instruction time by topic mastery, allowing her to differentiate the pacing of her core instruction. "These kids are working on similes; these kids are working on context clues. I tried to coordinate it," she said. She also used software reports during parent–teacher conferences to emphasize or clarify a point she wanted to make with parents about their child's progress.
>
> A teacher at another elementary school said she looked at the software reports often and used the data to decide how to group students in her class. She said she also looked at the software "to help with words for class and give students individualized spelling words based on where they are in the software." The reports helped her decide what to teach, based on where students were in the software and how they were doing. "I love using those reports and being able to see exactly where kids are," she said. "I can sit down with a parent in a conference, and there's no guessing on my part."

Developing a System to Motivate Software Use

Some of the software vendors recommend instituting a motivational system around software use—creating a visible chart showing modules completed, giving certificates for accomplishments on the software, or using software performance in grading. Some of the individual teachers in both the high-gain and the low-gain schools described setting up such systems, usually in the form of a public chart showing each student's record of software module completion. The difference between teachers in high-gain schools and those in low-gain schools in use of this technique was not significant. Moreover, when the correlation between this technique and gain score is computed for all EETI treatment classrooms, a negative relationship between this practice and student gains is found (perhaps because teachers whose students are not progressing resort to extrinsic rewards).

Table 12.5 summarizes the differences between teachers in high- and low-gain schools in terms of teacher-level software implementation practices.

Table 12.5 Teacher Implementation Practices in High- and Low-Gain Schools

Practice	Teachers in High-Gain Schools	Teachers in Low-Gain Schools
Teacher-Reported Practices a		
Met vendor software weekly usage guideline	64%	50%
Reviewed software reports for all students weekly	78%	17%
Integrated software use with other instruction	86%	77%
Instituted motivational system	64%	46%
Observed Practices b		
Managed classroom effectively	100%	17%
Facilitated learning during software use	67%	67%

a Number of teachers responding to interview item varied between 12 and 14 for the two sets of schools.
b Number of teachers observed and scored on a variable varied between 3 and 6 for the two sets of schools.

SCHOOL-LEVEL IMPLEMENTATION PRACTICES

In addition to teacher behaviors and choices that teachers make about how to implement software with their students, the school as a whole provides supports for software implementation. The interviews that researchers conducted with school staff participating in the follow-up study addressed some broader school implementation issues that had not been covered in the EETI data collection. These include integration of technology use with a schoolwide instructional vision, principal support for use of the software, and teacher collaboration around software use. Additional schoolwide practices related to software implementation that were documented as part of the effectiveness study include the technology infrastructure, technical support, and receipt of additional formal training on software use or implementation. High- and low-gain schools were contrasted in terms of all of these schoolwide practices.

Consistent instructional vision. In schools with a consistent instructional vision, the principal and the treatment teachers expressed similar coherent views of how the subject (reading or mathematics) should be taught and the role that the software should play in implementing that instructional vision. Such consistency can be illustrated by reports from the staff of a large middle school serving a low-income student body that included many students who were not yet fluent in English (Means et al., 2006):

> All of the interviewed staff indicated that their top priority was to achieve the state/district content standards on the schedule designated in the district's instructional guide and pacing chart. The principal and both software-using teachers noted in separate interviews that many of their students did not come in with the skills that the district's instructional guide assumed and that, although they were supposed to be teaching the more advanced skills in the district instructional guide, they also needed to work on basic skills for students who had not yet mastered them. They all cited the software as useful for this purpose. They thought it would be better if students acquired basic skills before being moved to more advanced mathematics, but had concluded that they had to teach both together and saw the software as a useful tool for doing so.

The majority of high-gain schools (four of seven) were coded as having a consistent instructional vision. In contrast, only two of six low-gain schools were judged to exhibit this kind of consistency. Lack of a consistent view of the software's role was illustrated by the staff in a low-gain school, as described below (Means et al., 2006):

> The principal had little involvement with the study and was unsure how well the software fit with current school-wide initiatives. One of the two teachers using the software taught low-skilled and English-language-learner students and said that the software would be good for honors students but not for his students because the language and concepts were too advanced. The other software-using teacher taught honors students and said that they got bored with it, but he expected that the software would be good for remediation.

Principal support. In addition to being instrumental in forging a consistent instructional vision, principals can provide support for use of instructional software, not just in the form of permission and supportive verbal statements but also in terms of concrete actions, such as giving the classes using the software priority access to computer resources and arranging for joint planning periods or other paid opportunities for teachers to gain proficiency with the software and to plan for its use. The majority of high-gain schools in the follow-up sample (five of seven) had principals who supported the software implementation in those ways; the majority of low-gain schools (four of six) did not.

Teacher collaboration. Beyond the support from the principal, support from one's colleagues appears to be another factor present in schools that achieve learning gains with technology. All seven of the high-gain schools that could be scored for this variable reported that their teachers collaborated and supported each other on use of the software product. Only one third of the low-gain schools (two of six) reported this kind of teacher collaboration.

Two teachers at an elementary school implementing the reading software illustrated the kind of teacher collaboration found in the high-gain schools (Means et al., 2006):

> Collaboration between the two teachers using the software at this elementary school was very close. The younger teacher, who was in her second year of teaching, "handles the technical side, does reports, registers kids." The older, veteran teacher mentored her younger colleague on instructional strategies for elementary reading. They planned together at the beginning of the year and got together throughout the year to look at software reports and discuss student progress. One of the teachers noted that they even "get in competition a little with the scores." The school's technology coordinator commented that "they work well together; they're both committed to the program."

A number of researchers have suggested that the presence of strong ties among teachers who view themselves as a learning community will facilitate the adoption of technology (Frank, Zhao, & Borman, 2004; Strudler & Hearrington, 2008). In these case studies, however, there was no difference between the proportions of high- and low-gain schools in the follow-up sample that were judged to emphasize teacher collaboration generally (five of seven high-gain schools and four of six low-gain schools described themselves as collaborative). This finding suggests that the focus of the collaboration, not just a generally supportive climate, is important.

Technology infrastructure and technical support. In implementing the EETI effectiveness study, the research team took steps to make sure that each school had the technology infrastructure needed to implement the software assigned to treatment classrooms. The study team worked with districts to identify hardware and software needs such as computers, headphones, memory, and operating system upgrades, and the study purchased the upgrades as needed. Thus, all of the schools in the case studies (as well as those in the larger EETI study) had technology infrastructures that were, at least in theory, adequate for running the assigned reading or mathematics software.

When we asked case study teachers about the technology support available to them, we found that high-gain schools nearly always had on-site technical support that teachers considered good (six of seven high-gain schools). Half of the case study low-gain schools (three of six) were similarly happy with their on-site support while half were not. Hence, the qualitative data suggest that the quality of on-site technology support, rather than its mere presence, is important and that good local support is not sufficient but may be necessary to ensure positive outcomes with technology.

Receipt of additional training and support. In a typical implementation of commercial software, the school or district purchasing the software has the option of obtaining training and support services from the vendor. In the EETI study, these services were provided by vendors as part of the agreement around their participation. All of the commercial vendors with a product in the study conducted formal initial training for the teachers who would be implementing their software. In addition to this formal training, vendors were permitted to provide additional formal training sessions during the school year, face-to-face informal support as part of school visits, or assistance through a help desk, e-mail, or a website. Somewhat larger proportions of the high-gain schools received additional formal training and face-to-face informal support from the software vendors, but the differences were not dramatic and the samples are small. A similarly large majority of teachers in both high- and low-gain schools reported having access to technical assistance in the form of a help desk, e-mail, or website supporting use of the software.

Table 12.6 summarizes the differences between high- and low-gain schools in terms of school-wide implementation practices.

Table 12.6 Proportion of Schools with Schoolwide Practices and Supports, by Gain Status

Practice or Support	High-Gain Schools (*n* = 7)	Low-Gain Schools (*n* = 6)
Consistent instructional vision	4 of 7	2 of 6
Principal support for software use	5 of 7	2 of 6
Teacher collaboration around software use	7 of 7	2 of 6
Satisfactory on-site technical support	6 of 7	3 of 6
Receipt of additional formal training	3 of 7	1 of 6
Receipt of informal face-to-face support	5 of 7	3 of 6
Access to help desk, e-mail, website	6 of 7	5 of 6

CHANGES IN IMPLEMENTATION PRACTICES FROM YEAR 1 TO YEAR 2

Many changes in implementation practices in teachers' second year with the software appeared to reflect teachers' increased knowledge and confidence around software use. Nearly half of the teachers reported that technology problems were reduced in their second year of software implementation. Teachers at six of the 13 follow-up schools reported fewer technology problems in Year 2. One of these schools had gained a technology coordinator, and two schools that had had major start-up delays in Year 1 did not have this same problem in their second year of implementation. Teachers also credited their own increased familiarity with technology and with the programs for a decrease in technology problems. Technology problems do not always disappear with experience, however; two schools said that they had had more rather than fewer technology problems in Year 2. In both cases, a change in the school's technology infrastructure required reconfiguration of the technology for running the software.

One might expect teachers' increasing comfort with the technology to lead to more software use in their second year of implementation, but this was not the case. Nine teachers from five different schools reported using the software for less time in Year 2 than in Year 1, and only one teacher reported increased use. Time pressures and competition with other school improvement initiatives were the most frequently cited reasons for reducing the amount of time devoted to software use during the second year of implementation. Three of the schools where there was less software use in the second year had introduced a new core curriculum in the area covered by the software. Teachers said that the new curriculum required adjustment on their part and integrating the software with the new curriculum was difficult. At one of these schools, for example, teachers felt the new curriculum required them to do more whole-class instruction, making it more difficult to find time for software use.

Discussion

The findings from this study generally are consistent with the usual recommendations for school-level supports for technology in the education literature but are less similar to common recommendations for practices within classrooms implementing technology. The four school-level practices for which the study found support were:

- Establishment of a consistent instructional vision
- Principal support for software use
- Teacher collaboration around software use
- Satisfactory on-site technical support

These recommendations are among those commonly made in the educational technology literature (as shown in Table 12.1).

The classroom-level practices receiving the strongest empirical support from this study were:

- Reviewing software reports for all students weekly
- Managing the classroom effectively

Similar practices can be found in Table 12.2 ("Teacher reviews software reports" and "Efficient routines established for shifting in and out of technology use"), but there are fewer citations for them in the literature than there are for other practices, such as a low student-to-computer ratio, that did not receive empirical support either in the qualitative study of 27 classrooms reported here or in the large EETI study involving 132 classrooms.

One implication of this study for classroom practice and software implementation efforts is that teachers should be urged to capitalize on the assessment data that instructional software makes available. Most instructional software will adapt the learner's experience to the results of embedded assessments automatically. But teachers can use the software assessment reports also to identify specific areas where they can do more to support students during their regular classroom instruction, as was described by a number of case study teachers. Software reports can also bring to light individual students' motivational issues or learning disabilities that might have gone unnoticed during whole-class instruction.

A second implication is that training and support around instructional software should pay more attention to the details of classroom management. Teachers work with classes of different sizes, in different physical settings, and with different kinds of students. One of the teachers in the EETI study, for example, taught pre-Algebra to a large class of students in a space intended as a lecture hall. Students were widely spaced out in seats with small flip-up arms designed to hold a pad of paper. Distributing laptop computers and juggling papers and computers at the same time under such conditions is a challenge. Teachers also have different habitual routines for organizing and orchestrating class activities. All of these factors can influence the ease with which students can be transitioned into and out of technology-based activities. As with professional development on other aspects of teaching, it would be helpful for teachers to be able to observe examples of efficient routines for transitioning in and out of software use within the kind of setting in which they teach, and then to try out their transition strategy in their own classroom and school, with the opportunity to receive feedback and suggestions for improvement from experienced software-using coaches.

The study has implications also for future research. It raises but does not resolve questions about how teachers can best facilitate their students' work as students are engaging with software designed for independent individual use. The literature on classroom implementation of technology highlights the role of the teacher as a facilitator of students' technology use. This facilitative role is usually described as a move toward student-centered instruction and away from the more typical teacher role of directing classroom activities. However, other than giving students more responsibility, there is actually very little guidance in the literature about the most effective teacher facilitation practices when students are working with software. In these case studies, researchers categorized an identical percentage (67%) of observed teachers in high- and low-gain schools as "facilitating" students' use of software. It would be premature to suggest that teachers' facilitative behaviors do not affect student-learning gains, but this null result does suggest a need for a more precisely defined concept of teacher facilitation during software use. In interviews, teachers report gaining insights into their students' thinking by observing or working with students who are engaged with instructional software. But how should the teacher interact with the student to best support his or her learning with the software? When should teachers give answers and when should they give hints to students struggling with the online content? Should teachers attend primarily to motivational and behavioral issues or treat their students' software use as a "teachable moment" for individual students? Establishing an empirical basis for making recommendations in these areas requires theory development around facilitation, the development of reliable measures of different aspects of facilitation, and a program of systematic research.

Given the relatively small number of case study schools and of software implementing teachers within those schools, findings from the present study should be interpreted with caution. Certainly failure to find significant differences between high- and low-gain schools in terms of an often-recommended implementation practice could be attributable to limited statistical power. But those implementation variables for which significant differences did emerge, especially in cases where the case study data and the larger EETI data set provide converging evidence, merit attention. Here we have evidence that the practice is associated with learning gains, not just more frequent use of technology.

The descriptive data presented in the appendixes also highlight larger issues having to do with the way teachers juggle the requirements of software implementation with everything else they are trying to do in the classroom. Case study interviews and observations point to the need for more contextualized studies and a broader view of technology implementation. Rather than treating technology as a "thing" which is present or absent, researchers and educators need to look at instructional activity systems in context. Any piece of hardware or software is but a part of the instruction that students are exposed to in a given domain. The importance of teacher management of transitions onto and off of software, teachers' articulation of connections between online and offline instruction, and teachers' struggles to fit technology-based learning activities into schedules dominated by core curricula that are not technology-based underline the importance of taking this broader view.

Building on the concept of an instructional regime, as described by Cohen and Ball (1999), educators and policymakers need to stop thinking of learning software as an intervention in and of itself and to think instead of broader instructional activity systems (Roschelle, Knudsen, & Hegedus, 2010) defined by:

- Learning content
- Learning activities, only some of which are technology-based
- Articulation between a given learning activity system and other systems the student is exposed to
- Teacher professional development and collaboration around implementation of the instructional activity system
- Assessments for learning
- Use of data to refine the instructional activity on an ongoing basis

Such a framework has obvious implications for intervention design and what may be less obvious implications for research. We need to get beyond the simplistic "what works" view of learning technology as a "pill" that will have the same effect on outcomes for anyone in any context. We have ample evidence that implementation practices matter, and the instructional activity system framework suggests basic categories for the kinds of data that should be collected in any study of a technology-supported intervention in action.

The learning technology field needs implementation research contrasting the student outcomes produced by different implementation strategies and practices for the same intervention, not just comparisons of treatment versus no-treatment conditions. Education policymakers and practitioners need to think about the implementation of technology-supported interventions as a process of iteration and refinement rather than as a pill to be selected on the basis of "what works" evidence. Partnerships between the teachers, schools, and districts implementing technology-supported reforms and those who design and research such reforms can support a process of collaborative elaboration and adaptation of the intervention to fit local circumstances, followed by a cycle of implementation with monitoring of both the implementation process and outcomes for students. Findings of the implementation cycle can then inform another round of intervention refinement, again followed by implementation, monitoring, and improvement. Only by defining, measuring, and analyzing implementation variables and context along with student outcomes (Means & Penuel, 2005) can we gain the understanding that will support the implementation of technology-supported interventions in a way that optimizes student learning.

Author Update

As more and more K–12 instruction involves a blending of online and classroom-based elements, the popularity of the particular mathematics and reading software products that we studied in 2005–06 is uncertain. I have no doubt, however, that the same kinds of opportunities and challenges we observed in software-using classrooms will continue, whatever new technologies teachers are using in the next decade.

Changing one's teaching practice to incorporate new technology-supported learning opportunities is hard work. Teachers in settings that provide social and institutional support—from encouragement and recognition, to the provision of technical support, to colleagues with whom to collaborate and reflect—will be more likely to integrate technology into their practice in meaningful ways.

The spread of blended learning—where portions of students' learning are done online and at least partially under student control, while other portions involve face-to-face interaction with the teacher and other students—is likely to exacerbate two of the challenges we observed. Blended learning calls for efficient activity scheduling and classroom management. The emerging capability of online systems to track not only current levels of skill mastery, as in the case of the software described in this article, but also user habits, preferences, and more fine-grained, diagnostic aspects of learner behavior, will open up new possibilities for teachers to use data from online systems to inform their practice.

Policymakers hope that the adoption of common core standards in mathematics, reading, and eventually science in many states will reduce instructional incoherence and the sense of competing priorities for instructional time—two of the challenges we observed in software-using classes. At the same time, however, the number of web-based instructional resources available free of charge is growing

Continued

geometrically. The issue of instructional coherence becomes even more important when teachers are mixing and matching disparate web-based resources to create learning opportunities for their students. Where we observed students struggling with differences in terminology and representations between one piece of software and one textbook, future researchers may see students confronted with five or six different sets of terms and symbols from that many different open educational resources. If asked to bet on the race between standardization resulting from common standards and divergence related to the web, I'll bet on the Internet.

References

Adelman, N., Donnelly, M. B., Dove, T., Tiffany-Morales, J., Wayne, A., & Zucker, A. (2002). *The integrated studies of educational technology: Professional development and teachers' use of technology.* Menlo Park, CA: SRI International.

Bakia, M., Means, B., Gallagher, L., Chen, E., & Jones, K. (2009). *Evaluation of the Enhancing Education through Technology Program: Final report.* Washington, DC: U.S. Department of Education.

Barnett, H. (2001). Successful K–12 technology planning: Ten essential elements. ERIC Digest, ED457858. ERIC Clearinghouse on Information and Technology, Syracuse, NY. Available at www.ericdigests.org/2002-2/ten.htm

Becker, H. J. (1994). How exemplary computer-using teachers differ from other teachers: Implications for realizing the potential of computers in schools. *Journal of Research on Computing in Education, 26,* 291–320.

Becker, H. J. (2000). Who's wired and who's not: Children's access to and use of computer technology. *The Future of Children, 10*(2), 44–75.

Black, P., & Wiliam, D. (1998). *Inside the black box: Raising standards through classroom assessment.* London, UK: King's College.

Brand, G. A. (1997). What research says: Training teachers for using technology. *Journal of Staff Development, 19*(1). Retrieved from www.learningforward.org/news/articleDetails.cfm?articleID=268 (membership required). A draft is available at http://wikieducator.org/images/0/04/Training_Teachers_to_Use_Computers.pdf

Cavalier, J. C., & Klein, J. D. (1998). Effects of cooperative versus individual learning and orienting activities during computer-based instruction. *Educational Technology Research and Development, 46*(1), 5–17.

Cohen, D. K., & Ball, D. L. (1999). *Instruction, capacity, and improvement.* CPRE Research Report No. RR-043. Philadelphia: University of Pennsylvania, Consortium for Policy Research in Education.

Cole, K., Simkins, M., & Penuel, W. R. (2002). Learning to teach with technology: Strategies for inservice professional development. *Journal of Technology and Teacher Education, 10*(3), 431–455.

Coley, R. J., Cradler, J., & Engel, P. K. (1997). *Computers and classrooms: The status of technology in U.S. schools.* Princeton, NJ: Educational Testing Service. Retrieved from www.ets.org/Media/Research/pdf/PICCOMPCLSS.pdf

Cuban, L. (2001). *Oversold and underused: Computers in the classroom.* Cambridge, MA: Harvard University Press.

Dynarski, M., Agodini, R., Heaviside, S., Novak, T., Carey, N., Means, B., et al., (2007). *Effectiveness of educational technology interventions.* Report prepared for Institute of Education Sciences, U.S. Department of Education. Princeton, NJ: Mathematica Policy Research, Inc.

eMINTS Evaluation Team. (2003, January). *Analysis of 2002 MAP results for eMINTS students.* Retrieved from http://emints.org/evaluation/reports/map2002.pdf

Ertmer, P. A. (1999). Addressing first- and second-order barriers to change: Strategies for technology integration. *Educational Technology Research and Development, 47*(4), 47–61.

Frank, K. A., Zhao, Y., & Borman, K. (2004). Social capital and the diffusion of innovations within organizations: Application to the implementation of computer technology in schools. *Sociology of Education, 77*(2), 148–171.

Glennan, T. K., & Melmed, A. (1996). *Fostering the use of educational technology: Elements of a national strategy.* Santa Monica, CA: Critical Technologies Institute, RAND.

Hansen, E. E., Llosa, L. L., & Slayton, J. (2004). *Evaluation of the Waterford Early Reading Program as a supplementary program in the*

Los Angeles Unified School District: 2002–03. Planning, Assessment and Research Division Publication No. 177. Los Angeles, CA: Los Angeles Unified School District, Program Evaluation and Research Branch.

Hill, J., & Reeves, T. (2004). *Change takes time: The promise of ubiquitous computing in schools. A report of a four year evaluation of the laptop initiative at Athens Academy.* Athens, GA: University of Georgia.

Jones, B. F., Valdez, G., Nowakowski, J., & Rasmussen, C. (1995). *Plugging in: Choosing and using educational technology.* Oak Brook, IL: North Central Educational Research Laboratory. (ERIC Document Reproduction Service No. ED415837)

Mann, D., Shakeshaft, C., Becker, J., & Kottkamp, R. (1998). *West Virginia story: Achievement gains from a statewide comprehensive instructional technology program.* Santa Monica, CA: Milken Exchange on Educational Technology.

Martin, W., Culp, K., Gersick, A., & Nudell, H. (2003, April). *Intel Teach to the Future: Lessons learned from the evaluation of a large-scale technology-integration professional development program.* Paper presented at the annual meeting of American Educational Research Association, Chicago, IL. Available at http://cct.edc.org/admin/publications/speeches/ITTF_AERA03.pdf

Means, B., Murphy, R., Shear, L., Gorges, T., Hu, P., & Sussex, W. (2006). *Implementing reading and mathematics software.* Menlo Park, CA: SRI International. Available at http://ctl.sri.com/publications/downloads/SW_Case_Studies_Final.pdf

Means, B., & Olson, K. (1995). *Technology and education reform: Technical research report.* Menlo Park, CA: SRI International.

Means, B., & Penuel, W. R. (2005). Research to support scaling up technology-based educational interventions. In C. Dede, J. P. Honan, & L. C. Peters (Eds.), *Scaling up success: Lessons from technology-based educational improvement* (pp. 176–197). San Francisco, CA: Jossey-Bass.

Moore, G. (1999). *Crossing the chasm: Marketing and selling high-tech products to mainstream consumers.* New York, NY: Harper Business Essentials.

Nunnery, J. A., Ross, S. M., & McDonald, A. (2006). A randomized experimental evaluation of the impact of Accelerated Reader/Reading Renaissance implementation on reading achievement in grades 3 to 6. *Journal of Education for Students Placed at Risk, 11*(1), 1–18.

O'Dwyer, L. M., Russell, M., & Bebell, D. (2004). Identifying teacher, school, and district characteristics associated with elementary teachers' use of technology: A multilevel perspective. *Education Policy Analysis Archives, 12*(48). Available at http://epaa.asu.edu/epaa/v12n48/v12n48.pdf

O'Dwyer, L. M., Russell, M., & Bebell, D. (2005). Identifying teacher, school, and district characteristics associated with middle and high school teachers' use of technology: A multilevel perspective. *Journal of Educational Computing Research, 33*(4), 369–393.

Office of Technology Assessment (OTA), U.S. Congress. (1995). *Teachers and technology: Making the connection* (OTA-HER-616). Washington, DC: U.S. Government Printing Office.

Powell, J. V., Aeby, V. G., Jr., & Carpenter-Aeby, T. (2003). A comparison of student outcomes with and without teacher facilitated computer-based instruction. *Computers & Education, 40*, 183–191.

Roschelle, J., Knudsen, J., & Hegedus, S. (2010). From new technological structures to curricular activity systems: Advanced designs for teaching and learning. In M. J. Jacobson & P. Reiman (Eds.), *Designs for learning environments for the future: International perspectives from the learning sciences* (pp. 233–262). New York, NY: Springer.

Sandholtz, J. H., Ringstaff, C., & Dwyer, D. C. (1997). *Teaching with technology: Creating student-centered classrooms.* New York, NY: Teachers College Press.

Sarama, J., Clements, D. H., & Henry, J. J. (1998). Network of influences in an implementation of a mathematics curriculum innovation. *International Journal of Computers for Mathematical Learning, 3*(2), 113–148.

Strudler, N., & Hearrington, D. (2008). Quality support for ICT in schools. In J. Voogt & G. Knezek (Eds.), *International handbook of information technology in primary and secondary education*, (pp. 579–596). New York, NY: Springer.

Sweet, J. R., Rasher, S. P., Abromitis, B. S., & Johnson, E. M. (2004). *Case studies of high-performing, high-technology schools: Final research report on schools with predominantly low-income, African-American, or Latino student populations.* Oak Brook, IL: North Central Regional Educational Laboratory.

U.S. Department of Education. (2000). *Does professional development change teaching practice? Results from a three-year study.* Washington, DC.: Author.

Van Dusen, L. M., & Worthen, B. R. (1995). Can integrated instructional technology transform the classroom? *Educational Leadership, 53*(2), 28–33.

Wenglinsky, H. (1998). *Does it compute? The relationship between educational technology and student achievement in mathematics* [Policy Information Report]. Princeton, NJ: Educational Testing Service Policy Information Center.

Yamagata-Lynch, L. (2003). How a technology professional development program fits into a teacher's work life. *Teaching and Teacher Education, 19*(6), 591–607.

Zhao, Y., Pugh, K., Sheldon, S., & Byers, J. (2002). Conditions for classroom technology innovations. *Teachers College Record, 104*(3), 482–515.

CHAPTER

13

Perspectives on the Integration of Technology and Assessment

James W. Pellegrino | University of Illinois at Chicago

Edys S. Quellmalz | WestEd

This paper considers uses of technology in educational assessment from the perspective of innovation and support for teaching and learning. It examines assessment cases drawn from contexts that include large-scale testing programs as well as classroom-based programs, and attempts that have been made to harness the power of technology to provide rich, authentic tasks that elicit aspects of integrated knowledge, critical thinking, and problem solving. These aspects of cognition are seldom well addressed by traditional testing programs using paper and pencil or computer technologies. The paper also gives consideration to strategies for developing balanced, multilevel assessment systems that involve articulating relationships among curriculum-embedded, benchmark, and summative assessments that operate across classroom, district, state, national, and international levels. It discusses the multiple roles for technology in an assessment-based information system in light of the decision support needed from the multiple actors who operate across levels of the education system. The paper concludes with a consideration of the current state of the field as well as the potential for technology to help launch a new era of integrated, learning-centered assessment systems.

Across the disciplines, technologies have expanded the phenomena that can be investigated, the nature of argumentation, and the use of evidence. Technologies allow representations of domains, systems, models, data, and their manipulation in ways that previously were not possible. Dynamic models of ecosystems or molecular structures help scientists visualize and communicate complex interactions. Models of population density permit investigations of economic and social issues. This move from static to dynamic models has changed the nature of inquiry among professionals as well as the way that academic disciplines can be taught. Correspondingly, a new generation of assessments is well on its way to transforming what, how, when, where, and why assessment occurs and its linkages to teaching and learning. Powered by the ever-increasing capabilities of technology, these 21st-century approaches to assessment expand the potential for tests to both probe and promote a broad spectrum of human learning, including the types of knowledge and competence advocated in various recent policy reports on education and the economy (e.g., NCEE, 2007; NRC, 2006).

Although early uses of technology in large-scale testing have focused on relatively straightforward logistical efficiencies and cost reductions (see e.g., Bennett, 2008; Quellmalz & Pellegrino, 2009), a new generation of innovative assessments is pushing the frontiers of measuring complex forms of learning. The computer's ability to capture student inputs permits collecting evidence of processes such as problem-solving sequences and strategy use as reflected by information selected, numbers of attempts, approximation to solutions, and time allocation. Such data can be combined with statistical and measurement algorithms to extract patterns associated with varying levels of expertise (e.g., Vendlinski & Stevens, 2002). Research in the learning sciences is simultaneously informing the design of innovative, dynamic, interactive assessment tasks and powerful scoring, reporting, and real-time feedback mechanisms. When coupled with technology, such knowledge has propelled various advances in adaptive testing, including knowledge and skills diagnosis, the provision of immediate feedback to teachers and students accompanied by scaffolding for improvement, and the potential for accommodations for special populations. Technology also supports movement toward the design of more balanced sets of coherent, nested assessments that operate across levels of educational systems.

Each of the preceding constitutes a major body of theory, research, and development and deserves major treatment that is well beyond the limits of the current article. This paper attempts to illustrate some of the major trends at work by examining a few of the emergent cases that have used technology to push the envelope with regard to a new generation of educational assessment. It seems clear that the use of assessment to support the attainment of many of our current goals for education improvement will require interdisciplinary partnerships and considerable additional research and development. It will also demand major shifts in education policies and practices in the designs of assessments, the models for testing, and the use of assessment data for various purposes, including student, teacher, and system-level accountability.

Technology-Enabled Assessments in State, National, and International Assessment Programs

Information and communications technologies such as web browsers, word processors, editing, drawing, simulations, and multimedia programs support a variety of research, design, composition, and communication processes. These same tools can expand the cognitive skills that can be assessed, including the processes of planning, drafting, composing, and revising. For example, the National Assessment of Educational Progress (NAEP) writing assessment in 2011 will require use of word processing and editing tools to compose essays. In professional testing, architecture examinees use computer-assisted design (CAD) programs as part of their licensure assessment. The challenge that such technology-based presentation and data capture contexts offers now lies in the design principles for eliciting complex learning, the analysis of complex forms of data, and their meaningful interpretation relative to models of the underlying components of competence and expertise.

The area of science assessment is perhaps leading the way in exploring the presentation and interpretation of complex, multifaceted problem types and assessment approaches. In 2006, the Programme for International Student Assessment (PISA) pilot tested a Computer-Based Assessment of Science to test knowledge and inquiry processes not assessed in the paper-based booklets. The assessment included such student explorations as the genetic breeding of plants. At the state level, Minnesota has an online science test with tasks engaging students in simulated laboratory experiments or investigations of phenomena such as weather or the solar system.

ETS pioneered the design of technology-based assessments for complex learning and performance (Bennett, Persky, Weiss, & Jenkins, 2007). An example of the type of item that Bennett et al. evaluated is shown in Figure 13.1. In this technology-based simulation task, eighth graders are asked to use a hot-air balloon simulation to design and conduct an experiment to determine the relationship between payload mass and balloon altitude. After completing the tutorial about the simulation tool interface, students select values for the independent variable payload mass. They can observe the balloon rise in the flight box and note changes in the values of the dependent variables of altitude, balloon volume, and time to final altitude. In another problem using the simulation, the amount of helium, another independent variable, is held constant to reduce the task's difficulty. Students can construct tables and graphs and draw conclusions by clicking on the buttons below the heading labeled Interpret Results. Figure 13.1 also shows the types of data that a student might obtain and plot prior to reaching a conclusion and writing a final response. As students work with the simulation, they can get help as needed in the form of (a) a glossary of science terms, (b) science help about the substance of the problem, and (c) computer help about the buttons and functions of the simulation interface that are built into the technology environment. Student performance can be used to derive measures of the student's computer skills, scientific inquiry exploration skills, and scientific inquiry synthesis skills within the context of physics.

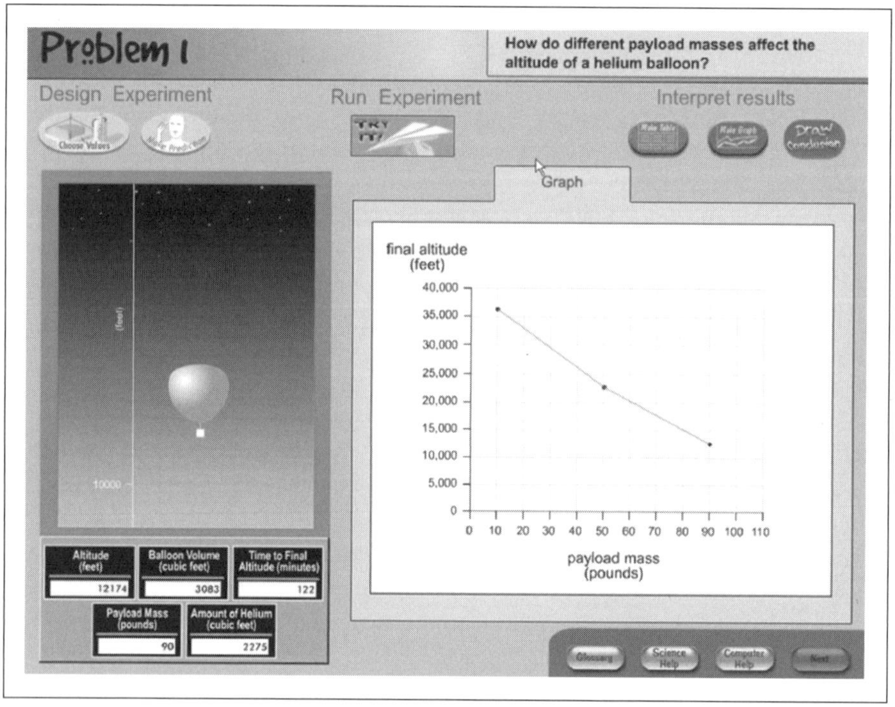

Figure 13.1 Example of large-scale science assessment task developed by ETS

The 2009 NAEP Science Framework and specifications drew upon ETS's work and other research in developing their rationale for the design and pilot testing of Interactive Computer Tasks (ICT) to test students' ability to engage in inquiry practices. Such innovative items were included in the 2009 NAEP science administration. The new 2014 Technology and Engineering Literacy Framework for NAEP will be entirely computer administered and will include specifications for interactive, simulation-based tasks involving problem solving, communication, and collaboration related to technology and society, design and systems, and information communications technology.

Large-scale testing programs such as those mentioned above are just beginning to explore the possibilities of using dynamic, interactive tasks for obtaining evidence of student content knowledge and reasoning. However, in the realm of high-stakes assessment for No Child Left Behind (NCLB) accountability, a number of regulatory, economic, and logistical issues have constrained the breadth and depth of the content and performance standards assessed in annual on-demand tests. Standard, multiple-choice item formats continue to dominate large-scale, computer-based, high-stakes testing, resulting in an overreliance on simple, highly structured problems that tap fact retrieval and the use of algorithmic solution procedures.

Technology-Enabled Assessments for Classroom Instructional Uses

A distinction has been made between assessments of the outcomes of learning, typically used for grading and accountability purposes (summative assessment), and assessments for learning, used to diagnose and modify the conditions of learning and instruction (formative assessment) (Stiggins, 2005). Research has repeatedly shown the formative use of assessment to significantly benefit student achievement (Black & Wiliam, 1998; Wiliam, 2007). Such effects depend on several classroom practice factors, including alignment of assessments with state standards, quality of the feedback provided to students, involvement of students in self-reflection and action, and teachers making adjustments to their instruction based on the assessment results (Black et al., 2004). Technologies are well suited to support many of the data collection, complex analysis, and individualized feedback and scaffolding features needed for the formative use of assessment (Brown, Hinze, & Pellegrino, 2008). Two illustrative projects, one drawn from science and the other from mathematics, rely on detailed analyses of subject matter domains and student thinking to provide in-depth assessment and feedback during instruction.

The DIAGNOSER project is based on the facets framework for mapping aspects of student knowledge (Hunt & Minstrell, 1996; Minstrell & Stimpton, 1996) combined with principles of guided inquiry (see Minstrell & Kraus, 2005). It has set out to do the difficult work of breaking down physics concepts into requisite knowledge sets and misconceptions (facets). The facet framework is based on the understanding that students have preconceptions about scientific concepts that are not necessarily unique. For example, students may think that magnets exert a force only when they touch an object, or that "cold" can flow out of something that feels cold. For each of a number of physics concepts appropriate for middle school to high school level courses, researchers have created a series of multiresponse items designed to have every facet represented at least once in a response choice. Figure 13.2 provides an example of an item available online in the DIAGNOSER system. Occasionally, the system asks students to provide their reasoning for a response by choosing an option, which encourages consistent scientific reasoning. Each topic contains two question sets, and instructors are supposed to use prescriptive activities between question sets. Other resources are provided as support materials.

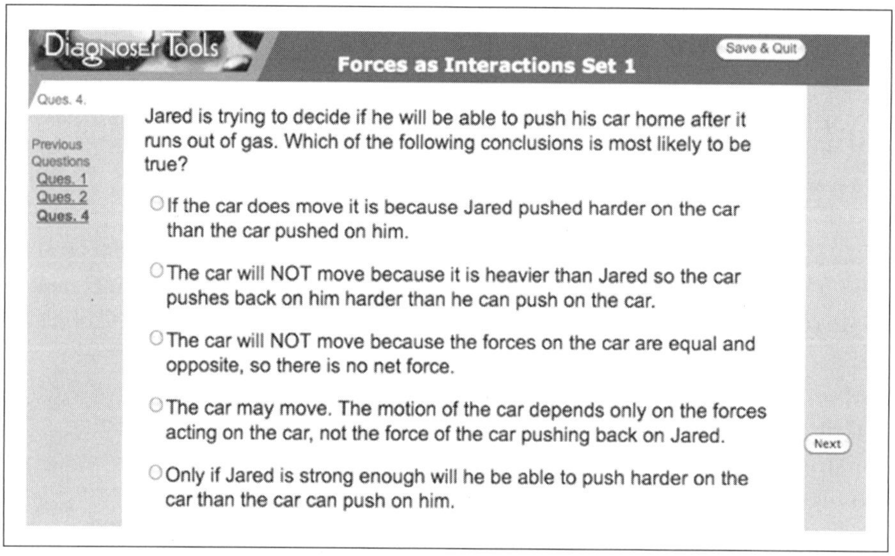

Figure 13.2 Example of a DIAGNOSER physics assessment item

Based on a student's response to an item such as that shown in Figure 13.2, as well as others in a set related to this topic area, the system diagnoses the student's level of understanding. Through the web-based system, students respond and receive immediate and cumulative constructive feedback. Teachers receive the results immediately and can refer to a series of prescriptive activities tailored to address each facet. It would be difficult to replicate the feedback system without the web-based design, which provides opportunities for self-regulated learning on the part of the student as well as targeted interventions on the part of the teacher. Providing two question sets along with supplemental material allows for intervention and re-assessment to work toward advancing student understanding. In a validation study in a Washington state district, students using DIAGNOSER outperformed their peers on items from the state science test.

Another example is the ASSISTment system, which is a pseudo-tutor for middle school level mathematics. Originally based on items from the Massachusetts state standardized test, researchers have developed a feedback system for each item through discussions with teachers. The system uses scaffolding questions, optional hints, and buggy messages (specific feedback given after student errors) for each item. Students must eventually reach the correct answer, and scaffolds/hints are limited to avoid giving away the answer (Feng, Heffernan, & Koedinger, 2006, 2009). Teachers receive feedback on student and class progress both on general summative measures (e.g., time to completion, percent correct) and on more specific knowledge components. Students also receive item-level analyses to identify specific issues with problems (Feng & Heffernen, 2005). Evaluation of the efficacy of ASSISTments has shown that performance is predictive of performance on randomly selected standardized test questions in paper-and-pencil format, and finer-grained models predict standardized-test performance better than typical scores (Feng et al., 2006, 2009), indicating that providing this analysis to teachers should be useful in interpreting students' skills. More than 60% of students self-report that the ASSISTments help them with the standardized tests, and there is some evidence that scaffolds help students transfer knowledge better than hints, especially on difficult problems.

In addition to assessment of student knowledge and skills in highly structured problems with one right answer, technology can also support the design of complex, interactive tasks that extend the range of knowledge, skills, and cognitive processes that can be assessed (Quellmalz & Haertel, 2004). For example, simulations can assess and promote understanding of complex systems by superimposing multiple representations and permitting manipulation of structures and patterns that otherwise might not be visible or even conceivable. Simulation-based assessments can probe basic foundational knowledge such as the functions of organisms in an ecosystem, and, more important, they can probe students' knowledge of how components of a system interact along with abilities to investigate the impacts of multiple variables changing at the same time (Quellmalz, Timms, & Buckley, 2009). Moreover, because simulations use multiple modalities and representations, students with diverse learning styles and language backgrounds may have better opportunities to demonstrate their knowledge than are possible in text-laden print tests.

In an ongoing program of research and development, WestEd's SimScientists projects (http://simscientists.org) are studying the suitability of simulation-based science assessments as summative assessments with the technical quality required for components of an accountability system (Quellmalz et al., 2008; Quellmalz, Timms, & Buckley, 2010). New SimScientists projects are also studying use of simulations for curriculum-embedded formative uses of assessment. Figures 13.3 and 13.4 present screenshots of tasks in a SimScientists summative, benchmark assessment designed to provide evidence of middle school students' understanding of ecosystems and inquiry practices after completing a regular curriculum unit on ecosystems.

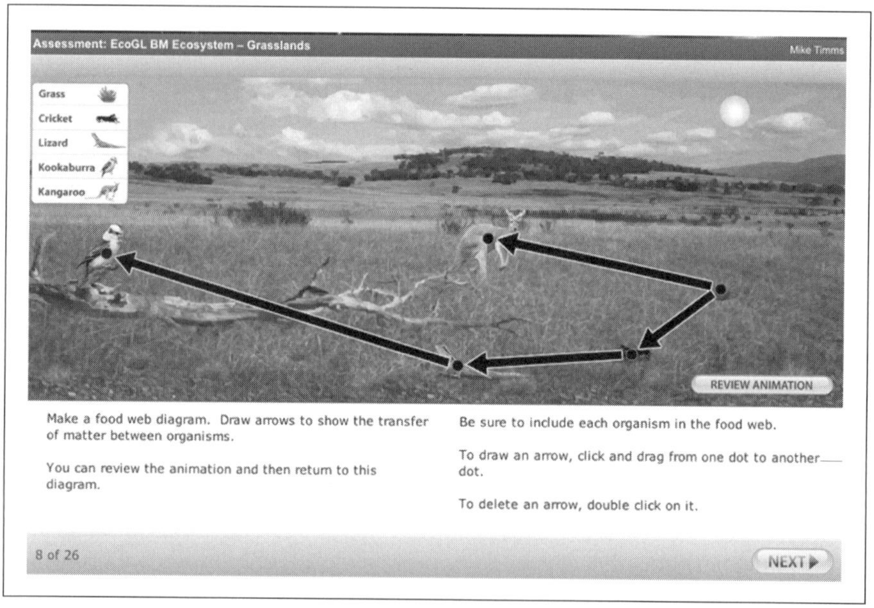

Figure 13.3 Screenshot of SimScientists ecosystems benchmark assessment showing a food web diagram interactively produced by a student after observing the behaviors of organisms in the simulated Australian grasslands environment

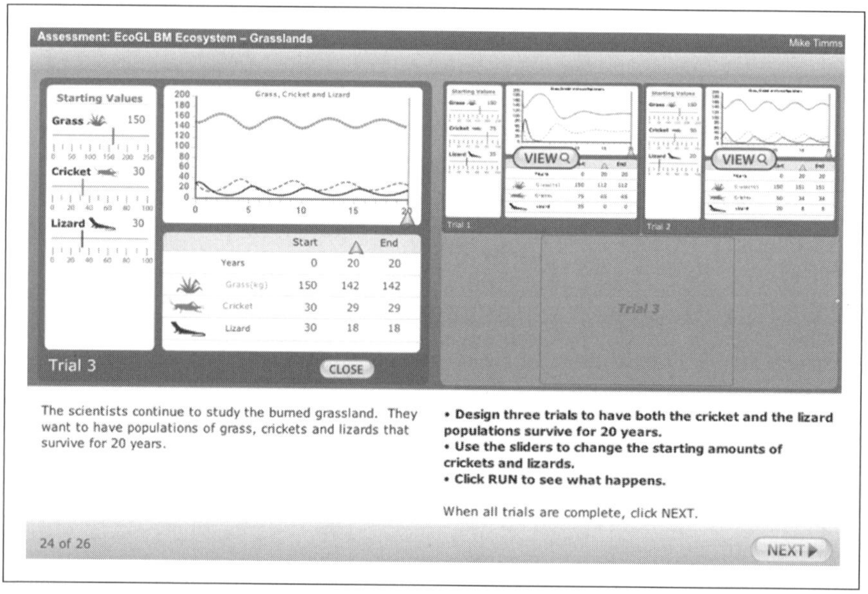

Figure 13.4 Screenshot of SimScientists ecosystems benchmark assessment showing a student's investigations with the interactive population model

Students are presented with the overarching problem of preparing a report to describe the ecology of an Australian grasslands ecosystem for an interpretive center. They investigate the roles and relationships of the animals, birds, insects, and grass by observing animations of the interactions among the organisms. Students draw a food web representing these interactions in the novel ecosystem. The assessment then presents sets of simulation-based tasks and items that focus on students' understanding of the emergent behaviors of the dynamic ecosystem by conducting investigations with the simulation to predict, observe, and explain what happens to population levels when numbers of particular organisms are varied. In a culminating task, students present their findings about the grasslands ecosystem.

In a companion set of curriculum embedded formative assessments situated in a different ecosystem, a mountain lake, the technological infrastructure identifies types of errors and follows up with feedback and graduated coaching. Figure 13.5 illustrates one of the levels of feedback and coaching that progresses from identifying that an error has occurred and asking the student to try again, to showing worked examples of investigations that met the specifications. For constructed responses, students self-assess by judging if their explanations meet criteria or match a sample response.

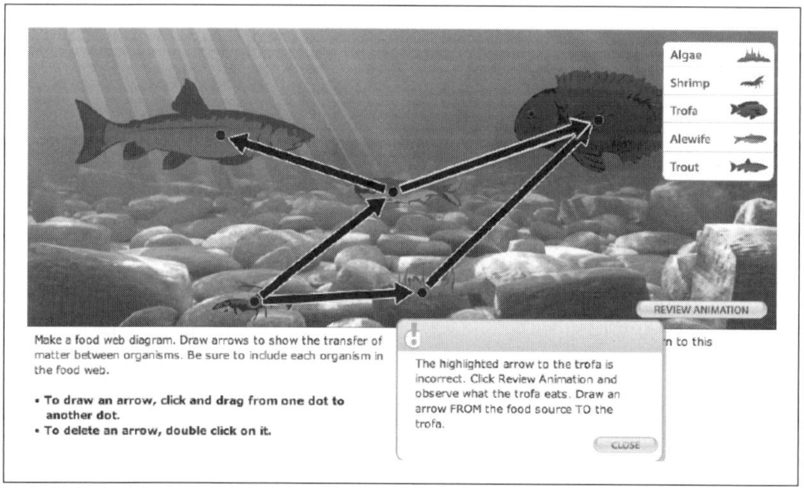

Figure 13.5 Screenshot of SimScientists ecosystems formative embedded assessment providing feedback and coaching following student errors in drawing food web arrows after observing the behaviors of organisms in the simulated mountain lake environment

These SimScientists examples illustrate ways that assessment tasks can take advantage of the affordances of simulations to represent generalizable, progressively complex models of science systems; present significant, challenging inquiry tasks; provide individualized feedback; customize scaffolding; and promote self-assessment and metacognitive skills. Reports that the SimScientists learning management system generates in the embedded assessments for teachers and students indicate the level of additional help students may need and classify students into groups for tailored follow-on offline reflection activities, which further guide students to use scientific discourse. The project promotes model-based reasoning about the common organization and behaviors of all ecosystems to transfer knowledge about ecosystem components, interactions, and emergent behaviors to examples of new ecosystems. Research in the SimScientists projects is studying the technical quality of the assessments, the potential of the end-of-unit assessments as components of a state science accountability system, and the impact of the curriculum-embedded assessments and feedback on student learning. Project designs such as these can document the validity and utility of technology-based assessments for both instructional and accountability purposes.

Technology and the Development of Multilevel Assessment Systems

It is widely recognized that states must aim for balanced state assessment systems in which district, classroom, and state tests are aligned and mutually reinforcing. In the National Research Council (NRC) report *Knowing What Students Know*, a balanced assessment system relies on a nested system of assessments that exhibits features of comprehensiveness, coherence, and continuity (Pellegrino, Chudowsky, & Glaser, 2001). Comprehensiveness is achieved by multiple measures of the full range of standards. Coherence involves a horizontal alignment of standards, goals, assessments, curriculum, and instruction as well as vertical alignment among assessments at different levels of the system. Continuity is achieved by going beyond annual, on-demand tests to multiple assessments over time and in time for teachers to tailor instruction. Indeed, underlying the introduction of the NCLB requirement for statewide testing is the assumption that, given timely access to information about student learning, teachers will draw inferences about areas of need and use research and standards for best practice to make sound decisions for improving learning. However, the disconnect between classroom assessments and large-scale tests tends to reduce the coherence of a statewide assessment system and interfere with sound instructional decision making.

Consensus is growing that better methods for capturing and connecting compelling evidence of student learning, both content knowledge and reasoning and inquiry skills, must be implemented across levels of the educational system. To this end, the National Science Foundation (NSF) funded the National Research Council to offer recommendations to states on their science assessment systems (see Wilson & Bertenthal, 2005). In a report commissioned by that project, Quellmalz and Moody (2004) proposed strategies for states to form collaboratives and use technology to create multilevel science assessment systems based on common standards and task design specifications. With the goal of helping schools and students meet federally mandated accountability goals, states are seeing formative assessment as a powerful tool for driving student achievement. Formative assessment is distinguished from summative, end-of-unit, and course benchmark assessments and from summative, interim, cross-unit assessments administered on a larger scale that are intended to describe the status of student performance periodically during the school year (Perie, Marion, & Gong, 2009; Quellmalz, Timms, & Buckley, 2010).

When well designed and implemented, classroom assessments that are used during instruction to monitor and improve progress and that are also administered following instruction to document learning and identify remaining needs can become credible components of a multilevel state assessment system. Technology-enhanced formative assessments during instruction can provide immediate, contingent feedback and adaptive coaching for reteaching of problematic knowledge and skills. Benchmark assessments following instruction can provide summative classroom-based assessments with technical quality that could be aggregated into the state accountability system.

Online authoring systems promise to streamline test design and reduce development costs (Mislevy & Haertel, 2007). The use of common specifications to design assessments at classroom, district, state, and national levels holds great promise for articulating the components of balanced assessment systems (Quellmalz & Moody, 2004). In addition, online design systems can support adaptations of assessments to offer accommodations for special populations while preserving the links between targeted standards and the designs of the tasks for eliciting evidence of achievement.

Technology's Multiple Roles in the Development of Assessment-Based Information Systems

Assessment programs should be designed to produce results that allow educators and policy makers to address a variety of questions about how a nation, state, district, school, program, group, or individual is performing. The goal is to make assessment results available to the right people, in the right form, at the right time so that assessment informs decisions and actions. Before individuals can answer questions, they must have the assessment results to work with. The goal is to collect the results in timely and efficient ways that allow educators and policy makers to answer their most important questions. Finally, it is not enough to answer questions; the answers must inform action. The goal is to help people use assessment results to make decisions about what actions to take. A technology infrastructure is a collection of tools and processes that help people achieve these goals.

There are a variety of roles that technology might play in this complex process. It is likely that a collection of tools, rather than a single tool, will fulfill these roles. However, information must flow appropriately between tools to support the differing needs of different people. Table 13.1 lists some of the roles that technology might play in the assessment process. Part of designing and implementing an assessment system for a school, district, or state is determining the appropriate roles for technology in that system.

Table 13.1 Functions of Technology in Supporting the Use of Assessment in Education

Collecting	Reporting	Using
Create assessment materials	Manage assessment data	Identify teaching resources
Tailor assessment administration	Analyze and interpret assessment data	Identify possible actions
Collect assessment data	Create reports	Design professional development
Score assessment performance	Distribute reports	Deliver professional development

Given the range of assessment tasks and data on student performance that are potentially available within the educational context, it is clear that the processes of collecting, scoring, and interpreting assessment data and then longitudinally tracking student performance are formidable. It is highly unlikely that any teacher, principal, or district or state administrator would be able to succeed in using all the assessment data available to him or her without the support of technology tools to assist in such a process across a variety of assessment levels and time frames. Thus, an important direction for development and implementation of assessment systems is the design of specific and general technology-based tools that can assist educators in managing the assessment process. Ideally, one would like to have a system with extensive diagnostic assessment capability.

The design and deployment of even simple technology tools must ultimately rely on a technology infrastructure that connects the classroom to powerful database management and information retrieval systems that operate within and across schools and systems. This is especially true when the classroom assessment data are viewed as part of a coordinated system of assessment data that would potentially include curriculum-embedded assessment information, unit and end-of-course benchmark assessment data, interim cross-unit summative status checks, and state-level test data. Further work addressing issues of technology and the design of a comprehensive assessment system involves consideration of information and how it needs to flow through this system. For example, who needs to use assessment data? What questions need to be answered? In what time frame do they need to be answered? What actions might they take based on these answers?

Conclusions, Implications, and Future Directions

It is an exciting time in the field of assessment for several reasons. First, individuals have realized that there are multiple roles for assessment to play in the educational process and that one of the most valuable roles is the formative function of assisting student learning. Second, cognitive research and theory have provided us with rich models and representations of how students understand many of the key principles in the curriculum, how students develop knowledge structures, and how to analyze and understand simple and complex aspects of student performance. Third, technology makes possible more flexible, tailored presentations to students of a much wider and richer array of tasks and environments where students can learn and where they can show us what they know and how they know it. Thus, there is an interesting and powerful confluence among theory, research, technology, and practice, especially when it comes to the integration of curriculum, instruction, and assessment.

In numerous areas of the curriculum, information technologies are changing what is taught, when and how it is taught, and what students are expected to be able to do to demonstrate their knowledge and skill. These changes in turn are stimulating people to rethink what is assessed, how that information is obtained, and how it is fed back into the educational process in a productive and timely way. This situation creates opportunities to center curriculum, instruction, and assessment around cognitive principles. With technology, assessment can become richer, timelier, and more seamlessly interwoven with multiple aspects of curriculum and instruction. As discussed earlier, the most useful kinds of assessment for enhancing student learning emphasize knowledge integration and extended reasoning, support a process of individualized instruction, allow for student interaction, collect rich diagnostic data, and provide timely feedback. The demands and complexity of these types of assessment can be quite substantial, but technology makes them feasible. Diagnostic assessments of individuals' learning, for example, must involve collecting, interpreting, and reporting significant amounts of information. No educator, whether a classroom teacher or other user of assessment data, could realistically be expected to handle the information flow, analysis demands, and decision-making burdens involved without technological support. Thus, technology removes some of the constraints that previously made high-quality formative assessment of complex performances difficult or impractical for a classroom teacher. The examples described above illustrate how technology can help infuse ongoing formative assessment into the learning process.

Clearly, we are just beginning to see how to harness technology to support the formative and summative functions of assessment. We still need to learn a great deal about the quality and efficacy of systems operating at both the large-scale level and the small-scale level. Not the least of the concerns facing us is the integration of assessment tools and practices into the educational system and teachers' practices. But we must also take note of the fact that extremely powerful information technologies are becoming as ubiquitous in educational settings as they are in other aspects of people's daily lives. Technologies are almost certain to continue to provoke fundamental changes in learning environments at all levels of the education system. Many of the implications of technology are beyond people's speculative capacity. Little more than 15 years ago, for example, few could have predicted the sweeping effects of the Internet and social networking on education and other segments of society. The range of computational devices and their applications is expanding exponentially, fundamentally changing how people think about communication, collaboration, problem solving, connectivity, information systems, educational practices, and the role of technology in society.

Although it is always risky to try to predict the future, it appears clear that advances in technology will continue to affect the world of education in powerful and provocative ways. The following scenario is adapted from one originally developed in Pellegrino et al. (2001). Many technology-driven advances in the design of learning environments, which include the integration of assessment with instruction, will continue to emerge and will reshape the terrain of what is both possible and desirable in education. Advances in curriculum, instruction, assessment, and technology are likely to continue to move educational practice toward more individualized and mastery-oriented approaches to learning, yet at the same time intertwine networking with resources, experts, and peers in problems requiring more complex forms of reasoning, problem solving, and collaboration. This evolution will occur across the K–16+ spectrum. To manage learning and instruction effectively, people will want and need to know considerably more about what has been mastered, at what level, by whom, with what levels of scaffolding.

Consider the possibilities that might arise if we integrate assessment into instruction in multiple curricular areas and collect the resultant information about student accomplishment and understanding with the aid of technology. In such a world, programs of on-demand external assessment, such as state achievement tests, might not be necessary. Instead, it might be possible to extract the information needed for summative and program evaluation purposes from data about student performance continuously available both in and out of the school context.

Technology could offer ways of creating, over time, a complex stream of data about how students think and reason, independently and collaboratively, while engaged in important learning activities. We could extract information for assessment purposes from this stream and use it to serve both classroom and external assessment needs, including providing customized feedback to students for reflection about their knowledge and skills, learning strategies, and habits. To realize this vision, additional research on the problem and data representations and analysis methods best suited for different learning goals, audiences, and different assessment objectives would clearly be needed—and is certainly doable.

We can therefore imagine a future in which the audit function of assessments external to the classroom would be significantly reduced or even unnecessary because the information needed to assess students, at the levels of description appropriate for various monitoring purposes, could be mined from the data streams generated by students in and out of their classrooms. A metaphor for such a radical shift in how one "does the business of educational assessment" exists in the world of retail outlets, ranging from small businesses to supermarkets to department stores. No longer do these businesses have to close down once or twice a year to take inventory of their stock. Rather, with the advent of automated checkouts and barcodes for all items, these enterprises have access to a continuous stream of information that can be used to monitor inventory and the flow of items. Not only can business continue without interruption, but the information obtained is far richer, enabling stores to monitor trends and aggregate the data into various kinds of summaries. Similarly, with new assessment technologies, schools would no longer have to interrupt the normal instructional process at various times during the year to administer external tests to students, nor would they have to spend significant amounts of time preparing for specific external tests peripheral to the ongoing activities of teaching and learning.

Extensive technology-based systems that link curriculum, instruction, and assessment at the classroom level might enable a shift from today's assessment systems, which use different kinds of assessments for different purposes, to a balanced design that would ensure the three critical features of comprehensiveness, coherence, and continuity. In such a design, assessments would provide a variety of evidence to support educational decision making (comprehensiveness). The information provided at differing levels of responsibility and action would be linked back to the same underlying conceptual model of student learning (coherence) and would provide indications of student growth over time (continuity).

Clearly, technological advances will allow for the attainment of many of the goals that educators, researchers, policymakers, teachers, and parents have envisioned for assessment as a viable source of information for educational improvement. When we implement powerful technology-based systems in classrooms, rich sources of information about intellectually significant student learning will be continuously available across wide segments of the curriculum and for individual learners over extended periods of time. This is exactly the kind of information we now lack, making it difficult to use assessment to truly support learning. The major issue is not whether this type of innovative assessment design, data collection, and information analysis is feasible in the future. Rather, the issue is how the world of education anticipates and embraces this possibility, and how it will explore the resulting options for effectively using assessment information to meet the multiple purposes served by current assessments and, most important, to enhance student learning.

Author Update

It would be hard to imagine any aspect of the education landscape that is developing and changing more rapidly than applications of technology to important educational assessment challenges. In fact, many of the trends, examples, and issues highlighted in this chapter have only become more significant given recent developments. Below we reflect on what is happening in four influential areas that collectively are supporting and accelerating the transformation of technology-enabled assessment.

At the level of national technology and assessment policy, the U.S. Department of Education's 2010 Race-To-The-Top (RTTT) assessment initiative has set forth a vision and provided substantial funding for a new generation of multilevel, technology-enhanced assessment systems. Multi-state assessment consortia have begun four-year plans to harness technology to create balanced assessment systems incorporating adaptive testing, automated scoring, integration of multiple interim assessments, and web-based shared collections of classroom-based performance assessments. Complementing the RTTT effort is the vision in the U.S. Department of Education's 2010 National Technology Plan (NETP) for applying technology to "measure what matters" and use assessment results to support continuous improvement across PK–16+.

Continued

Much of what is contemplated in both RTTT and NETP relies on intelligent and adaptive uses of technology to assess the forms of knowledge and competence deemed important for the 21st century. The latter have been articulated in the Grade 6–12 standards for science education released by the College Board and in the framework for K–12 science education standards soon to be released by the National Research Council. These efforts in science complement the Common Core State Standards released during 2010 for English Language Arts and Mathematics. All these documents focus on educational targets that involve deeper understanding of core disciplinary knowledge that is intimately connected to practices of disciplinary reasoning. The definition and assessment of the important learning outcomes intended in these standards inevitably rests on applications of technology to collect and interpret the processes and products that students will be asked to generate to demonstrate their learning and competence. This will occur in the classroom for normal instructional processes and in contexts designed for summative evaluation purposes, including what is anticipated by the RTTT assessment effort.

As highlighted in our article, technology is also becoming the engine driving delivery, scoring, and reporting for a variety of national and international assessment programs. This includes the National Assessment of Educational Progress (NAEP) examinations for 2011 Writing, the 2014 new assessment of Technology and Engineering Literacy, and the 2015 Science assessment. These large-scale assessments will harness technology in a variety of ways including innovative, interactive task and item formats for science inquiry, for problem solving, and for evaluating transmedia literacy. Internationally, the IEA will administer an assessment of Information Communication Technology (ICT), and in 2015 PISA Science will include a range of science reasoning tasks administered and scored by computer as part of the new science framework, as well as expanding the problem solving framework to include computer-based problem solving tasks performed by individuals as well as collaborative groups.

Continued

Many of the trends that we describe above will need to rely on related advances in research and development concerned with developing and clarifying methods for studying the construct and instructional validities of this new generation of assessment tasks and formats, most especially their capacity for yielding information that supports the processes of learning and teaching. Research on classroom instructional uses of transformative assessments is accumulating evidence of their instructional utility, feasibility, and technical quality, but much remains to be done. The same can be said about the importance of work on refining and applying psychometric methods for purposes of analyzing the complex performance data that can be derived from rich interactive task formats. Suffice it to say that although the promise of technology-enhanced assessment for documenting and supporting learning and teaching that was overviewed in our article is increasing, it is clear that we have much to learn about how best to do so in ways that are productive for students, teachers, and schools. Fortunately, the opportunities and venues in which to do such work are expanding at an exponential rate.

References

Bennett, R. E. (2008). *Technology for large-scale assessment.* ETS Report No. RM-08-10. Princeton, NJ: Educational Testing Service.

Bennett, R. E., Persky, H., Weiss, A. R., & Jenkins, F. (2007). *Problem solving in technology-rich environments: A report from the NAEP Technology-Based Assessment Project (NCES 2007–466).* Washington, DC: National Center for Education Statistics, U.S. Department of Education. Retrieved from http://nces.ed.gov/pubsearch/pubsinfo.asp?pubid=2007466

Black, P., Harrison, C., Lee, C., Marshall, B., & Wiliam, D. (2004). Working inside the black box: Assessment for learning in the classroom. *Phi Delta Kappan, 86*(1), 8–21.

Black, P., & Wiliam, D. (1998). *Inside the black box: Raising standards through classroom assessment.* London, UK: King's College.

Brown, J., Hinze, S., & Pellegrino, J. W. (2008). Technology and formative assessment. In T. Good (Ed.), *21st Century Education.* Vol 2. Technology (pp. 245–255). Thousand Oaks, CA: Sage.

Feng, M., & Heffernan, N. T. (2005). Informing teachers live about student learning: Reporting in the ASSISTment system. *Technology, Instruction, Cognition and Learning, 3,* 1–14.

Feng, M., Heffernan, N. T., & Koedinger, K. (2006). Predicting state test scores better with intelligent tutoring systems: Developing metrics to measure assistance required. In M. Ikeda, K. Ashley, & T-W. Chan (Eds.), *Proceedings of the Eighth International Conference on Intelligent Tutoring Systems* (pp. 31–40). Berlin, Germany: Springer-Verlag.

Feng, M., Heffernan, N. T., & Koedinger, K. R. (2009). Addressing the assessment challenge in an online system that tutors as it assesses. User Modeling and User-Adapted Interaction: *The Journal of Personalization Research (UMUAI), 19*(3), 243–266.

Hunt, E., & Minstrell, J. (1996). Effective instruction in science and mathematics: Psychological principles and social constraints. *Issues in Education: Contributions from Educational Psychology, 2,* 123–162.

Minstrell, M., & Kraus, P. (2005). Guided inquiry in the classroom. In J. Bransford & S. Donovan (Eds.), *How students learn history, mathematics, and science in the classroom* (pp. 475–515). Washington, DC: National Academy Press.

Minstrell, J., & Stimpton, V. (1996). A classroom environment for learning: Guiding students' reconstruction of understanding and reasoning. In L. Schauble & R. Glaser (Eds.), *Innovations in learning: New environments for education* (pp. 175–202). Mahwah, NJ: Lawrence Erlbaum.

Mislevy, R., & Haertel, G. D. (2007). Implications of evidence-centered designs for educational testing. *Educational Measurement: Issues and Practices, 25*(4), 6–20.

National Center on Education and the Economy (NCEE). (2007). *Tough choices or tough times: Report of the new commission on the skills of the American workforce.* Washington, DC: Jossey-Bass.

National Research Council (NRC). (2006). *Rising above the gathering storm: Energizing and employing America for a brighter economic future.* Committee on Prospering in the Global Economy in the 21st Century: An Agenda for Science and Technology. Committee on Science, Engineering, and Public Policy. Washington, DC: National Academy Press.

Pellegrino, J., Chudowsky, N., & Glaser, R. (Eds.) (2001). *Knowing what students know: The science and design of educational assessment.* National Research Council's Committee on the Foundations of Assessment. Washington, DC: National Academy Press.

Perie, M., Marion, S., & Gong, B. (2009). Moving towards a comprehensive assessment system: A framework for considering interim assessments. *Educational Measurement: Issues and Practice, 28*(3), 5–13.

Quellmalz, E. S., DeBarger, A. H., Haertel, G., Schank, P., Buckley, B., Gobert, J., Horwitz, P., & Ayala, C. (2008). Exploring the role of technology-based simulations in science assessment: The Calipers Project. In J. Coffey, R. Douglas, & C. Stearns (Eds.), *Science assessment: Research and practical approaches* (pp. 191–202). Washington, DC: National Science Teachers Association.

Quellmalz, E. S., & Haertel, G. (2004). *Technology supports for state science assessment systems.* Paper commissioned by the National Research Council Committee on Test Design for K–12 Science Achievement.

Quellmalz, E. S., & Moody, M. (2004). *Models for multi-level state science assessment systems.* Report commissioned by the National Research Council Committee on Test Design for K–12 Science Achievement.

Quellmalz, E. S., & Pellegrino, J. W. (2009). Technology and testing. *Science, 323*, 75–79.

Quellmalz, E. S., Timms, M., & Buckley, B. (2009). *Using science simulations to support powerful formative assessments of complex science learning.* Paper presented at the annual meeting of the American Educational Research Association. San Diego, CA.

Quellmalz, E. S., Timms, M. J., & Buckley, B. C. (2010). The promise of simulation-based science assessment: The Calipers project. *International Journal of Learning Technologies, 5*(3), 243–265.

Stiggins, R. (2005). From formative assessment to assessment for learning: A path to success in standards-based schools. *Phi Delta Kappan, 85*(4), 324–328.

Vendlinski, T., & Stevens, R. (2002). Assessing student problem-solving skills with complex computer-based tasks. *Journal of Technology, Learning, and Assessment, 1*(3). Retrieved from www.jtla.org; http://escholarship.bc.edu/cgi/viewcontent.cgi?article=1010&context=jtla

Wiliam, D. (2007). Keeping learning on track. In F. K. Lester, Jr. (Ed.), *Second handbook of mathematics teaching and learning* (pp. 1051–1098). Greenwich, CT: Information Age Publishing.

Wilson, M. R., & Bertenthal, M. W. (Eds.) (2005). *Systems for state science assessment.* Washington, DC: National Academy Press.

Index

Page numbers followed by f (for example, 71f) indicate figures.
Page numbers followed by t (for example, 199t) indicate tables.

A

achievement gap, 130
ACOT (Apple Classrooms of Tomorrow), 87–88, 132–133, 151
adaptation stage, in Stages of Instructional Evolution, 87
administrator group concerns profile, 163–164, 163f, 164f
  See also teacher concerns study
adoption models, technology, 87, 153, 154–155, 155t
adoption stage, in Stages of Instructional Evolution, 87
Adventure of the American Mind, An, 42
affordances, 240, 241
algebra. *See* student learning study
American history. *See* multimedia software study
American Memory collection, 42, 46, 53
  See also historical thinking study
Anderson-Inman, L., 220
Anytime, Anywhere Learning program, 107, 151
AP/Honors students, historical thinking skills of, 55–56, 57, 58–59
Apple Classrooms of Tomorrow (ACOT), 87–88, 132–133, 151
appropriation stage, in Stages of Instructional Evolution, 87
archives, online, 43–44
assessments
  criteria for student artifacts, 72t
  ecosystems unit, 291, 292f, 293–294, 293f
  formative, 289–291, 290f, 293–294, 293f, 295
  simulation-based, 291, 292f, 293–294, 293f
  summative, 289, 291, 292f, 293
  technology-enabled, 285–302
    about, 286–287
    abstract, 285
    for classroom instructional uses, 289–291, 290f, 292f, 293–294, 293f
    conclusions and implications, 297–298
    future directions, 298–300
    mathematics, 291
    multilevel systems, 294–295
    physics, 289–290, 290f
    state, national, and international programs, 287–289, 288f
    technology's role in development of assessment-based information systems, 295–297, 296t
    update, 300–302
    See also science assessment, technology-enabled
ASSISTment system, 291
Awareness stage, in Stages of Concern, 155, 155t

B

Barab, S., 6
barriers to technology integration, 10–11
basic operations and concepts, in NETS for Students, 86
Beaufort (SC) Learning with Laptops initiative, 109
Bebell, D., 118
blended learning, 280
budget, professional development in, 10

C

case studies, urban elementary school, 9–40
  abstract, 9
  appendix, 40
  conclusion, 33–36
  context, 13–14
  future research implications, 35
  interview questions, 40
  introduction, 10–11
  method and data sources, 14–16
  purpose of study, 11–12
  results, 16–27

Central Elementary School (pseudonym), 20–23
Michigan Street Elementary School (pseudonym), 23–27
Rosa Parks Elementary School (pseudonym), 16–20
scaffolding technology integration, 27–33
alignment with school curriculum/mission, 28–30
public/private roles for technology, 32–33
teacher leadership, 30–32
significance of study, 12–13
update, 36–37
CBAM (Concerns-Based Adoption Model), 153, 154–155, 155t
Center for Research and Information Technology and Organizations, 90–91, 91f, 100
CEO Forum, 150
change as process, 168–169
Chicago public schools, 91–92, 100
CIP scale. *See* Current Instructional Practices (CIP) scale
Classroom Connectivity in Mathematics and Science study, 123
classroom instructional uses of technology-enabled assessment, 289–291, 290f, 292f, 293–294, 293f
classroom management, 266–267, 277
"Close of a Career in New York, The" (photo), 54–57, 55f
cognitive load, 240–241, 242
See also electronic scaffolding study
collaboration, teacher, 274
communication, elaborated, 72t
communication tools. *See* technology communication tools
Computer-Based Assessment of Science, 287
Computer-Supported Intentional Learning Environments (CSILE), 199–200
computers, handheld. *See* mobile computing devices in K-9 classrooms
concept mapping, 190, 193
conceptual knowledge, 199–200, 206–209, 207t
conceptual scaffolds, 190
conceptual understanding levels, 78, 78t
Concerns-Based Adoption Model (CBAM), 153, 154–155, 155t
confidence levels in using technology, 242, 247, 250–251, 250t, 252, 253
See also electronic scaffolding study
Consortium on Chicago School Research, 91–92, 100
constructivism, 10, 131, 132–133
See also teacher technology use and instructional practices study
corroboration, as historical thinking skill, 48, 57–59, 58f
CSILE (Computer-Supported Intentional Learning Environments), 199–200
Current Instructional Practices (CIP) scale
described, 88, 136, 136t
Level of Technology Implementation scores and, 141–142, 143
Los Angeles Unified School District study, 89
Personal Computer Use scores and, 142–143
teacher levels, predominant, 140–141, 141f
curriculum, alignment with, 28–30

D

decision-making tools. *See* technology problem-solving and decision-making tools
Delta Rural Systemic Initiative, 134
Dewey, John, 131
DIAGNOSER project, 289–290, 290f
digitized primary sources. *See* historical thinking study
"directed" prompts, 202
Dodge, T., 6
domain knowledge, 200–201

E

ecosystems unit assessment, 291, 292f, 293–294, 293f
educational games, 4
educational reform, 3, 11
educational resources, open, 123
educational technology integration. *See* technology integration
educational technology research, 1–7
challenges for, 1, 2–5
future agenda for, 5–6
need for, 1–2
Educational Testing Service (ETS), 287–288, 288f
Effectiveness of Educational Technology Interventions (EETI), 261, 262
See also student learning study
electronic scaffolding study, 239–254
abstract, 239
discussion and implications, 251–253
introduction, 240–242
methodology, 243–247
context of study, 243

Filamentality and HyperStudio, 243–244, 244f, 245f
instruments, 246–247
research procedures, 245–246
results, 247–251, 248t, 249t, 250t
update, 254
electronic text, supported, 220
elementary school teachers, technology use by, 96–97, 96f, 99
elementary schools. *See* case studies, urban elementary school; mobile computing devices in K-9 classrooms; technology in K-12 schools study
English teachers, technology use by, 97–98, 97f, 99–100
Enhancing Education through Technology Act of 2001, 85, 101
entry stage, in Stages of Instructional Evolution, 87
epistemic games, 4
equity, in one-to-one computing initiatives, 109
ETS (Educational Testing Service), 287–288, 288f
evidence, citing, as historical thinking skill, 48, 57–59, 58f

F

facilitation, 267–268
Filamentality. *See* electronic scaffolding study
first-grade students. *See* student learning study
Florida Department of Education, 93, 102
Florida Digital Educators, 102
Florida teachers. *See* technology in K-12 schools study
formative assessment, 289–291, 290f, 293–294, 293f, 295

G

Gaining Early Awareness and Readiness for Undergraduate Programs (GEAR UP) federal grant program, 153, 154, 165
games, epistemic/educational, 4
"generic" prompts, 202
Germany, laptop program in, 118–119
grant coordinators, 18, 21, 25

H

handheld computers. *See* mobile computing devices in K-9 classrooms
Henrico County Public Schools (VA) one-to-one initiative, 151–152
Higgins, J., 118
high school students. *See* historical thinking study; student learning study
high school teachers, technology use by, 96–97, 96f, 99
high schools. *See* technology in K-12 schools study
historical images
student use of, 44
teacher use of, 45
historical thinking study, 41–66
abstract, 41
appendix, 65–66
conclusions, 59–60
future research implications, 60
introduction, 42–45
methods, 46–48, 47t
research questions, 45
results, 48–59
historical thinking skills exhibited by students, 54–59, 55f, 58f
student description of current history or social studies class, 48–53
sample screens and student questionnaire, 65–66
update, 62
history. *See* multimedia software study
Honors/AP students, historical thinking skills of, 55–56, 57, 58–59
Horney, M., 220
Hotlists, in Filamentality, 243, 244, 246, 247, 249
HyperStudio. *See* electronic scaffolding study

I

Ignite! Early American History. *See* multimedia software study
Impact level, in Stages of Concern, 155, 155t
implementation practices. *See* school-level implementation practices; teacher implementation practices
implementation studies, one-to-one computing initiative, 112–113
inferencing, as historical thinking skill, 48, 54–57, 55f
infrastructure, technology, 274–275
Innovations Configurations, in Concerns-Based Adoption Model, 154
inquiry-based learning. *See* learning, web-based

instructional activity systems, 279
Instructional Evolution Model, 151
instructional practices. *See* teacher technology use and instructional practices study
instructional technology consultants, 17
instructional uses of technology-enabled assessment, 289–291, 290f, 292f, 293–294, 293f
instructional vision, consistent, 272–273
iNtegrating Technology for inQuiry (NTeQ), 117
integration of technology. *See* technology integration
interactive multimedia, 218–219
International Society for Technology in Education (ISTE), 85–86
Internet-based learning. *See* learning, web-based
Internet-based question prompts. *See* question prompts, web-based
invention stage, in Stages of Instructional Evolution, 87
Inventory of Teacher Technology Skills, 102
ISTE (International Society for Technology in Education), 85–86

J

Jackson, C., 6

K

knowledge
  conceptual, 199–200, 206–209, 207t
  domain, 200–201
  See also learning, web-based; question prompts, web-based
knowledge integration, 199–200, 206–209, 207t
knowledge integration prompts, 203, 204, 206–209, 207t, 210

L

laptop programs
  classroom uses of, 114–115, 114t
  student learning, potential for, 108–110
  technology literacy, effects on, 118–119
  writing skills, effects on, 119
  See also one-to-one computing initiatives research synthesis; teacher concerns study
leadership, teacher, 25, 30–32
learning
  blended, 280
  constructivism and, 131
  resource-based, 180–181
  See also learning, web-based; student learning study
learning, web-based, 177–193
  abstract, 177
  conclusions, 190–192
  future research recommendations, 191–192
  introduction, 178–186
    data sources, 182–184, 183t, 184t
    design of study, 182
    hopes and cautions, 178
    method, 181–182
    procedures, 185–186
    scaffolds in resource-based learning, 180–181
    WebQuests, 179–180
  results, 186–190
    relationship between task procedures, resources, and student performance, 188–190
    site design features, 187–188, 189t
    task scaffolding, 186–187, 187t
  update, 193
Learning with Laptops initiative, 109
Levels of Technology Implementation (LoTi)
  Current Instructional Practices scores and, 141–142, 143
  described, 88–89, 135, 135t
  Los Angeles Unified School District study, 89
  teacher levels, predominant, 138–139, 139f
Los Angeles Unified School District, 89

M

Maine one-to-one computing initiative, 113, 116, 118
Mangement stage, in Stages of Concern, 155, 155t, 166
map of Seymour (CT), 57–59, 58f
mathematics assessment, technology-enabled, 291
mathematics software. *See* student learning study
mathematics teachers, technology use by, 97–98, 97f, 99, 100
McKenzie, J., 144
media-focused research, 219
memory, working, 240

metacognitive scaffolds, 190
metacognitive strategies, 201
Microsoft's Anytime, Anywhere Learning program, 107, 151
middle school students. *See* historical thinking study; multimedia software study
middle school teachers, technology use by, 96–97, 96f, 99
  See also teacher concerns study
middle schools
  ecosystems unit assessment, 291, 292f, 293–294, 293f
  mathematics assessment, 291
  See also mobile computing devices in K-9 classrooms; technology in K-12 schools study
mission, alignment with, 28–30
mobile computing devices in K-9 classrooms, 67–81
  abstract, 67
  advantages of, 68–69
  background, 68–69
  conclusions, 79–80
  disadvantages of, 69, 80
  future research recommendations, 80
  methodology, 70–72
    data sources and analyses, 70–72, 72t
    subjects and settings, 70
  results, 72–79
    learning processes, 77–79, 78t
    student motivation to learn and engagement in learning, 76–77
    student use of mobile computing devices, 72–76, 73t, 74t, 75t
  update, 81
multilevel assessment systems, 294–295
multimedia
  defined, 218
  interactive, 218–219
  learning, contributions to, 218–219
  rubric for slide shows, 182, 183t
multimedia software study, 217–234
  abstract, 217
  discussion, 230–233
    implications and future research, 232–233
    limitations of study, 231
  introduction and purpose of study, 218–221
    interactive media focus, 218–219
    supportive resource focus, 219–220
    teaching history and social studies, 221
    technology-supported social studies learning, 221
  method, 222–229
    data analysis, 229
    data collection, 226–228
    early American history software, 222
    participants, 223–225, 224t
    research design, 222–223
    use of American history software, 228
  results, 229–230
    posttest, 230
    pretest, 229
  update, 234

N

National Assessment of Educational Progress (NAEP), 287, 288, 301
National Center for Education Statistics, 89–90, 98–99
National Education Technology Plan, 300–301
National Educational Technology Standards (NETS) for Students, 85–86
  See also technology in K-12 schools study
National Research Council, 294, 295, 301
NEGD (Non-Equivalent Group Design), 226, 230, 231
NETS (National Educational Technology Standards) for Students, 85–86
  See also technology in K-12 schools study
No Child Left Behind Act of 2001, 85, 223, 231, 232
Non-Equivalent Group Design (NEGD), 226, 230, 231
NTeQ (iNtegrating Technology for inQuiry), 117

O

observation, as historical thinking skill, 48, 54–57, 55f
one-to-one computing initiatives
  classroom uses of laptops in, 114–115, 114t
  defined, 107–108
  equity in, 109
  Henrico County Public Schools (VA), 151–152
  implementation studies, 112–113
  literature review, 151–152
  Maine, 113, 116, 118
  outcome studies, 112, 118–119
  scale of, 113–114

one-to-one computing initiatives research synthesis, 105–123
abstract, 105
discussion and conclusion, 119–121
future research recommendations, 120–121
introduction, 106–107
methodology used for research synthesis, 111–113
criteria for inclusion, 112–113
process for finding and selecting articles, 112
process for synthesizing results, 113
scope of synthesis, 112
one-to-one initiatives, defined, 107–108
outcome studies findings, 118–119
synthesis findings, 113–118
classroom uses of laptops in one-to-one initiatives, 114–115, 114t
goals of one-to-one initiatives, 113
professional development, role in fostering implementation, 110–111, 116–117, 117t, 120
scale of one-to-one initiatives, 113–114
teacher attitudes and beliefs, role in implementation, 110–111, 115–116, 115t
technical support, role in fostering implementation, 111, 117–118
theoretical framework, 108–111
implementation conditions, 110–111
wireless laptop computing potential for student learning, 108–110
update, 123
See also teacher concerns study
online archives, 43–44
open educational resources, 123
operations and concepts, in NETS for Students, 86
outcome studies, one-to-one computing initiative, 112, 118–119

P

Papert, Seymour, 132
Perceived Task Effort (PTE), 240–241, 242, 246–247, 249–250, 249t, 251–253
See also electronic scaffolding study
Personal Computer Use (PCU) scale
Current Instructional Practices scores and, 142–143
described, 88, 137, 137t
teacher levels, predominant, 139–140, 140f
physics assessment, technology-enabled, 289–290, 290f
Piaget, Jean, 131
Picturing Modern America, 45
PISA (Programme for International Student Assessment), 287, 301
poverty, 11, 130
preservice teachers, 37, 179–180
See also question prompts, web-based
primary sources. *See* historical thinking study
primary student teachers. *See* electronic scaffolding study
principals
as agents of technology growth and development, 18–19, 22, 25–26
school-level implementation practices and, 273
teacher leadership and, 25, 30–32
technology integration, role in, 34–35
technology integration, scaffolding, 27–28, 29–30, 32
problem solving, ill-structured, 200–201, 205, 206–210, 207t
See also question prompts, web-based
problem-solving prompts, 203, 204, 206–208, 207t, 209, 210
problem-solving tools. *See* technology problem-solving and decision-making tools
procedural scaffolds, 190
productivity tools. *See* technology productivity tools
professional development
one-to-one computing initiatives and, 110–111, 116–117, 117t, 120
teacher concerns, alignment with, 167–168
in technology budget, 10
technology integration and, 33–34, 35–36
Programme for International Student Assessment (PISA), 287, 301
Project Hiller, 115–116
prompts
"directed," 202
"generic," 202
knowledge integration, 203, 204, 206–209, 207t, 210
problem-solving, 203, 204, 206–208, 207t, 209, 210
See also question prompts, web-based
PTE (Perceived Task Effort), 240–241, 242, 246–247, 249–250, 249t, 251–253

Q

question prompts, web-based, 197–213
abstract, 197
discussion, 209–210
future research recommendations, 211–212
implications, 210–211
introduction, 198
methodology, 203–206
experimental study, 204–205
participants, 203
qualitative study, 206
purpose of study, 202–203
results, 206–209
qualitative findings, 208–209
quantitative outcomes, 206–207, 207t
theoretical framework, 199–202
knowledge integration, 199–200
problem solving, ill-structured, 200–201
question prompts as scaffolding strategies, 201–202
update, 213

R

Race-To-The-Top (RTTT) assessment initiative, 300, 301
reading software. *See* student learning study
reform, 3, 11
research
media-focused, 219
scientifically based, 223, 231, 232
See also educational technology research; one-to-one computing initiatives research synthesis
research tools. *See* technology research tools
resource-based learning, 180–181
RTTT (Race-To-The-Top) assessment initiative, 300, 301
rubrics
multimedia slide shows, 182, 183t
website evaluation, 183–184, 184t, 188, 189t
rural schools, challenges facing, 130
See also teacher technology use and instructional practices study
Russell, M., 118

S

scaffolded knowledge integration (SKI) framework, 199
scaffolding technology integration, 27–33
alignment with school curriculum/mission, 28–30
public/private roles for technology, 32–33
teacher leadership, 30–32
scaffolds
conceptual, 190
metacognitive, 190
procedural, 190
in resource-based learning, 180–181
strategic, 190
See also electronic scaffolding study; learning, web-based; question prompts, web-based
Schaumburg, H., 118–119
school curriculum/mission, alignment with, 28–30
school level differences in technology integration, 96–97, 96f, 96t, 99
school-level implementation practices
recommended, 259–260t
student learning study results, 272–275, 275t, 276–277
instructional vision, consistent, 272–273
principal support, 273
teacher collaboration, 274
technology infrastructure and technical support, 274–275
training and support, additional, 275
school reform, 3, 11
School Technology and Readiness Report, 150
science assessment, technology-enabled
future, 301
multilevel programs, 295
SimScientists, 291, 292f, 293–294, 293f
state, national, and international programs, 287–288, 288f
science teachers, technology use by, 97–98, 97f, 99, 100
scientifically based research, 223, 231, 232
Scrapbooks, in Filamentality, 243, 244, 246, 247, 249
selection-maturation threat, 226, 230
Self level, in Stages of Concern, 155, 155t, 164–165
seventh grade students. *See* multimedia software study
seventh grade teachers. *See* teacher concerns study
Seymour (CT) map, 57–59, 58f
SimScientists, 291, 292f, 293–294, 293f

simulation-based assessments, 291, 292f, 293–294, 293f
SKI (scaffolded knowledge integration) framework, 199
social, ethical, and human issues, in NETS for Students, 86
social studies learning, technology-supported, 221
social studies teachers, technology use by, 97–98, 97f, 100
sources, primary. *See* historical thinking study
Stages of Concern, 154–155, 155t
Stages of Concern Questionnaire, 156, 174–176
Stages of Instructional Evolution, 87
stages of technology integration, 86–89
statistical power, 231
strategic scaffolds, 190
student/computer ratios in classrooms, 118
student learning study, 257–281
  about, 258, 259–260t, 260–263, 263t, 264t
  abstract, 257
  discussion, 276–279
  future research recommendations, 278
  method, 265
  results, 265–277
    changes in implementation practices from Year 1 to Year 2, 276
    school-level implementation practices, 272–275, 275t, 276–277
    teacher implementation practices, 266–272, 272t, 277
  update, 280–281
student teachers, primary. *See* electronic scaffolding study
Student Tool for Technology Literacy, 102
students
  as agents of technology growth and development, 19–20, 23, 26
  high school (*See* historical thinking study; student learning study)
  historical images, use of, 44
  mobile computing device use in K-9 classrooms, 72–76, 73t, 74t, 75t
    assignments by class, 72–73, 73t
    usage by class, 73–74, 73t, 74t
    usage by gender, 75, 75t
  motivation to learn and engagement in learning, 76–77
  public/private roles for technology, 32, 33
  as technical support providers in one-to-one computing initiatives, 118
  technology integration, role in, 35
subject area differences in technology integration, 97–98, 97f, 97t, 99–100
summative assessment, 289, 291, 292f, 293
support, technical, 111, 117–118, 275
supported electronic text, 220

T

Task level, in Stages of Concern, 155, 155t, 164–165
task scaffolding. *See* learning, web-based
teacher concerns study, 149–176
  abstract, 149
  appendix, 174–176
  conclusion, 169–170
  discussion, 164–169
    change as process, 168–169
    giving teachers voice in innovation adoption, 168
    implications, 166
    limitations of current study, 169
    overview, 164–166
    professional development and teacher concerns, alignment of, 167–168
  introduction, 150
  literature review, 150–152
    one-to-one computing access, 151–152
  method, 153–159
    Concerns-Based Adoption Model, 154–155, 155t
    data analysis, 158–159, 158t, 159t
    data collection, 157–158
    one-legged interviews, 156–157
    open-ended questions, 156
    participants and setting, 153–154
    research tools, 154
    Stages of Concern Questionnaire, 156
  purpose, 152
  results, 159–164
    administrator group concerns profile, 163–164, 163f, 164f
    teacher concerns group profile, 160–163, 160f, 161f, 161t, 162f
  Stages of Concern Questionnaire, 156, 174–176
  theoretical framework, 153
  update, 171
  See also one-to-one computing initiatives research synthesis

teacher implementation practices
recommended, 260t
student learning study results, 266–272, 272t, 277
classroom management, 266–267, 277
instruction, articulation and integration of, 268–270
software data, using to inform instruction, 270–271, 277
software use, developing system to motivate, 271–272
software use, facilitation during, 267–268
software use, level of, 266
teacher leadership, 25, 30–32
teacher technology use and instructional practices study, 129–146
abstract, 129
constructivism and learning, 131
future research, 144–145
introduction, 130
methodology, 134–138
instrumentation, 135–137, 135t, 136t, 137t
limitations, 138
population, 134
research questions, 133–134
results and discussion, 138–143, 139f, 140f, 141f
technology and constructivism, 132–133
update, 146
teachers
as agents of technology growth and development, 17, 19, 22, 25–26
attitudes and beliefs of, 110–111, 115–116, 115t
collaboration between, 274
elementary school, 96–97, 96f, 99
English, 97–98, 97f, 99–100
Florida (*See* technology in K-12 schools study)
high school, 96–97, 96f, 99
historical image use by, 45
innovation adoption, voice in, 168
math, 97–98, 97f, 99, 100
middle school, 96–97, 96f, 99 (*See also* teacher concerns study)
preservice, 37, 179–180 (*See also* question prompts, web-based)
primary student (*See* electronic scaffolding study)
public/private roles for technology, 32, 33
science, 97–98, 97f, 99, 100
social studies, 97–98, 97f, 100
technology integration, role in, 35
Teaching, Learning, and Computing (TLC) study, 90–91, 91f, 100
technical support, 111, 117–118, 275
technology
assessment-based information systems, role in developing, 295–297, 296t
constructivism and, 10, 132–133
public/private roles for, 32–33
technology adoption models, 87, 153, 154–155, 155t
technology budget, professional development in, 10
technology communication tools
in NETS for Students, 86
teacher use of, school level differences in, 96f, 96t, 97, 99
teacher use of, subject area differences in, 97f, 97t, 98
technology competencies, in NETS for Students, 85–86
technology in K-12 schools study, 83–102
abstract, 83
concluding remarks, 101
discussion, 98–100
limitations of study, 100
literature review, 84–92
National Educational Technology Standards, 85–86
technology integration stages, 86–89
technology integration surveys, 89–92, 91f
method, 92–95
data collection, 93–94
instrumentation, 93
respondent sample, 94, 94t, 95t
overview, 84
results, 95–98, 95t
school level differences, 96–97, 96f, 96t, 99
subject area differences, 97–98, 97f, 97t, 99–100
update, 102
technology infrastructure, 274–275
technology integration
barriers to, 10–11
conditions supporting, 11
poverty and, 11
professional development and, 33–34, 35–36
reform and, 3, 11
stages of, 86–89
See also scaffolding technology integration
technology literacy, laptop program effects on, 118–119

technology problem-solving and decision-making tools
in NETS for Students, 86
teacher use of, school level differences in, 96, 96f, 96t, 99
teacher use of, subject area differences in, 97f, 97t, 98, 99
technology productivity tools
in NETS for Students, 86
teacher use of, school level differences in, 96f, 96t, 97
teacher use of, subject area differences in, 97f, 97t, 98
technology research tools
in NETS for Students, 86
teacher use of, school level differences in, 96f, 96t, 97, 99
teacher use of, subject area differences in, 97f, 97t, 98, 99
technology specialists
as agents of technology growth and development, 17, 21, 22, 25
teacher leadership and, 31
technology integration, role in, 34–35
Texas Instruments Navigator system, 123
text transformations, 219
Thomas, M. K., 6
TLC (Teaching, Learning, and Computing) study, 90–91, 91f, 100
training, additional, 275
Tuzun, H., 6

U

Union City, NJ, 11
Unrelated level, in Stages of Concern, 155, 155t
urban elementary school case studies. *See* case studies, urban elementary school
U.S. Department of Education, 2, 3, 300–301

V

vision, instructional, 272–273
Vygotsky, L. S., 131

W

Web-based Inquiry Service Environment (WISE), 199
web-based learning. *See* learning, web-based
web-based question prompts. *See* question prompts, web-based
WebQuests, 178, 179–180, 190
See also learning, web-based
websites
design features of, 187–188, 189t, 191
evaluation rubric for, 183–184, 184t, 188, 189t
usability guidelines for, 191
Weiser, Mark, 68
Wineburg, Sam, 43
WISE (Web-based Inquiry Service Environment), 199
working memory, 240
writing, 77–78, 119